Guides to the

Evaluation
of
Permanent Impairment

2nd Edition

AMERICAN MEDICAL ASSOCIATION

Additional copies may be purchased from:
Order Department OP-254
American Medical Association
P.O. Box 10946
Chicago, Illinois 60610

NEA:83-86(B):254:3/85 10M

Foreword

In 1956 the Board of Trustees of the American Medical Association (AMA) created an *ad hoc* Committee on Medical Rating of Physical Impairment to establish a series of practical guides for the rating of physical impairment of the various organ systems. As the scope of the Committee's work broadened, its name was changed to the Committee on Rating of Mental and Physical Impairment. From 1958 to 1970 the Committee published 13 separate "Guides to the Evaluation of Permanent Impairment" in *The Journal of the American Medical Association.*

In 1971 the AMA reviewed the Committee's Guides and published them as a single volume. By providing clinically sound and reproducible criteria for rating permanent impairment, the Guides have continued to be useful to physicians, attorneys and adjudicators in fulfilling their responsibilities to patients, clients and applicants seeking benefits from agencies and programs serving the disabled.

In 1981 the AMA's Council on Scientific Affairs undertook a review of the Guides and established an advisory panel to determine the need for revision. At the suggestion of these consultants, 12 expert panels were established to update the clinical information that supports the impairment ratings. This second edition of the Guides is the result of their efforts combined with the efforts of many on the AMA's staff.

In this edition there are many changes. The chapter on the extremities, spine and pelvis contains four new tables assigning impairment ratings to orthopedic conditions not mentioned in the first edition. Two chapters on the central and peripheral nervous systems in the first edition have become one, and the new chapter contains a section on impairment due to sleep and arousal disorders. This relatively recent field of clinical endeavor may be unfamiliar to users of the Guides; therefore, an appendix is included that briefly describes categories of sleep and arousal abnormalities, and gives examples of the impairments they may cause.

The chapter on the respiratory system has been modified extensively to include physiologic tests that reflect more accurately the degree of impairment. The chapter on the cardiovascular system is divided into sections on valvular heart disease, hypertensive cardiovascular disease, cardiomyopathies, arrhythmias and peripheral vascular disease. Specific impairment criteria are given for each.

The chapter on the endocrine system features revised criteria for impairment due to diabetes mellitus. The chapters on the hematopoietic system, the visual system, the ear, nose and throat, the digestive system, the skin, and the reproductive and urinary systems have been modified to include more modern clinical examples and measurement techniques.

Finally, the chapter on mental and behavioral disorders is written not only to stand by itself, but to be used in the assessment of mental impairment that may result from physical impairment. It emphasizes the need for rehabilitation before a rating of permanent impairment can be assigned.

The Guides continue to espouse the philosophy that all physical and mental impairments affect the whole person, and therefore, all impairment ratings should be combined to be expressed as impairment of the whole person. This is done with the aid of a "Combined Values Chart."

The AMA strongly urges that all readers become familiar with the proper use of the Guides and the proper terminology in the fields of impairment and disability. All users should read the Preface to the Guides and the two appendices on report preparation and terminology before using the Guides.

In addition to the members of the committees who devoted their time and gave of their knowledge to the revision of the Guides, many medical specialty societies, individual practitioners, and governmental agencies helped AMA's expert panels and staff add new and relevant information in this second edition.

The AMA acknowledges the contributions of the following members of the various panels whose efforts are largely responsible for the preparation of this new edition.

American Medical Association Council on Scientific Affairs
John R. Beljan, MD
George Bohigian, MD
Theodore Cooper, MD
William D. Dolan, MD
Ira R. Friedlander, MD
Ray W. Gifford, Jr, MD, Chairman
Michael B. Kastan
John H. Moxley, III, MD, Vice Chairman
Joseph H. Skom, MD
Rogers J. Smith, MD
James B. Snow, Jr, MD
C. John Tupper, MD

American Medical Association Staff
Leonard D. Fenninger, MD, Vice President,
    Group on Medical Education and Scientific Policy
Betty Jane Anderson, JD, Associate General Counsel
Richard J. Jones, MD, Secretary,
    Council on Scientific Affairs
Environmental and Occupational Health Program
    Theodore C. Doege, MD, MS, Program Director
    Jermyn F. McCahan, MD, Senior Editor
    Alan L. Engelberg, MD, MPH, Editor
    Leatha A. Tiggelaar, Coordinator
    Cathy A. Campbell
    Barbara S. Jansson
    Nancy T. O'Connor

Panel Members
Robert M. Adams, MD, Stanford University,
    Palo Alto, CA
Robert G. Addison, MD, Northwestern University,
    Chicago, IL
William H. Anderson, MD,
    University of Louisville, Louisville, KY
Budd Appleton, MD, private practice,
    St. Paul, MN
Ronald A. Arky, MD, Harvard University,
    Boston, MA
John L. Bell, MD, Northwestern University,
    Chicago, IL
Harvey W. Bender, Jr, MD, Vanderbilt University,
    Nashville, TN
Donald J. Birmingham, MD, Wayne State University,
    Detroit, MI
Bernard R. Blais, MC, Captain, United States
    Department of the Navy, Washington, DC

Robert W. Cantrell, MD, University of Virginia,
    Charlottesville, VA
Leon A. Carrow, MD, Northwestern University,
    Chicago, IL
Francis I. Catlin, MD, Baylor College of Medicine,
    Houston, TX
Oliver H. Dabezies, Jr, MD, Tulane University,
    New Orleans, LA
Gilbert Daniels, MD, Harvard University,
    Boston, MA
Jane Desforges, MD, Tufts University, Boston, MA
Robert Dluhy, MD, Harvard University, Boston, MA
Marvin I. Dunn, MD, University of Kansas,
    Kansas City, KS
Jack R. Ewalt, MD, Veterans Administration,
    Washington, DC
Thomas W. Farmer, MD, University of
    North Carolina, Chapel Hill, NC
Daniel D. Federman, MD, Harvard University,
    Boston, MA
Donald I. Feinstein, MD, University of Southern
    California, Los Angeles, CA
Gerald F. Fletcher, MD, Emory University,
    Atlanta, GA
James C. Folsom, MD, ICD-International Center for
    the Disabled, New York, NY
Eugene P. Frenkel, MD, University of Texas,
    Dallas, TX
Edward E. Gaensler, MD, University Hospital,
    Boston, MA
Gerald A. Gellin, MD, University of California,
    San Francisco, CA
David Y. Graham, MD, Baylor University,
    Houston, TX
Norton J. Greenberger, MD, University of Kansas,
    Kansas City, KS
Donald W. Hammersley, MD, American Psychiatric
    Association, Washington, DC
William S. Haubrich, MD, Scripps Clinic and
    Research Foundation, La Jolla, CA
Alexander H. Hirschfeld, MD, University of
    California at San Francisco, San Francisco, CA
J. O'Neal Humphries, MD, University of
    South Carolina, Columbia, SC
Bernard Jacobs, MD, Cornell University,
    New York, NY
Donald J. Joseph, MD, University of Missouri,
    Columbia, MO
William J. Kane, MD, Northwestern University,
    Chicago, IL
Paul E. Kaplan, MD, Northwestern University,
    Chicago, IL
Irving Kass, MD, University of Nebraska
    College of Medicine, Omaha, NE (deceased)
Arthur H. Keeney, MD, University of Louisville,
    Louisville, KY

Robert I. Kohut, MD, Wake Forest University, Winston-Salem, NC

Joseph Majzoub, MD, Harvard University, Boston, MA

C. G. Toby Mathias, MD, University of California, San Francisco, CA

Richard F. Mayer, MD, University of Maryland, Baltimore, MD

Alan A. McLean, MD, International Business Machines Corporation, New York, NY

Michael P. McQuillen, MD, Medical College of Wisconsin, Milwaukee, WI

Arthur T. Meyerson, MD, Mount Sinai School of Medicine, New York, NY

William C. Morgan, MD, West Virginia University, Charleston, WV

John F. Mullan, MD, University of Chicago, Chicago, IL

Henry L. Nadler, MD, Wayne State University, Detroit, MI

Joseph F. Novak, MD, University of Pittsburgh, PA

Kurt Nussbaum, MD, Johns Hopkins University, Baltimore, MD

Vincent J. O'Conor, Jr, MD, Northwestern University, Chicago, IL

Desmond S. O'Doherty, MD, Georgetown University, Washington, DC

Bertram Pepper, MD, Rockland Community Mental Health Center, Pomona, NY

E. Chester Ridgway, MD, Harvard University, Boston, MA

James L. A. Roth, MD, University of Pennsylvania, Philadelphia, PA

Marvin A. Sackner, MD, University of Miami, Miami, FL

Joseph Sataloff, MD, Jefferson University, Philadelphia, PA

Gordon C. Sauer, MD, University of Kansas, Kansas City, KS

Sid J. Shafer, MD, University of Illinois, Chicago, IL

George M. Smith, MD, private consultant, Bethesda, MD

James B. Snow, Jr, MD, University of Pennsylvania, Philadelphia, PA

Arthur J. Spielman, PhD, Albert Einstein College of Medicine, Bronx, NY

John A. Spittell, Jr, MD, Mayo Clinic, Rochester, MN

James S. Taylor, MD, Cleveland Clinic Foundation, Cleveland, OH

Gennaro M. Tisi, MD, University of California, San Diego, CA

Theodore A. Tromovitch, MD, University of California, San Francisco, CA

Ralph O. Wallerstein, MD, University of California, San Francisco, CA

Hans Weill, MD, Tulane University, New Orleans, LA

Elliott D. Weitzman, MD, Cornell University, White Plains, NY (deceased)

Charles W. Whitmore, MD, LLB, Health Sciences Education and Research Corporation, Lynchburg, VA

Charles F. Wooley, MD, Ohio State University, Columbus, OH

Dewey K. Ziegler, MD, University of Kansas, Kansas City, KS

Preface

Introduction

Evaluation and rating of permanent medical impairment has long been recognized as an important subject because of the administrative, financial and social consequences of decisions about people whose health is no longer intact. Because of the complexity of the subject, and the lack of sufficient analysis and definition of concepts, there has been confusion and uncertainty about the role of physicians and the scope of their responsibilities. Also, confusion continues to exist about the differences between "medical impairment" and "disability."

Only a physician may carry out an authoritative medical evaluation that assesses an individual's health. Other physicians often are requested to review the evaluation, in order to ensure that the diagnoses or clinical impressions accord with established medical diagnostic criteria and that conclusions and recommendations are consistent with the accepted principles of medical practice. While the medical decision-making process is not an adversary one, the results of it are frequently used in an adversary arena.

The principal use of a medical rating of permanent impairment is in a nonmedical setting, and it is important to distinguish between conclusions and recommendations of a medical nature for which the physician is responsible, and those of a nonmedical nature that have social, administrative, economic, and legal consequences beyond the domain of medicine. The *Guides to the Evaluation of Permanent Impairment* provide a structured set of medical criteria that comprise a reference with which to establish well-formulated medical ratings of permanent impairment.

As users study the Guides, they will observe that because of differences in approaches and methods, practitioners of the various medical specialties use different kinds of criteria to rate permanent impairment of the various body systems. Some criteria, such as those for orthopedic or ophthalmologic impairments, are quantitative, while others depend on the practitioner's ability to select from a range of impairments that is not quantitatively precise, as with psychiatric problems.

Before medical evaluation is undertaken to determine a rating of permanent impairment, the user should review the applicable chapter of the Guides in its entirety, in order to ascertain the methodology involved and the nature of the particular criteria. Regardless of the degree of impairment, the value and credibility of the rating will depend on the accuracy of the clinical observations, the thoroughness with which the patient's medical history and record is analyzed, the logic by which relevant factors are incorporated into a decision relating the medical findings to the criteria in the Guides, and the clarity and completeness of the report.

The user of the Guides must give careful attention to the definitions listed in the Glossary. It is particularly important to understand the distinction between a patient's *medical impairment*, which is an alteration of health status assessed by medical means, and the patient's *disability*, which is an alteration of the patient's capacity to meet personal, social, or occupational demands, or to meet statutory or regulatory requirements, which is assessed by nonmedical means. In a particular case, the existence of permanent medical impairment does not automatically support the presumption that there is disability as well. Rather, disability results when medical impairment leads to the individual's inability to meet demands that pertain to nonmedical fields and activities.

A permanent impairment rating that is derived from use of the Guides may serve as a starting point for determinations about the consequences of the impairment, such as a disability rating or a legal entitlement, a starting point that is based on the most advanced and comprehensive application of current medical knowledge. The approach that has been taken in the AMA's Guides will provide for standardized communications of medical information about the impact of a medical impairment on an individual's activities of daily living.

The principal objective of the Guides is to define as precisely as possible the meaning of medical and nonmedical statements that are made by physicians about individuals whose health is impaired, and the ways in which these statements are understood and used. The purpose of the Guides is to make clear these distinctions in such a way as to meet the needs of all people whose health impairments have caused impairment of their capacities to engage in their activities of daily living and to meet their personal, social, or occupational demands.

Use of the Guides

Before using the Guides, the reader should become acquainted with the terms defined in the Glossary.

Each chapter contains recommended percentage values related to criteria established for the body system that the chapter considers. Although the editors are cognizant that terms such as "slight," "moderate," and "marked" are used by many physicians, administrative bodies, and jurisdictions, the editors prefer the use of numerical values because of difficulties in discussing and interpreting such subjective terms. The numerical values in this edition represent a practical way of calculating and expressing medical impairment by comparing clinical findings with specific clinical criteria. Uniform, reproducible methods of determining impairment are explained and illustrated with examples. The methods require a minimum of computation.

Generally, when a single permanent impairment is present, the percent of impairment may be read directly from the text, or it can be related to a part of the body or to the "whole person" by referring to appropriate tables. When two or more impairments exist, the value of each impairment is determined separately and related to the "whole person," using the Combined Values Chart. The Combined Values Chart is based on the principle that each impairment acts not on the whole person, but on the unimpaired portion that remains after other impairments, alone or in combination, have been taken into account. The final value, the "impairment of the whole person," is independent of the order in which the impairment values are combined.

Rating Permanent Impairment — Steps and Procedures

Medical evaluation: The first step in rating permanent impairment is to make a thorough medical evaluation with particular attention to reviewing the history of the medical condition(s). Then, a thorough physical examination should be done, supported by appropriate tests and diagnostic procedures. The history, the physical examination, and the laboratory tests and other diagnostic procedures should characterize all important abnormalities and justify all conclusions about the individual's present clinical status.

The examining physician should review the appropriate chapter of the Guides, in order to determine the extent of the examination necessary to obtain enough clinical information to rate the impairment.

Analysis of the findings: The second step is analysis of the history and the clinical and laboratory findings to determine the nature and extent of the loss, loss of use of, or derangement of the affected body parts, systems or functions.

Comparison of the results of analysis with the medical impairment criteria: The third step is the comparison of the results of the analysis with the criteria that are specified in the Guides for the particular body part, system, or function. This process is distinct from the prior clinical evaluation and need not be performed by the same physician doing the evaluation. Given sufficient data from a clinical evaluation that is based on the criteria of the Guides and that utilizes generally accepted and standardized methods, a knowledgeable physician may compare the clinical findings on a particular patient with the criteria of the Guides.

Rating of the whole person: The final step in rating medical impairment takes into account all relevant considerations in order to reach a "whole person" impairment rating. The final impairment value, whether the result of single or combined impairments, may be expressed in terms of the nearest 5%.

Impairment should not be considered "permanent" until maximum medical rehabilitation has been achieved, and until, in the physician's best clinical judgment, the impairment is static or well-stabilized. A physician who re-evaluates an individual's impairment must be aware that change may have occurred, even though the previous evaluator considered the impairment to be "permanent" at that time. For instance, the condition may have become worse as a result of aggravation (see Glossary for definition) or clinical progression, or it may have improved; regardless, the evaluator should assess the current state of the impairment in accordance with the criteria in the Guides.

The concept of "permanency" in disability programs may vary considerably; it usually relates to a provision in a contract, policy, or regulation in which the time limit for permanency of disability is defined.

Valid quantification of any change in impairment rating will depend on the reliability of the previous rating. If there was no valid rating previously, the adequacy of previous documentation about the condition could be used to estimate a rating according to the criteria in the Guides. If the rater does not have sufficient information to measure change accurately, the rater should not attempt to do so.

If *apportionment* is needed (see Glossary for definition), the analysis must consider the nature of the impairment and its possible relationship to each alleged factor and provide an explanation of the medical basis for all conclusions and opinions. To establish that a factor could have contributed to the impairment, the analysis and explanation should include, in accordance with scientific and epidemiologic principles, reference to the minimum exposure and to its timing that would have been necessary for the factor to have contributed to the impairment, and a discussion of the pathophysiology of the particular condition and of pertinent host characteristics.

Support for a conclusion that a factor did contribute to an impairment must rely on documentation of circumstances under which the factor was present, and verification that the actual type and extent of the exposure was of sufficient duration and had the necessary temporal relationship to the medical condition. The existence of medical impairment alone does not create a presumption of contribution by any factor with which the impairment is often associated. The establishment of nexus is a legal or administrative matter, not a medical matter.

Reports

The narrative report supporting the medical rating of impairment is a document that may be used in a variety of settings, including legal proceedings, in which decisions will be made about the award of significant sums of money. Significant weight is sometimes given to the opinion of the physician, whether or not that opinion is supported adequately by documentation. In order to avoid undue reliance on assertions by physicians, and to preclude the resolution of conflict of opinions between physicians by third parties who for nonmedical reasons give greater weight to the opinion of one physician than to another, the rating physician should provide clear and well-reasoned conclusions about medical matters that are supported by complete and accurate data.

The report that supports a permanent impairment rating should contain sufficient information to allow a knowledgeable reviewer to understand the rating and to assess its validity for its intended use. Appendix A specifies the kinds of information a report should contain to ensure its completeness.

Use of Permanent Impairment Ratings in Disability Determinations

Because a principal purpose for rating permanent impairment has to do with disability rating for workers' compensation programs, disability insurance, or social security disability payments, a major concern is how the ratings will be used for administrative or legal purposes. The permanent impairment rating should be understood as an assessment of health status that is made in accordance with established, accepted medical criteria. Each administrative or legal system that uses permanent impairment as a basis for disability rating should define its own process for translating the rating into an estimate of the degree to which the individual's capacity to meet personal, social, or occupational demands, or to meet statutory or regulatory requirements, is limited by the impairment.

In any particular case, a permanent impairment rating may be used by two or more different systems separately to determine entitlement to different benefits. While the entitlements and benefits may differ, there is only one health status. Therefore, the rating of permanent impairment should be uniform and should not vary with the circumstances of its occurrence nor with the geographic location of the patient. Nor should the opinion of physicians about nonmedical issues influence the outcome. The Guides pertain to medical issues, and when they are used properly, permanent impairment can be rated with reasonable accuracy and uniformity.*

There are various formulas that are used in the evaluation of *permanent disability*. These formulas, usually administrative devices that are used to establish permanent partial or total disability by inference from a knowledge of permanent impairment, represent estimates of the average loss of wage earning capacity or of actual wages to be expected in a population of workers. While a permanent impairment rating that is determined in accordance with the principles listed in these Guides may be used in such a fashion, it is clear that not all permanent impairments will result in the same estimates about the degree of disability in all cases.

---

*Glass DS, Wardle MG: Reliability and validity of American Medical Association's guides to ratings of permanent impairment. JAMA 1982; 248 : 2292-2296.

The physician who makes a determination about impairment must keep in mind that a permanent impairment rating is not the same as a disability rating. Permanent medical impairment is related directly to the health status of the individual, whereas disability can be determined only within the context of the personal, social, or occupational demands, or statutory or regulatory requirements that the individual is unable to meet as a result of the impairment. Accordingly, the physician must understand the nature of the conclusions contained in the report, specify any limitations about their use, and refrain from speculating about nonmedical consequences of an impairment.

In general, it is not possible for a physician, using medical information alone, to make reliable predictions about the ability of an individual to perform tasks or to meet functional demands. A physician can determine, however, whether or not a particular medical condition has become permanent because it is static or well-stabilized. When it is stable, there is no medical reason to expect that the individual will gain or lose future functional ability. When functional ability is assessed by a standardized nonmedical procedure in a vocational rehabilitation facility or in an occupational setting, the physician may have confidence in the determination.

While medical information is of little value in predicting functional ability or the lack of it, an appropriate use of knowledge about an individual's health may be of help in explaining an observed performance failure. However, in such a case, the analysis should consider whether or not the specific medical condition can cause the type of observed failure, which is a medical decision, and whether or not in the particular case it *did* cause the failure, which is not a medical decision.

Beyond the patient's performance of a specific task, a physician may have good medical reasons to be concerned about risks to the patient or others that may be associated with the patient's medical condition, for example, the likelihood of the patient's sudden incapacitation, of subtle incapacitation, of further impairment, or of transmitting a communicable disease. When the physician has justifiable concern about any of these possible outcomes, the recommendation of restrictions or of accommodations may be medically warranted, or limitation of activities may be medically justified.

While a physician properly may make an inference about degree of risk based on medical information, it is not proper for the physician to determine the acceptability of that risk. Such a decision is of a personal, social, legal, economic, business, or insurance nature and is properly made by nonphysicians based on nonmedical considerations.

Table of Contents

Chapter 1

The Extremities, Spine and Pelvis

Introduction

This chapter includes sections on the upper extremity, the lower extremity, the spine and the pelvis. Each section considers techniques of measurement, includes tables for impairments due to restriction of active motion, ankylosis, amputations and fractures, and describes methods for combining and relating various impairments.

The upper extremity, the lower extremity, the spine and the pelvis are each to be considered *a unit of the whole person*. The upper extremity may be divided into four sections: the hand, wrist, elbow, and shoulder. The normal hand has five digits: the thumb, index, middle, ring, and little fingers. The thumb has three joints: interphalangeal, metacarpophalangeal, and carpometacarpal. Each finger has three joints: the distal interphalangeal, proximal interphalangeal, and metacarpophalangeal joints.

The lower extremity may be divided into four sections: the foot; hind foot, which includes the ankle and subtalar joints; knee; and hip. The foot has five digits: the great toe and the second, third, fourth and fifth toes. The great toe has two joints, the interphalangeal and the metatarsophalangeal joints. The second, third, fourth and fifth toes all have three joints, the distal interphalangeal, proximal interphalangeal, and metatarsophalangeal joints.

The spine may be divided into the cervical, thoracic, and lumbar regions. The cervical region has seven vertebrae, C1-C7. The thoracic region has twelve vertebrae, T1-T12. The lumbar region has five vertebrae, L1-L5. There may be congenital variations in the number of vertebrae. For the purpose of measuring restricted motion, the spine is divided into the cervical region and the thoracolumbar region.

The pelvis is composed of the two innominate bones that form the sides and the front and the sacrum and coccyx that form the rear.

Techniques of measurement should be simple, practical and scientifically sound. A large and a small portable goniometer are useful and are the only medical devices necessary. Suggested types of these devices for measuring angles of fixation and ranges of motion of joints are illustrated in the text. Procedures for testing restriction of active motion and ankylosis are described in detail and also are illustrated. The contralateral normal joint should serve as the standard against which the impaired joint is measured.

To determine restriction of motion, several measurements are necessary. If the patient cannot assume the prescribed neutral position for each joint, then the degree of deviation from the prescribed neutral position should be recorded, which is the degree of *ankylosis* of the joint. Next, the full range of active motion, that is, the range throughout which the patient can move the part, should be carried out by the patient and measured by the examiner. Finally, if possible, the examiner should complete the range of motion of the joint (passive motion) and record the results.

Additional testing procedures may be desirable in specific cases. However, in most instances the measurement techniques described in this chapter are adequate. The measurements are converted to impairments by referring to the appropriate tables of the chapter.

The criteria used to develop the relative impairment ratings in this chapter involve analysis of anatomic and physiological factors underlying the function of the joint, and observation of the following interrelationships:

a. observed range of motion compared with "normal" or "expected" motion;

b. angles of fixation, if there is ankylosis;

c. the extremities and spine and the whole person;

d. the spinal regions and the whole person;

1

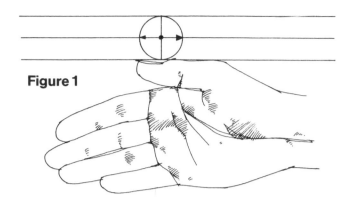

Figure 1

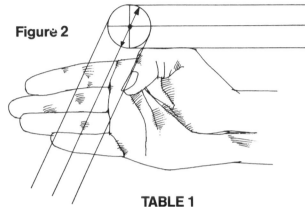

Figure 2

TABLE 1
IMPAIRMENT DUE TO AMPUTATION, ABNORMAL MOTION AND ANKYLOSIS OF THE INTERPHALANGEAL JOINT OF THE THUMB

Impairment of Thumb

Amputation—At Joint 75%

Abnormal Motion

Average range of FLEXION-EXTENSION is 80 degrees
Value to total range of joint motion is 100%

Flexion from neutral position (0°) to:	Degrees of Joint Motion LOST	Degrees of Joint Motion RETAINED	Impairment of Thumb
0°	80	0	45%
10°	70	10	39
20°	60	20	34
30°	50	30	28
40°	40	40	23
50°	30	50	17
60°	20	60	11
70°	10	70	6
80°	0	80	0

Ankylosis

Joint ankylosed at:	
0° (neutral position)	45%
10°	43
20°	40
30°	38
*40°	35
50°	45
60°	55
70°	65
80° (full flexion)	75

*position of function

e. the hand, wrist, elbow, and shoulder and the upper extremity;

f. the foot, ankle, knee, and hip and the lower extremity;

g. the digits and the hand or foot;

h. the joints and the digits.

In establishing the values for amputation, consideration was given both to loss of motor function and loss of sensation. However, in establishing the values for ankylosis and restricted motion of the hand, no consideration was given for loss of sensation. Therefore, when evaluating impairment due to loss of sensation of the hand, it is necessary to refer to Chapter 2.

Nonpreferred Upper Extremity—Since the basic tasks of everyday living are more dependent upon the preferred upper extremity than upon the nonpreferred one, dysfunction of the nonpreferred extremity results in less impairment than dysfunction of the preferred. Therefore, when the impairment of an upper extremity has been determined to be between 5% and 50%, the value should be reduced by 5% if the impairment is of the nonpreferred extremity. If the determined value is 51% to 100%, the value should be reduced by 10% if the impairment is of the nonpreferred extremity. For example, a 60% impairment would become 60% — (60% x 10%) = 54%.

Before using the information in this chapter, the reader is urged to consult the Preface to the Guides, which provides a general discussion of the purpose of the Guides, and of the situations in which they are useful; and discusses techniques for the evaluation of the patient and for report preparation.

The Upper Extremity

Interphalangeal Joint of Thumb — Flexion and Extension

Abnormal Motion

1. Place the patient's hand in the neutral position (Figure 1).

2. Center the goniometer over the dorsum of the interphalangeal joint (Figure 2). Record the goniometer reading.

3. With the patient flexing the interphalangeal joint as far as possible (Figure 2), follow the range of motion with the goniometer arm. Record the angle that subtends the arc of motion.

4. Consult the abnormal motion section of Table 1 to determine the impairment of the thumb.

Example: 40° active flexion from neutral position (0°) or from maximum extension is equivalent to 23% impairment of the thumb.

Ankylosis

1. Place the goniometer base as if measuring the neutral position (Figure 1). Measure the deviation from the neutral position with the goniometer arm and record the reading.

2. Consult the ankylosis section of Table 1 to determine the impairment of the thumb.

Example: An interphalangeal joint with ankylosis at 40° flexion is equivalent to 35% impairment of the thumb.

Metacarpophalangeal Joint of Thumb — Flexion and Extension

Abnormal Motion

1. Place the patient's hand in the neutral position (Figure 3).

2. Center the goniometer adjacent to the metacarpophalangeal joint·(Figure 3). Record the goniometer reading.

3. With the patient flexing the metacarpophalangeal joint as far as possible (Figure 4), follow the range of motion with the goniometer arm. Record the angle that subtends the arc of motion.

4. Consult the abnormal motion section of Table 2 to determine the impairment of the thumb.

Example: 50° active flexion from neutral position (0°) or from maximum extension is equivalent to 9% impairment of the thumb.

Ankylosis

1. Place the goniometer base as if measuring the neutral position (Figure 3). Measure the deviation from the neutral position with the goniometer arm and record the reading.

2. Consult the ankylosis section of Table 2 to determine the impairment of the thumb.

Example: Metacarpophalangeal joint with ankylosis at 50° flexion is equivalent to 70% impairment of the thumb.

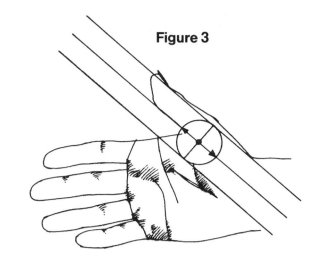

Figure 3

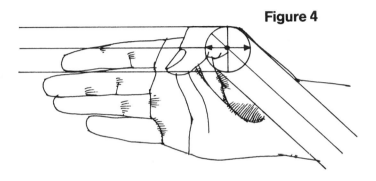

Figure 4

TABLE 2
IMPAIRMENT DUE TO AMPUTATION, ABNORMAL MOTION AND ANKYLOSIS OF THE METACARPOPHALANGEAL JOINT OF THE THUMB

	Impairment of Thumb
Amputation—At Joint	100%

Abnormal Motion

Average range of FLEXION-EXTENSION is 60 degrees
Value to total range of joint motion is 100%

Flexion from neutral position (0°) to:	Degrees of Joint Motion LOST	RETAINED	Impairment of Thumb
0°	60	0	55%
10°	50	10	46
20°	40	20	37
30°	30	30	27
40°	20	40	18
50°	10	50	9
60°	0	60	0

Ankylosis

Joint ankylosed at:

0° (neutral position)	55%
10°	49
*20°	43
30°	52
40°	61
50°	70
60° (full flexion)	80

*position of function

3

TABLE 3
IMPAIRMENT DUE TO AMPUTATION, ABNORMAL MOTION AND ANKYLOSIS OF THE CARPOMETACARPAL JOINT OF THE THUMB

Impairment of Thumb

Amputation—At Joint with all or part of
  metacarpal bone 100%

Abnormal Motion

Average range of FLEXION-EXTENSION is 45 degrees

Flexion from neutral position (0°) to:	Degrees of Joint Motion LOST	RETAINED	Impairment of Thumb
0°	15	0	15%
10°	5	10	5
15°	0	15	0

Extension from neutral position (0°) to:	LOST	RETAINED	
0°	30	0	15%
10°	20	10	10
20°	10	20	5
30°	0	30	0

Ankylosis

Joint ankylosed at:

0° (neutral position)	30%
10°	55
15° (full extension)	80

Joint ankylosed at:

0° (neutral position)	30%
10°	47
20°	63
30° (full extension)	80

TABLE 4
RELATIONSHIP OF IMPAIRMENT OF THE THUMB TO IMPAIRMENT OF THE HAND

% Impairment of Thumb		Hand		% Impairment of Thumb		Hand
0 – 1	=	0		49 – 51	=	20
2 – 3	=	1		52 – 53	=	21
4 – 6	=	2		54 – 56	=	22
7 – 8	=	3		57 – 58	=	23
9 – 11	=	4		59 – 61	=	24
12 – 13	=	5		62 – 63	=	25
14 – 16	=	6		64 – 66	=	26
17 – 18	=	7		67 – 68	=	27
19 – 21	=	8		69 – 71	=	28
22 – 23	=	9		72 – 73	=	29
24 – 26	=	10		74 – 76	=	30
27 – 28	=	11		77 – 78	=	31
29 – 31	=	12		79 – 81	=	32
32 – 33	=	13		82 – 83	=	33
34 – 36	=	14		84 – 86	=	34
37 – 38	=	15		87 – 88	=	35
39 – 41	=	16		89 – 91	=	36
42 – 43	=	17		92 – 93	=	37
44 – 46	=	18		94 – 96	=	38
47 – 48	=	19		97 – 98	=	39
				99 – 100	=	40

NOTE: Impairment of the hand contributed by the thumb may be rounded to the nearest 5 percent only when it is the *sole* impairment involved.

Consult Table 9 for converting hand impairment to upper extremity impairment.

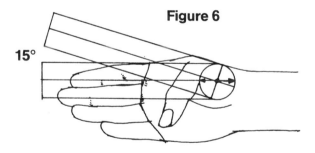

Figure 6

15°

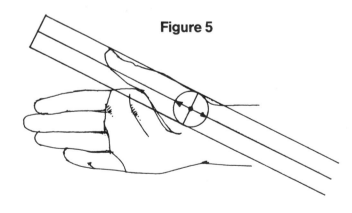

Figure 5

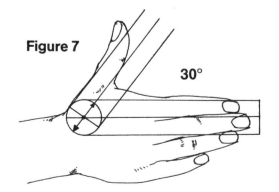

Figure 7

30°

Carpometacarpal Joint of Thumb — Flexion and Extension

Abnormal Motion

1. Place the patient's hand in the neutral position (Figure 5).

2. Place the goniometer adjacent to the carpometacarpal joint. Record the goniometer reading.

3. With the patient flexing the thumb (Figure 6), follow the range of motion of the goniometer arm. Record the angle that subtends the arc of motion.

4. With the patient extending the thumb from the index finger in the plane of the palm, follow the range of motion with the goniometer arm (Figure 7). Record the angle that subtends the arc of motion.

5. Consult the abnormal motion section of Table 3 to determine the impairment of the thumb.

6. Add the impairment values of flexion and extension; their sum represents impairment due to flexion and extension of the carpometacarpal joint of the thumb.

Ankylosis

1. Place the goniometer base as if measuring the neutral position (Figure 5). Measure the deviation from the neutral position with the goniometer arm and record the reading.

2. Consult the ankylosis section of Table 3 to determine the impairment of the thumb.

NOTE: Abduction and adduction of the carpometacarpal joint of the thumb is associated with the ability to flex and extend the joint. This association has been taken into consideration in establishing the percentages of impairment for flexion and extension.

Thumb — Multiple Joints

If more than one joint is impaired, measure separately and record the impairment of the thumb contributed by each joint. Then combine the impairment values using the Combined Values Chart to ascertain the impairment of the thumb.

Examples:

Description	% Impairment of Thumb
1. Ankylosis	
(a) Interphalangeal joint with ankylosis at 40° flexion	35 (Table 1)
(b) Metacarpophalangeal joint with ankylosis at 50° flexion	70 (Table 2)
(70 combined with 35 = 81)	81
2. Ankylosis and Restricted Motion	
(a) Interphalangeal joint with ankylosis at 40° flexion	35 (Table 1)
(b) Metacarpophalangeal joint restricted to 50° active flexion from neutral position or from maximum extension	9 (Table 2)
(35 combined with 9 = 41)	41
3. Restricted Motion	
(a) Interphalangeal joint with 40° flexion from neutral position or from maximum extension	23 (Table 1)
(b) Metacarpophalangeal joint with 50° active flexion from neutral position or from maximum extension	9 (Table 2)
(c) Carpometacarpal joint with 10° active flexion and 20° active extension	10 (Table 3)
(23 combined with 9 = 30; 30 combined with 10 = 37)	37
4. Amputation and Restricted Motion	
(a) Amputated interphalangeal joint	75 (Table 1)
(b) Metacarpophalangeal joint with 50° active flexion from neutral position or from maximum extension	9 (Table 2)
(75 combined with 9 = 77)	77

TABLE 5
IMPAIRMENT DUE TO AMPUTATION, ABNORMAL MOTION AND ANKYLOSIS OF THE DISTAL INTERPHALANGEAL JOINT OF ANY FINGER

	Impairment of Finger
Amputation—At Joint	45%

Abnormal Motion
Average range of FLEXION-EXTENSION is 70 degrees
Value to total range of joint motion is 100%

Flexion from neutral position (0°) to:	Degrees of Joint Motion LOST	Degrees of Joint Motion RETAINED	Impairment of Finger
0°	70	0	45%
10°	60	10	38
20°	50	20	32
30°	40	30	26
40°	30	40	19
50°	20	50	13
60°	10	60	6
70°	0	70	0

Ankylosis

Joint ankylosed at:

0° (neutral position)	45%
10°	41
20°	38
30°	34
*40°	30
50°	35
60°	40
70° (full flexion)	45

*position of function

Distal Interphalangeal Joint of Any Finger— Flexion and Extension

Abnormal Motion

1. Place the patient's hand in the neutral position (Figure 8).

2. Center the goniometer over the dorsum of the distal interphalangeal joint (Figure 8). Record the goniometer reading.

3. With the patient flexing the distal interphalangeal joint as far as possible (Figure 9), follow the range of motion with the goniometer arm. Record the angle that subtends the arc of motion.

4. Consult the abnormal motion section of Table 5 to determine the impairment of the finger.

Example: 40° active flexion from neutral position (0°) or from maximum extension is equivalent to 19% impairment of the finger.

Ankylosis

1. Place the goniometer base as if measuring the neutral position (Figure 8). Measure the deviation from neutral position with the goniometer arm and record the reading.
2. Consult the ankylosis section of Table 5 to determine the impairment of the finger.

Example: Ankylosis of the distal interphalangeal joint at 40° is equivalent to 30% impairment of the finger.

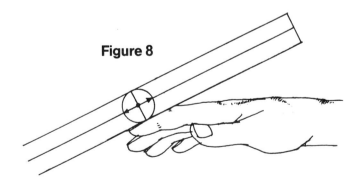

Figure 8

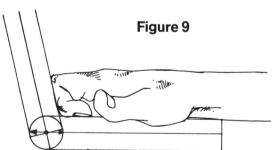

Figure 9

Proximal Interphalangeal Joint of Any Finger— Flexion and Extension

Abnormal Motion

1. Place the patient's hand in the neutral position (Figure 10).

2. Center the goniometer over the dorsum of the proximal interphalangeal joint (Figure 10), and record the reading.

3. With the patient flexing the proximal interphalangeal joint as far as possible (Figure 11), follow the range of motion with the goniometer arm. Record the angle that subtends the arc of motion.

4. Consult the restricted motion section of Table 6 to determine the impairment of the finger.

Example: 40° active flexion from neutral position (0°) or from maximum extension is equivalent to 36% impairment of the finger.

Ankylosis

1. Place the goniometer base as if measuring the neutral position (Figure 10). Measure the deviation from the neutral position with the goniometer arm and record the reading.

2. Consult the ankylosis section of Table 6 to determine the impairment of the finger.

Example: Ankylosis of the proximal interphalangeal joint at 40° flexion is equivalent to 50% impairment of the finger.

TABLE 6
IMPAIRMENT DUE TO AMPUTATION, ABNORMAL MOTION AND ANKYLOSIS OF THE PROXIMAL INTERPHALANGEAL JOINT OF ANY FINGER

	Impairment of Finger
Amputation—At Joint	80%

Abnormal Motion
Average range of FLEXION-EXTENSION is 100 degrees
Value to total range of joint motion is 100%

Flexion from neutral position (0°) to:	Degrees of Joint Motion LOST	Degrees of Joint Motion RETAINED	Impairment of Finger
0°	100	0	60%
10°	90	10	54
20°	80	20	48
30°	70	30	42
40°	60	40	36
50°	50	50	30
60°	40	60	24
70°	30	70	18
80°	20	80	12
90°	10	90	6
100°	0	100	0

Ankylosis

Joint ankylosed at:

0° (neutral position)	60%
10°	58
20°	55
30°	53
*40°	50
50°	55
60°	60
70°	65
80°	70
90°	75
100° (full flexion)	80

*position of function

Figure 11

Figure 10

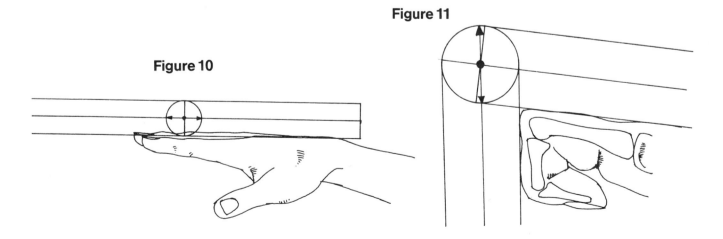

7

TABLE 7
IMPAIRMENT DUE TO AMPUTATION, ABNORMAL MOTION AND ANKYLOSIS OF THE METACARPOPHALANGEAL JOINT OF ANY FINGER

Impairment of Finger

Amputation—At Joint 100%

Abnormal Motion

Average range of FLEXION-EXTENSION is 90 degrees
Value to total range of joint motion is 100%

Flexion from neutral position (0°) to:	Degrees of Joint Motion LOST	Degrees of Joint Motion RETAINED	Impairment of Finger
0°	90	0	55%
10°	80	10	49
20°	70	20	43
30°	60	30	37
40°	50	40	31
50°	40	50	24
60°	30	60	18
70°	20	70	12
80°	10	80	6
90°	0	90	0

Ankylosis

Joint ankylosed at:

0° (neutral position)	55%
10°	52
20°	48
*30°	45
40°	54
50°	63
60°	72
70°	82
80°	91
90° (full flexion)	100

*position of function

NOTE: In ulnar nerve injuries, loss of function of the intrinsic muscles of the hand produces impairment of the abductor-adductor mechanism of the fingers. Evaluation of impairment of the ulnar nerve is set forth in Chapter 2.

TABLE 8
RELATIONSHIP OF IMPAIRMENT OF THE FINGERS TO IMPAIRMENT OF THE HAND

% Impairment of Index Finger		Hand	% Impairment of Middle Finger		Hand
0	– 1 =	0	0	– 2 =	0
2	– 5 =	1	3	– 7 =	1
6	– 9 =	2	8	– 12 =	2
10	– 13 =	3	13	– 17 =	3
14	– 17 =	4	18	– 22 =	4
18	– 21 =	5	23	– 27 =	5
22	– 25 =	6	28	– 32 =	6
26	– 29 =	7	33	– 37 =	7
30	– 33 =	8	38	– 42 =	8
34	– 37 =	9	43	– 47 =	9
38	– 41 =	10	48	– 52 =	10
42	– 45 =	11	53	– 57 =	11
46	– 49 =	12	58	– 62 =	12
50	– 53 =	13	63	– 67 =	13
54	– 57 =	14	68	– 72 =	14
58	– 61 =	15	73	– 77 =	15
62	– 65 =	16	78	– 82 =	16
66	– 69 =	17	83	– 87 =	17
70	– 73 =	18	88	– 92 =	18
74	– 77 =	19	93	– 97 =	19
78	– 81 =	20	98	– 100 =	20
82	– 85 =	21	**Ring Finger**		**Hand**
86	– 89 =	22	0	– 4 =	0
90	– 93 =	23	5	– 14 =	1
94	– 97 =	24	15	– 24 =	2
98	– 100 =	25	25	– 34 =	3
Little Finger		**Hand**	35	– 44 =	4
0	– 9 =	0	45	– 54 =	5
10	– 29 =	1	55	– 64 =	6
30	– 49 =	2	65	– 74 =	7
50	– 69 =	3	75	– 84 =	8
70	– 89 =	4	85	– 94 =	9
90	– 100 =	5	95	– 100 =	10

NOTE: Impairment of the hand contributed by the finger may be rounded to the nearest 5 percent only when it is the *sole* impairment involved.

Consult Table 9 for converting hand impairment to upper extremity impairment.

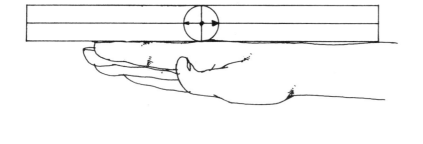

Figure 12

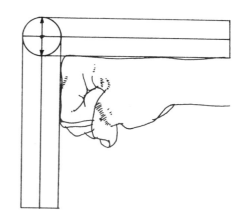

Figure 13

Metacarpophalangeal Joint of Any Finger — Flexion and Extension

Abnormal Motion

1. Place the patient's hand in the neutral position (Figure 12).

2. Center the goniometer over the dorsum of metacarpophalangeal joint and record the reading.

3. With the patient attempting to make a fist (Figure 13), follow the range of motion with the goniometer arm and record the angle that subtends the arc of motion.

4. Consult the abnormal motion section of Table 7 to determine the impairment of the finger.

Example: $30°$ active flexion from neutral position $(0°)$ or from maximum extension is equivalent to 37% impairment of the finger.

Ankylosis

1. Place the goniometer base as if measuring the neutral position (Figure 12). Measure the deviation from the neutral position with the goniometer arm and record the reading.

2. Consult the ankylosis section of Table 7 to determine the impairment of the finger.

Example: Ankylosis of the metacarpophalangeal joint at $30°$ flexion is equivalent to 45% impairment of the finger.

Any Finger — Multiple Joints

If two or more joints are involved, measure separately and record the impairment contributed by each joint. Then combine the impairment values using the Combined Values Chart to ascertain impairment of the entire finger.

Examples:

	Description	% Impairment of Finger
1.	**Ankylosis**	
	(a) Distal interphalangeal joints with ankylosis at $40°$	30 (Table 5)
	(b) Proximal interphalangeal joint with ankylosis at $40°$	50 (Table 6)
	(30 combined with 50 = 65)	65

2. Amputation, Ankylosis, and Restricted Motion

   (a) Distal interphalangeal joint amputated . 45 (Table 5)

   (b) Proximal interphalangeal joint with ankylosis at $40°$ . . . . 50 (Table 6)

   (c) Metacarpophalangeal joint with $30°$ active flexion from neutral position or from maximum extension . . . . 37 (Table 7)

   (45 combined with 50 = 73; 73 combined with 37 = 83) 83

Hand

If two or more digits of the hand are involved, measure separately and record the impairment of each digit. Then record the impairment of the hand that is contributed by each digit. Finally, add all values. The sum of these values represents the impairment of the hand.

Example:

Description	% Impairment of Hand
10% impairment of thumb	4 (Table 4)
20% impairment of index finger	5 (Table 8)
30% impairment of middle finger	6 (Table 8)
40% impairment of ring finger	4 (Table 8)
50% impairment of little finger	3 (Table 8)
(4 + 5 + 6 + 4 + 3 = 22)	22

Finally, consult Table 9 to ascertain the impairment of the upper extremity that is contributed by the hand. In the example, the 22% impairment of the hand is equivalent to 20% impairment of the upper extremity.

The relationship of impairment of the hand to amputation or to ankylosis of multiple digits in any of three positions is found in Table 10.

9

TABLE 9
RELATIONSHIP OF IMPAIRMENT OF THE HAND TO IMPAIRMENT OF THE UPPER EXTREMITY

Hand	=	% Impairment of Upper Extremity	Hand	=	% Impairment of Upper Extremity	Hand	=	% Impairment of Upper Extremity	Hand	=	% Impairment of Upper Extremity	Hand	=	% Impairment of Upper Extremity	Hand	=	% Impairment of Upper Extremity
0	=	0	18	=	16	35	=	32	53	=	48	70	=	63	88	=	79
1	=	1	19	=	17	36	=	32	54	=	49	71	=	64	89	=	80
2	=	2				37	=	33				72	=	65			
3	=	3	20	=	18	38	=	34	55	=	50	73	=	66	90	=	81
4	=	4	21	=	19	39	=	35	56	=	50	74	=	67	91	=	82
			22	=	20				57	=	51				92	=	83
5	=	5	23	=	21	40	=	36	58	=	52	75	=	68	93	=	84
6	=	5	24	=	22	41	=	37	59	=	53	76	=	68	94	=	85
7	=	6				42	=	38				77	=	69			
8	=	7	25	=	23	43	=	39	60	=	54	78	=	70	95	=	86
9	=	8	26	=	23	44	=	40	61	=	55	79	=	71	96	=	86
10	=	9	27	=	24	45	=	41	62	=	56	80	=	72	97	=	87
11	=	10	28	=	25	46	=	41	63	=	57	81	=	73	98	=	88
12	=	11	29	=	26	47	=	42	64	=	58	82	=	74	99	=	89
13	=	12				48	=	43				83	=	75			
14	=	13	30	=	27	49	=	44	65	=	59	84	=	76	100	=	90
			31	=	28				66	=	59						
15	=	14	32	=	29	50	=	45	67	=	60	85	=	77			
16	=	14	33	=	30	51	=	46	68	=	61	86	=	77			
17	=	15	34	=	31	52	=	47	69	=	62	87	=	78			

NOTE: Impairment of the upper extremity contributed by the hand may be rounded to the nearest 5 percent only when it is the sole impairment involved. Consult Table 20 for converting upper extremity impairment to whole person impairment.

TABLE 10
IMPAIRMENT OF THE HAND DUE TO AMPUTATION OR ANKYLOSIS OF DIGIT(S) IN THREE POSITIONS

Digit(s) Involved	Digit Amputated	Full Extension	Position of Function	Full Flexion	Digit(s) Involved	Digit Amputated	Full Extension	Position of Function	Full Flexion
Thumb	40	30	25	38	Index	25	23	20	25
Thumb, Index	65	53	45	63	Index, Middle	45	41	36	45
Thumb, Index, Middle	85	71	61	83	Index, Middle, Ring	55	50	44	55
Thumb, Index, Ring	75	62	53	73	Index, Middle, Little	50	46	40	50
Thumb, Index, Little	70	58	49	68	Index, Middle, Ring, Little	60	55	48	60
Thumb, Index, Middle, Ring	95	80	69	93	Index, Ring	35	32	28	35
Thumb, Index, Middle, Little	90	76	65	88	Index, Ring, Little	40	37	32	40
Thumb, Index, Ring, Little	80	67	57	78	Index, Little	30	28	24	30
Thumb, Index, Middle, Ring, Little	100	85	73	98	Middle	20	18	16	20
Thumb, Middle	60	48	41	58	Middle, Ring	30	27	24	30
Thumb, Middle, Ring	70	57	49	68	Middle, Ring, Little	35	32	28	35
Thumb, Middle, Little	65	53	45	63	Middle, Little	25	23	20	25
Thumb, Middle, Ring, Little	75	62	53	73	Ring	10	9	8	10
Thumb, Ring	50	39	33	48	Ring, Little	15	14	12	15
Thumb, Ring, Little	55	44	37	53	Little	5	5	4	5
Thumb, Little	45	35	29	43					

Wrist Joint—Dorsi-flexion

Abnormal Motion

1. Place the patient in the neutral position (Figure 14). Note the pronation of the forearm.

2. Center the goniometer beneath the patient's wrist (Figure 14). Record the reading with the goniometer arm between the patient's middle and ring fingers.

3. With the patient dorsi-flexing the wrist as far as possible (Figure 15), follow the range of motion with the goniometer arm. Record the angle that subtends the arc of motion.

4. Consult the abnormal motion section of Table 11 to determine the impairment of the upper extremity.

Example: 30° active dorsi-flexion from neutral position (0°) or any 30° arc of retained active dorsi-flexion is equivalent to 5% impairment of the upper extremity.

Ankylosis

1. Place the goniometer base as if measuring the neutral position (Figure 14). Measure the deviation from neutral position with the goniometer arm and record the reading.

2. Consult the ankylosis section of Table 11 to determine the impairment of the upper extremity.

Example: A wrist joint ankylosis of 30° dorsi-flexion is equivalent to 25% impairment of the upper extremity.

TABLE 11
IMPAIRMENT DUE TO AMPUTATION, ABNORMAL MOTION AND ANKYLOSIS OF THE WRIST JOINT—DORSI-FLEXION

Impairment of Upper Extremity

Amputation—At Joint 90%

Abnormal Motion

Average range of DORSI-PALMAR FLEXION is 130 degrees
Value to total range of joint motion is 70%

Dorsi-flexion from neutral position (0°) to:	Degrees of Joint Motion LOST	Degrees of Joint Motion RETAINED	Impairment of Upper Extremity
0°	60	0	10%
10°	50	10	8
20°	40	20	6
30°	30	30	5
40°	20	40	3
50°	10	50	2
60°	0	60	0

Ankylosis

Joint ankylosed at:

0° (neutral position)	30%
10°	28
20°	27
*30°	25
40°	47
50°	68
60° (full dorsi-flexion)	90

*position of function

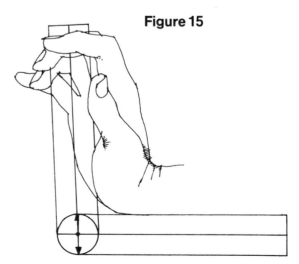

Figure 15

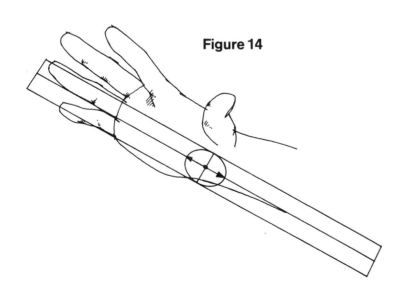

Figure 14

TABLE 12
IMPAIRMENT DUE TO AMPUTATION, ABNORMAL MOTION AND ANKYLOSIS OF THE WRIST JOINT—PALMAR-FLEXION

Impairment of Upper Extremity

Amputation—At Joint 90%

Abnormal Motion

Average range of DORSI-PALMAR FLEXION is 130 degrees
Value to total range of joint motion is 70%

Palmar-flexion from neutral position (0°) to:	Degrees of Joint Motion LOST	RETAINED	Impairment of Upper Extremity
0°	70	0	11%
10°	60	10	10
20°	50	20	8
30°	40	30	6
40°	30	40	5
50°	20	50	3
60°	10	60	2
70°	0	70	0

Ankylosis

Joint ankylosed at:

0° (neutral position)	30%
10°	39
20°	47
30°	56
40°	64
50°	73
60°	81
70° (full flexion)	90

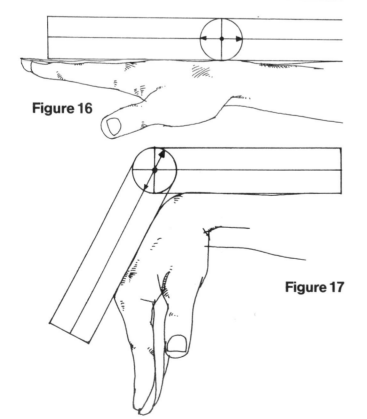

Figure 16

Figure 17

Wrist Joint—Palmar-flexion

Abnormal Motion

1. Place the patient in the neutral position (Figure 16). Note the pronation of the forearm.

2. Center the goniometer on the patient's wrist (Figure 16). Record the goniometer reading.

3. With the patient palmar-flexing the wrist as far as possible (Figure 17), follow the range of motion with the goniometer arm. Record the angle that subtends the arc of motion.

4. Consult the abnormal motion section of Table 12 to determine the impairment of the upper extremity.

Example: Active palmar-flexion of 30° from neutral position (0°) or any 30° arc of retained active palmar-flexion is equivalent to 6% impairment of the upper extremity.

5. To determine the overall impairment of the wrist joint, add the impairment values for dorsi-flexion and palmar-flexion. The sum of these values is equivalent to the impairment of the upper extremity due to those abnormal motions of the wrist.

Ankylosis

1. Place the goniometer base as if measuring the neutral position (Figure 16). Measure deviation from the neutral position with the goniometer arm and record the reading.

2. Consult the ankylosis section of Table 12 to determine the impairment of the upper extremity.

Example: Ankylosis of the wrist joint at 30° of palmar-flexion is equivalent to 56% impairment of the upper extremity.

Wrist Joint—Radial and Ulnar Deviation (Adduction-Abduction)

Abnormal Motion

1. Place the patient in the neutral position (Figure 18). Note the pronation of the hand and forearm.

2. Center the goniometer over the wrist with its arm lying directly over the third metacarpal bone (Figure 18). Record the goniometer reading.

3. Radial deviation: Starting from the neutral position with the patient deviating the wrist to the radial side as far as possible (Figure 19), follow the range of motion with the goniometer arm over the third metacarpal bone and record the angle that subtends the arc of motion.

4. Ulnar deviation: With the patient deviating the wrist as far as possible to the ulnar side (Figure 20), follow the range of motion with the goniometer arm over the third metacarpal bone and record the angle that subtends the arc of motion.

5. Consult the abnormal motion section of Table 13 to determine the impairment of the upper extremity.

Example: 10° active radial deviation from neutral position (0°) or any 10° arc of retained active radial deviation is equivalent to 2% impairment of the upper extremity.

6. To determine the impairment of the upper extremity, add the values for radial and ulnar deviation. The sum of the values represents impairment of the upper extremity contributed by abnormalities in radial and ulnar deviation of wrist.

Ankylosis

1. Place the goniometer base as if measuring the neutral position (Figure 18). Measure deviation from the neutral position with the goniometer arm and record the reading.

2. Consult the ankylosis section of Table 13 to determine the impairment of the upper extremity.

Example: A wrist joint with ankylosis at 20° ulnar deviation is equivalent to 70% impairment of the upper extremity.

TABLE 13
IMPAIRMENT DUE TO AMPUTATION, ABNORMAL MOTION AND ANKYLOSIS OF THE WRIST JOINT—ADDUCTION-ABDUCTION

Impairment of Upper Extremity

Amputation—At Joint 90%

Abnormal Motion

Average range of RADIAL-ULNAR DEVIATION (adduction-abduction) is 50 degrees
Value to total range of joint motion is 30%

Radial deviation from neutral position (0°) to:	Degrees of Joint Motion LOST	RETAINED	Impairment of Upper Extremity
0°	20	0	4%
10°	10	10	2
20°	0	20	0

Ulnar deviation from neutral position (0°) to:			
0°	30	0	5%
10°	20	10	4
20°	10	20	2
30°	0	30	0

Ankylosis

Joint ankylosed at:

*0° (neutral position)	30%
10°	60
20° (full radial deviation)	90

Joint ankylosed at:

*0° (neutral position)	30%
10°	50
20°	70
30° (full ulnar deviation)	90

*position of function

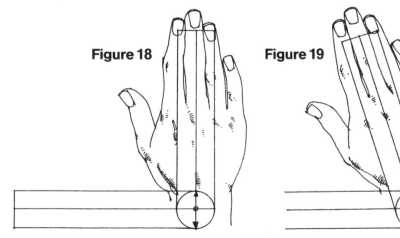

Figure 18   **Figure 19**

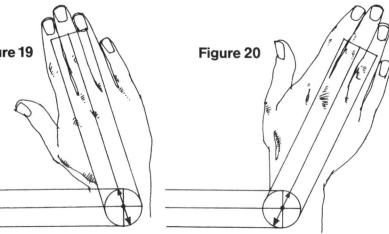

Figure 20

Wrist Joint — Two Ranges of Motion

Abnormal Motion

Measure separately and record the impairment of the upper extremity contributed by each range of motion. Then, add the impairment values contributed by the ranges of motion. Their sum represents impairment of the upper extremity that is contributed by abnormal motions of the wrist joint.

Example:

Description	% Impairment of Upper Extremity
20° active dorsi-flexion	6 (Table 11)
20° active palmar-flexion	8 (Table 12)
10° active radial deviation	2 (Table 13)
10° active ulnar deviation	4 (Table 13)
(6 + 8 + 2 + 4 = 20)	20

Ankylosis

Measure separately and record the impairment of the upper extremity that is contributed by ankylosis in each position. The largest impairment value due to ankylosis is the impairment of the upper extremity that is contributed by the ankylosis of the wrist joint.

Example:

Description	% Impairment of Upper Extremity
Ankylosis at 30° dorsi-flexion	25 (Table 11)
Ankylosis at 10° radial deviation	60 (Table 13)

The largest impairment value due to ankylosis is 60%; therefore, the upper extremity is 60% impaired by the ankylosed wrist joint.

TABLE 14
IMPAIRMENT DUE TO AMPUTATION, ABNORMAL MOTION AND ANKYLOSIS OF THE ELBOW JOINT—FLEXION-EXTENSION

Impairment of Upper Extremity

Amputation—At Joint 95%

Abnormal Motion

Average range of FLEXION-EXTENSION is 150 degrees
Value to total range of joint motion is 60%

Retained active flexion of:	Impairment of Upper Extremity
0°	39%
10°	36
20°	34
30°	31
40°	29
50°	26
60°	23
70°	21
80°	18
90°	16
100°	13
110°	10
120°	8
130°	5
140°	3
150°	0

Extension to:	
0° (neutral position)	0%
10°	2
20°	4
30°	6
40°	8
50°	10
60°	12
70°	14

	Impairment of Upper Extremity
80°	16%
90°	18
100°	20
110°	22
120°	24
130°	26
140°	28
150°	30

Ankylosis

Joint ankylosed at:	
0° (neutral position)	65%
10°	64
20°	62
30°	61
40°	59
50°	58
60°	56
70°	55
80°	53
90°	52
*100°	50
110°	59
120°	68
130°	77
140°	86
150° (full flexion)	95

*position of function

In the case of bilateral ankylosis of the elbows, position of function would not necessarily be the same for both elbows; however, the corresponding impairment of the whole person can be computed by using the above figures and the conversion figures in Table 20.

Elbow Joint — Flexion and Extension

Abnormal Motion

1. Place the patient in the neutral position (Figure 21). Note supination of the forearm.

2. Center the goniometer next to the elbow joint (Figure 22). Record the goniometer reading with the goniometer arm along the axis of the forearm. Also record any deviation of extension from the neutral position.

3. With the patient flexing the arm (Figure 21), follow the range of motion with the goniometer arm. Record the angle that subtends the arc of motion.

4. Consult the abnormal motion section of Table 14. ADD the percentages of impairment for loss of flexion and limitation of extension to determine the impairment of the upper extremity.

Example: 100° active flexion from neutral position (0°) is equivalent to 13% impairment of the upper extremity.

Example: 100° active flexion from 30° extension limitation is equivalent to 19% impairment of the upper extremity; 13% is due to the flexion loss, and 6% is due to the limitation of extension.

NOTE: There also may be impairment of elbow rotation, which should be added.

Ankylosis

1. Place the goniometer base as if measuring the neutral position (Figure 22). Measure the deviation from the neutral position with the goniometer arm and record the reading.

2. Consult the ankylosis section of Table 14 to determine the impairment of the upper extremity.

Example: An elbow joint with ankylosis at 100° flexion is equivalent to 50% impairment of the upper extremity.

Figure 21

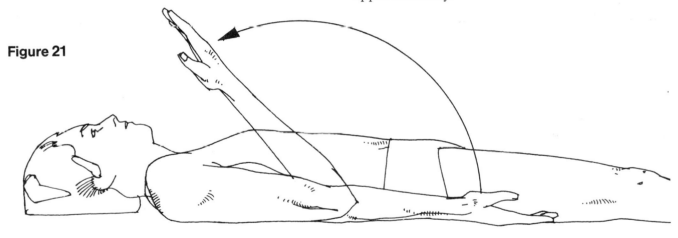

Figure 22

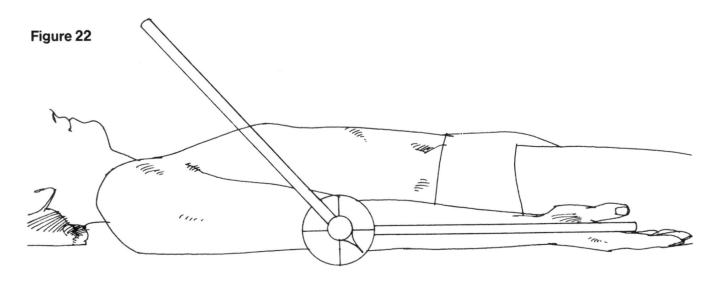

Elbow Joint — Rotation

Abnormal Motion

1. Place the patient in the neutral position (Figure 23). Note the vertical positioning of the forearm. The goniometer is not used in this measurement.

2. Supination: With patient supinating the forearm (Figure 24), record the range of motion as estimated by the arc described by the plane of the hand as it turns.

3. Pronation: With patient pronating the forearm (Figure 25), record the range of motion as estimated by the arc described by the plane of the hand as it turns.

4. Consult the abnormal motion section of Table 15 to determine the impairment of the upper extremity.

Example: 20° active pronation from neutral position (0°) or any 20° arc of retained active pronation is equivalent to 10% impairment of the upper extremity.

5. ADD the impairment values contributed by abnormalities of pronation and supination. The sum of these values is the impairment of the upper extremity due to abnormal rotation of the elbow.

NOTE: There may also be impairment of elbow flexion and extension, which should be added.

Ankylosis

1. Estimate the angle of ankylosis by estimating the angle of the plane of the hand.

2. Consult the ankylosis section of Table 15 to determine the impairment of the upper extremity.

Example: An elbow joint with ankylosis at mid-rotation (neutral position) is equivalent to 65% impairment of the upper extremity.

Figure 24

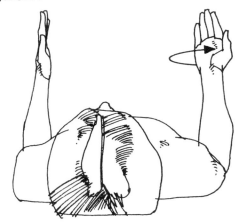

Figure 25

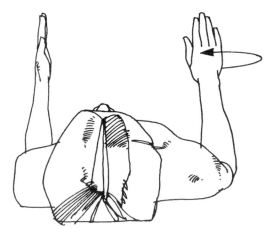

Figure 23

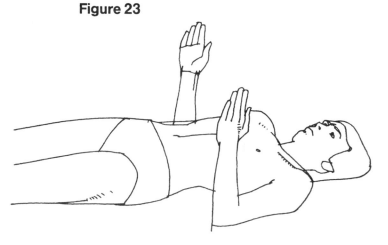

Elbow Joint — Two Ranges of Motion Involved

Abnormal Motion

Measure separately and record the impairment of the upper extremity contributed by each range of motion. Then, add the impairment values contributed by the ranges of motion. Their sum represents the impairment of the upper extremity contributed by the elbow joint.

Example:

Description	% Impairment of Upper Extremity
20° active pronation	10 (Table 15)
20° active supination	10 (Table 15)
100° active flexion	<u>13</u> (Table 14)
(10 + 10 + 13 = 33)	33

Ankylosis

1. Measure separately and record the impairment of the upper extremity that is contributed by ankylosis in each position.

2. The largest impairment value due to ankylosis represents the impairment of upper extremity contributed by the elbow joint.

Example:

Description	% Impairment of Upper Extremity
Ankylosis at 100° flexion	50 (Table 14)
Ankylosis at 20° pronation	73 (Table 15)

The larger impairment value is 73%; therefore, the upper extremity shows 73% impairment because of elbow joint ankylosis.

TABLE 15
IMPAIRMENT DUE TO AMPUTATION, ABNORMAL MOTION AND ANKYLOSIS OF THE ELBOW JOINT—ROTATION

Impairment of Upper Extremity

Amputation—At Joint. 95%

Abnormal Motion

Average range of ROTATION is 160 degrees
Value to total range of joint motion is 40%

Pronation from neutral position (0°) to:	Degrees of Joint Motion LOST	RETAINED	Impairment of Upper Extremity		Ankylosis Joint ankylosed at:	Impairment of Upper Extremity
0°	80	0	13%		*0° (neutral position)	65%
10°	70	10	11		10°	69
20°	60	20	10		20°	73
30°	50	30	8		30°	76
40°	40	40	7		40°	80
50°	30	50	5		50°	84
60°	20	60	3		60°	88
70°	10	70	2		70°	91
80°	0	80	0		80° (full pronation)	95

Supination from neutral position (0°) to:	LOST	RETAINED	Impairment		Joint ankylosed at:	
0°	80	0	13%		*0° (neutral position)	65%
10°	70	10	11		10°	69
20°	60	20	10		20°	73
30°	50	30	8		30°	76
40°	40	40	7		40°	80
50°	30	50	5		50°	84
60°	20	60	3		60°	88
70°	10	70	2		70°	91
80°	0	80	0		80° (full supination)	95

*position of function

Shoulder Joint — Forward Elevation

Abnormal Motion

1. Place the patient in the neutral position (Figure 26). Note pronation of the forearm.

2. Center the goniometer next to the shoulder joint (Figure 27). Record the goniometer reading with the goniometer arm along axis of the upper arm.

3. With the patient elevating both arms as far as possible (Figure 26), follow the range of motion with the goniometer arm. Record the angle that subtends the arc of motion in the tested arm.

4. Consult the abnormal motion section of Table 16 to determine the impairment of the upper extremity.

Example: 30° active forward elevation from neutral position (0°) or any 30° arc of retained active forward elevation is equivalent to 13% impairment of the upper extremity.

5. ADD the impairment values contributed by forward elevation and backward elevation. The sum of these values is the impairment of the upper extremity that is contributed by abnormalities of forward and backward elevation of the shoulder.

Ankylosis

1. Place the goniometer base as if measuring the neutral position (Figure 27). Measure the deviation from neutral position with the goniometer arm and record the reading.

2. Consult the ankylosis section of Table 16 to determine the impairment of the upper extremity.

Example: A shoulder joint with ankylosis at 30° forward elevation is equivalent to 40% impairment of the upper extremity.

Shoulder Joint — Backward Elevation

Abnormal Motion

1. Place the patient in the neutral position (Figure 28). Note supination of the forearm.

2. Center the goniometer next to the shoulder joint (Figure 29). Record the goniometer reading with the goniometer arm along the axis of the upper arm.

3. With the patient elevating both arms as far as possible (Figure 28), follow the range of motion

---

TABLE 16
IMPAIRMENT DUE TO AMPUTATION, ABNORMAL MOTION AND ANKYLOSIS OF THE SHOULDER JOINT—FORWARD ELEVATION

Impairment of Upper Extremity

Amputation—At Joint 100%

Abnormal Motion

Average range of FORWARD-BACKWARD ELEVATION is 190 degrees
Value to total range of joint motion is 33%

Forward elevation from neutral position (0°) to:	Degrees of Joint Motion LOST	RETAINED	Impairment of Upper Extremity
0°	150	0	16%
10°	140	10	15
20°	130	20	14
30°	120	30	13
40°	110	40	12
50°	100	50	11
60°	90	60	9
70°	80	70	8
80°	70	80	7
90°	60	90	6
100°	50	100	5
110°	40	110	4
120°	30	120	3
130°	20	130	2
140°	10	140	1
150°	0	150	0

Ankylosis Joint ankylosed at:	Impairment of Upper Extremity
0° (neutral position)	60%
10°	53
20°	47
*30°	40
40°	45
50°	50
60°	55
70°	60
80°	65
90°	70
100°	75
110°	80
120°	85
130°	90
140°	95
150° (full forward elevation)	100

*position of function

with the goniometer arm. Record the angle that subtends the arc of motion in the tested arm.

4. Consult the abnormal motion section of Table 17 to determine the impairment of the upper extremity.

Example: 30° active backward elevation from neutral position (0°) or any 30° arc of retained active backward elevation is equivalent to 1% impairment of the upper extremity.

5. ADD the impairment values contributed by forward elevation and backward elevation of the shoulder. The sum represents the impairment of the upper extremity that is contributed by abnormal forward and backward elevation of the shoulder.

Ankylosis

1. Place the goniometer base as if measuring the neutral position (Figure 29). Measure the deviation from the neutral position with the goniometer arm and record the reading.

2. Consult the ankylosis section of Table 17 to determine the impairment of the upper extremity.

Example: A shoulder joint with ankylosis at 10° backward elevation is equivalent to 70% impairment of the upper extremity.

Figure 26

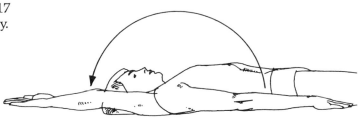

Figure 27

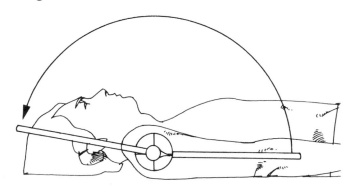

Figure 28

Figure 29

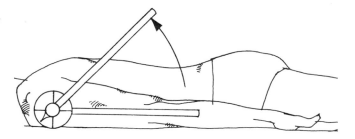

TABLE 17
IMPAIRMENT DUE TO AMPUTATION, ABNORMAL MOTION AND ANKYLOSIS OF THE SHOULDER JOINT—BACKWARD ELEVATION

Impairment of Upper Extremity

Amputation—At Joint 100%

Abnormal Motion

Average range of FORWARD-BACKWARD
ELEVATION is 190 degrees
Value to total range of joint motion is 33%

Backward elevation from neutral position (0°) to:	Degrees of Joint Motion LOST	RETAINED	Impairment of Upper Extremity
0°	40	0	4%
10°	30	10	3
20°	20	20	2
30°	10	30	1
40°	0	40	0

Ankylosis

Joint ankylosed at:

0° (neutral position)	60%
10°	70
20°	80
30°	90
40° (full backward elevation)	100

TABLE 18
IMPAIRMENT DUE TO AMPUTATION, ABNORMAL MOTION AND ANKYLOSIS OF THE SHOULDER JOINT—ABDUCTION-ADDUCTION

Impairment of Upper Extremity

Amputation—At Joint 100%

Abnormal Motion

Average range of ABDUCTION-ADDUCTION is 180 degrees
Value to total range of joint motion is 33%

Abduction from neutral position (0°) to:	Degrees of Joint Motion		Impairment of Upper Extremity
	LOST	RETAINED	
0°	150	0	17%
10°	140	10	16
20°	130	20	14
30°	120	30	13
40°	110	40	12
50°	100	50	11
60°	90	60	10
70°	80	70	9
80°	70	80	8
90°	60	90	7
100°	50	100	6
110°	40	110	4
120°	30	120	3
130°	20	130	2
140°	10	140	1
150°	0	150	0

Adduction from neutral position (0°) to:			
0°	30	0	3%
10°	20	10	2
20°	10	20	1
30°	0	30	0

Ankylosis

Joint ankylosed at:

0° (neutral position)	60%
10°	56
20°	51
30°	47
40°	42
*45°	40
50°	43
60°	49
70°	54
80°	60
90°	66
100°	71
110°	77
120°	83
130°	89
140°	94
150° (full abduction)	100

Joint ankylosed at:

0° (neutral position)	60%
10°	73
20°	87
30° (full adduction)	100

*position of function

Shoulder Joint — Abduction and Adduction

Abnormal Motion

1. Place the patient in the neutral position (Figure 30). Note the position of the forearm.

2. Center the goniometer over the shoulder joint (Figure 30). Record the reading with the goniometer arm along the axis of the patient's arm.

3. Abduction: With the patient abducting both arms as far as possible (Figure 31), follow the range of motion with the goniometer arm. Record the angle that subtends the arc of motion in the tested arm.

4. Adduction: Rotate the goniometer to the position indicated in Figure 32. Starting from the neutral position, with the patient moving the arm to be tested across the abdomen (Figure 33), follow the range of motion with the goniometer arm. Record the angle that subtends the arc of motion.

5. Consult the abnormal motion section of Table 18 to determine the impairment of the upper extremity.

Example: 20° active abduction from neutral position (0°) or any 20° arc of retained active abduction is equivalent to 14% impairment of upper extremity.

6. ADD the impairment values contributed by abduction and adduction. Their sum is the impairment of the upper extremity due to abnormal abduction and adduction of the shoulder.

Ankylosis

1. Place the goniometer base as if measuring the neutral position (Figure 30). Measure the deviation from the neutral position with the goniometer arm and record the reading.

2. Consult the ankylosis section of Table 18 to determine the impairment of the upper extremity.

Example: A shoulder joint with ankylosis at 45° abduction is equivalent to 40% impairment of the upper extremity.

Figure 34

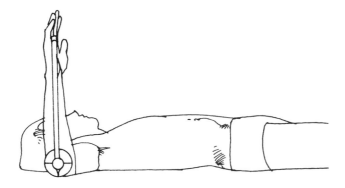

Figure 35

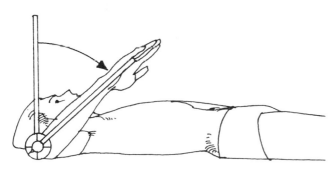

Figure 36

Figure 37

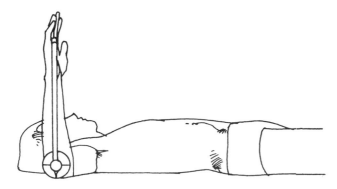

Shoulder Joint—Rotation

Abnormal Motion

1. Place the patient in the neutral position (Figure 34). Note the position of the forearm.

2. Center the goniometer next to the elbow joint (Figure 34). Record the reading with the goniometer arm parallel to the axis of the forearm. Consider 90° or a vertical position of the goniometer arm as the neutral point (0°).

3. External rotation: With the patient attempting to touch the dorsal surface of the forearm to the table top (Figure 35), follow the range of motion with the goniometer arm. Record the angle that subtends the arc of motion.

4. Internal rotation: Starting from the neutral position, with patient attempting to touch the volar surface of the forearm to the table top (Figure 36), follow the range of motion with the goniometer arm. Record the angle that subtends the arc of motion.

5. Consult the abnormal motion section of Table 19 to determine the impairment of the upper extremity.

Example: 20° active external rotation from neutral position (0°) or any 20° arc of retained active external rotation is equivalent to 11% impairment of the upper extremity.

6. ADD the impairment values due to abnormal external and internal rotation. Their sum represents impairment of the upper extremity due to abnormal rotation of the shoulder.

Ankylosis

1. Place the goniometer base as if measuring the neutral position (Figure 37). Measure the deviation from the neutral position with the goniometer arm and record the reading.

2. Consult the ankylosis section of Table 19 to determine the impairment of the upper extremity.

Example: A shoulder joint with ankylosis at 20° external rotation is equivalent to 40% impairment of the upper extremity.

Figure 30

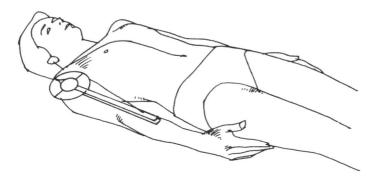

Figure 31

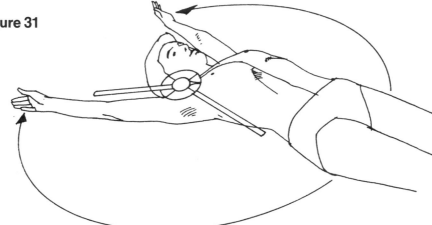

Figure 32

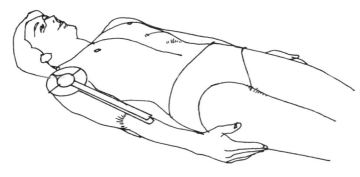

Figure 33

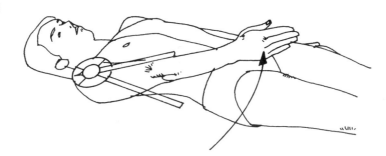

TABLE 19
IMPAIRMENT DUE TO AMPUTATION, ABNORMAL MOTION AND ANKYLOSIS OF THE SHOULDER JOINT—ROTATION

Impairment of Upper Extremity

Amputation—At Joint 100%

Abnormal Motion

Average range of ROTATION is 130 degrees
Value to total joint motion is 33%

Internal rotation from neutral postition (0°) to:	Degrees of Joint Motion LOST	Degrees of Joint Motion RETAINED	Impairment of Upper Extremity
0°	40	0	6%
10°	30	10	5
20°	20	20	3
30°	10	30	2
40°	0	40	0

External rotation from neutral position (0°) to:	LOST	RETAINED	
0°	90	0	14%
10°	80	10	12
20°	70	20	11
30°	60	30	9
40°	50	40	8
50°	40	50	6
60°	30	60	5
70°	20	70	3
80°	10	80	2
90°	0	90	0

Ankylosis

Joint ankylosed at:

0° (neutral position)	60%
10°	70
20°	80
30°	90
40° (full int. rotation)	100

Joint ankylosed at:

0° (neutral position)	60%
10°	50
*20°	40
30°	49
40°	57
50°	66
60°	74
70°	83
80°	91
90° (full ext. rotation)	100

*position of function

TABLE 20
RELATIONSHIP OF IMPAIRMENT OF THE UPPER EXTREMITY TO IMPAIRMENT OF THE WHOLE PERSON

% Impairment of Upper Extremity	Whole Person	% Impairment of Upper Extremity	Whole Person	% Impairment of Upper Extremity	Whole Person
0 =	0	35 =	21	70 =	42
1 =	1	36 =	22	71 =	43
2 =	1	37 =	22	72 =	43
3 =	2	38 =	23	73 =	44
4 =	2	39 =	23	74 =	44
5 =	3	40 =	24	75 =	45
6 =	4	41 =	25	76 =	46
7 =	4	42 =	25	77 =	46
8 =	5	43 =	26	78 =	47
9 =	5	44 =	26	79 =	47
10 =	6	45 =	27	80 =	48
11 =	7	46 =	28	81 =	49
12 =	7	47 =	28	82 =	49
13 =	8	48 =	29	83 =	50
14 =	8	49 =	29	84 =	50
15 =	9	50 =	30	85 =	51
16 =	10	51 =	31	86 =	52
17 =	10	52 =	31	87 =	52
18 =	11	53 =	32	88 =	53
19 =	11	54 =	32	89 =	53
20 =	12	55 =	33	90 =	54
21 =	13	56 =	34	91 =	55
22 =	13	57 =	34	92 =	55
23 =	14	58 =	35	93 =	56
24 =	14	59 =	35	94 =	56
25 =	15	60 =	36	95 =	57
26 =	16	61 =	37	96 =	58
27 =	16	62 =	37	97 =	58
28 =	17	63 =	38	98 =	59
29 =	17	64 =	38	99 =	59
30 =	18	65 =	39	100 =	60
31 =	19	66 =	40		
32 =	19	67 =	40		
33 =	20	68 =	41		
34 =	20	69 =	41		

NOTE: Impairment of the whole person contributed by the upper extremity may be rounded to the nearest 5 percent only when it is the *sole* impairment involved.

Shoulder Joint — Two or More Ranges of Motion

Abnormal Motion

Measure separately and record the impairment of the upper extremity contributed by each range of motion. Then, add the impairment values of the upper extremity contributed by ranges of motion. Their sum is the impairment of the upper extremity contributed by the shoulder joint.

Example:

Description	% Impairment of Upper Extremity
Three Ranges of Motion	
30° active forward elevation	13 (Table 16)
30° active backward elevation	1 (Table 17)
20° active abduction	14 (Table 18)
20° active adduction	1 (Table 18)
20° active internal rotation	3 (Table 19)
20° active external rotation	11 (Table 19)
(13 + 1 + 14 + 1 + 3 + 11 = 43)	43

Ankylosis

1. Measure separately and record the impairment of the upper extremity contributed by ankylosis in each position. The largest impairment value for ankylosis is the impairment of the upper extremity that is contributed by the shoulder joint.

Example:

Description	% Impairment of Upper Extremity
Ankylosis at 60° forward elevation	55 (Table 16)
Ankylosis at 20° external rotation	40 (Table 19)

The largest impairment value is 55%; therefore, upper extremity is 55% impaired by ankylosis of the shoulder joint.

Upper Extremity — Involvement of Multiple Units

Measure separately and record the impairment of the upper extremity that is contributed by each unit (hand, wrist joint, elbow joint, and shoulder joint). Then, combine the impairment values using the Combined Values Chart to ascertain the impairment of the upper extremity.

Example:

Description	% Impairment of Upper Extremity
Hand impaired at 44%	40 (Table 9)
Wrist impaired	30
Elbow impaired	20
(40 combined with 30 = 58; 58 combined with 20 = 66)	66

Finally, consult Table 20 to determine the impairment of the whole person that is due to impairment of the upper extremity.

Impairment values for amputation of various parts of the upper extremity are found in Table 21.

TABLE 21
IMPAIRMENTS OF DIGITS, HAND, UPPER EXTREMITY AND WHOLE PERSON DUE TO AMPUTATIONS

		% Impairment of:		
	Digit	Hand	Upper* Extremity	Whole Person
Forequarter amputation				70
Disarticulation at shoulder joint			100	60
Amputation of arm above deltoid insertion			100	60
Amputation of arm between deltoid insertion and elbow joint			95	57
Disarticulation at elbow joint			95	57
Amputation of forearm below elbow joint proximal to insertion of biceps tendon			95	57
Amputation of forearm below elbow joint distal to insertion of biceps tendon		100	90	54
Disarticulation at wrist joint		100	90	54
Midcarpal or mid-metacarpal amputation of hand		100	90	54
Amputation of all fingers except thumb at metacarpophalangeal joints		60	54	32
Amputation of thumb at metacarpophalangeal joint				
or with resection of carpometacarpal bone	100	40	36	22
At interphalangeal joint	75	30	27	16
Amputation of index finger at metacarpophalangeal joint				
or with resection of metacarpal bone	100	25	23	14
At proximal interphalangeal joint	80	20	18	11
At distal interphalangeal joint	45	11	10	6
Amputation of middle finger at metacarpophalangeal joint				
or with resection of metacarpal bone	100	20	18	11
At proximal interphalangeal joint	80	16	14	8
At distal interphalangeal joint	45	9	8	5
Amputation of ring finger at metacarpophalangeal joint				
or with resection of metacarpal bone	100	10	9	5
At proximal interphalangeal joint	80	8	7	4
At distal interphalangeal joint	45	5	5	3
Amputation of little finger at metacarpophalangeal joint				
or with resection of metacarpal bone	100	5	5	3
At proximal interphalangeal joint	80	4	4	2
At distal interphalangeal joint	45	2	2	1

*If the non-preferred upper extremity is involved, reduce the impairment rating by 5% or 10% (see text).

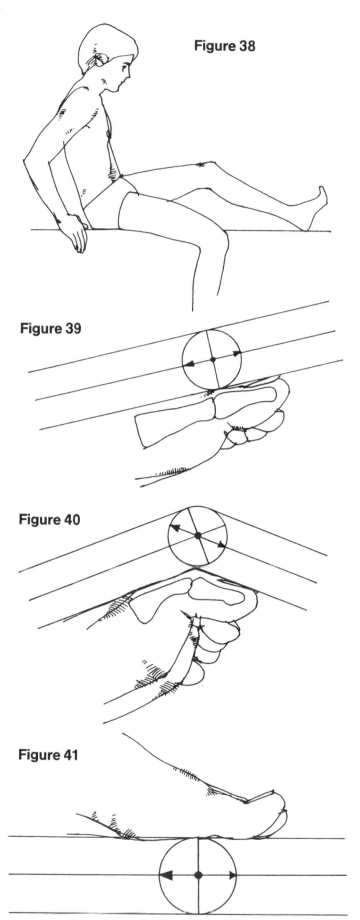

Figure 38

Figure 39

Figure 40

Figure 41

The Lower Extremity

Interphalangeal Joint of the Great Toe — Flexion and Extension

Abnormal Motion

1. Place the patient's foot in the neutral position (Figure 38). Note the 45° angle of the knee and the 90° angle of the ankle.

2. Center the goniometer next to the interphalangeal joint (Figure 39). Record the goniometer reading.

3. With the patient plantar-flexing the great toe as far as possible (Figure 40), follow the range of motion with the goniometer arm. Record the angle that subtends the arc of motion.

4. Consult the abnormal motion section of Table 22 to determine the impairment of the great toe.

Example: 10° active flexion from neutral position or from maximum extension is equivalent to 30% impairment of the great toe.

Ankylosis

1. Place the goniometer base as if measuring the neutral position (Figure 39). Measure the deviation from the neutral position with the goniometer arm and record the reading.

2. Consult the ankylosis section of Table 22 to determine the impairment of the great toe.

Example: The interphalangeal joint with ankylosis at 10° flexion is equivalent to 55% impairment of the great toe.

Figure 42

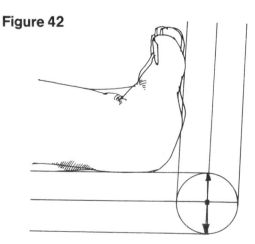

Metatarsophalangeal Joint of the Great Toe — Dorsi-flexion

Abnormal Motion

1. Place the patient in the neutral position (Figure 38). Note the 45° angle of the knee and the 90° angle of the ankle.

2. Center the goniometer over the metatarsophalangeal joint (Figure 41). Record the goniometer reading.

3. With the patient dorsi-flexing the great toe, follow the range of motion with the goniometer arm (Figure 42). Record the angle that subtends the arc of motion.

4. Consult the abnormal motion section of Table 23 to determine the impairment of the great toe.

Example: 20° active dorsi-flexion from neutral position (0°) or any 20° arc of retained active dorsi-flexion is equivalent to 21% impairment of the great toe.

5. ADD the impairment values of the great toe contributed by dorsi-flexion and plantar-flexion. Their sum is the impairment of the great toe contributed by abnormal motions of the metatarsophalangeal joint.

Ankylosis

1. Place the goniometer base as if measuring the neutral position (Figure 39). Measure the deviation from neutral position with the goniometer arm and record the reading.

2. Consult the ankylosis section of Table 23 to determine the impairment of the great toe.

Example: The metatarsophalangeal joint with ankylosis at 20° dorsi-flexion is equivalent to 62% impairment of the great toe.

TABLE 22
IMPAIRMENT DUE TO AMPUTATION, ABNORMAL MOTION AND ANKYLOSIS OF THE INTERPHALANGEAL JOINT OF THE GREAT TOE

	Impairment of Great Toe
Amputation—At Joint	75%

Abnormal Motion
Average range of FLEXION-EXTENSION is 30 degrees
Value to total range of joint motion is 100%

Flexion from neutral position (0°) to:	Degrees of Joint Motion LOST	RETAINED	Impairment of Great Toe
0°	30	0	45%
10°	20	10	30
20°	10	20	15
30°	0	30	0

Ankylosis

Joint ankylosed at:

	Impairment of Great Toe
*0° (neutral position)	45%
10°	55
20°	65
30° (full flexion)	75

*position of function

TABLE 23
IMPAIRMENT DUE TO AMPUTATION, ABNORMAL MOTION AND ANKYLOSIS OF THE METATARSOPHALANGEAL JOINT OF THE GREAT TOE—DORSI-FLEXION

	Impairment of Great Toe
Amputation—At Joint	100%

Abnormal Motion
Average range of DORSI-PLANTAR FLEXION is 80 degrees
Value to total range of joint motion is 100%

Dorsi-flexion from neutral position (0°) to:	Degrees of Joint Motion LOST	RETAINED	Impairment of Great Toe
0°	50	0	34%
10°	40	10	28
20°	30	20	21
30°	20	30	14
40°	10	40	7
50°	0	50	0

Ankylosis

Joint ankylosed at:

	Impairment of Great Toe
0° (neutral position)	55%
*10°	49
20°	62
30°	74
40°	87
50° (full dorsi-flexion)	100

Arthroplasty at joint: same loss as for ankylosis.

*position of function

27

TABLE 24
IMPAIRMENT DUE TO AMPUTATION, ABNORMAL MOTION AND ANKYLOSIS OF THE GREAT TOE—PLANTAR-FLEXION

	Impairment of Great Toe
Amputation—At Joint............................	100%

Abnormal Motion

Average range of DORSI-PLANTAR FLEXION is 80 degrees
Value to total range of joint motion is 100%

Plantar-flexion from neutral position (0°) to:	Degrees of Joint Motion LOST	RETAINED	Impairment of Great Toe
0°	30	0	21%
10°	20	10	14
20°	10	20	7
30°	0	30	0

Ankylosis

Joint ankylosed at:

0° (neutral position)...........	55%
10°	70
20°	85
30° (full plantar flexion)	100

TABLE 25
RELATIONSHIP OF IMPAIRMENT OF THE GREAT TOE TO IMPAIRMENT OF THE FOOT

% Impairment of Great Toe		Foot	% Impairment of Great Toe		Foot
0	— 2	= 0	53	— 57	= 10
3	— 8	= 1	58	— 62	= 11
9	— 13	= 2			
14	— 19	= 3	63	— 68	= 12
			69	— 73	= 13
20	— 24	= 4	74	— 79	= 14
25	— 30	= 5	80	— 84	= 15
31	— 35	= 6			
36	— 41	= 7	85	— 90	= 16
			91	— 95	= 17
42	— 46	= 8	96	— 100	= 18
47	— 52	= 9			

NOTE: Impairment of the foot contributed by the great toe may be rounded to the nearest 5% only when it is the *sole* impairment involved.
Consult Table 34 for converting foot impairment to lower extremity impairment.

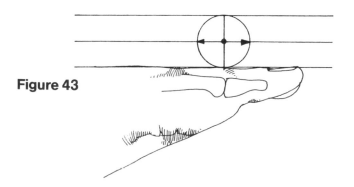

Figure 43

Metatarsophalangeal Joint of the Great Toe—Plantar-flexion

Abnormal Motion

1. Place the patient in the neutral position (Figure 38).

2. Center the goniometer over the metatarsophalangeal joint (Figure 43). Record the goniometer reading. Note that the goniometer is rotated 180° from its position for testing dorsi-flexion.

3. With the patient plantar-flexing the great toe (Figure 44), follow the range of motion with the goniometer arm. Record the angle that subtends the arc of motion.

4. Consult the abnormal motion section of Table 24 to determine the impairment of the great toe.

Example: 20° active plantar-flexion from neutral position (0°) or any 20° arc of active plantar-flexion is equivalent to 7% impairment of the great toe.

5. ADD the impairment values contributed by abnormalities of dorsi-flexion and plantar-flexion. Their sum represents impairment of the great toe contributed by the metatarsophalangeal joint.

Ankylosis

1. Place the goniometer base as if measuring the neutral position (Figure 43). Measure the deviation from the neutral position with the goniometer arm and record the reading.

2. Consult the ankylosis section of Table 24 to determine the impairment of the great toe.

Example: The metatarsophalangeal joint with ankylosis at 20° plantar-flexion is equivalent to 85% impairment of the great toe.

Figure 44

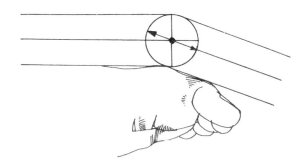

Great Toe—Both Joints Involved

Measure separately and record the impairment of the great toe contributed by each joint. Then, combine the impairment values using the Combined Values Chart to determine the impairment of the great toe contributed by both joints.

Example:

Description	% Impairment of Great Toe
Interphalangeal joint with ankylosis at 10° flexion	55 (Table 22)
Metatarsophalangeal joint with ankylosis at 20° dorsi-flexion	62 (Table 23)
(62 combined with 55 = 83)	83

Example:

Description	% Impairment of Great Toe
Amputated interphalangeal joint	75 (Table 22)
Metatarsophalangeal joint with 20° active dorsi-flexion from neutral position (0°)	21 (Table 23)
Metatarsophalangeal joint with 20° active plantar-flexion from neutral position (0°)	7 (Table 24)
(21 + 7 = 28; 28 combined with 75 = 82)	82

Finally, consult Table 25 to determine impairment of the foot that is contributed by the great toe; in these examples, the impairment of the foot would be 15%.

Distal Interphalangeal Joint of the Second through Fifth Toes—Dorsi- and Plantar-flexion

Abnormal Motion

1. Abnormal motion is not measurable.

Ankylosis

1. Place the goniometer base as if measuring the neutral position (Figure 45). Measure the deviation from the neutral position with the goniometer arm (Figure 46), and record the reading.

2. Consult the ankylosis section of Table 26 to determine the impairment of the toe.

TABLE 26
IMPAIRMENT DUE TO AMPUTATION, ABNORMAL MOTION AND ANKYLOSIS OF THE DISTAL INTERPHALANGEAL JOINT OF THE 2nd THROUGH 5th TOE—DORSI-PLANTAR-FLEXION

	Impairment of Toe
Amputation—At Joint	45%

Abnormal Motion

No functional value

Ankylosis Joint ankylosed in:	Impairment of Toe
Dorsi-flexion	45%
*Neutral position	30
Plantar-flexion (hammer toe) . . .	45

*position of function

Figure 45

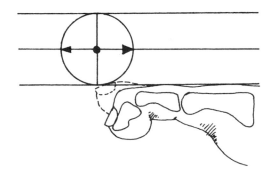

Figure 46

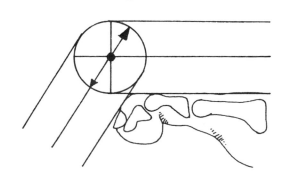

29

TABLE 27
IMPAIRMENT DUE TO AMPUTATION, ABNORMAL MOTION AND ANKYLOSIS OF THE PROXIMAL INTERPHALANGEAL JOINT OF THE 2nd THROUGH 5th TOE—DORSI-PLANTAR-FLEXION

	Impairment of Toe
Amputation—At Joint	80%

Abnormal Motion

No functional value

Ankylosis

Joint ankylosed in:	Impairment of Toe
Dorsi-flexion	80%
*Neutral position	45
Plantar-flexion	80

*position of function

Proximal Interphalangeal Joint of the Second through Fifth Toes — Dorsi- and Plantar-flexion

Abnormal Motion

1. Abnormal motion is not measurable.

Ankylosis

1. Place the goniometer base as if measuring the neutral position (Figure 47). Measure the deviation from the neutral position with the goniometer arm (Figure 48), and record the reading.

2. Consult the ankylosis section of Table 27 to determine the impairment of the toe.

Figure 47

Figure 48

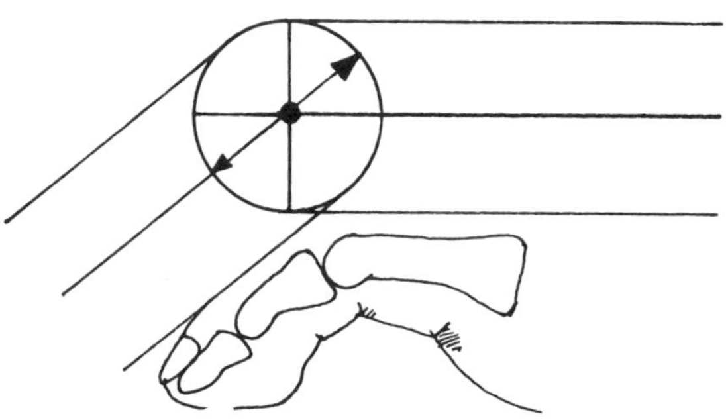

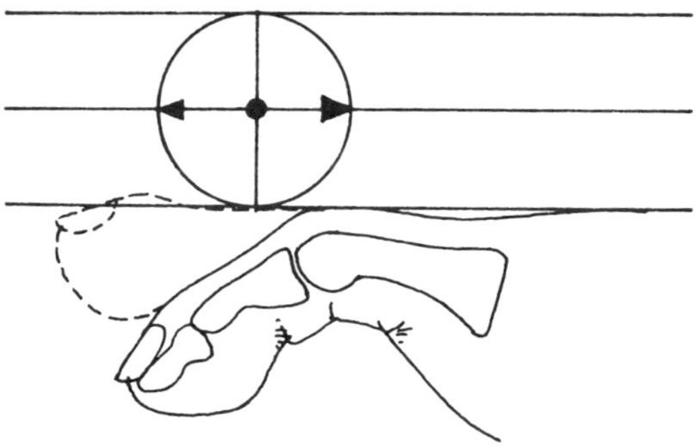

Figure 49

| (a) | (b) | (c) | (d) |

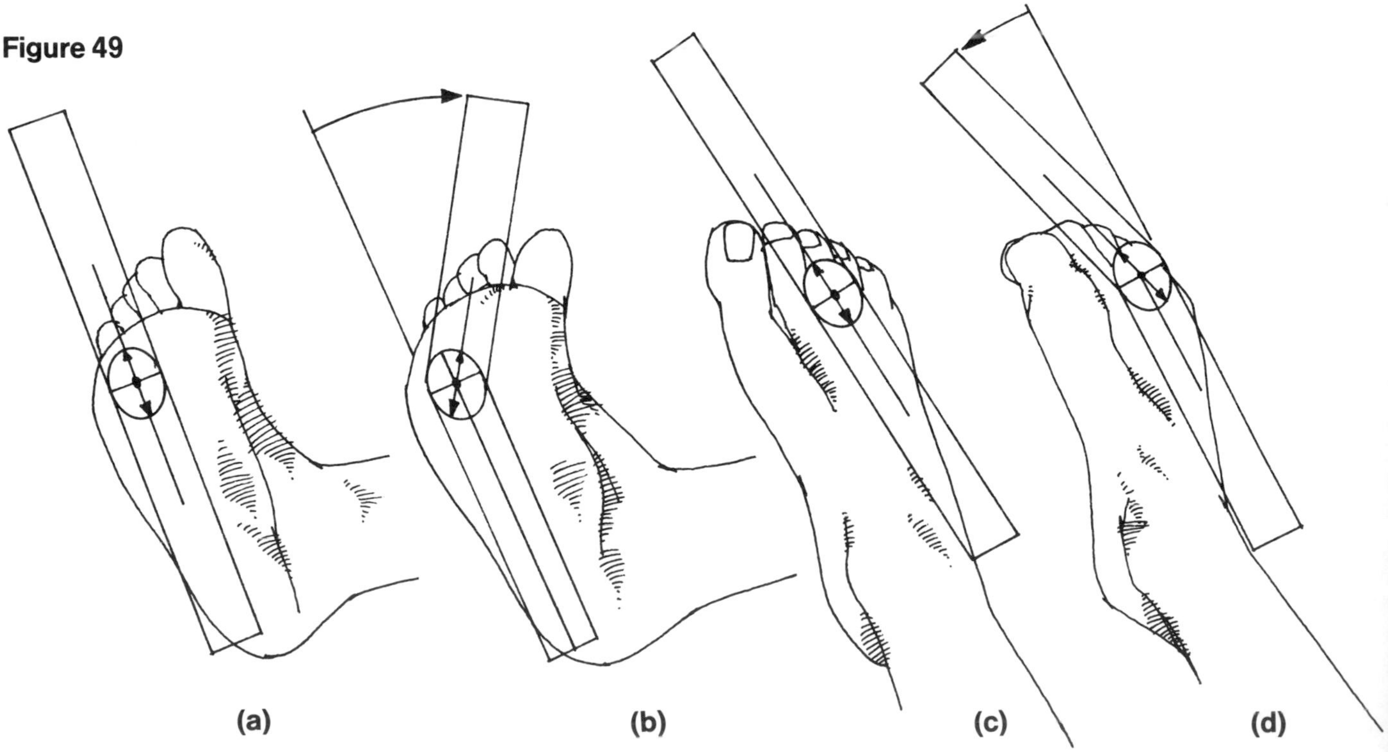

30

Metatarsophalangeal Joint of the Second through Fifth Toes — Dorsi- and Plantar-flexion

Abnormal Motion

1. Place patient in the neutral position (Figure 38).

2. Dorsi-flexion: Center the goniometer beneath the metatarsophalangeal joint of the toe being tested (Figure 49a). Record the goniometer reading. With the patient dorsi-flexing the toe as far as possible (Figure 49b), follow the range of motion with the goniometer arm. Record the angle that subtends the arc of motion.

3. Plantar-flexion: Center the goniometer over the metatarsophalangeal joint of the toe being tested (Figure 49c). Record the goniometer reading. Starting from the neutral position with patient plantar-flexing the toe as far as possible (Figure 49d), follow the range of motion with the goniometer arm. Record the angle that subtends the arc of motion.

4. Consult the abnormal motion section of Tables 28-31 to determine the impairment of the toe.

Example: 20° active dorsi-flexion from neutral position (0°) or any 20° arc of retained active dorsi-flexion is equivalent to 14% impairment of the second toe (Table 28).

5. ADD the toe impairment values contributed by dorsi-flexion and plantar-flexion. The sum of these values is the impairment of the toe.

Ankylosis

1. Place the goniometer base as if measuring the neutral position (Figure 49a or 49c). Measure the deviation from the neutral position with goniometer arm and record the reading.

2. Consult the ankylosis section of Tables 28-31 to determine the impairment of the toe.

Example: A metatarsophalangeal joint with ankylosis at 20° dorsi-flexion is equivalent to 75% impairment of the second toe (Table 28).

TABLE 28
IMPAIRMENT DUE TO AMPUTATION, ABNORMAL MOTION AND ANKYLOSIS OF THE METATARSOPHALANGEAL JOINT OF THE SECOND TOE—DORSI-PLANTAR FLEXION

Impairment of Second Toe

Amputation—At Joint 100%

Abnormal Motion

Average range of DORSI-PLANTAR FLEXION is 70 degrees
Value to total range of joint motion is 100%

Dorsi-flexion from neutral position (0°) to:	Degrees of Joint Motion LOST	Degrees of Joint Motion RETAINED	Impairment of Second Toe
0°	40	0	29%
10°	30	10	21
20°	20	20	14
30°	10	30	7
40°	0	40	0

Plantar-flexion from neutral position (0°) to:	Degrees of Joint Motion LOST	Degrees of Joint Motion RETAINED	Impairment of Second Toe
0°	30	0	21%
10°	20	10	14
20°	10	20	7
30°	0	30	0

Ankylosis Joint ankylosed at:	Impairment of Second Toe
*0° (neutral position)	50%
10°	63
20°	75
30°	88
40° (full dorsi-flexion)	100

Joint ankylosed at:	
*0° (neutral position)	50%
10°	67
20°	83
30° (full plantar-flexion)	100

*position of function

Second through Fifth Toes — Two or More Joints

Measure separately and record the impairment of the toe contributed by each joint. Then, combine the impairment values using the Combined Values Chart to determine the impairment of the toe contributed by two or more joints.

Example: Second Toe

Description	% Impairment of Toe
Amputated distal interphalangeal joint	45 (Table 26)
Proximal interphalangeal joint with ankylosis in neutral position	45 (Table 27)
Metatarsophalangeal joint with 20° active dorsi-flexion from neutral position	14 (Table 28)
Metatarsophalangeal joint with 20° active plantar-flexion from neutral position	7 (Table 28)

(14 + 7 = 21; 21 combined with 45 = 57; 57 combined with 45 = 76). 76

Finally, consult Table 32 to determine the impairment of the foot contributed by the toe. In the example, foot impairment would be 2%.

Foot — Involvement of Two or More Toes

Measure separately and record the impairment of each toe involved. Then, measure separately and record the impairment of the foot as contributed by each toe.

ADD all the impairment values. Their sum equals the impairment of the foot.

Example

Description	% Impairment of Foot
10% impairment of great toe	2 (Table 25)
20% impairment of second toe	1 (Table 32)
30% impairment of third toe	1 (Table 32)
40% impairment of fourth toe	1 (Table 32)
50% impairment of fifth toe	2
(2 + 1 + 1 + 1 + 2 = 7)	7

Finally, consult Table 33 to determine the impairment of the foot that is contributed by combinations of impairment of the toes, and consult Table 34 to determine the impairment of the lower extremity.

For example, mid-tarsal joint ankylosis results in 10% impairment of the foot and 7% impairment of the lower extremity.

TABLE 29
IMPAIRMENT DUE TO AMPUTATION, ABNORMAL MOTION AND ANKYLOSIS OF THE METATARSOPHALANGEAL JOINT OF THE THIRD TOE—DORSI-PLANTAR FLEXION

	Impairment of Third Toe
Amputation—At Joint	100%

Abnormal Motion

Average range of DORSI-PLANTAR FLEXION is 50 degrees
Value to total range of joint motion is 100%

Dorsi-flexion from neutral position (0°) to:	Degrees of Joint Motion LOST	Degrees of Joint Motion RETAINED	Impairment of Third Toe
0°	30	0	30%
10°	20	10	20
20°	10	20	10
30°	0	30	0

Plantar-flexion from neutral position (0°) to:			
0°	20	0	20%
10°	10	10	10
20°	0	20	0

Ankylosis

Joint ankylosed at:

*0° (neutral position)	50%
10°	67
20°	83
30° (full dorsi-flexion)	100

Joint ankylosed at:

*0° (neutral position)	50%
10°	75
20° (full plantar-flexion)	100

*position of function

TABLE 30
IMPAIRMENT DUE TO AMPUTATION, ABNORMAL MOTION AND ANKYLOSIS OF THE METATARSOPHALANGEAL JOINT OF THE FOURTH TOE—DORSI-PLANTAR FLEXION

Impairment of Fourth Toe

Amputation—At Joint 100%

Abnormal Motion

Average range of DORSI-PLANTAR FLEXION is 30 degrees
Value to total range of joint motion is 100%

Dorsi-flexion from neutral position (0°) to:	Degrees of Joint Motion LOST	RETAINED	Impairment of Fourth Toe
0°	20	0	33%
10°	10	10	17
20°	0	20	0

Plantar-flexion from neutral postition (0°) to:			
0°	10	0	17%
10°	0	10	0

Ankylosis

Joint ankylosed at:

*0° (neutral position)	50%
10°	75
20° (full dorsi-flexion)	100

Joint ankylosed at:

*0° (neutral position)	50%
10° (full plantar-flexion)	100

*position of function

TABLE 31
IMPAIRMENT DUE TO AMPUTATION, ABNORMAL MOTION AND ANKYLOSIS OF THE METATARSOPHALANGEAL JOINT OF THE FIFTH TOE—DORSI-PLANTAR FLEXION

Impairment of Fifth Toe

Amputation—At Joint 100%

Abnormal Motion

Average range of DORSI-PLANTAR FLEXION is 20 degrees
Value to total range of joint motion is 100%

Dorsi-flexion from neutral position (0°) to:	Degrees of Joint Motion LOST	RETAINED	Impairment of Fifth Toe
0°	10	0	50%
10°	0	10	0

Plantar-flexion from neutral position (0°) to:			
0°	10	0	50%
10°	0	10	0

Ankylosis

Joint ankylosed at:

0° (neutral position)	50%
10° (full dorsi-flexion)	100

Joint ankylosed at:

0° (neutral position)	50%
10° (full plantar-flexion)	100

TABLE 32
RELATIONSHIP OF IMPAIRMENTS OF SECOND THROUGH FIFTH TOES TO IMPAIRMENT OF THE FOOT

% Impairment of	
Each Toe	Foot
0- 16	0
17- 49	1
50- 83	2
84-100	3

NOTE: Impairment of the foot contributed by the toe may be rounded to the nearest 5 percent only when it is the *sole* impairment involved.

Consult Table 33 for converting foot impairment to lower extremity impairment.

33

Hind Foot (Ankle Joint Primarily) — Dorsi- and Plantar-flexion

Abnormal Motion

1. Place the patient in the neutral position (Figure 50).

2. Center the goniometer over the lateral malleolus (Figure 51). Note that the goniometer base lies along the axis of the tibia. Record the goniometer reading with the goniometer arm parallel to the sole of the foot.

3. Dorsi-flexion: With the patient dorsi-flexing the foot as far as possible, follow the range of motion with the goniometer arm. Record the angle that subtends the arc of motion.

4. Plantar-flexion: Starting from the neutral position with the patient plantar-flexing the foot as far as possible, follow the range of motion with the goniometer arm. Record the angle that subtends the arc of motion.

5. Retest the range of dorsi- and plantar-flexion of the foot with the knee flexed to 45°. If the arcs of motion are different from those obtained in steps 3 and 4, then the averages of the results represent the angles to be used in determining the impairment of the lower extremity.

6. Consult the abnormal motion section of Table 35 to determine the impairment of the lower extremity.

Example: 10° active dorsi-flexion from neutral position (0°) or any 10° arc of retained active dorsi-flexion is equivalent to 4% impairment of the lower extremity.

7. ADD impairment values contributed by dorsi-flexion and plantar-flexion. Their sum is the impairment of the lower extremity contributed by abnormalities of dorsi-flexion and plantar-flexion of the ankle.

NOTE: There may also be impairment of inversion or eversion, the value for which should be added (see below).

Ankylosis

1. Place the goniometer base as if measuring the neutral position (Figure 50). Measure the deviation from the neutral position with the goniometer arm and record the reading.

2. Consult the ankylosis section of Table 35 to determine the impairment of the lower extremity.

Example: An ankle joint with ankylosis at 10° dorsi-flexion is equivalent to 50% impairment of the lower extremity.

TABLE 33
IMPAIRMENT OF THE FOOT DUE TO AMPUTATION AND ANKYLOSIS OF MULTIPLE DIGITS

Digit(s) Involved	% Impairment of Foot			
	Amputated	Ankylosed in		
		Position		
		Full Extension	of Function	Full Flexion
Great	18	14	13	18
Great, Second	21	17	15	21
Great, Second, Third	24	20	17	24
Great, Second, Fourth	24	20	17	24
Great, Second, Fifth	24	20	17	24
Great, Second, Third, Fourth	27	23	19	27
Great, Second, Third, Fifth	27	23	19	27
Great, Second, Fourth, Fifth	27	23	19	27
Great, Second, Third, Fourth, Fifth	30	26	21	30
Great, Third	21	17	15	21
Great, Third, Fourth	24	20	17	24
Great, Third, Fifth	24	20	17	24
Great, Third, Fourth, Fifth	27	23	19	27
Great, Fourth	21	17	15	21
Great, Fourth, Fifth	24	20	17	24
Great, Fifth	21	17	15	21
Second	3	3	2	3
Second, Third	6	6	4	6
Second, Third, Fourth	9	9	4	9
Second, Third, Fifth	9	9	6	9
Second, Third, Fourth, Fifth	12	12	8	12
Second, Fourth	6	6	4	6
Second, Fourth, Fifth	9	9	6	9
Second, Fifth	6	6	4	6
Third	3	3	2	3
Third, Fourth	6	6	4	6
Third, Fourth, Fifth	9	9	6	9
Third, Fifth	6	6	4	6
Fourth	3	3	2	3
Fourth, Fifth	6	6	4	6
Fifth	3	3	2	3

34

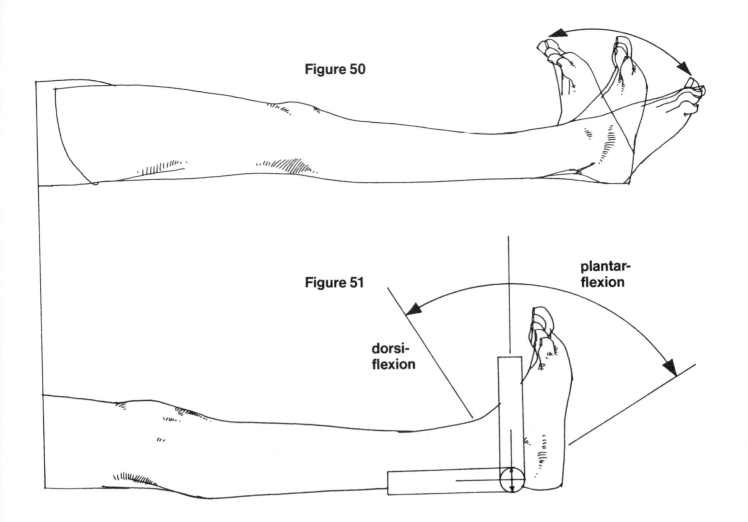

Figure 50

Figure 51

dorsi-
flexion

plantar-
flexion

TABLE 34
RELATIONSHIP OF IMPAIRMENT OF THE FOOT TO IMPAIRMENT OF THE LOWER EXTREMITY

Foot	% Impairment of Lower Extremity	Foot	% Impairment of Lower Extremity	Foot	% Impairment of Lower Extremity	Foot	% Impairment of Lower Extremity	Foot	% Impairment of Lower Extremity	Foot	% Impairment of Lower Extremity
0 =	0	20 =	14	40 =	28	60 =	42	75 =	53	90 =	63
1 =	1	21 =	15	41 =	29	61 =	43	76 =	53	91 =	64
2 =	1	22 =	15	42 =	29	62 =	43	77 =	54	92 =	64
3 =	2	23 =	16	43 =	30	63 =	44	78 =	55	93 =	65
4 =	3	24 =	17	44 =	31	64 =	45	79 =	55	94 =	66
5 =	4	25 =	18	45 =	32	65 =	46	80 =	56	95 =	67
6 =	4	26 =	18	46 =	32	66 =	46	81 =	57	96 =	67
7 =	5	27 =	19	47 =	33	67 =	47	82 =	57	97 =	68
8 =	6	28 =	20	48 =	34	68 =	48	83 =	58	98 =	69
9 =	6	29 =	20	49 =	34	69 =	48	84 =	59	99 =	69
10 =	7	30 =	21	50 =	35	70 =	49	85 =	60	100 =	70
11 =	8	31 =	22	51 =	36	71 =	50	86 =	60		
12 =	8	32 =	22	52 =	36	72 =	50	87 =	61		
13 =	9	33 =	23	53 =	37	73 =	51	88 =	62		
14 =	10	34 =	24	54 =	38	74 =	52	89 =	62		
15 =	11	35 =	25	55 =	39						
16 =	11	36 =	25	56 =	39						
17 =	12	37 =	26	57 =	40						
18 =	13	38 =	27	58 =	41						
19 =	13	39 =	27	59 =	41						

NOTE: Impairment of the lower extremity as contributed by the foot may be rounded to the nearest 5% only when it is the *sole* impairment involved.

Consult Table 44 for converting lower extremity impairment to whole person impairment.

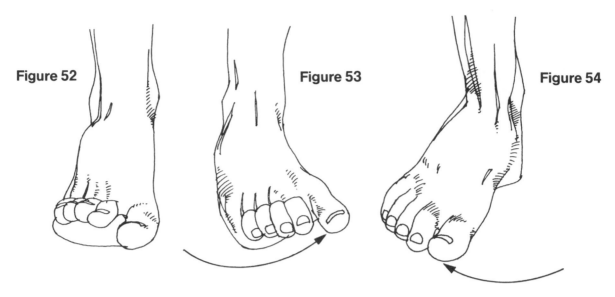

Figure 52

Figure 53

Figure 54

TABLE 35
IMPAIRMENT DUE TO AMPUTATION, ABNORMAL MOTION AND ANKYLOSIS OF THE HIND FOOT (ANKLE JOINT)—DORSI-PLANTAR FLEXION

	Impairment of Lower Extremity
Amputation—At Joint	70%

Abnormal Motion

Average range of DORSI-PLANTAR FLEXION is 60 degrees
Value to total range of joint motion is 70%

	Degrees of Joint Motion		Impairment of Lower
Dorsi-flexion from neutral position (0°) to:	LOST	RETAINED	Extremity
0°	20	0	7%
10°	10	10	4
20°	0	20	0

Plantar-flexion from neutral position (0°) to:			
0°	40	0	14%
10°	30	10	11
20°	20	20	7
30°	10	30	4
40°	0	40	0
Ankle instability due to lateral collateral ligament loss			25
Ankle instability due to medial collateral ligament loss			15

Ankylosis

Joint ankylosed at:	
*0° (neutral position)	30%
10°	50
20° (full dorsi-flexion)	70

Joint ankylosed at:	
*0° (neutral position)	30%
10°	40
20°	50
30°	60
40° (full plantar-flexion)	70
Arthroplasty of joint: same loss as for maximum ankylosis.	

*position of function

TABLE 36
IMPAIRMENT DUE TO AMPUTATION, ABNORMAL MOTION AND ANKYLOSIS OF THE HIND FOOT (SUBTALAR JOINT)—INVERSION-EVERSION

	Impairment of Lower Extremity
Amputation—At Joint	70%

Abnormal Motion

Average range of INVERSION-EVERSION is 50 degrees
Value to total range of joint motion is 30%

	Degrees of Joint Motion		Impairment of Lower
Inversion from neutral position (0°) to:	LOST	RETAINED	Extremity
0°	30	0	5%
10°	20	10	4
20°	10	20	2
30°	0	30	0

Eversion from neutral position (0°) to:			
0°	20	0	4%
10°	10	10	2
20°	0	20	0

Ankylosis

Joint ankylosed at:	
*0° (neutral position)	10%
10°	43
20°	57
30° (full inversion)	70

Joint ankylosed at:	
*0° (neutral position)	10%
10°	50
20° (full eversion)	60

*position of function

Hind Foot (Subtalar Joint Primarily) — Inversion and Eversion

Abnormal Motion

1. Place the patient in the neutral position (Figure 52). The plane of the foot is at a right angle to the lower leg. The goniometer is not used.

2. Inversion: Starting from the neutral position with the patient inverting the foot (Figure 53), record the range of motion by estimating the arc described by the plantar surface of the foot as it turns.

3. Eversion: With the patient everting the foot (Figure 54), record the range of motion by estimating the arc described by the plantar surface of the foot as it turns.

4. Consult the abnormal motion section of Table 36 to determine the impairment of the lower extremity.

Example: A foot with 20° inversion from neutral position (0°) or any 20° arc of retained active inversion is equivalent to 2% impairment of the lower extremity.

5. ADD impairment values contributed by inversion and eversion. Their sum represents the impairment of the lower extremity contributed by abnormal inversion and eversion of the subtalar joint.

NOTE: There may also be impairment of dorsi- and plantar-flexion of the ankle, which should be added to impairment of inversion and eversion of the subtalar joint.

Ankylosis

1. Estimate the angle of ankylosis by observing the angle of the plane formed by the plantar surface of the foot.

2. Consult the ankylosis section of Table 36 to determine the impairment of the lower extremity.

Example: A subtalar joint with ankylosis of 20° inversion is equivalent to 57% impairment of the lower extremity.

Hind Foot — Two Ranges of Motion

Abnormal Motion

Measure separately and record the impairment of the lower extremity that is contributed by each range of motion. ADD the impairment values of the lower extremity contributed by all ranges of motion. Their sum is the impairment of the lower extremity contributed by the ankle and subtalar joints.

Example

Description	% Impairment of Lower Extremity
10° active dorsi-flexion	4 (Table 35)
10° active plantar-flexion	11 (Table 35)
10° active inversion	4 (Table 36)
10° active eversion	2 (Table 36)
(4 + 11 + 4 + 2 = 21)	21

Ankylosis

Measure separately and record the impairment of the lower extremity that is contributed by ankylosis in each position. The larger impairment value represents the impairment of the lower extremity that is contributed by ankylosis of the ankle and subtalar joints.

Example:

Description	% Impairment of Lower Extremity
Ankylosis at 10° dorsi-flexion	50 (Table 35)
Ankylosis at 10° inversion	43 (Table 36)

The largest value is 50%; therefore, the lower extremity has 50% impairment due to the ankylosis.

Figure 55

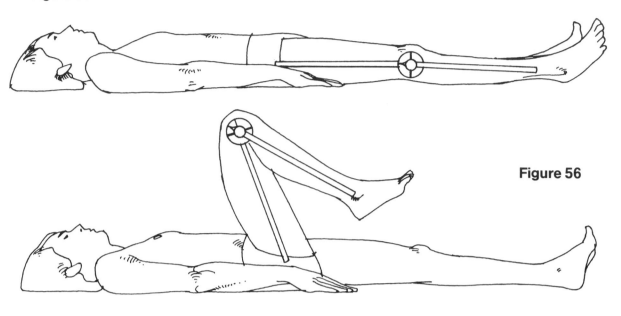

Figure 56

TABLE 37
IMPAIRMENT DUE TO AMPUTATION, ABNORMAL MOTION AND ANKYLOSIS OF THE KNEE JOINT

	Impairment of Lower Extremity
Amputation—At Joint	90%

Abnormal Motion*
Average range of FLEXION-EXTENSION is 150 degrees
Value to total range of joint motion is 100%

Retained active flexion of:	Impairment of Lower Extremity
0°	53%
10°	49
20°	46
30°	42
40°	39
50°	35
60°	32
70°	28
80°	25
90°	21
100°	18
110°	14
120°	11
130°	7
140°	4
150°	0

*If an orthosis is required for knee stability, there is 50% impairment of the lower extremity although there might be full range of motion of the knee joint.

Hyperextension to:	Impairment Of Lower Extremity
0°(neutral position)	0%
10°	1
20°	7
30°	17
40°	27
50° to 150° (full flexion)	90

Ankylosis

Joint ankylosed at:	
0° (neutral position)	53%
**10°	50
20°	60
30°	70
40°	80
50° to 150° (full flexion)	90

**position of function

Knee Joint — Flexion and Extension

Abnormal Motion

1. Place the patient in the neutral position (Figure 55).

2. Center the goniometer next to the knee joint (Figure 55). Record the goniometer reading with one arm of the goniometer along the axis of the femur and the other arm along the axis of the lower leg. Maintain these relationships of the arms as motion is carried out. Record any deviation from the neutral position, which would indicate limitation of knee joint extension.

3. With the patient flexing the knee as far as possible, follow the range of motion with the goniometer arm. Record the angle that subtends the arc of motion (Figure 56).

4. Retest the flexion of the knee with the patient in a sitting position. If the arc of motion is different from that obtained in step 3, then the average of the results represents the value to be used in determining impairment of the lower extremity.

5. Consult the abnormal motion section of Table 37. ADD the percentages for flexion loss and limitation of extension to determine impairment of the lower extremity.

NOTE: If there is inability to extend the knee for weight-bearing purposes beyond 50°, the degree of impairment is equivalent to that for amputation and no additional impairment value should be given for flexion loss.

Example: 70° flexion from neutral position (0°) is equivalent to 28% impairment of the lower extremity.

Example: Flexion to 100° with extension limited to 30° is equivalent to 45% impairment of the lower extremity (28% plus 17%, Table 37).

Ankylosis

1. Place the goniometer base as if measuring the neutral position (Figure 55). Measure the deviation from neutral position with goniometer arm extending along the lower leg and record the reading.

2. Consult the ankylosis section of Table 37 to determine the impairment of the lower extremity.

Example: A knee joint with ankylosis at 20° flexion is equivalent to 60% impairment of the lower extremity.

Table 38 lists impairment ratings for other disorders of the knee.

TABLE 38
IMPAIRMENT RATINGS OF THE LOWER EXTREMITY FOR OTHER DISORDERS OF THE KNEE

Disorder	Impairment of Lower Extremity*	
1. Patellectomy (with loss of power)	15-20%, combined with impairment for loss of motion**	
2. Meniscectomy (with loss of shock absorption)	10% for one meniscus 25% for both menisci	combined with impairment for loss of motion
3. Knee replacement arthroplasty	40%, if in optimum position	
4. Patella replacement only	Same as for patellectomy	
5. Post-traumatic patellar irregularity or arthritis	Up to 20% according to deformity	
6. Anterior cruciate ligament loss	10-20%, combined with impairment for loss of motion	
7. Posterior cruciate ligament loss	25%, combined with impairment for loss of motion	
8. Collateral ligament loss	15% for moderate instability 25% for marked instability	
9. Post-traumatic varus deformity (if over 15°)	20%, combined with impairment for loss of motion	
10. Post-traumatic valgus deformity (if over 20°)	20%, combined with impairment for loss of motion	

*See Table 37 for impairment ratings for loss of motion

**The combining of any impairment value in this table with impairment for loss of motion is to be done using the Combined Values Chart

Hip Joint — Forward Flexion

Abnormal Motion

1. Place the patient in the neutral position (Figure 57) with the opposite hip flexed and held to lock the pelvis. The leg to be tested is extended in a relaxed position.

2. Place the goniometer next to the hip joint (Figure 58). Record the goniometer reading.

3. With the patient flexing the hip to be tested as far as possible (Figure 59), follow the range of motion with the goniometer arm until the superior iliac spine begins to move. Record the angle that subtends the arc of motion.

4. Consult the abnormal motion section of Table 39 to determine the impairment of the lower extremity.

Example: 20° forward flexion from neutral position (0°) or any 20° arc of retained active forward flexion is equivalent to 14% impairment of the lower extremity.

Ankylosis

1. Place the goniometer base as if measuring the neutral position (Figure 57). Measure the deviation from neutral position with the goniometer arm and record the reading.

2. Consult the ankylosis section of Table 39 to determine the impairment of the lower extremity.

Example: A hip joint with ankylosis at 25° forward flexion is equivalent to 50% impairment of the lower extremity.

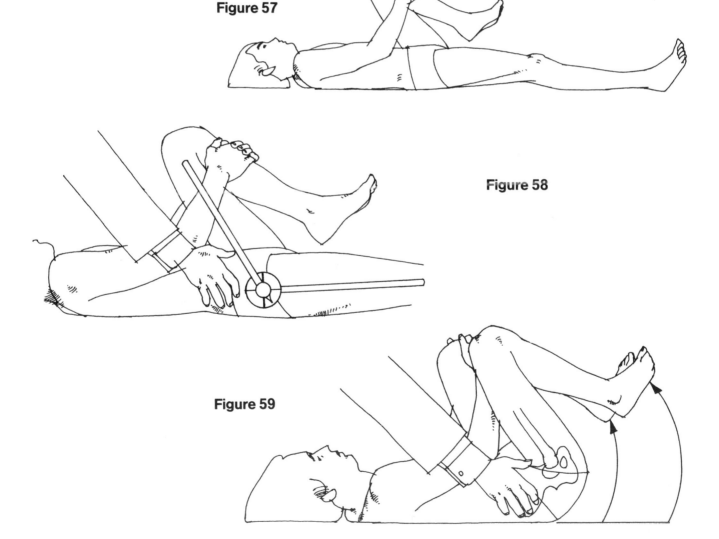

Figure 57

Figure 58

Figure 59

Hip Joint — Backward Extension

Abnormal Motion

1. Place the patient in the neutral position (Figure 60).

2. Center the goniometer next to the hip (Figure 60) and record the reading.

3. With the patient raising the leg as far as possible (Figure 61), follow the range of motion with the goniometer arm. Record the angle that subtends the arc of motion.

4. Consult the abnormal motion section of Table 40 to determine the impairment of the lower extremity.

Example: 20° active backward extension from neutral position (0°) or any 20° arc of retained active backward flexion is equivalent to 2% impairment of the lower extremity.

5. ADD the impairment values contributed by forward flexion and backward extension. Their sum represents the impairment of the lower extremity contributed by abnormal forward flexion and backward extension of the hip.

Ankylosis

1. Place the goniometer base as if measuring the neutral position (Figure 60). Measure the deviation from neutral position with the goniometer arm and record the reading.

TABLE 39
IMPAIRMENT DUE TO AMPUTATION, ABNORMAL MOTION AND ANKYLOSIS OF THE HIP JOINT—FORWARD FLEXION

	Impairment of Lower Extremity
Amputation—At Joint	100%

Abnormal Motion

Average range of FORWARD FLEXION—BACKWARD EXTENSION is 130 degrees
Value to total range of joint motion is 33%

Forward flexion from neutral position (0°) to:	Degrees of Joint Motion LOST	RETAINED	Impairment of Lower Extremity
0°	100	0	18%
10°	90	10	16
20°	80	20	14
30°	70	30	12
40°	60	40	11
50°	50	50	9
60°	40	60	7
70°	30	70	5
80°	20	80	4
90°	10	80	2
100°	0	100	0

Ankylosis

Joint ankylosed at:

0° (neutral position)	70%
10°	62
20°	54
*25°	50
30°	53
40°	60
50°	67
60°	73
70°	80
80°	87
90°	93
100° (full forward flexion)	100

*position of function

Figure 60

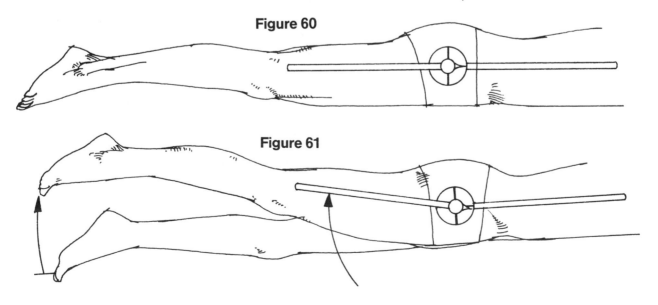

Figure 61

41

2. Consult the ankylosis section of Table 40 to determine the impairment of the lower extremity.

Example: A hip joint with ankylosis at 20° backward extension is equivalent to 90% impairment of the lower extremity.

TABLE 40
IMPAIRMENT DUE TO AMPUTATION, ABNORMAL MOTION AND ANKYLOSIS OF THE HIP JOINT—BACKWARD EXTENSION

	Impairment of Lower Extremity
Amputation—At Joint	100%

Abnormal Motion

Average range of FORWARD FLEXION—BACKWARD EXTENSION is 130 degrees
Value to total range of joint motion is 33%

	Degrees of Joint Motion		Impairment of Lower
Backward extension from neutral position (0°) to:	LOST	RETAINED	Extremity
0°	30	0	5%
10°	20	10	4
20°	10	20	2
30°	0	30	0

Ankylosis

Joint ankylosed at:

0° (neutral position)	70%
10°	80
20°	90
30° (full backward ext.)	100

Hip Joint—Abduction and Adduction

Abnormal Motion

1. Place the patient on a table in the neutral position (Figure 62) with the opposite hip flexed and held to lock the pelvis. The leg to be tested is extended in a relaxed position.

2. Center the goniometer over the hip joint (Figure 62). Record the goniometer reading. Consider 90° as the neutral point.

3. Abduction: With the patient abducting the thigh as far as possible (Figure 63), follow the range of motion with the goniometer arm. Record the angle that subtends the arc of motion.

4. Adduction: Starting from the neutral position with the patient swinging the leg across the body as far as possible (Figure 64), follow the range of motion with the goniometer arm. Record the angle that subtends the arc of motion.

5. Consult the abnormal motion section of Table 41 to determine the impairment of the lower extremity.

Example: 20° abduction from neutral position or any 20° arc of retained active abduction is equivalent to 8% impairment of the lower extremity.

6. ADD the lower extremity impairment values contributed by abduction and adduction. Their sum represents impairment of the lower extremity that is contributed by abnormal abduction and adduction of the hip.

Ankylosis

1. Place the goniometer base as if measuring the neutral position (Figure 62). Measure the deviation from the neutral position with the goniometer arm and record the reading.

2. Consult the ankylosis section of Table 41 to determine the impairment of the lower extremity.

Example: A hip joint with ankylosis at 20° abduction is equivalent to 85% impairment of the lower extremity.

TABLE 41
IMPAIRMENT DUE TO AMPUTATION, ABNORMAL MOTION AND ANKYLOSIS OF THE HIP JOINT—ABDUCTION-ADDUCTION

Impairment of Lower Extremity

Amputation—At Joint 100%

Abnormal Motion

Average range of ABDUCTION-ADDUCTION is 60 degrees
Value to total range of joint motion is 33%

Abduction from neutral position (0°) to:	Degrees of Joint Motion		Impairment of Lower Extremity
	LOST	RETAINED	
0°	40	0	16%
10°	30	10	12
20°	20	20	8
30°	10	30	4
40°	0	40	0

Adduction from neutral position (0°) to:			
0°	20	0	8%
10°	10	10	4
20°	0	20	0

Ankylosis

Joint ankylosed at:

*0° (neutral position)	70%
10°	78
20°	85
30°	93
40° (full abduction)	100

Joint ankylosed at:

*0° (neutral position)	70%
10°	85
20° (full adduction)	100

*position of function

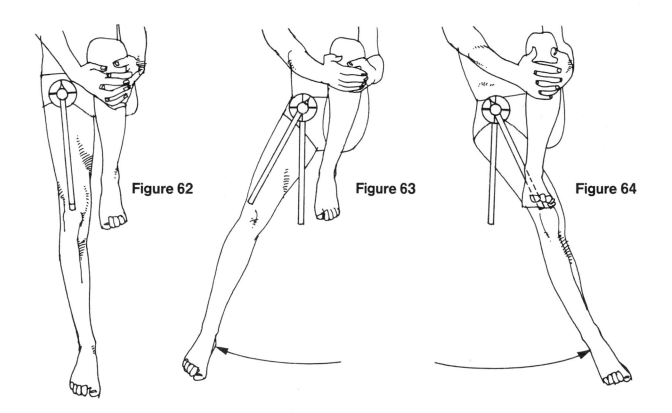

Figure 62   **Figure 63**   **Figure 64**

TABLE 42
IMPAIRMENT DUE TO AMPUTATION, ABNORMAL MOTION AND ANKYLOSIS OF THE HIP JOINT—ROTATION

Impairment of
Lower Extremity

Amputation—At Joint 100%

Abnormal Motion
Average range of ROTATION is 90 degrees
Value to total range of joint motion is 33%

Internal rotation from neutral position (0°) to:	Degrees of Joint Motion LOST	RETAINED	Impairment of Lower Extremity
0°	40	0	10%
10°	30	10	8
20°	20	20	5
30°	10	30	3
40°	0	40	0

External rotation from neutral position (0°) to:			
0°	50	0	13%
10°	40	10	10
20°	30	20	8
30°	20	30	5
40°	10	40	3
50°	0	50	0

Ankylosis

Joint ankylosed at:

*0° (neutral position)	70%
10°	78
20°	85
30°	93
40° (full int. rotation)	100

Joint ankylosed at:

*0° (neutral position)	70%
10°	76
20°	82
30°	88
40°	94
50° (full ext. rotation)	100

*position of function

TABLE 43
IMPAIRMENT OF THE LOWER EXTREMITY DUE TO OTHER DISORDERS OF THE HIP JOINT

Disorder	Impairment of Lower Extremity*
1. Arthroplasty (in optimum position)	20%
2. Non-union of hip fracture	30%
3. Avascular necrosis of the hip	30%
4. Loose hip prosthesis	40%

*These ratings should be combined with the ratings for loss of motion to determine impairments of the lower extremity (Table 39-42), using the Combined Values Chart.

Hip Joint — Rotation

Abnormal Motion

1. Place the patient in the neutral position (Figure 65).

2. Center the goniometer over the middle of the heel (Figure 65). Record the goniometer reading with the goniometer arm lying between the second and third toes. Consider 90° as the neutral point.

3. External rotation: With the patient externally rotating the hip as far as possible (Figure 66), follow the range of motion with the goniometer arm. Record the angle that subtends the arc of motion.

4. Internal rotation: Starting from the neutral position with the patient internally rotating the hip as far as possible (Figure 66), follow the range of motion with the goniometer arm. Record the angle that subtends the arc of motion.

5. Consult the abnormal motion section of Table 42 to determine the impairment of the lower extremity.

Example: 20° active external rotation from neutral position (0°) or any 20° arc of retained active external rotation is equivalent to 8% impairment of the lower extremity.

6. ADD the impairment values contributed by internal and external rotation. Their sum is the impairment of the lower extremity contributed by rotation of the hip.

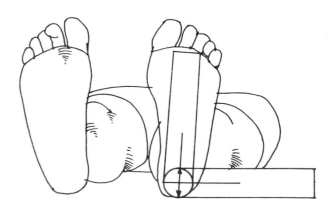

Figure 65

Ankylosis

1. Place the goniometer base as if measuring the neutral position (Figure 65). Measure the deviation from neutral position with the goniometer arm and record the reading.

2. Consult the ankylosis section of Table 42 to determine the impairment of the lower extremity.

Example: A hip joint with ankylosis at 20° internal rotation is equivalent to 85% impairment of the lower extremity.

Hip Joint — Two or More Ranges of Motion

Abnormal Motion

Measure separately and record the impairment of the lower extremity contributed by each range of motion. ADD the impairment values contributed by ranges of motion. Their sum is the impairment of the lower extremity contributed by the hip joint.

Example:

Description	% Impairment of Lower Extremity
10° active forward flexion	16 (Table 39)
10° active backward extension	4 (Table 40)
10° active abduction	12 (Table 41)
10° active adduction	4 (Table 41)
(16 + 4 + 12 + 4=36)	36

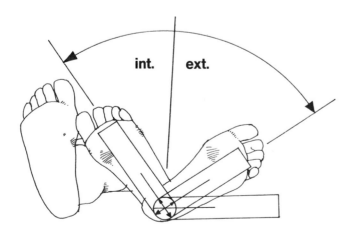

Figure 66

Ankylosis

Measure separately and record the impairment of the lower extremity contributed by ankylosis in each position. The larger impairment due to ankylosis is the impairment of the lower extremity contributed by the hip joint.

Example:

Description	% Impairment of Lower Extremity
Ankylosis at 25° forward flexion	50 (Table 39)
Ankylosis at 20° internal rotation	85 (Table 42)

The larger impairment value is 85%; therefore, the impairment rating is 85%.

Table 43 lists impairment values due to other disorders of the hip joint.

Lower Extremity — Involvement of Multiple Units

Measure separately and record the impairment of the lower extremity contributed by each unit (foot, ankle and subtalar joints, knee joint and hip joint). Then, combine the impairment values using the Combined Values Chart.

Example:

Description	% Impairment of Lower Extremity
Foot impaired at 57%	40 (Table 34)
Hindfoot (ankle) impaired	30
Knee impaired	20
(40 combined with 30 = 58; 58 combined with 20 = 66)	66

Finally, consult Table 44 to determine the impairment of the whole person that is contributed by the lower extremity.

Impairment values for amputations of various parts of the lower extremity are found in Table 45.

TABLE 44
RELATIONSHIP OF IMPAIRMENT OF THE LOWER EXTREMITY TO IMPAIRMENT OF THE WHOLE PERSON

% Impairment of Lower Extremity	Whole Person	% Impairment of Lower Extremity	Whole Person	% Impairment of Lower Extremity	Whole Person	% Impairment of Lower Extremity	Whole Person	% Impairment of Lower Extremity	Whole Person	% Impairment of Lower Extremity	Whole Person
0 =	0	25 =	10	50 =	20	75 =	30	85 =	34	95 =	38
1 =	0	26 =	10	51 =	20	76 =	30	86 =	34	96 =	38
2 =	1	27 =	11	52 =	21	77 =	31	87 =	35	97 =	39
3 =	1	28 =	11	53 =	21	78 =	31	88 =	35	98 =	39
4 =	2	29 =	12	54 =	22	79 =	32	89 =	36	99 =	40
5 =	2	30 =	12	55 =	22	80 =	32	90 =	36	100 =	40
6 =	2	31 =	12	56 =	22	81 =	32	91 =	36		
7 =	3	32 =	13	57 =	23	82 =	33	92 =	37		
8 =	3	33 =	13	58 =	23	83 =	33	93 =	37		
9 =	4	34 =	14	59 =	24	84 =	34	94 =	38		
10 =	4	35 =	14	60 =	24						
11 =	4	36 =	14	61 =	24						
12 =	5	37 =	15	62 =	25						
13 =	5	38 =	15	63 =	25						
14 =	6	39 =	16	64 =	26						
15 =	6	40 =	16	65 =	26						
16 =	6	41 =	16	66 =	26						
17 =	7	42 =	17	67 =	27						
18 =	7	43 =	17	68 =	27						
19 =	8	44 =	18	69 =	28						
20 =	8	45 =	18	70 =	28						
21 =	8	46 =	18	71 =	28						
22 =	9	47 =	19	72 =	29						
23 =	9	48 =	19	73 =	29						
24 =	10	49 =	20	74 =	30						

NOTE: In case of shortening due to overriding or malalignment or fracture deformities, but not to include flexion or extension deformities, combine the following values with other functional sequelae, using the Combined Values Chart.

0 – ½ inch =	5% of lower extremity
½ – 1 inch =	10% of lower extremity
1 – 1½ inch =	15% of lower extremity
1½ – 2 inch =	20% of lower extremity

NOTE: Impairment of whole person contributed by lower extremity may be rounded to the nearest 5 percent only when it is the *sole* impairment involved.

TABLE 45
IMPAIRMENT OF THE DIGITS, FOOT, LOWER EXTREMITY AND WHOLE PERSON DUE TO AMPUTATIONS

	% Impairment of			
	Digit	Foot	Lower Extremity	Whole Person
Hemipelvectomy				50
Disarticulation at hip joint			100	40
Amputation above knee joint with short thigh stump (3″ or less below tuberosity of ischium)			100	40
Amputation above knee joint with functional stump			90	36
Disarticulation at knee joint			90	36
Gritti-Stokes amputation			90	36
Amputation below knee joint with short stump (3″ or less below intercondylar notch)			90	36
Amputation below knee joint with functional stump			70	28
Amputation at ankle (Syme)		100	70	28
Partial amputation of foot (Chopart's)		75	53	21
Mid-metatarsal amputation		50	35	14
Amputation of all toes at metatarsophalangeal joints		30	21	8
Amputation of *Great Toe*				
With resection of metatarsal bone		30	21	8
At metatarsophalangeal joint	100	18	13	5
At interphalangeal joint	75	14	10	4
Amputation of *Lesser Toe* (2nd-5th)				
With resection of metatarsal bone		5	4	2
At metatarsophalangeal joint	100	3	2	1
At proximal interphalangeal joint	80	2	1	0
At distal interphalangeal joint	45	1	1	0

The Spine

Vertebrae — Fractures

The following table applies to compression of the body of a vertebrae:

Amount of Compression	% Impairment of Whole Person
25%	3
50%	6
>50%	10

Fracture of posterior elements is rated at 3% impairment.

Impairments contributed by the compression of a body of a vertebra and the fracture of the posterior elements are combined, not added.

NOTE: Non-union of a fractured posterior element would cause a 3% impairment of the whole person. The pedicles, laminae, articular process, and transverse process are included in the above impairment rating involving fracture of posterior elements.

Two or More Vertebrae

Measure separately and record the impairment of the whole person that is contributed by each vertebra. Then, combine the impairment values, using the Combined Values Chart. Neurological involvement also should be evaluated, and the results should be combined with the impairment rating related to the vertebrae (see Chapter 2).

Example:

Description	% Impairment of Whole Person
First vertebrae with 50% compression of body	6
First vertebrae with fracture of posterior elements	3
Second vertebrae with 75% compression of body	10
Third vertebrae with 50% compression of body	6
Third vertebrae with fracture of pedicle	3
(6 combined with 3 = 9; 9 combined with 10 = 18; 18 combined with 6 = 23; 23 combined with 3 = 25)	25

Vertebrae — Dislocations or Subluxations

A reduced dislocation or subluxation of one vertebrae is rated at 5% impairment of the whole person. If two or more vertebrae are dislocated and reduced, their impairments are combined. For example, if three vertebrae are dislocated, the impairment rating would be 15 (5 combined with 5 = 10; 10 combined with 5 = 15).

An unreduced dislocation or subluxation causes temporary impairment until it is reduced; then the physician should evaluate permanent impairment on the basis of the patient's condition with the reduced dislocation or subluxation. If no reduction is possible, then the physician should evaluate impairment on the basis of restricted motion and concomitant neurological findings in the spinal region involved, according to the criteria shown below and in Chapter 2.

Ankylosis of Cervical, Thoracic and Lumbar Regions

The examiner may choose to determine impairment of the spine due to ankylosis of the cervical, thoracic or lumbar regions by one of two methods: (1) using the goniometer and referring to the appropriate table involving the region of the spine being tested (see below), or (2) using appropriate radiographs to determine the number and position of the vertebrae with ankylosis and referring to Table 46.

Cervical Region — Flexion and Extension

Abnormal Motion

1. Place the patient in the neutral position (Figure 67).

2. Center the goniometer (Figure 67), with its base in line with the superior border of the larynx (C5) and its arm extended vertically along the mastoid process. Record the goniometer reading.

3. Flexion: With the patient bending the head as far forward as possible (Figure 68), follow the range of motion with the goniometer arm. Keep the goniometer arm along the mastoid process. Record the angle that subtends the arc of motion.

4. Extension: Starting from the neutral position with the patient bending the head as far backward as possible (Figure 69), follow the range of motion with the goniometer arm. Keep the goniometer arm vertical along the mastoid process. Record the angle that subtends the arc of motion.

5. Consult the abnormal motion section of Table 47 to determine the impairment of the whole person.

Example: 30° active flexion from neutral position (0°) or any 30° arc of retained active flexion is equivalent to 1% impairment of the whole person.

6. ADD the impairment values contributed by flexion and extension. Their sum is the impairment of the whole person that is contributed by flexion and extension abnormalities of the cervical region.

Ankylosis

1. Place the goniometer base as if measuring the neutral position (Figure 67). Measure the deviation from the neutral position with the goniometer arm and record the reading.

2. Consult the ankylosis section of Table 47 to determine the impairment of the whole person.

Example: A cervical region with ankylosis at 30° flexion is equivalent to 23% impairment of the whole person.

Consult Table 46 if radiographic methods are chosen to determine impairment due to ankylosis.

TABLE 46
IMPAIRMENT OF CERVICAL, THORACIC AND LUMBAR REGIONS DUE TO ANKYLOSIS, DETERMINED BY RADIOGRAPHIC METHODS

Favorable (neutral) Position	% Impairment of Whole Person	Unfavorable Position	% Impairment of Whole Person
Any 2 cervical	2	Any 2 cervical	4
Any 3 cervical	5	Any 3 cervical	10
Any 4 cervical	7	Any 4 cervical	14
Any 5 cervical	9	Any 5 cervical	18
Any 6 cervical	12	Any 6 cervical	24
Any 7 cervical	14	Any 7 cervical	28
C7 and T1	2	C7 and T1	4
Any 2 thoracic	1	Any 2 thoracic	2
Any 3 thoracic	2	Any 3 thoracic	4
Any 4 thoracic	3	Any 4 thoracic	5
Any 5 thoracic	4	Any 5 thoracic	7
Any 6 thoracic	5	Any 6 thoracic	9
Any 7 thoracic	5	Any 7 thoracic	11
Any 8 thoracic	6	Any 8 thoracic	13
Any 9 thoracic	7	Any 9 thoracic	15
Any 10 thoracic	8	Any 10 thoracic	16
Any 11 thoracic	9	Any 11 thoracic	18
Any 12 thoracic	12	Any 12 thoracic	20
T12 and L1	3	T12 and L1	6
Any 2 lumbar	3	Any 2 lumbar	6
Any 3 lumbar	6	Any 3 lumbar	12
Any 4 lumbar	9	Any 4 lumbar	18
Any 5 lumbar	12	Any 5 lumbar	24
C1—C7	14	C1—C7	28
T1—T12	10	T1—T12	20
L1—L5	12	L1—L5	24
C1—T12	23	C1—T12	28
T1—L5	21	T1—L5	39
C1—L5	32	C1—L5	56

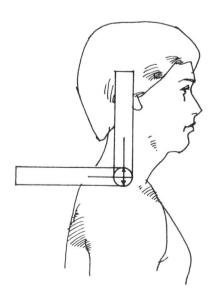

Figure 67

48

TABLE 47
IMPAIRMENT DUE TO ABNORMAL MOTION AND ANKYLOSIS OF THE CERVICAL REGION— FLEXION-EXTENSION

Abnormal Motion

Average range of FLEXION-EXTENSION is 90 degrees
Value to total range of cervical motion is 40%

Flexion from neutral position (0°) to:	Degrees of Cervical Motion		Impairment of Whole Person
	LOST	RETAINED	
0°	45	0	4%
15°	30	15	3
30°	15	30	1
45°	0	45	0

Extension from neutral position (0°) to:			
0°	45	0	4%
15°	30	15	3
30°	15	30	1
45°	0	45	0

Ankylosis

Region ankylosed at:

*0° (neutral position)	14%
15°	19
30°	23
45° (full flexion)	35

Region ankylosed at:

*0° (neutral position)	14%
15°	19
30°	30
45° (full extension)	60

*position of function

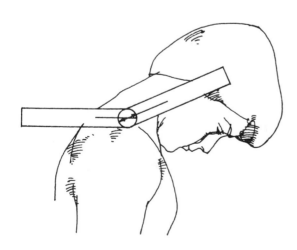

Figure 68

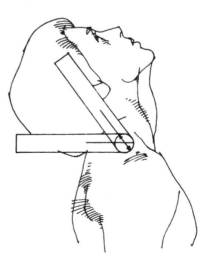

Figure 69

Cervical Region — Lateral Flexion and Bending

Abnormal Motion

1. Place the patient in the neutral position (Figure 70). Note the lateral extension or abduction of the arms to steady the shoulders.

2. Center the goniometer over the back of the neck (Figure 70), with the base on the vertebra prominans and the goniometer arm along midline of the neck. Record the goniometer reading.

3. Left lateral flexion: Starting from the neutral position with the patient bending the neck to the left as far as possible (Figure 71), follow the range of motion with the goniometer arm. Record the angle that subtends the arc of motion.

4. Right lateral flexion: Starting from the neutral position with the patient bending the neck to the right as far as possible (Figure 71), follow the range of motion with the goniometer arm. Record the angle that subtends the arc of motion.

5. Consult the abnormal motion section of Table 48 to determine the impairment of the whole person.

Example: 30° active left lateral flexion from neutral position (0°) or any 30° arc of retained active left lateral flexion is equivalent to 1% impairment of the whole person.

6. ADD the impairment values contributed by left lateral flexion and right lateral flexion. Their sum represents the impairment of the whole person that is contributed by abnormal lateral flexion of the cervical region.

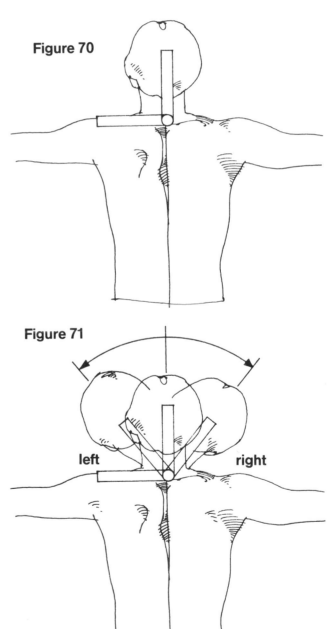

Figure 70

Figure 71

left   right

TABLE 48
IMPAIRMENT DUE TO ABNORMAL MOTION AND ANKYLOSIS OF THE CERVICAL REGION— LATERAL FLEXION

Abnormal Motion

Average range of LATERAL FLEXION (lateral bending) is 90 degrees
Value to total range of cervical motion is 25%

Right lateral flexion from neutral position (0°) to:	Degrees of Cervical Motion LOST	Degrees of Cervical Motion RETAINED	Impairment of Whole Person
0°	45	0	3%
15°	30	15	2
30°	15	30	1
45°	0	45	0

Left lateral flexion from neutral position (0°) to:			
0°	45	0	3%
15°	30	15	2
30°	15	30	1
45°	0	45	0

Ankylosis

Region ankylosed at:

*0° (neutral position)	15%
15°	20
30°	25
45° (full right lat. flexion)	30

Region ankylosed at:

*0° (neutral position)	15%
15°	20
30°	25
45° (full left lat. flexion)	30

*position of function

Ankylosis

1. Place the goniometer base as if measuring the neutral position (Figure 70). Measure the deviation from the neutral position with the goniometer arm and record the reading.

2. Consult the ankylosis section of Table 48 for the cervical region to determine the impairment of the whole person.

Example: A cervical region with ankylosis at 30° right lateral flexion is equivalent to 25% impairment of the whole person.

Consult Table 46 if radiographic methods are chosen to determine impairment due to ankylosis.

Cervical Region — Rotation

Abnormal Motion

1. Place the patient in the neutral position (Figure 72); the examiner should prevent motion of the shoulders by placing the hands on the patient's shoulders. The goniometer is not used.

2. With patient rotating the head to the right and left as far as possible (Figure 73), record the range of motion in each direction, estimating the arc described by the chin as it turns from the neutral position.

3. Consult the abnormal motion section of Table 49 to determine the impairment of the whole person.

Example: 20° active left rotation from neutral position (0°) or any 20° arc of retained active left rotation is equivalent to 3% impairment of the whole person.

4. ADD the impairment values contributed by left rotation and right rotation. Their sum is the impairment of the whole person that is contributed by abnormal rotation of the cervical region.

Ankylosis

1. Estimate by the position of the chin the angle at which the cervical region is ankylosed.

2. Consult the ankylosis section of Table 49 to determine the impairment of the whole person.

Example: A cervical region with ankylosis at 20° right rotation is equivalent to 17% impairment of the whole person.

Consult Table 46 if radiographic methods are chosen to determine impairment due to ankylosis.

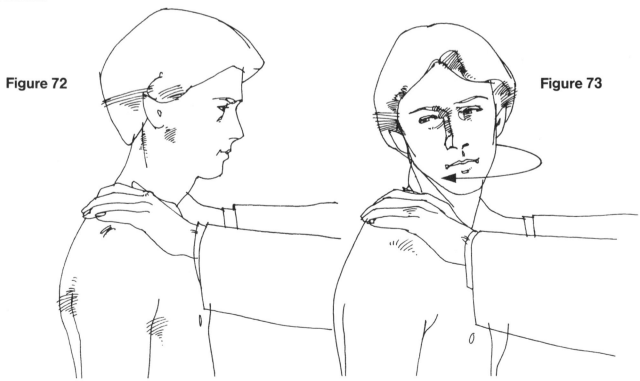

Figure 72

Figure 73

TABLE 49
IMPAIRMENT DUE TO ABNORMAL MOTION AND ANKYLOSIS OF THE CERVICAL REGION— ROTATION

Abnormal Motion

Average range of ROTATION is 160 degrees
Value to total range of cervical motion is 35%

Right rotation from neutral position (0°) to:	Degrees of Cervical Motion		Impairment of Whole Person
	LOST	RETAINED	
0°	80	0	4%
20°	60	20	3
40°	40	40	2
60°	20	60	1
80°	0	80	0

Left rotation from neutral position (0°) to:			
0°	80	0	4%
20°	60	20	3
40°	40	40	2
60°	20	60	1
80°	0	80	0

Ankylosis

Region ankylosed at:

*0° (neutral position)	14%
20°	17
40°	21
60°	25
80° (full right rotation)	28

Region ankylosed at:

*0° (neutral position)	14%
20°	17
40°	21
60°	25
80° (full left rotation)	28

*position of function

TABLE 50
IMPAIRMENT DUE TO ABNORMAL MOTION AND ANKYLOSIS OF THE THORACOLUMBAR REGION—FLEXION-EXTENSION

Abnormal Motion

Average range of FLEXION-EXTENSION is 120 degrees
Value to total range of thoracolumbar motion is 40%

Flexion from neutral position (0°) to:	Degrees of Thoracolumbar Motion		Impairment of Whole Person
	LOST	RETAINED	
0°	90	0	9%
10°	80	10	8
20°	70	20	7
30°	60	30	6
40°	50	40	5
50°	40	50	4
60°	30	60	3
70°	20	70	2
80°	10	80	1
90°	0	90	0

Extension from neutral position (0°) to:			
0°	30	0	3%
10°	20	10	2
20°	10	20	1
30°	0	30	0

Ankylosis

Region ankylosed at:

*0° (neutral position)	20%
10°	22
20°	24
30°	27
40°	29
50°	31
60°	34
70°	36
80°	38
90° (full flexion)	40

Region ankylosed at:

*0° (neutral position)	20%
10°	27
20°	34
30° (full extension)	40

*position of function

Thoracolumbar Region — Flexion and Extension

Abnormal Motion

1. Place the patient in the neutral position (Figure 74). The arm is raised and adducted only to show placement of the goniometer.

2. Center the goniometer along the mid-axillary line at level of the lowest rib (Figure 74). Record the goniometer reading.

3. Flexion: With patient bending as far forward as possible (Figure 75), follow the range of motion, keeping the goniometer arm along the mid-axillary line. Note that the goniometer base is to be kept in line with the femur. Record the angle that subtends the arc of motion.

4. Extension: Starting from the neutral position with the patient bending as far backward as possible, follow the range of motion with the goniometer arm. Record the angle that subtends the arc of motion.

5. Consult the abnormal motion section of Table 50 to determine the impairment of the whole person.

Example: 20° active flexion from neutral position (0°) or any 20° arc of retained active flexion is equivalent to 7% impairment of the whole person.

6. ADD the impairment values contributed by flexion and extension. Their sum represents the impairment of the whole person that is contributed by flexion and extension abnormalities of the thoracolumbar region.

Ankylosis

1. Place the goniometer base as if measuring the neutral position (Figure 74). Measure the deviation from the neutral position with the goniometer arm and record the reading.

2. Consult the ankylosis section of Table 50 to determine the impairment of the whole person.

Example: A thoracolumbar region with ankylosis at 20° flexion is equivalent to 24% impairment of the whole person.

Consult Table 46 if radiographic methods are chosen to determine impairment due to ankylosis.

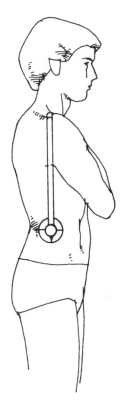

Figure 74

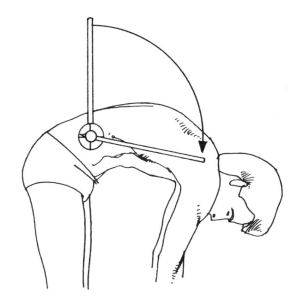

Figure 75

Thoracolumbar Region — Lateral Flexion (Lateral Bending)

Abnormal Motion

1. Place the patient in the neutral position (Figure 76).

2. Center the goniometer with the base over the posterior superior iliac spines and the goniometer arm along the midline of spine (Figure 76). Record the goniometer reading.

3. Left lateral flexion: With the patient bending to the left as far as possible (Figure 77), follow the range of motion with the goniometer arm. Record the angle that subtends the arc of motion.

4. Right lateral flexion: Starting from the neutral position with the patient bending to right as far as possible (Figure 78), follow the range of motion with the goniometer arm. Record the angle that subtends the arc of motion.

5. Consult the abnormal motion section of Table 51 to determine the impairment of the whole person.

Example: 10° active left lateral flexion from neutral position (0°) or any 10° arc of retained left lateral flexion is equivalent to 4% impairment of the whole person.

6. ADD the impairment values contributed by left lateral flexion and right lateral flexion. Their sum represents impairment of the whole person due to lateral flexion abnormalities of the thoracolumbar region.

Ankylosis

1. Place the goniometer base as if measuring the neutral position (Figure 76). Measure the deviation from the neutral position with the goniometer arm and record the reading.

2. Consult the ankylosis section of Table 51 to determine the impairment of the whole person.

Example: A thoracolumbar region with ankylosis at 10° right lateral flexion is equivalent to 27% impairment of the whole person.

Consult Table 45 if radiographic methods are chosen to determine impairment of the whole person.

TABLE 51
IMPAIRMENT DUE TO ABNORMAL MOTION AND ANKYLOSIS OF THE THORACOLUMBAR REGION—LATERAL FLEXION

Abnormal Motion
Average range of LATERAL FLEXION
(lateral bending) is 60 degrees
Value to total range of thoracolumbar motion is 25%

Right lateral flexion from neutral position (0°) to:	Degrees of Thoracolumbar Motion LOST	RETAINED	Impairment of Whole Person
0°	30	0	6%
10°	20	10	4
20°	10	20	2
30°	0	30	0
Left lateral flexion from neutral position (0°) to:			
0°	30	0	6%
10°	20	10	4
20°	10	20	2
30°	0	30	0

Ankylosis

Region ankylosed at:	
*0° (neutral position)	20%
10°	27
20°	34
30° (full right lat. flex.)	40
Region ankylosed at:	
*0° (neutral position)	20%
10°	27
20°	34
30° (full left lat. flex.)	40

*position of function

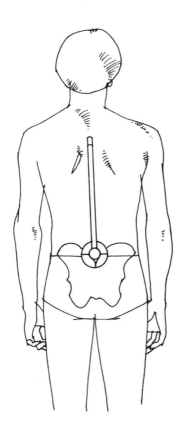

Figure 76

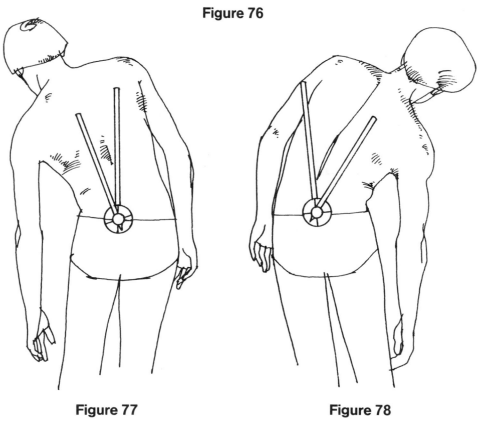

Figure 77   **Figure 78**

Thoracolumbar Region — Rotation

Abnormal Motion

1. Place the patient in the neutral position (Figure 79); the examiner should prevent motion of the pelvis. The goniometer is not used.

2. With the patient twisting to the right and left as far as possible (Figure 80), record the range of motion in each direction, estimating the arc described by the plane of the chest as it turns from the neutral position.

3. Consult the abnormal motion section of Table 52 to determine the impairment of the whole person.

Example: 10° active left rotation from neutral position (0°) or any 10° arc of retained active left rotation is equivalent to 4% impairment of the whole person.

4. ADD the impairment values contributed by left rotation and right rotation. Their sum is the impairment of the whole person due to abnormal rotation of the thoracolumbar region.

Ankylosis

1. Estimate by the position of an imaginary plane through the front of the body the angle of ankylosis of the thoracolumbar region.

2. Consult the ankylosis section of Table 52 to determine the impairment of the whole person.

Example: A thoracolumbar region with ankylosis at 10° right rotation is equivalent to 27% impairment of the whole person.

Consult Table 46 if radiographic methods are chosen to determine impairment of the whole person.

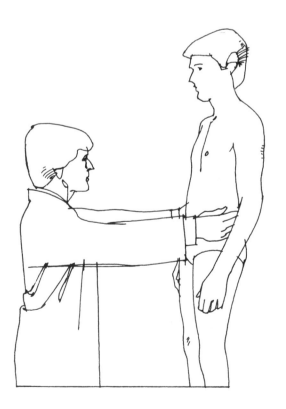

Figure 79

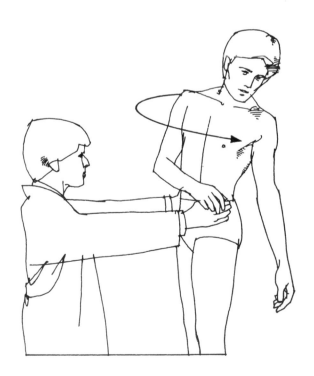

Figure 80

Spinal Region—
Two or More Ranges of Motion Involved

Abnormal Motion

Measure separately and record the impairment as contributed by each range of motion of the spine. Then, ADD the impairment values contributed by all ranges of motion of the spine. Their sum is the impairment of the whole person that is contributed by the spinal region.

Example: Cervical Region

Description	% Impairment of Whole Person
30° active flexion	1 (Table 47)
30° active extension	1 (Table 47)
60° active right rotation	1 (Table 49)
60° active left rotation	1 (Table 49)
(1 + 1 + 1 + 1 = 4)	4

TABLE 52
IMPAIRMENT DUE TO ABNORMAL MOTION AND ANKYLOSIS OF THE THORACOLUMBAR REGION—ROTATION

Abnormal Motion

Average range of ROTATION is 60 degrees
Value to total range of thoracolumbar motion is 35%

Right rotation from neutral position (0°) to:	Degrees of Thoracolumbar Motion LOST	RETAINED	Impairment of Whole Person
0°	30	0	6%
10°	20	10	4
20°	10	20	2
30°	0	30	0

Left rotation from neutral position (0°) to:			
0°	30	0	6%
10°	20	10	4
20°	10	20	2
30°	0	30	0

Ankylosis

Region ankylosed at:
*0° (neutral position)	20%
10°	27
20°	34
30° (full right rotation)	40

Region ankylosed at:
*0° (neutral position)	20%
10°	27
20°	34
30° (full left rotation)	40

*position of function

Ankylosis

Measure separately and record the impairment contributed by ankylosis in each position of the spinal region. The largest impairment value for ankylosis is the impairment of the whole person contributed by the spinal region.

Example: Cervical Region

Description	% Impairment of Whole Person
Ankylosis at 30° flexion	23 (Table 47)
Ankylosis at 20° right rotation	17 (Table 49)

The largest impairment value for ankylosis is 23%; therefore, the patient has 23% impairment due to ankylosis of the cervical region.

TABLE 53
IMPAIRMENT DUE TO OTHER DISORDERS OF THE SPINE

Disorder	% Impairment of the Whole Person
A. Spondylolysis and Spondylolisthesis	
1. Grade I or II spondylolysis and spondylolisthesis with aggravation, persistent muscle spasm, rigidity and pain resulting from trauma	20
2. Grade III or IV spondylolysis or spondylolisthesis with persistent muscle spasm, rigidity and pain, aggravated by trauma	30
B. Intervertebral Disc Lesions	
1. Non-operated, clinically established disc derangement without residuals	0
2. Operated, disc removed without residuals	5
3. Operated or non-operated, clinically established disc derangement with residuals	5*

*This impairment rating should be combined with the appropriate value(s) for residuals based on:

(a) Ankylosis (fusion) in spinal area or extremities;
(b) Abnormal motion in spinal area or extremities;
(c) Fractures of vertebrae;
(d) Spinal cord injuries, with resulting neurologic impairment (Chapter 2);
(e) Spinal nerve root injuries, with resulting neurologic impairment (Chapter 2);
(f) Any combination of the above, using the Combined Values Chart

Spinal Region — Two or More Conditions

Measure separately and record the percentage of impairment contributed by each condition. Then, combine the impairment values, using the Combined Values Chart, to determine the impairment of the whole person contributed by two or more conditions.

Example: Spinal disorder with multiple conditions

Description	% Impairment of Whole Person
L1 fraction with 50% compression of body	6
L1 fracture with fracture of transverse process	3
L2 fracture with 75% compression of body	10
Cervical region motion restrictions:	
30° flexion	1 (Table 47)
30° extension	1 (Table 47)
30° right lateral flexion	1 (Table 48)
30° left lateral flexion	1 (Table 48)
20° right rotation	3 (Table 49)
20° left rotation	3 (Table 49)
(1 + 1 + 1 + 1 + 3 + 3 = 10)	10
Non-operated cervical disc derangement without residuals	0 (Table 53)
(6 combined with 3 = 9; 9 combined with 10 = 18; 18 combined with 10 = 26)	26

Other Conditions of the Spine

Table 53 provides impairment values for other conditions of the spine.

Pelvis

The following shows impairment values associated with conditions of the pelvis.

Example:

Disorder	% Impairment of Whole Person
1. Healed fracture *without* displacement or residuals	0
2. Healed fracture *with* displacement, without residuals involving:	
a. Single ramus	0
b. Rami, bilateral	0
c. Ilium	0
d. Innominate	0
e. Symphysis pubis, without separation	5
f. Sacrum	5
g. Coccyx	0
3. Healed fracture *with* displacement, deformity and residuals:	
a. Single ramus	0
b. Rami, bilateral	5
c. Ilium	2
d. Innominate, displaced 1 inch or more	10
e. Symphysis pubis, displaced or separated	15
f. Sacrum, into sacro-iliac joint	10
g. Coccyx, non-union or excision	5
h. Fracture into acetabulum; evaluate on basis of restricted motion of hip joint.	

The impairment value for hemipelvectomy is 50% of the whole person (Table 45).

References

1. Joint Motion—Method of Measuring and Recording. Chicago, IL, American Academy of Orthopedic Surgeons, 1965.

2. McBride ED: Disability Evaluation and Principles of Treatment of Compensable Injuries, 6th ed, Philadelphia, PA, Lippincott, 1963.

3. Rice CO: Calculation of Industrial Disabilities of the Extremities and the Back, 2nd ed, Springfield, IL, Thomas, 1968.

4. Rothman RH, Simeone FA, eds: The Spine. Philadelphia, PA, Saunders 1975.

5. Kelikian H, Kelikian AS: Disorders of the Ankle. Philadelphia, PA, Saunders, 1984.

6. Cervical Spine Research Society, Cervical Spine Research Editorial Subcommittee, et al, eds: The Cervical Spine. Philadelphia, PA, Lippincott, 1983.

7. Bunnel S: Surgery of the Hand, 5th ed revised by Boyes JH, Philadelphia, PA, Lippincott, 1970.

Chapter 2

The Nervous System

Introduction

This chapter provides criteria for the evaluation of permanent impairment resulting from dysfunction of the brain, spinal cord, and cranial and peripheral nerves.

Before using the information in this chapter, the reader is urged to consult the Preface to the Guides, which provides a general discussion of the purpose of the Guides, and of the situations in which they are useful; and discusses techniques for the evaluation of the patient and for report preparation.

The Central Nervous System

Special Considerations: The emphasis in this chapter is upon organic deficits of the central nervous system (CNS) as demonstrated by loss of function. Categories for evaluating impairment are established in the chapter in terms of restrictions or limitations of the patient's ability to perform the activities of daily living and not in terms of specific diagnoses. However, before evaluating or classifying the impairment of any patient, the physician must establish, if possible, an accurate neurological diagnosis.

Evaluation of CNS impairment is difficult because of the complex relationships between the brain and the mind. It is impossible to avoid consideration of associated mental, emotional and personality processes. When appropriate, Chapter 12 should be used in conjunction with this chapter.

An example of the relationship between the brain and the mind would be found in the evaluation of persistent headache. The etiologies of chronic, persistent headache range from tension to intracranial tumor. The subjective sensation of distress or discomfort may be treated easily with rest or analgesics, or the problem may resist effective therapy. The patient's reaction to headache pain is colored by his or her past experiences and motivations of the moment. Persistence of the pain may alter a person's

affect or behavior and interfere with his or her ability to carry out the activities of daily living. Thus, the chapter on behavioral disorders may be useful in evaluating impairment due to headaches.

When a patient has clinical findings indicative of both brain and spinal cord impairment, evaluation should be made of each, and the percentages of impairment should be combined by using the Combined Values Chart.

The Brain

The brain is a central regulatory organ and mediator of voluntary acts that includes areas in which consciousness, sensations, emotions, memory and judgment are integrated. Permanent impairment can result from various disorders. The effects on the patient with the established disorder provide the criteria by which the permanent impairment is evaluated.

The more common categories of impairment resulting from brain disorders and the order in which they will be discussed are: (1) sensory and motor disturbances; (2) communication disturbances; (3) complex, integrated disturbances of cerebral function; (4) emotional disturbances; (5) disturbances of consciousness; (6) episodic neurological disorders; and (7) sleep and arousal disorders.

More than one category of impairment may result from brain disorders. In such cases the various degrees of impairment from the several categories are not added or combined, but the largest value, or greatest percentage of the 7 categories of impairment, is used to represent the impairment for all of the types.

For example, a patient was determined to have a communication impairment of 35%, a complex integrated cerebral-function impairment of 15%, an emotional disturbance resulting in an impairment rating of 30%, and a disturbance of consciousness resulting in an impairment rating of 5%. The patient's impairment of brain function would be rated at 35% of the whole person and not at the sum of the values, 85%, or at "the combined value" of 64%.

1. Sensory and Motor Disturbances—A patient seldom has an isolated sensory or motor disturbance, if the brain is involved. Evaluation of such disturbances is based on their ultimate effects on the activities of daily living. In evaluating the degree of impairment the physician should determine whether the disturbance is unilateral or bilateral and whether the preferred side is affected.

Sensory: When sensory disturbances are evaluated, consideration should be given to (1) pain and dysesthesias; (2) disorders in the recognition of the size, shape, and form of objects (astereognosis); (3) disturbances of two-point and position sense; (4) paresthesias of central origin; and (5) disturbances that might be identified by more elaborate testing, such as disorders of body image.

Organic lesions involving the optic nerve, optic chiasm, optic tracts, optic radiations, or the optic cortex may result in disturbances in the visual fields, such as homonymous hemianopsia, homonymous quadrantanopsia (superior and inferior), and bitemporal hemianopsia. Such lesions should be evaluated in terms of loss of the visual fields as described in Chapter 6. Lesions that cause central scotomata are, of course, manifested by disturbances in central vision and are evaluated as disturbances of central visual acuity.

It is recognized that certain isolated disturbances, such as thalamic pain, phantom limb sensations, or other subjective disturbances of the body image, may result in impairment. Evaluation of the effects of such disturbances calls for critical judgment on the part of examiners.

Motor: These disorders include hemiparesis and hemiplegias and variations thereof. The most common condition is hemiparesis, which may be of variable severity and responsible for different ratings of impairment, depending on how the patient's daily activities are affected. In addition, there is a large list of motor disorders that includes, but is not limited to: (1) involuntary movement such as tremor, athetosis, chorea, or hemiballism; (2) disturbances of tone and posture; (3) various forms of akinesia and bradykinesia such as Parkinsonism, in which voluntary and semiautomatic movement may be severely impaired; (4) impairment of associated and cooperative (synergistic) movements, as in certain

diseases of the basal ganglia; (5) complex manual and gait disturbances, including the ataxias, especially those of frontal and cerebellar origin; and (6) motor seizure disorders, including generalized, focal, akinetic and myoclonic seizures.

Evaluation: The evaluation of sensory and motor impairments due to brain disorders should be based on the patient's ability to perform various functions, for example, standing, walking, using the upper extremities, controlling bladder and bowel, breathing, and speaking. Methods of evaluating these functions are described in sections of this chapter with the cranial nerves or spinal cord, or in other chapters of the Guides. When more than one function is involved, the percentage of impairment is derived by combining appropriate values by using the Combined Values Chart.

2. Language Disturbances—The part of the speaking that involves the structures of the brain stem is discussed in detail in Chapter 7 and briefly in the cranial nerves section of this chapter. Here the concern is with the central mechanism for language comprehension, storage, and production, which is mediated by the brain and disturbance of which has to do with the clinical conditions known as aphasia and dysphasia.

Forms of disturbed communication, such as agraphia, alexia, or acalculia, are reflected in the following criteria for evaluating the impairment of communication due to brain damage. These criteria consider not only the comprehension and understanding of language by the patient, but also the patient's ability to produce discernible and appropriate language symbols.

Description	% Impairment of the Whole Person
1. Minimal disturbance in comprehension and production of language symbols of daily living	0-15
2. Moderate impairment in comprehension and production of language symbols for daily living	20-45
3. CANNOT comprehend language symbols, therefore has an unintelligible or inappropriate production of language for daily living	50-90
4. CANNOT comprehend OR produce language symbols sufficient for daily living	95

3. Disturbances of Complex, Integrated Cerebral Functions — Disturbances of these functions constitute the well-known organic brain syndrome. The resulting deficits may include defects in orientation; ability to abstract or understand concepts; memory, both immediate and remote; judgment; ability to initiate decisions and perform planned action; and acceptable social behavior.

The restrictions placed on patients with established organic brain syndromes provide criteria by which the permanent impairment may be evaluated. These criteria are:

Description	% Impairment of the Whole Person
1. There is a degree of impairment of complex integrated cerebral functions, but there is ability to carry out most activities of daily living as well as before onset	5-15
2. There is a degree of impairment of complex integrated cerebral functions such that daily activities need some supervision and/or direction	20-45
3. There is a degree of impairment of complex integrated cerebral functions that limits daily activities to directed care under confinement at home or in other domicile	50-90
4. There is such a severe degree of impairment of complex integrated cerebral functions that the individual is unable to care for self in any situation or manner	95

4. Emotional Disturbances — Emotional disturbances may be one of the results of organic brain damage. These disturbances may range from irritability to outbursts of severe rage and aggression, or at the other extreme, to an absence of normal emotional response. The abnormalities include inappropriate euphoria, depression, degrees of fluctuation of emotional state, impairment of normal emotional interactions with others, involuntary laughing and crying, akinetic mutism, and other disturbances in the emotional sphere. The criteria for evaluating such disturbances are:

Description	% Impairment of the Whole Person
1. There is mild to moderate emotional disturbance under unusual stress	5-15
2. There is mild to moderate emotional disturbance under ordinary stress	20-45
3. There is moderate to severe emotional disturbance under ordinary to minimal stress, which requires sheltering	50-90
4. There is severe emotional disturbance that continually endangers self or others	95

5. Consciousness Disturbances — Disturbances of consciousness that are not covered in the episodic disorders or in the sleep and arousal disorders, which are described below, include organic confusional state (hyper- or hypoactive), stupor (poorly organized responses to noxious stimuli), and coma (no response).

Determination of grades of impairment of consciousness may be made by judging the patient's reaction to noxious stimuli; this may vary from a well-organized reaction to none at all.

Description	% Impairment of the Whole Person
1. Neurological disorder results in mild alteration in the state of consciousness	5-35
2. Neurological disorder results in moderate alteration in the state of consciousness	40-70
3. Neurological disorder results in a state of stupor	75-90
4. Neurological disorder results in a state of coma	95

6. Episodic Neurological Disorders — Episodic neurological disorders include, but are not limited to, syncope, epilepsy, and the convulsive disorders. Criteria for evaluating such impairments are based on the frequency, severity, and duration of attacks as they affect the patient's performance of the activities of daily living. These criteria are:

Description	% Impairment of the Whole Person
1. An episodic neurological disorder is of slight severity and under such control that most of the activities of daily living can be performed	5-15
2. An episodic neurological disorder is of such severity as to interfere moderately with the activities of daily living	20-45

3. An episodic neurological disorder is of such severity and constancy as to limit activities to supervised or protected care or confinement 50-90

4. An episodic neurological disorder is of such severity and constancy as to totally incapacitate the individual in terms of daily living 95

7. Sleep and Arousal Disorders—The disorders of sleep and arousal include such syndromes as the disorders of initiating and maintaining sleep, or insomnia; disorders of excessive somnolence, including those associated with sleep-induced respiratory impairment; disorders of the sleep-wake schedule; and dysfunctions associated with sleep, sleep stages or parasomnias.

The categories of impairment that may arise from sleep disorders relate to (1) nervous system, with reduced daytime attention, concentration and other cognitive capacities; (2) mental and behavioral factors, including depression, irritability, interpersonal difficulties and social problems; and (3) cardiovascular system, with systemic and pulmonary hypertension, cardiac enlargement and congestive heart failure, cardiac arrhythmias, and polycythemia.

In assessing permanent impairment due to sleep and arousal disorders, the physician must complete a thorough diagnostic evaluation and allow time for appropriate treatment to take effect. The physician should then evaluate the remaining permanent impairment of each affected organ system and combine the impairment ratings using the Combined Values Chart. The criteria for the cardiovascular and for the mental and behavioral impairments are found in Chapters 4 and 12, respectively. The criteria for central nervous system impairment due to excessive daytime sleepiness are:

Description	% Impairment of the Whole Person

1. There is reduced daytime alertness due to sleepiness or sleep episodes, or disturbed nocturnal sleep affecting complex integrated cerebral functions, but ability remains to carry out most activities of daily living 5-15

2. There is reduced daytime alertness due to sleepiness or sleep episodes, or disturbed nocturnal sleep affecting complex integrated cerebral functions that requires some supervision to carry out activities of daily living 20-45

3. There is reduced daytime alertness due to sleepiness or sleep episodes, or disturbed nocturnal sleep that significantly limits activities of daily living and requires supervision by caretakers 50-90

4. There is such a severe reduction of daytime alertness due to sleepiness or sleep episodes or disturbed nocturnal sleep, that activities of daily living are severely limited so as to cause the patient to be unable to care for self in any situation or manner 95

In Appendix C is a discussion of sleep and arousal disorders that includes a diagnostic classification, description of tests, and examples of affected patients.

The Spinal Cord

The spinal cord is concerned with sensory, motor and visceral functions. Permanent impairment can result from various disorders affecting these functions. The restrictions placed upon the patient who has an established spinal cord disorder provide criteria by which the permanent impairment may be evaluated.

The more common impairments resulting from spinal cord disorders and the order in which they will be discussed, involve: (1) station and gait; (2) use of upper extremities; (3) respiration; (4) urinary bladder function; (5) anorectal function; and (6) sexual function.

Sensory disturbances including the loss of touch, pain, temperature, vibration, or position senses, and paresthesias and phantoms, may be a part of spinal cord disorders. Autonomic (vegetative) disorders, such as disturbance of sweating, circulation, and temperature regulation, may also occur in the course of spinal cord disorders. The rating of impairment due to such sensory disturbances or autonomic disorders should be determined by the amount of functional impairment according to the criteria given below.

Accompanying disorders, such as trophic lesions, urinary calculi, osteoporosis, nutritional disturbances, infections, and reactive psychological states may occur. The degree to which any of these augment impairment from a condition of the spinal cord should be based on the criteria given in the chapters of the Guides that deal with those disorders.

1. Station and Gait—The ability to stand and walk

provides criteria for evaluating spinal cord disorders affecting the lower extremities. These criteria are:

Description	% Impairment of the Whole Person
1. Patient can rise to a standing position and can walk BUT has difficulty with elevations, grades, steps and distances	5-20
2. Patient can rise to a standing position and can walk with difficulty BUT is limited to level surfaces. There is variability as to the distance the patient can walk	25-35
3. Patient can rise to a standing position and can maintain it with difficulty BUT cannot walk	40-60
4. Patient cannot stand without a prosthesis or the help of others	65

2. Use of Upper Extremities—Because the basic tasks of everyday living are more dependent upon the preferred upper extremity, dysfunction or loss of the preferred extremity results in greater impairment than impairment of the nonpreferred extremity.

Evaluation of impairment of the preferred extremity should be subject to periodic review, because the originally non-preferred extremity sometimes becomes as accomplished as the originally preferred extremity. The criteria for the evaluation of spinal cord impairment affecting ONLY one upper extremity are:

Description	% Impairment of the Whole Person	
	Preferred Extremity	Nonpreferred Extremity
1. Can use the involved extremity for self care, grasping, and holding BUT has difficulty with digital dexterity	5-10	0-5
2. Can use the involved extremity for self care, can grasp and hold objects with difficulty, BUT has no digital dexterity	15-25	10-15
3. Can use the involved extremity BUT has difficulty with self care activities	30-35	20-25
4. CANNOT use the involved extremity for self care	40-60	30-40

When the spinal-cord disorder affects both upper extremities, the resulting impairment to the whole person is greater than a simple combination of the values of "preferred" and "nonpreferred." The criteria for evaluating spinal-cord disorders affecting both upper extremities are:

Description	% Impairment of the Whole Person
1. Can use both upper extremities for self care, grasping, and holding BUT has difficulty with digital dexterity	5-15
2. Can use both upper extremities for self care, can grasp and hold objects with difficulty BUT has *no* digital dexterity	20-40
3. Can use both upper extremities BUT has difficulty with self care activities	45-80
4. CANNOT use upper extremities	85

3. Respiration—Respiration in this guide is limited to the individual's ability to perform the act of breathing. Criteria for evaluating the limitations placed on the patient with respiratory difficulty due to spinal cord disorders are:

Description	% Impairment of the Whole Person
1. Capable of spontaneous respiration BUT has difficulty in activities of daily living that require extra exertion	5-20
2. Capable of spontaneous respiration BUT of a degree that restricts patient to sitting, standing, or limited ambulation	25-50
3. Capable of spontaneous respiration BUT of a degree that limits patient to bed existence	75-90
4. No capacity for spontaneous respiration	95

4. Urinary Bladder Function—The ability to control bladder emptying provides the criteria for evaluating permanent bladder impairment resulting from spinal cord disorders. These criteria are:

Description	% Impairment of the Whole Person
1. Patient has varying degrees of voluntary bladder control BUT is impaired by urgency	5-10

2. Patient has good bladder reflex activity BUT no voluntary control (limited capacity with intermittent emptying times) 15-20

3. Patient's bladder has poor reflex activity (intermittent dribbling) and no voluntary control 25-35

4. Patient has no reflex or voluntary control of the bladder (continuous dribbling) 40-60

5. Anorectal Function—The ability to control anorectal emptying provides criteria for evaluating the permanent impairment resulting from spinal cord disorders. These criteria are:

Description	% Impairment of the Whole Person
1. Anorectum has reflex regulation BUT only limited voluntary control	0-5
2. Anorectum has reflex regulation BUT no voluntary control	10-15
3. Anorectum has no reflex regulation and no voluntary control	20-25

6. Sexual Function—Sexual capability and awareness of sexual function provide the criteria for evaluating permanent impairment resulting from spinal cord disorders. These criteria are:

Description	% Impairment of the Whole Person (Ages 40-65 Yr)
1. Sexual function is possible BUT with varying degrees of difficulty of erection or ejaculation in males, or awareness in both sexes	5-10
2. Reflex sexual function is possible BUT there is no awareness	10-15
3. There is no sexual function	20

These values may be increased by 50% of the given value for those below the age of 40 years, and decreased by 50% for those over the age of 65 years. For instance, in a 25-year-old man, a 50% increase of a 20% impairment would yield a 30% impairment of function.

Table 1 summarizes the percentage values for the impairment of the spinal cord and brain.

TABLE 1
SPINAL CORD AND BRAIN IMPAIRMENT VALUES

A. Spinal Cord and/or Brain	% Impairment of the Whole Person		
Station and gait			
Can stand but walks with difficulty	5-20		
Can stand but walks only on the level . . .	25-35		
Can stand but cannot walk	40-60		
Can neither stand nor walk	65		
Use of upper extremities	(Preferred Extremity)	(Nonpreferred Extremity)	(Both)
Some difficulty with digital dexterity	5-10	0- 5	5-15
Has no digital dexterity	15-25	10-15	20-40
Has difficulty with self care	30-35	20-25	45-80
Cannot carry out self care	40-60	30-40	85
Respiration			
Difficulty only where extra exertion required	5-20		
Restricted to limited ambulation	25-50		
Restricted to bed	75-90		
Has no spontaneous respiration	95		
Urinary bladder function			
Impairment in form of urgency	5-10		
Good reflex activity without voluntary control	15-20		
Poor reflex activity and no voluntary control	25-35		
No reflex or voluntary control	40-60		
Anorectal function			
Limited voluntary control	0- 5		
Has reflex regulation but no voluntary control	10-15		
No reflex regulation or voluntary control	20-25		
Sexual function	age— (below 40)	(40-65)	(over 65)
Mild difficulties	8-15	5-10	3- 5
Reflex function possible but no awareness	15-23	10-15	5- 8
No sexual function	30	20	10

B. Brain	% Impairment of the Whole Person
Language disturbances	
Mild difficulties	0-15
Comprehends but cannot produce sufficient or appropriate language	20-45
Cannot comprehend or produce intelligible or appropriate language . . .	50-90
Cannot comprehend or produce langauge	95
Complex integrated cerebral function disturbances	
Can carry out daily living tasks	5-15
Needs some supervision	20-45
Needs confinement	50-90
Cannot care for self	95
Emotional disturbances	
Only present under unusual stress	5-15
Present in mild to moderate degree under ordinary stress	20-45
Present in moderate to severe degree under ordinary stress	50-90
Severe degree; continually endangers self or others	95
Consciousness disturbances	
Mild alterations	5-35
Moderate alterations	40-70
Stupor	75-90
Coma	95
Episodic neurological disorders	
Slight interference with daily living	5-15
Moderate interference with daily living . .	20-45
Requires constant supervision or confinement	50-90
Totally incapacitated for daily living	95
Sleeping arousal disorders	
Slight interference with daily activities . . .	5-15
Requires some supervision to carry out daily activities	20-45
Requires supervision of care by caretakers	50-90
Patient unable to care for self	95

The Cranial Nerves

The cranial nerves are discussed in this chapter by their respective names. Reference also is made to them in other chapters dealing with specific organs, such as the eye and the ear.

Twelve pairs of cranial nerves emerge from the base of the brain. These are identified by Roman numerals I through XII and by their names. Some of the nerves are mixed, having sensory, autonomic, and motor fibers, while others have only one or two types of fibers.

Ratings of impairments that involve these nerves are made as follows:

I—Olfactory: The olfactory nerve is concerned with the sense of smell. In cases of complete bilateral involvement with total inability to detect any odors (anosmia), the impairment is placed at 3% of the whole person. Parosmia, or perversion of the sense of smell, may be sufficiently disturbing to constitute an impairment, and the physician should consider that fact when evaluating olfactory nerve function. The value of 3% for anosmia would be combined with the value of any other permanent impairment of the patient.

II—Optic: The optic nerve is concerned with the sense of vision. Impairment resulting from the complete destruction of an optic nerve, which causes total loss of vision in one eye, is rated at 24% of the whole person. Impairment of the whole person from complete loss of both optic nerves, which causes total blindness, would be 85%. Evaluation of partial impairments of the optic nerve is considered in Chapter 6.

III—Oculomotor: IV—Trochlear; and VI—Abducens: These nerves are responsible for the motility of the eyeballs and for regulating the size of the pupil.

If there is loss of any one of these nerves or of combinations of them, with resulting inability to perceive a single image (permanent diplopia), the condition is equivalent to the loss of vision in one eye and the impairment is set at 24% of the whole person. This is true in patients who can correct the affected eye by covering the other eye.

In instances where loss of function of the eyeball musculature secondary to nerve involvement requires special positioning of the head for effective vision, consideration should be given to combining appropriate values for impairment to locomotion, station, and so forth. If partial visual impairment must be evaluated, Chapter 6 should be consulted.

V—Trigeminal: This is a mixed nerve with sensory fibers to the face, cornea, anterior scalp, nasal and oral cavities, tongue, and the supratentorial dura mater; and with motor fibers to the muscles of mastication.

Sensation in the area served by the trigeminal nerve, including the cornea, is tested with the usual techniques of evaluating tactile appreciation and pain. Loss of sensation on one side results in some dysfunction, and this should be evaluated at 3% to 10% impairment of the whole person. Bilateral trigeminal sensory loss, which is rare, is more disturbing, and the impairment of the whole person in that instance would be 20% to 35%. The impairment rating for loss of sensation of the trigeminal nerve is to be combined with any impairment rating for pain and for motor loss.

Intractable unilateral or bilateral trigeminal neuralgia, "tic douloureux," may entail impairment ranging from 10% to 50% of the whole person, depending on the frequency and severity of the attacks.

Impairment from the pain of "atypical trigeminal neuralgia" is to be made on the basis of how much the neuralgia interferes with daily activities of the patient and would be in the range of 0% to 20% impairment of the whole person.

Motor involvement of the trigeminal nerve not only affects chewing, but also causes difficulty in speaking and swallowing. This is particularly true when there is bilateral damage. Complete loss of the motor function of one trigeminal nerve would be rated at 3% to 5% impairment of the whole person. Complete bilateral motor loss would result in 30% to 45% impairment of the whole person, depending on the difficulty with speech and swallowing that the patient experiences.

Methods of evaluating speech impairment and ability to swallow are set forth in greater detail in Chapter 7.

VII—Facial: This is a mixed nerve with a sensory component carrying tactile sensory supply to a part of the external ear, the external auditory canal, tympanic membrane, soft palate and adjacent pharynx, and taste fibers to the anterior two-thirds of the tongue; motor fibers to the muscles of expression and to the accessory muscles of mastication and deglutition; and special fibers to the lacrimal and salivary glands.

Sensory loss from damage to one or even both facial nerves would not interfere with the patient's performance of daily activities, and in that instance no impairment rating would be given. Since taste also is mediated by the ninth nerve, it is unlikely that even loss of both facial nerves would result in a complete loss of taste. If total loss of taste were to occur, the rating would be 3% impairment of the whole person.

Unilateral motor loss of the facial nerve causes the individual to have some difficulty with facial expression, blinking, chewing, and the control of salivation. Also the face is distorted. The permanent impairment in complete unilateral motor loss is 10% to 15% impairment of the whole person.

Bilateral motor loss of the facial nerve constitutes a more severe handicap, and the impairment of the whole person would be 30% to 45%. These values are established on the basis of the difficulties in food-taking and speech and are correlated with impairment values for the ninth, tenth, eleventh, and twelfth cranial nerves and with evaluations made in Chapter 7.

VIII—Auditory: This so-called single nerve actually consists of two separate components, a cochlear nerve that is concerned with hearing and a vestibular nerve that affects equilibrium.

Unilateral loss of hearing is much less of an impairment than is bilateral or total loss. Complete loss of one cochlear nerve carries a rating of impairment of 6% of the whole person, and complete bilateral loss of hearing has a rating of 35%. Tinnitus alone does not result in permanent impairment. However, tinnitus in the presence of a unilateral hearing loss may impair speech discrimination, and 3% to 5% should be added to the rating for the hearing loss. The procedure for evaluating hearing loss is given in Chapter 7.

The total loss of one vertibular nerve rarely results in permanent disturbance of equilibrium, and therefore, no percentage of permanent impairment is given. Total bilateral loss of the vestibular nerves is usually compensated to some degree by other neural mechanisms. The permanent impairment of the whole person may range from 0% to 25%, depending on the extent of such compensation. The full classification for vestibular impairment is given in Chapter 7.

IX—Glossopharyngeal; X—Vagus; and XI—Cranial Accessory: The glossopharyngeal and the vagus are mixed nerves that supply sensory fibers chiefly

TABLE 2
VALUES FOR IMPAIRMENT OF CRANIAL NERVES

	% Impairment of the Whole Person
I. Olfactory	
Complete unilateral loss	0
Complete bilateral loss	3
II. Optic	
Complete unilateral loss	24
Complete bilateral loss	85
III, IV, VI. Oculomotor, Trochlear, Abducens (Alone or in Combinations)	
Complete loss of ability to perceive single image, but with a condition which can be corrected by covering one eye and then having clear vision	24
V. Trigeminal	
Complete unilateral sensory loss	3-10
Complete bilateral sensory loss	20-35
Intractable typical trigeminal neuralgia, or tic douloureux	10-50
Atypical facial neuralgia	0-20
Complete unilateral motor loss	3-5
Complete bilateral motor loss	30-45
VII. Facial	
Complete loss of taste (unlikely)	3
Complete unilateral paralysis	10-15
Complete bilateral paralysis	30-45
VIII. Auditory REFER TO CHAPTER 7	
IX, X, XI. Glossopharyngeal, Vagus, Cranial Accessory	
Swallowing impairment due to any one or two combinations of these nerves	
diet restricted to semi-solids	5-10
diet restricted to liquids	20-30
diet by tube feeding or gastrostomy	40-60
Speech REFER TO CHAPTER 7	
XII. Hypoglossal	
Unilateral paralysis	0
Bilateral paralysis	
Swallowing impairment	
diet restricted to semi-solids	5-10
diet restricted to liquids	20-30
diet by tube feeding or gastrostomy	40-60
Speech impairment REFER TO CHAPTER 7	

to the posterior part of the tongue, pharynx, larynx, and trachea. Motor fibers innervate the pharynx and the larynx. Autonomic fibers supply the thoracic and upper abdominal viscera.

The cranial accessory nerves assist the vagus in supplying some of the muscles of the larynx.

Sensory impairment of the glossopharyngeal and vagus nerves is difficult to evaluate and should be judged by how it contributes to the impairment of swallowing, breathing, speaking, and visceral function.

The glossopharyngeal nerves may be the source of severe neuralgia. This, however, is usually curable. In those rare cases where residual impairment results, the physician should assign a value that is consistent with other established values and that is based on the severity of the neuralgia and the degree to which it interferes with the daily activities of the patient.

The impairment of swallowing due to disorders of one or of a combination of these nerves may be evaluated as follows:

Description	% Impairment of the Whole Person
1. The diet is restricted to semi-solid foods or to soft foods	5-10
2. The diet is limited to liquid foods	20-30
3. The taking of food is by tube or by gastrostomy	40-60

The impairment of speech due to disorders of one or of combinations of these nerves is discussed in detail in Chapter 7.

XII—Hypoglossal: This is the motor nerve to the tongue. Unilateral loss of the function of this nerve does not ordinarily result in significant impairment.

Bilateral loss results in impairment of the functions of swallowing and speech. Evaluation of these impairments is based on the same criteria as for the glossopharyngeal, vagus, and cranial accessory nerves.

Table 2 is a summary of the percentage values for the impairments of the cranial nerves.

The Peripheral Spinal Nerves

The peripheral spinal nerves constitute an intricate conduction system that serves as the conductor of neural impulses traveling in both directions between the spinal cord and other tissues of the body and through which many important bodily functions are regulated. For descriptive purposes, the peripheral spinal nerves may be classified according to their site of origin from the spinal cord and their function (Table 3). The dermatomes are shown in Figures 1 and 2.

The peripheral spinal nerves consist of 31 pairs of symetrically arranged nerves, each leaving and entering the spinal cord via two roots. Functionally, the peripheral spinal nerves can be divided into three main groups of fibers: (a) sensory (afferent) fibers that carry impulses arising from various receptors in the skin, muscles, tendons, ligaments, bones and joints to the central nervous system; (b) motor (efferent) fibers; the large alpha motor neuron fibers conduct impulses from the spinal cord to skeletal muscle fibers; the small gamma motor neuron fibers carry impulses to muscle spindles for feedback control; and (c) autonomic fibers, which are efferent and are concerned with the control of smooth muscles and glandular activities.

In evaluating peripheral nerve function, it is important to recognize two important concepts: (a) the metabolism of peripheral nerves occurs primarily in the cell body (neuron), either in the spinal cord, brainstem or in ganglions, and the peripheral parts of the nerves are dependent on neuronal function and on the process of axoplasmic transport of essential factors between the cell body and the nerve terminals; and (b) there are "trophic" effects of interactions between nerve fibers and other cells which are illustrated by skeletal muscle atrophy following immobilization in spite of intact peripheral nerves, or "disuse atrophy."

Disorders of autonomic nerve function may impair an organ or body system. The chapter that is concerned with the body system affected should be consulted when determining the degree of impairment due to these disorders.

Permanent impairment related to a peripheral spinal nerve may be described as a condition that persists after maximum medical efforts have been made in rehabilitation and after the passing of a reasonable period of time that would permit optimal regeneration and other physiologic adjustments.

Method of Evaluation—In order to evaluate impairment resulting from the effects of peripheral spinal nerve lesions, it is necessary to determine the extent of loss of function due to (a) sensory deficit, pain or discomfort; and (b) loss of muscle strength and altered fine motor control of muscles of the part. Although atrophy, vasomotor and trophic changes, reflex changes, and certain characteristic deformities are also effects of peripheral nerve lesions, it is not necessary to evaluate all of these separately, because they would be reflected in the

Table 3
ORIGINS AND FUNCTIONS OF THE PERIPHERAL NERVES

Plexus and Nerve Root Origins	Nerves of Plexus	Primary Branches	Secondary Branches	Function
Cervical (Cervical 1 to 4)	Lesser occipital			Sensory to skin behind ear and over posterior aspect of mastoid process
	Great auricular			Sensory to skin over parotid gland, angle of jaw, lobule of ear, and anterior aspect of mastoid process
	Cervical Cutaneous			Sensory to skin over anterolateral aspect of neck
	Supraclaviculars			Sensory to skin over medial infraclavicular region, pectoralis major, and deltoid
	Muscular branches	Unnamed		Motor to Rectus capitus lateralis and anterior, Longus capitus, Longus colli, hyoid musculature. Sterno cleidomastoid, Trapezius, Levator scapulae, Scalenus medius
	Phrenic			Sensory to costal and mediastinal pleura and pericardium, Motor to diaphragm
Brachial (Cervical 5 to 8 and Thoracic 1)	Muscular branches	Unnamed		Motor to Longus colli, scaleni, and Subclavius
	Dorsal scapular			Motor to Rhomboideus major and minor, Levator scapulae
	Long thoracic			Motor to Serratus anterior
	Suprascapular			Motor to Supraspinatus and Infraspinatus
	Lateral anterior thoracic			Motor to Pectoralis major
	Medial anterior thoracic			Motor to Pectoralis major and minor
	Upper subscapular			Motor to Subscapularis
	Lower subscapular			Motor to Teres major and Subscapularis
	Thoracodorsal			Motor to Latissimus dorsi
	Axillary	Posterior	Lateral brachial cutaneous	Motor to Teres minor and posterior part of Deltoid / Sensory to skin over lower two-thirds of Deltoid
		Anterior		Motor to Deltoid
	Medial brachial cutaneous			Sensory to anteromedial surface of arm (with intercostobrachial)
	Medial antebrachial cutaneous			Sensory to anteromedial surface of arm and ulnar surface of forearm
	Musculocutaneous	Unnamed		Motor to Coracobrachialis, Biceps brachii, Brachialis
		Lateral antebrachial cutaneous		Sensory to radial surface of forearm
	Median	Unnamed		Motor to Pronator teres, Flexor carpi radialis, Palmaris longus, Flexor digitorum sublimus, Abductor pollicis brevis, Opponens pollicis, superficial head of Flexor pollicis brevis
		Volar Interosseous		Motor to radial half of Flexor digitorum profundus, Flexor pollicis longus, Pronator quadratus
		Palmar		Sensory to radial surface of palm
		Common volar digitals	Proper volar digitals	Sensory to palmar surface of thumb, index, middle and radial half of ring fingers, and dorsal surface of distal halves of thumb, index, middle and radial half of ring fingers. Motor to first and second Lumbricals
	Ulnar	Unnamed		Motor to Flexor carpi ulnaris, ulnar half of Flexor digitorum profundus
		Palmar cutaneous, dorsal and superficial palmar		Sensory to ulnar half of hand, little finger and ulnar half of ring finger. Motor to Palmaris brevis (Superficial palmar n.)
		Deep palmar		Motor to Adductor pollicis, deep head of Flexor pollicis brevis, Abductor digiti quinti, Flexor digiti quinti brevis, Opponens digiti quinti, third and fourth Lumbricals, all Interossei
	Radial	Unnamed		Motor to Triceps, Anconeus, Brachioradialis, Extensor carpi radialis longus, Brachialis
		Ulnar collateral		Motor to medial head of Triceps brachii
		Posterior brachial cutaneous		Sensory to posteromedial surface of arm (with intercostobrachial)
		Dorsal antebrachial cutaneous		Sensory to dorsal surface of arm and forearm and distal lateral one-third of arm
		Superficial and dorsal digitals		Sensory to dorsum of radial one-half of wrist and hand; thumb, index, middle and radial one-half of ring finger
		Deep (Dorsal Interosseous)		Motor to Extensor carpi radialis brevis, Supinator, Extensor digitorum communis, Extensor digiti quinti proprius, Extensor carpi ulnaris, Extensor pollicis longus, Abductor pollicis longus, Extensor indicis proprius

Table 3
ORIGINS AND FUNCTIONS OF THE PERIPHERAL NERVES—CONTINUED

Plexus and Nerve Root Origins	Nerves of Plexus	Primary Branches	Secondary Branches	Function
No Plexus Formed (Thoracic) 2 to 11)	Intercostobrachial			Sensory to medial aspect of arm (with Dorsal and Medial Brachial Cutaneous) Branches run directly to intercostal and anterior abdominal musculature and to skin over the thorax and abdomen
	Iliohypogastric			Sensory to skin over hypogastric and lateral gluteal regions
	Ilioinguinal			Sensory to skin over upper medial aspect of thigh and genitalia
	Genitofemoral	External spermatic		Sensory to skin over scrotum and adjacent thigh. Motor to Cremaster
		Lumboinguinal		Sensory to skin over upper anterior aspect of thigh
	Lateral femoral cutaneous			Sensory to skin over entire lateral aspect of thigh
	Obturator			Motor to Adductor longus, brevis and magnus, Obturator externis, Gracilis
	Muscular branches	Unnamed		Motor to Psoas major and minor, Quadratus femoris, Gemellus inferior and superior, Piriformis, and Obturator internus
	Femoral	Anterior femoral cutaneous		Sensory to skin over anterior and medial aspects of thigh and knee
		Saphenous		Sensory to skin over medial and anterior aspects of leg and dorsum of foot to base of first metatarsal
		Unnamed		Motor to Iliacus, Pectineus, Sartorius, Quadriceps femoris
	Superior gluteal			Motor to Gluteus minimus and medius, Tensor fasciae latae
	Inferior gluteal			Motor to Gluteus maximus
Lumbosacral (Thoracic 12, Lumbar 1 to 5 and Sacral 1 to 4)	Posterior femoral cutaneous			Sensory to skin over inferior aspect of buttock, entire posterior aspect of thigh, politeal space, perineum, external genitalia
	Sciatic	Unnamed		Motor to Hamstrings (Biceps femoris, Semitendinosus, Semimembranosus): Adductor magus
		Tibial	Unnamed	Motor to Gastrocnemius, Plantaris, Soleus, Popliteus, Tibialis posterior, Flexor digitorum longus, Flexor hallucis longus
			Sural	Sensory to skin over posterolateral aspect of leg and lateral aspect of foot and heel
			Medial calcaneal	Sensory to skin over heel and medial aspect of sole
			Medial plantar	Sensory to skin over medial aspect sole, great toe, 2nd, 3rd and medial aspects of 4th toe. Motor to Abductor hallucis, Flexor digitorum brevis, Flexor hallucis brevis, 1st Lumbrical
			Lateral plantar	Sensory to skin over lateral aspect of sole and 5th and lateral half of 4th toes. Motor to Quadratus plantae, Abductor digiti quinti, Flexor digiti quinti brevis, all Interossei, 2nd, 3rd, & 4th Lumbricals, Adductor hallucis
		Common peroneal	Unnamed	Sensory to skin over upper 1/3 of lateral aspect of leg below knee
			Superficial peroneal	Sensory to skin over anterolateral aspect of leg and dorsum of foot and toes except for area between great and 2nd toes. Motor to Peroneus longus and brevis
			Deep peroneal	Sensory to skin on dorsum of foot between great toe and 2nd toe. Motor to Tibialis anterior, Extensor digitorum longus and brevis, Peroneus tertius, Extensor hallucis longus, 1st and 2nd Interossei dorsalis
	Pudendal (plexus)	Unnamed		Motor to Levator ani, Coccygeus, and Sphincter ani externus
		Inferior hemorrhoidal		Sensory to skin of genitalia and anus. Motor to Sphincter ani externus
		Perineal		Sensory to skin of scrotum (Labium majus). Motor to Transversus perinei superficialis and profundus, Bulbocavernosus, Ischiocavernosus, Sphincter urethrae membranacae
		Dorsal n. of penis (clitoris)		Sensory to penis (clitoris)
Coccygeal (Sacral 4,5 and Coccygeal 1)	Anococcygeal			Sensory to skin in the region of the coccyx

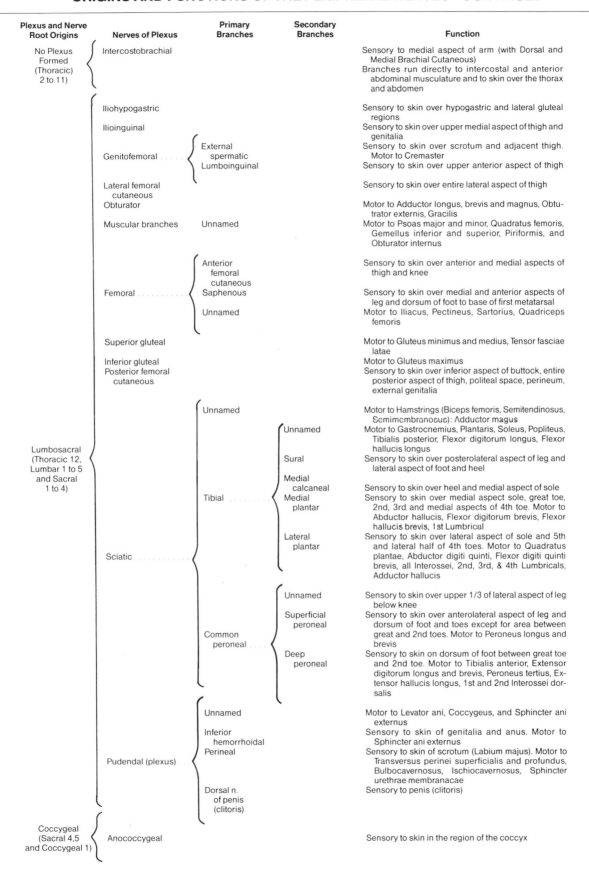

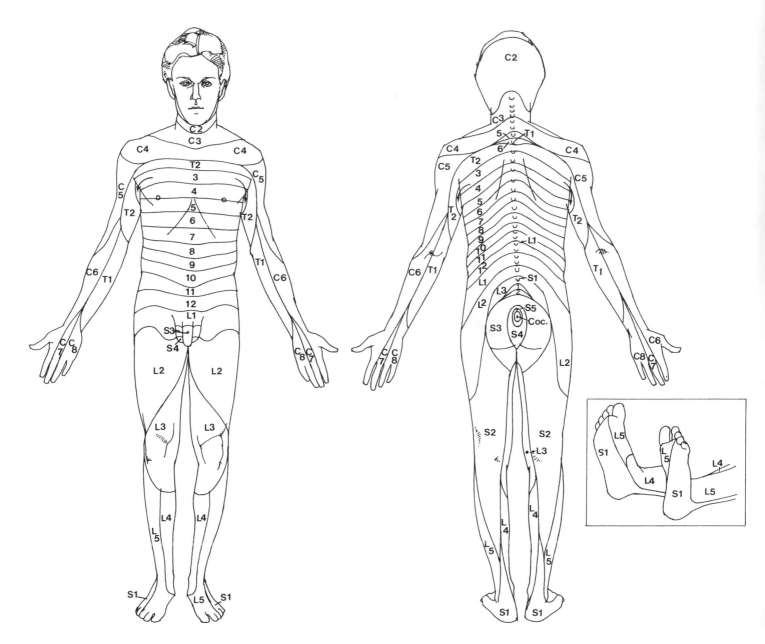

Figure 1.

The Segmental Innervation of the Skin from the Anterior Aspect. The uppermost dermatome adjoins the cutaneous field of the mandibular division of the trigeminal nerve. The arrows indicate the lateral extensions of dermatome T3.

Source: Haymaker W, Woodhall B: *Peripheral Nerve Injuries: Principles of Diagnosis*, ed 2. Philadelphia, W. B. Saunders Co, 1953, p 28. Copyright ©W. B. Saunders Co, 1953. Reproduced with permission.

Figure 2.

The Dermatomes from the Posterior View. Note the absence of cutaneous innervation by the first cervical segment. Arrows in the axillary regions indicate the lateral extent of dermatome T3; those in the region of the vertebral column point to the first thoracic, the first lumbar and the first sacral spinous processes.

Source: Haymaker W, Woodhall B: *Peripheral Nerve Injuries: Principles of Diagnosis*, ed 2. Philadelphia, W. B. Saunders Co, 1953, p 26. Copyright ©W. B. Saunders Co, 1953. Reproduced with permission.

sensory disturbance, loss of muscle strength, or altered fine motor control.

Restrictions of motion and ankyloses may result from peripheral spinal nerve impairments. Consideration was given to such impairments when the percentage values set forth in this section were derived. Therefore, if an impairment results strictly from a peripheral nerve lesion, the evaluator *should not* apply both the impairment values from Chapter 1 relating to the extremities and back and those from this chapter, because this would result in a duplication and a multiplying of the impairment rating. However, when restricted motion or ankylosis occurs in conjunction with sensory involvement or muscle weakness, then values from Chapter 1 may be combined with values of this chapter using the Combined Values Chart.

It is necessary for the physician to establish as accurately as possible which peripheral spinal nerves are involved in an impairment before determining the percentage of permanent impairment. The diagnosis is based firmly on the patient's signs and symptoms. With a carefully obtained history, a thorough medical and neurological examination, and appropriate laboratory aids, the physician should be able to describe the amount of pain, discomfort, and loss of sensation occurring in the areas innervated by the affected nerve, and also the amount of muscle strength and fine motor control that has been lost.

Pain: A subjective sensation of distress or agony, called "pain," may be associated with peripheral spinal nerve impairment. Pain may be defined as a unique complex made up of afferent stimuli interacting with the emotional or affective state of the individual and modified by that individual's past experience and present state of mind. The two constituents, neural stimulation and central reaction, are extremely variable in make-up and duration.

The pain associated with peripheral spinal nerve impairment, and particularly with that of the median, sciatic, and tibial nerves, sometimes has a constant burning quality. This pain is described as a major or a minor causalgia in accordance with its severity, and it is evaluated on the same percentage basis as are other types of pain. Major causalgia that persists despite appropriate treatment can result in loss of function of the affected extremity and impairment that is as great as 100%.

In evaluating pain that is associated with peripheral

spinal nerve disorders, the physician should consider: (1) how the pain interferes with the individual's performance of the activities of daily living; (2) to what extent the pain follows the defined anatomical pathways of the root (dermatome), plexus, or peripheral nerve; and (3) to what extent the description of the pain indicates that it is caused by the peripheral spinal nerve impairment; that is, the pain should correspond to other kinds of disturbances of the involved nerve or nerve root.

Complaints of pain that cannot be substantiated as above are not considered within the scope of this chapter. The examiner must determine whether the sensory or motor deficit is due to involvement of one or more nerve roots or of one or more peripheral nerves in order to use the appropriate table. Table 6 relates to nerve roots, Table 7 relates to the brachial and lumbosacral plexuses, and Tables 8, 9, 12, 13 and 14 relate to the peripheral nerves.

TABLE 4
GRADING SCHEME AND PROCEDURE FOR DETERMINING IMPAIRMENT OF AFFECTED BODY PART DUE TO PAIN, DISCOMFORT, OR LOSS OF SENSATION

a. Grading Scheme

Description	Grade
1. No loss of sensation or no spontaneous abnormal sensations	0%
2. Decreased sensation with or without pain, which is forgotten during activity	5-25%
3. Decreased sensation with or without pain, which interferes with activity	30-60%
4. Decreased sensation with or without pain, which may prevent activity (minor causalgia)	65-80%
5. Decreased sensation with severe pain, which may cause outcries as well as prevent activity (major causalgia)	85-95%
6. Decreased sensation with pain, which may prevent all activity	100%

b. Procedure

1. Identify the area of involvement, using the dermatome chart.
2. Identify the nerve(s) that innervate the area(s).
3. Find the value for maximum loss of function of the nerve(s) due to pain or loss of sensation or pain, using the appropriate table.*
4. Grade the degree of decreased sensation or pain according to the grading scheme above.
5. Multiply the value of the nerve (from the appropriate table) by the degree of decreased sensation or pain.

*Table 6 for nerve roots; Table 7 for brachial and lumbosacral plexuses; Tables 8, 9, 12-14 for peripheral nerves.

A grading scheme and procedure for determining impairment of a body part that is affected by pain, discomfort, or loss of sensation are found in Tables 4a and 4b, respectively.

Example: Following an injury to his elbow, a worker, after reaching maximum medical rehabilitation, was left with pain and a loss of sensation that prevented activity and caused minor causalgia in the medial aspect of his right forearm (preferred side).

1. Area of involvement is medial aspect of right forearm; see Figures 1 and 2.
2. Nerve involved is medial antibrachial cutaneous nerve; see Table 3.
3. Maximum loss of function due to loss of sensation or pain is 5%; see Table 9.
4. Gradation of decreased sensation or pain is 65%-80%; see Table 4.
5. Therefore, impairment of the upper extremity is 80% x 5%, or 4%.

Strength: Involvement of peripheral spinal nerves or nerve roots may lead to paralysis or to weakness of the muscles supplied by them as well as to characteristic sensory changes. In the case of weakness, the patient often will attempt to substitute stronger muscles to accomplish the desired motion. Thus, the physician should have an understanding of the muscles that are involved in the performance of the various movements of the body and its parts.

Muscle testing, including tests for strength, duration, repetition of contraction, and function, aids evaluation of the functions of specific nerves. Muscle testing is based on the principle of gravity and resistance, that is, the ability to raise a segment of the body through its range of motion against gravity and to hold the segment at the end of its range of motion against resistance. In interpreting muscle testing, comparable muscle functions on both sides of the body should be considered.

A grading scheme and procedure for determining impairment of a body part that is affected by loss of strength are found in Tables 5a and 5b, respectively.

Example: A work-related injury of a patient's right knee resulted in surgery and prolonged therapy. Following maximum medical rehabilitation, the examining physician found that the patient could extend his leg fully against gravity and some resistance.

1. Motion involved is extension of the knee.
2. Muscle performing motion is quadriceps femoris; see Table 3.
3. Maximum loss of nerve due to loss of strength of femoral nerve is 30%; see Table 14.
4. Gradation of loss of strength is 5% to 20%; see Table 5.
5. Therefore, impairment of the lower extremity is 20% x 30%, or 6%.

After the individual values for loss of function due to sensory deficit, pain, or discomfort, and loss of function due to loss of strength have been determined, the impairment to the part of the body or to the whole person is calculated by combining the values using the Combined Values Chart.

Special Consideration—Since the basic tasks of everyday living are more dependent upon the preferred upper extremity, dysfunction of the

TABLE 5
GRADING SCHEME AND PROCEDURE FOR DETERMINING IMPAIRMENT OF AFFECTED BODY PART DUE TO LOSS OF STRENGTH

a. Grading Scheme

Description	Grade
1. Complete range of motion against gravity and full resistance	0%
2. Complete range of motion against gravity and some resistance, or reduced fine movements and motor control	5-20%
3. Complete range of motion against gravity, and only without resistance	25-50%
4. Complete range of motion with gravity eliminated	55-75%
5. Slight contractibility, but no joint motion	80-90%
6. No contractibility	100%

b. Procedure

1. Identify the motion involved, such as flexion, extension, etc.
2. Identify the muscle(s) performing the motion.
3. Determine the nerve(s) that innervate the muscle(s), and find the value for maximum percent loss, due to loss of strength, according to the appropriate table.*
4. Grade degree of loss of strength according to the grading scheme above.
5. Multiply the value of the nerve (from the appropriate table) by the degree of loss of strength.

*Table 6 for nerve roots; Table 7 for brachial and lumbosacral plexuses; Tables 8, 9, 12-14 for peripheral nerves.

nonpreferred upper extremity results in less impairment than dysfunction of the preferred extremity. The percentage values in this chapter for the upper extremity are in terms of the preferred extremity. Therefore, when the impairment of an upper extremity has been determined to be between 5% and 50%, this value should be reduced by 5%, if the impairment is of the nonpreferred upper extremity. If the value is 51% to 100% impairment of the upper extremity, the value should be reduced by 10% for the nonpreferred extremity before converting to whole person impairment. For example, a 40% impairment of the upper extremity would be reduced to 40% − (40% x 5%) = 38% if the impairment were in the nonpreferred extremity. This procedure does not apply to the lower extremity.

Determination of Impairment — The order in which permanent impairment of the peripheral spinal nerves will be discussed is (1) the spinal nerve roots; (2) the spinal nerve plexuses; and (3) the named spinal nerves.

The Spinal Nerve Roots

The roots of the spinal nerves can be impaired by various diseases or by injuries that produce partial or complete, and unilateral or bilateral, effects. The degree of permanent impairment resulting from a spinal nerve root dysfunction would be reflected in the loss of function of the named spinal nerves having fibers from the specific nerve root. Since the named spinal nerves have fibers from more than one root, a dysfunction affecting two or more roots that supply fibers to the same nerves usually will be more impairing than a combination of the individual root impairment values (see section on brachial plexus).

Impairment ratings for the spinal nerve roots can be determined by combining appropriate values found by using a later section entitled, "The Named Spinal Nerves." Table 6 provides values for the spinal nerve roots that are most frequently involved in permanent impairment. The values given are for unilateral involvement only. Where there is bilateral involvement, the values should be combined, using the Combined Values Chart at the end of the book.

Values for impairment of a specific spinal nerve root that is not mentioned should be determined by taking into consideration the values that are suggested for a nerve having fibers from the specific nerve root. The reader should refer to the "The Named Spinal Nerves."

TABLE 6
UNILATERAL SPINAL NERVE ROOT IMPAIRMENT

Nerve Root Impaired	Maximum % Loss of Function Due to Sensory Deficit, Pain or Discomfort	Maximum % Loss of Function Due to Loss of Strength	% Impairment of Upper Extremity*
C-5	5	30	0-34
C-6	8	35	0-40
C-7	5	35	0-38
C-8	5	45	0-48
T-1	5	20	0-24

Nerve Root Impaired			% Impairment of Lower Extremity*
L-3	5	20	0-24
L-4	5	34	0-37
L-5	5	37	0-40
S-1	5	20	0-24

*See Tables 4 and 5 for grading schemes for deriving the percent impairment of the upper or lower extremity due to sensory deficit or loss of strength. See Tables 11 and 15 for converting extremity impairments to whole person impairment. Conversion to whole person impairment should be made ONLY when all impairments involving the upper extremity have been combined.

Example: A 42-year-old right-handed man fell 30 feet and landed on his upper back. He complained of neck pain radiating down his right arm. Examination revealed 20% sensory loss of the C5 area and 50% loss of strength of the muscles innervated by C5.

1. 20% of 5% (see Table 6) equals 1% loss of function due to sensory deficits, pain or discomfort.
2. 50% of 30% equals 15% loss of function due to loss of strength.
3. 1% combined with 15% equals 16% impairment of the right upper extremity.
4. 16% impairment of the preferred upper extremity equals 10% impairment of the whole person (see Table 11).

The Spinal Nerve Plexuses

Impairment due to plexus injury or disease can be determined by evaluating the various functions that are lost. For convenience, values have been set forth for some of the more commonly recognized instances of plexus involvement, for example, the brachial plexus and lumbosacral plexus.

The brachial plexus innervates the shoulder girdle and upper extremity. It is formed by the anterior primary divisions of the fifth, sixth, seventh, and eighth cervical and first thoracic roots. Through anastamoses, these roots unite to form three primary trunks (Figure 3). The clinical importance of the trunks lies in the fact that lesions of them give rise to easily recognized syndromes of the upper trunk, middle trunk, and lower trunk.

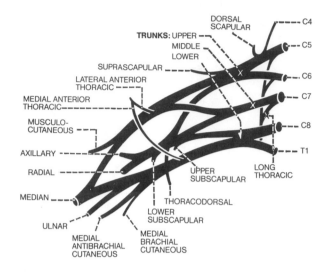

Figure 3-Brachial Plexus

The major nerves of the lower extremity and of the pelvic girdle are derived from the lumbosacral plexus (Figure 4). Thus, that plexus involves not only the lower extremity, but also bowel, bladder, and reproductive functions and trunk stabilization. Percentages for unilateral brachial and lumbosacral impairments are given in Table 7.

TABLE 7
UNILATERAL BRACHIAL AND
LUMBOSACRAL PLEXUS IMPAIRMENT

	Maximum % Loss of Function Due to Sensory Deficit, Pain or Discomfort	Maximum % Loss of Function Due to Loss of Strength	% of Impairment Upper Extremity*	Whole Person
Brachial Plexus	100	100	0-100	0-60
Upper Trunk (C-5, C-6) (Duchenne-Erb)	25	70	0-78	0-47
Middle Trunk (C-7)	5	35	0-38	0-23
Lower Trunk (C-8, T-1) (Klumpke-Dejerine)	20	70	0-76	0-46
Lumbosacral Plexus	40	50		0-70

*See Tables 4 and 5 for grading schemes for deriving the percent impairment of the upper extremity due to sensory deficit or loss of strength. See Tables 11 and 15 for converting impairment of the extremities to impairment of the whole person. Conversion to whole person impairment should be made ONLY when all impairments involving the one upper extremity have been combined.

The Named Spinal Nerves

The named spinal nerves most frequently associated with impairments are grouped below according to the involved parts of the body, that is, the head, neck and diaphragm; upper extremity; trunk, inguinal region, and perineum; and lower extremity. By consulting the sections below, the physician can determine how the clinical findings can be translated into percentages of loss of function of the part and of the whole person. The absence from the sections of some of the named spinal nerves and the absence of certain impairment values indicate that impairment associated with the particular nerve seldom occurs or is considered to be of little significance.

TABLE 8
SPECIFIC UNILATERAL SPINAL NERVE
IMPAIRMENT AFFECTING THE HEAD AND NECK

Nerve	Maximum % Loss of Function Due to Sensory Deficit, Pain, or Discomfort	Maximum % Loss of Function Due to Loss of Strength	% Impairment of the Whole Person*
Greater occipital	5	0	0- 5
Lesser occipital	3	0	0- 3
Great auricular	3	0	0- 3
Accessory (spinal accessory)	0	10	0-10

*See Tables 4 & 5 for grading schemes for determining impairment of the whole person due to sensory deficit or loss of strength.

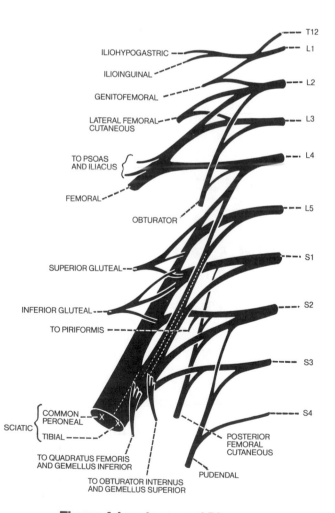

Figure 4-Lumbosacral Plexus

TABLE 9—SPECIFIC UNILATERAL SPINAL NERVE IMPAIRMENT AFFECTING THE UPPER EXTREMITY

Nerve	Maximum % Loss of Function Due to Sensory Deficit, Pain, or Discomfort	Maximum % Loss of Function Due to Loss of Strength	% Impairment of Upper Extremity*		% Impairment of the Digit
Anterior thoracics (pectoral)	0	5	0- 5		
Axillary (circumflex)	5	35	0-38		
Dorsal scapular	0	5	0- 5		
Long thoracic (posterior thoracic n., external respiratory n. of Bell, n. to serratus anterior)	0	15	0-15		
Medial antibrachial cutaneous	5	0	0- 5		
Medial brachial cutaneous	5	0	0- 5		
Median (above midforearm)	40	55	0-73		
Median (below midforearm)	40	35	0-61		
Branch to radial side of thumb	4	0	0- 4	=	0-11
Branch to ulnar side of thumb	8	0	0- 8	=	0-23
Branch to radial side of index finger	8	0	0- 8	=	0-37
Branch to ulnar side of index finger	3	0	0- 3	=	0-13
Branch to radial side of middle finger	7	0	0- 7	=	0-42
Branch to ulnar side of middle finger	2	0	0- 2	=	0-12
Branch to radial side of ring finger	3	0	0- 3	=	0-34
Musculocutaneous	5	25	0-29		
Radial (musculospiral) (upper arm with loss of triceps) wrist placed in position of function	5	55	0-57		
Radial (musculospiral) (with sparing of triceps) wrist placed in position of function	5	40	0-43		
Subscapular (upper and lower)	0	5	0- 5		
Suprascapular	5	15	0-19		
Thoracodorsal (long subscapular; nerve to latissimus dorsi)	0	10	0-10		
Ulnar (above midforearm)	10	35	0-42		
Ulnar (below midforearm)	10	25	0-33		
Branch to ulnar side of ring finger	2	0	0- 2	=	0-24
Branch to radial side of little finger	2	0	0- 2	=	0-49
Branch to ulnar side of little finger	2	0	0- 2	=	0-49

*See Tables 4 & 5 for grading schemes for determining impairment of upper extremity due to sensory deficit or loss of strength.

For upper extremity impairments between 5% and 50% involving the nonpreferred extremity, the value should be reduced by 5%; for upper extremity impairments between 51% and 100%, the value should be reduced by 10%. See text for examples.

See Table 11 for converting impairment of upper extremity to impairment of whole person.

NOTE: Conversion to whole person impairment should be made ONLY when all impairments involving the one upper extremity have been combined.

TABLE 10—RELATIONSHIP OF DIGIT IMPAIRMENT TO HAND AND UPPER EXTREMITY IMPAIRMENT

	Digit	Hand	Upper Extremity		Digit	Hand	Upper Extremity		Digit	Hand	Upper Extremity		Digit	Hand	Upper Extremity
Thumb	0- 1	= 0	= 0	Index Finger	0- 1	= 0	= 0	Middle Finger	0- 2	= 0	= 0	Ring Finger	0- 4	= 0	= 0
	2- 3	= 1	= 1		2- 5	= 1	= 1		3- 7	= 1	= 1		5-14	= 1	= 1
	4- 6	= 2	= 2		6- 9	= 2	= 2		8-12	= 2	= 2		15-24	= 2	= 2
	7- 8	= 3	= 3		10-13	= 3	= 3		13-17	= 3	= 3		25-34	= 3	= 3
	9-11	= 4	= 4		14-17	= 4	= 4		18-22	= 4	= 4		35-44	= 4	= 4
	12-13	= 5	= 5		18-21	= 5	= 5		23-27	= 5	= 5		45-54	= 5	= 5
	14-16	= 6	= 5		22-25	= 6	= 5		28-32	= 6	= 5				
	17-18	= 7	= 6		26-29	= 7	= 6		33-37	= 7	= 6	Little Finger	0- 9	= 0	= 0
	19-21	= 8	= 7		30-33	= 8	= 7		38-42	= 8	= 7		10-29	= 1	= 1
	22-23	= 9	= 8		34-37	= 9	= 8		43-47	= 9	= 8		30-49	= 2	= 2
	24-26	=10	= 9		38-41	=10	= 9		48-52	=10	= 9		50-69	= 3	= 3
	27-28	=11	=10		42-45	=11	=10						70-89	= 4	= 4
	29-31	=12	=11		46-49	=12	=11								

Figure 5-Motor Innervation of the Upper Extremity

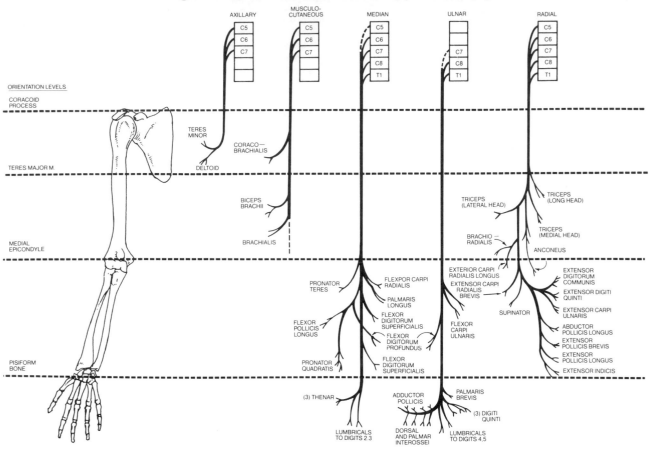

Figure 6-Motor Innervation of the Lower Extremity

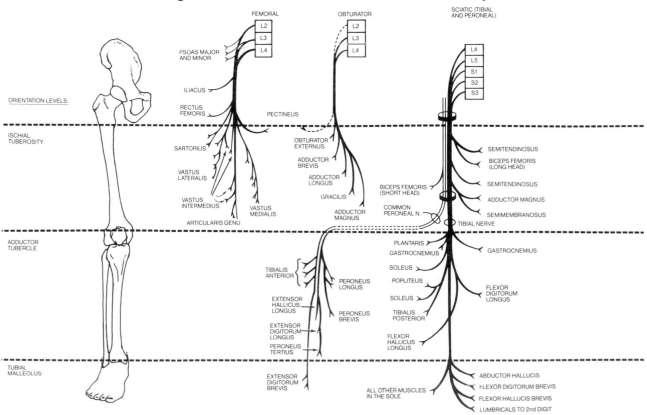

The percentages are expressed in terms of unilateral involvement. When there is bilateral involvement, the unilateral impairments should be determined separately and each converted to whole person impairment. Finally, the unilateral values are combined by using the Combined Values Chart.

Figures 5 and 6 are schematic diagrams of the major peripheral nerves of the upper and lower extremities.

Head, Neck and Diaphragm

A unilateral phrenic nerve disorder would result in minimal to no functional impairment, inasmuch as the patient would compensate and continue to carry on the activities of daily living. The impairment to the whole person for unilateral phrenic involvement would be 0% to 5%. On the other hand, bilateral phrenic involvement would result in a demonstrable reduction in ventilatory function and would be evaluated in terms of the criteria set forth in the section on the central nervous system.

Table 8 presents impairment due to loss of function of specific nerves to the head and neck.

Upper Extremity

Example: A patient sustained an injury at the wrist of the preferred extremity that affected the median nerve. After reaching maximum medical rehabilitation, he says he can use his hand for self care, grasping and holding, but he experiences some difficulty with digital dexterity. There is an 80% loss of sensation with pain that prevents activity with his thumb, index and middle fingers. The ring finger is not affected. Muscle testing of the fingers reveal complete range of motion against gravity with some resistance, which is the equivalent of a 20% loss of function due to loss of strength. The evaluation of impairment is:

Description	% Impairment of			
	Digit	Hand	Upper Extremity	Whole Person
Loss of function of the upper extremity due to sensory deficit and pain associated with median nerve injury (Tables 9 & 10)				
(a) branch to radial side of thumb	9			
(b) branch to ulnar side of thumb	18			
(9 combined with 18=25)	25	= 10	= 9	
(c) branch to radial side of index finger	30			
(d) branch to ulnar side of index finger	10			
(30 combined with 10=37)	37	= 9	= 8	
(e) branch to radial side of middle finger	34			
(f) branch to ulnar side of middle finger	10			
(34 combined with 10=41)	41	= 8	= 7	
Loss of function of upper extremity due to sensory deficit of median nerve (9 combined with 8, combined with 7=22)			22	
Loss of function of upper extremity due to loss of strength from median nerve involvement (20% loss of strength X 35%, which is maximum loss of function due to injury to median nerve below midforearm=7%) (Table 9)			7	
Impairment of upper extremity due to sensory and motor deficits (22 combined with 7=27)			27	
Impairment of whole person (Table 11)				16

NOTE: If this injury had involved the nonpreferred extremity, the impairment to the upper extremity would be reduced by 5% (27%-(27% X 5%) =26%), but the impairment of the whole person would have remained at 16% (Table 11).

Trunk, Inguinal Region, and Perineum

Evaluation of impairment of intercostal and abdominal nerves, which derive from T2-L1, is based on the number of nerves involved. The percentages in Table 12 are in terms of complete loss of function in the involved nerves. The percentages for bilateral impairment are derived by combining the figures for unilateral impairment by means of the Combined Values Chart. Where intercostal neuralgia persists, the impairment of the whole person is 0% to 3%.

Unilateral involvement of the iliohypogastric nerve would result in loss of function due to sensory deficit, pain, or discomfort of 0% to 3%. Unilateral involvement of the ilioinguinal nerve would result in loss of function due to sensory deficit, pain, or discomfort of 0% to 5% (Table 13).

Unilateral involvement of the pudendal nerve, including the branches to the inferior hemorrhoidal nerve, perineal nerve, and dorsal nerve of the penis or clitoris, would result in loss of function due to sensory deficit, pain, or discomfort of 0% to 5% and loss of strength of 0% to 5%, which combine to impairment of the whole person of 0% to 10%. Bilateral involvement, however, would result in impairment percentages of 0% to 20% for loss of function due to sensory deficit, pain, or discomfort, and loss of strength of 0% to 20%, which combine to 0% to 36% impairment of the whole person. Involvement of the coccygeal nerve would result in loss of function due to sensory deficit, pain, or discomfort of 0% to 5%.

Lower Extremity

Example: A patient suffered a simple fracture of the lower third of the femur with involvement of the sciatic nerve. After maximal medical rehabilitation, he still has some inability to extend his toes or dorsiflex his foot, unless gravity is eliminated. He can plantar-flex against gravity and against some resistance. These losses of strength are determined to be equivalent to a 60% loss of strength due to involvement of the deep common peroneal nerve, and a 20% loss of strength due to involvement of the tibial nerve. There is also complete sensory loss over the posterolateral aspect of the leg and over the lateral aspect of the foot and heel, which is deter-

mined to be equivalent to a 100% loss of sensation due to sural nerve involvement. The evaluation of impairment would be determined as follows from Table 14:

Description	% Impairment of	
	Lower Extremity	Whole Person
Loss of function due to involvement of		
(a) deep common peroneal nerve (60% gradation in loss of strength x 25%, which is the maximum value for loss of function=15%)	15	
(b) tibial nerve (20% gradation in loss of strength x 35%, which is the maximum loss of function=7%)	7	
Loss of function of lower extremity due to loss of strength (15 + 7 = 21)	21	
Loss of function of lower extremity due to sensory deficit from sural nerve involvement (100 x 5)	5	
Impairment of lower extremity (21 combined with 5 = 25)	25	
Impairment of whole person (Table 15)		10

NOTE: If, as a result of the fracture and not of the sciatic nerve injury, a permanent ankylosis of the knee were to occur, the impairment value for ankylosis, as set forth in Chapter 1, would be combined with the above peripheral spinal nerve impairment value.

TABLE 11—RELATIONSHIP OF IMPAIRMENT OF THE UPPER EXTREMITY TO IMPAIRMENT OF THE WHOLE PERSON

% Impairment of		% Impairment of		% Impairment of		% Impairment of		% Impairment of	
Upper Extremity	Whole Person	Upper Extremity	Whole Person	Upper Extremity	Whole Person	Upper Extremity	Whole Person	Upper Extremity	Whole Person
0 = 0		20 = 12		40 = 24		60 = 36		80 — 48	
1 = 1		21 = 13		41 = 25		61 = 37		81 = 49	
2 = 1		22 = 13		42 = 25		62 = 37		82 = 49	
3 = 2		23 = 14		43 = 26		63 = 38		83 = 50	
4 = 2		24 = 14		44 = 26		64 = 38		84 = 50	
5 = 3		25 = 15		45 = 27		65 = 39		85 = 51	
6 = 4		26 = 16		46 = 28		66 = 40		86 = 52	
7 = 4		27 = 16		47 = 28		67 = 40		87 = 52	
8 = 5		28 = 17		48 = 29		68 = 41		88 = 53	
9 = 5		29 = 17		49 = 29		69 = 41		89 = 53	
								90 = 54	
10 = 6		30 = 18		50 = 30		70 = 42		91 = 55	
11 = 7		31 = 19		51 = 31		71 = 43		92 = 55	
12 = 7		32 = 19		52 = 31		72 = 43		93 = 56	
13 = 8		33 = 20		53 = 32		73 = 44		94 = 56	
14 = 8		34 = 20		54 = 32		74 = 44		95 = 57	
15 = 9		35 = 21		55 = 33		75 = 45		96 = 58	
16 = 10		36 = 22		56 = 34		76 = 46		97 = 58	
17 = 10		37 = 22		57 = 34		77 = 46		98 = 59	
18 = 11		38 = 23		58 = 35		78 = 47		99 = 59	
19 = 11		39 = 23		59 = 35		79 = 47		100 = 60	

NOTE: Impairment of whole person contributed by upper extremity may be rounded to the nearest 5% ONLY when it is the *sole* impairment involved.

TABLE 12—IMPAIRMENT OF THORACIC (DORSAL) NERVE

	% Impairment of the Whole Person	
	Unilateral Involvement	Bilateral Involvement
Any 2 thoracic (dorsal) nerves	0- 5	0-10
Any 2 to 5 thoracic (dorsal) nerves . .	5-15	10-28
Any 5 or more thoracic (dorsal) nerves	15-35	28-58

TABLE 13—UNILATERAL SPINAL NERVE IMPAIRMENT AFFECTING INGUINAL REGION

Nerve	Maximum % Loss of Function Due to Sensory Deficit, Pain, or Discomfort	Maximum % Loss of Function Due to Loss of Strength	% Impairment of the Whole Person*
Iliohypogastric . .	3	0	0-3
Ilioinguinal . . .	5	0	0-5

*See Tables 4 & 5 for grading schemes for determining impairment of the whole person due to sensory deficit or loss of strength.

TABLE 14—SPECIFIC UNILATERAL SPINAL NERVE IMPAIRMENT AFFECTING THE LOWER EXTREMITY

Nerve	Maximum % Loss of Function Due to Sensory Deficit, Pain, or Discomfort	Maximum % Loss of Function Due to Loss of Strength	% Impairment of Lower Extremity*	Nerve	Maximum % Loss of Function Due to Sensory Deficit, Pain, or Discomfort	Maximum % Loss of Function Due to Loss of Strength	% Impairment of Lower Extremity*
Femoral (anterior crural)	5	35	0-38	Common peroneal (lateral, or external popliteal)	5	35	0-38
Femoral (anterior crural) (below iliacus nerve)	5	30	0-34	Deep (above midshin)	0	25	0-25
Genitofemoral (genito crural)	5	0	0- 5	Deep (below midshin) anterior tibial	0	5	0- 5
Inferior gluteal	0	25	0-25	Superficial	5	10	0-14
Lateral femoral cutaneous	10	0	0-10	Tibial nerve (medial, or internal popliteal)			
N. to obturator internus muscle				Above knee	15	35	0-45
N. to piriformis muscle	0	10	0-10	Posterior tibial (midcalf and knee)	15	25	0-33
N. to quadratus femoris muscle				Below midcalf	15	15	0-28
N. to superior gemellus muscle				Lateral plantar branch	5	5	0-10
Obturator	0	10	0-10	Medial plantar branch	5	5	0-10
Posterior cutaneous of thigh	5	0	0- 5	Sural (external saphenous)	5	0	0- 5
Superior gluteal	0	20	0-20				
Sciatic (above hamstring innervation)	25	75	0-81				

*See Tables 4 & 5 for grading schemes for determining impairment of the lower extremity due to sensory deficit or loss of strength.

See Table 15 for converting impairment of lower extremity to impairment of whole person. NOTE: Conversion to whole person impairment should be made ONLY when all impairments involving the one lower extremity have been completed.

TABLE 15—RELATIONSHIP OF IMPAIRMENT OF THE LOWER EXTREMITY TO IMPAIRMENT OF THE WHOLE PERSON

% Impairment of Lower Extremity	Whole Person	% Impairment of Lower Extremity	Whole Person	% Impairment of Lower Extremity	Whole Person	% Impairment of Lower Extremity	Whole Person	% Impairment of Lower Extremity	Whole Person
0 =	0	20 =	8	40 =	16	60 =	24	80 =	32
1 =	0	21 =	8	41 =	16	61 =	24	81 =	32
2 =	1	22 =	9	42 =	17	62 =	25	82 =	33
3 =	1	23 =	9	43 =	17	63 =	25	83 =	33
4 =	2	24 =	10	44 =	18	64 =	26	84 =	34
5 =	2	25 =	10	45 =	18	65 =	26	85 =	34
6 =	2	26 =	10	46 =	18	66 =	26	86 =	34
7 =	3	27 =	11	47 =	19	67 =	27	87 =	35
8 =	3	28 =	11	48 =	19	68 =	27	88 =	35
9 =	4	29 =	12	49 =	20	69 =	28	89 =	36
10 =	4	30 =	12	50 =	20	70 =	28	90 =	36
11 =	4	31 =	12	51 =	20	71 =	28	91 =	36
12 =	5	32 =	13	52 =	21	72 =	29	92 =	37
13 =	5	33 =	13	53 =	21	73 =	29	93 =	37
14 =	6	34 =	14	54 =	22	74 =	30	94 =	38
15 =	6	35 =	14	55 =	22	75 =	30	95 =	38
16 =	6	36 =	14	56 =	22	76 =	30	96 =	38
17 =	7	37 =	15	57 =	23	77 =	31	97 =	39
18 =	7	38 =	15	58 =	23	78 =	31	98 =	39
19 =	8	39 =	16	59 =	24	79 =	32	99 =	40
								100 =	40

Note: Impairment of whole person contributed by lower extremity may be rounded to the nearest 5% only when it is the *sole* impairment involved.

References

1. Baker AB, Baker LH (eds): *Clinical Neurology*, vol 1-3. Philadelphia, Harper and Row Publishers Inc, 1982.

2. Merritt HH: *A Textbook of Neurology*, ed 6. Philadelphia, Lea and Febiger, 1979.

3. Sunderland S: *Nerves and Nerve Injuries*. Edinburgh, Churchill Livingstone, 1978.

4. Strub RL, Black FW: *The Mental Status Examination in Neurology*, Philadelphia, FA Davis, 1977.

Chapter 3

The Respiratory System

Introduction

The major topics of this chapter are evaluation of respiratory impairment and impairment resulting from breathing abnormalities that occur during sleep.

Before using the information in this chapter, the reader is urged to consult the Preface to the Guides, which provides a general discussion of the purpose of the Guides, and of the situations in which they are useful; and discusses techniques for the evaluation of the patient and for report preparation.

Evaluation of Impairment Due to Respiratory Disease

General Considerations

There are several classification schemes used to define the degree of respiratory impairment. Some of these are based on actual values of pulmonary function tests, while others use predicted values. One scheme is based on severity of dyspnea. This chapter represents an attempt to develop criteria that would help standardize assessment of respiratory impairment.

The criteria presented in this chapter are based on those developed by the Component Committee for Disability Criteria of the American Lung Association and approved by its medical section, the American Thoracic Society (ATS). The criteria are intended to apply to occupational as well as to non-occupational respiratory disease. The latter may include conditions such as hypoventilation states, vascular occlusive disease and chest wall weakness.

Personal and Medical History

Identification: The physician should record basic information about the patient, including name, address, age, sex, social security number, telephone number, and date and place of birth. Information about ethnicity, marital status, highest grade completed in school, and regularity and extent of exercise may be helpful in selected situations.

Dyspnea: The physician should ask specific questions about whether or not dyspnea is increasing in severity, because one of the manifestations of reduced lung function and impairment is shortness of breath. The severity of dyspnea can be estimated by obtaining information about activities that lead to shortness of breath, such as the distance walked, the number of stairs climbed, etc (Table 1).

Dyspnea may not be used as the sole criterion for evaluation of impairment. The causes of dyspnea are multiple and complex. Individual responses to a given degree of dyspnea vary and are influenced by factors unrelated to the extent of lung disease, such as difficulty in verbal communication, preoccupation with health, socioeconomic status and educational background. Therefore, the symptom of dyspnea should be considered along with other physiologic and personal factors.

Cough and sputum production: Although cough occurs frequently in patients with chronic obstructive pulmonary diseases (COPD), only some patients will meet the accepted criterion of chronic bronchitis: cough that is productive of sputum each day for at least three months out of the year for at least two consecutive years, without other apparent causes. Thus, a detailed description of sputum volume, color, odor and consistency, and how often it is expectorated, is important.

Wheezing: The hallmark of reversible airway obstruction is the wheeze. In addition to asthma, foreign bodies or tumors in airways can cause wheezing, but in the latter instances the wheezing is usually confined to one area of the chest. Wheezing may occur in patients with congestive heart failure; in such cases it is of brief duration and associated with obvious signs of cardiovascu-

TABLE 1—CLASSES OF RESPIRATORY IMPAIRMENT

	Class 1 0% No Impairment	Class 2 10-25% Mild Impairment	Class 3 30-45% Moderate Impairment	Class 4** 50-100% Severe Impairment
DYSPNEA	The subject may or may not have dyspnea. If dyspnea is present, it is for non-respiratory reasons or it is consistent with the circumstances of activity.	Dyspnea with fast walking on level ground or when walking up a hill; patient can keep pace with persons of same age and body build on level ground but not on hills or stairs.	Dyspnea while walking on level ground with person of the same age or walking up one flight of stairs. Patient can walk a mile at own pace without dyspnea, but cannot keep pace on level ground with others of same age and body build.	Dyspnea after walking more than 100 meters at own pace on level ground. Patient sometimes is dyspneic with less exertion or even at rest.
	or	or	or	or
TESTS OF VENTILATORY FUNCTION*				
FVC FEV_1 FEV_1/FVC ratio (as percent)	Above the lower limit of normal for the predicted value as defined by the 95% confidence interval. (See Tables 2-7 and text for methods of calculation.)	Below the 95% confidence interval but greater than 60% predicted for FVC, FEV_1 and FEV_1/FVC ratio.	Less than 60% predicted, but greater than: 50% predicted for FVC 40% predicted for FEV_1 40% actual value for FEV_1/FVC ratio.	Less than: 50% predicted for FVC 40% predicted for FEV_1 40% actual value for FEV_1/FVC ratio 40% predicted for D_{CO}.
	or	or	or	or
$\dot{V}O_2$ Max	Greater than 25 ml/(kg·min)	Between 20-25 ml/(kg·min)	Between 15-20 ml/(kg·min)	Less than 15 ml/(kg·min)

*FVC is Forced Vital Capacity. FEV_1 is Forced Expiratory Volume in the first second. At least one of the three tests should be abnormal to the degree described for Classes 2, 3, and 4.

**An asthmatic patient who, despite optimum medical therapy, has had attacks of severe bronchospasm requiring emergency room or hospital care on the average of six times per year is considered to be severely impaired. See text.

lar decompensation. Wheezing should be described in terms of frequency, whether it occurs as paroxysms along with shortness of breath, when during the day or time of year it occurs, what are the possible factors involved, and whether it limits the patient's capacity to function.

Environmental exposure, tobacco usage and chronological occupational data: A detailed history of the patient's employment in chronological order should be obtained. It is easiest to begin with the most recent job and work back to the earliest job. The examiner should ask about the specific activities in each job, rather than about only the job title. An employee should be questioned about exposures to dusts, gases, vapors and fumes. The specific information required involves (1) the year he or she was first exposed to an agent; (2) the extent of the exposure; (3) the total number of years of exposure; (4) his or her estimate of the hazard that the agent posed; and (5) the number of years since exposure ceased.

Subjects should be classified as non-smokers, present smokers, and ex-smokers; the latter are those who have stopped for at least one year. The smoking history should list type(s) of tobacco smoked (cigarette, pipe or cigar) and should emphasize cigarette smoking history. The history should include information about the age at which the patient started to smoke, the brands used, and if and when the use of cigarettes was discontinued. The cumulative dose of exposure should be estimated in terms of "pack-years," which is the product of the usual number of packs of cigarettes the patient smoked per day and the total number of years the patient was a smoker. The maximum level of tobacco use should be described.

Data on environmental exposures and use of tobacco are especially important when the examining physician is asked to give an opinion on *apportionment.* The reader should consult the Preface for a discussion of apportionment.

Physical Examination

The physician should note the patient's position when the blood pressure and the heart and respiratory rates are recorded. The physician should check for the following: *en bloc* movement of the chest, use of the sternocleidomastoid and other accessory muscles of respiration, paradoxical movement of the intercostal spaces posterolaterally, and an attempt to elevate the chest cage by fixing the shoulders and leaning forward. The physician should record the degree of thoracic muscle wasting, the position and extent of diaphragmatic motion, and the presence of paradoxical movement between the rib cage and the abdomen.

Description of the patient's breathing: The physician should record depth of breathing and the presence of tachypnea, hyperpnea, labored breathing at rest, inability to complete sentences because of dyspnea, as well as exhalation through pursed lips. Duration of forced expiratory flow following a maximal inspiration can be measured while listening over the trachea with a stethoscope. Normally the duration is less than four seconds, but it may be several times longer in a patient with airflow obstruction.

Cyanosis and clubbing: The physician should note the presence of cyanosis of the buccal mucosa or lips; if there is a normal hemoglobin concentration, cyanosis may not be seen until the arterial blood oxygen saturation is less than 75%. Clubbing, almost invariably absent in patients with COPD alone, may occur when lung abscess, empyema, bronchiectasis or asbestosis is present as well.

Adventitious lung sounds: The physician should note the character of the lung sounds during the patient's quiet, deep breathing. Noting the relative duration of expiration and inspiration and listening to the quality and intensity of breath sounds can provide valuable information concerning obstruction to airflow. Intensity of breath sounds correlates well with pulmonary function measurements.

Intensity and location of wheezing, rhonchi and rales should be described, as well as whether they are heard during inspiration, expiration, or both. Crackles may be present in two-thirds of patients with chronic interstitial disease such as asbestosis and desquamative interstitial pneumonia. These crackles usually occur during late inspiration. Early inspiratory crackles may be heard in diseases of airflow obstruction and particularly in bronchiolitis obliterans.

Cor pulmonale: The physician should look for evidence of cor pulmonale, which may be associated with conditions such as chronic bronchitis and emphysema and with chronic diffuse interstitial disease. If right heart failure accompanies cor pulmonale, neck vein distension occurs above the manubrium sterni when the patient lies supine: the veins fill from below, and their volume does not decrease when the thorax is elevated 45 degrees from the horizontal. If the patient has such a sign, the physician should perform a thorough cardiovascular examination and determine an impairment rating for cardiovascular disease, which should be combined with the impairment rating for pulmonary disease using the Combined Values Chart.

Chest roentgenograms: Minimal radiographic examination should consist of posterior-anterior (PA) and lateral views taken on deep inspiration. Chest radiographic findings often correlate poorly with physiologic findings in diseases of airflow limitation such as asthma and emphysema. No correlation between ability to work and roentgenographic findings has been noted.

If there is obstructive disease, the chest radiograph should be described in terms of hyperinflation, loss of vascular markings, presence of bullae, flattened diaphragms, and an increase in the retrosternal air space, sternophrenic angle, and PA diameter. Cardiac abnormalities or evidence of cor pulmonale with enlargement of the pulmonary arc segment with small distal pulmonary arterial branches should be noted.

In interstitial diseases with small rounded or irregular opacities, such as coal workers' pneumoconiosis or asbestosis, respectively, the correlation between physiologic and radiographic abnormalities is poor. The only exception is when there is radiographic evidence of progressive massive fibrosis (PMF). As the PMF intensifies, there is frequently a significant reduction in the ventilatory capacity.

The physician should be familiar with the 1980 International Labor Organization (ILO) Classification of Pneumoconioses, and use that Classification in describing radiographic findings.

Physiologic Test of Pulmonary Function: Techniques, Use and Interpretation

Forced expiratory maneuvers (simple spirometry): A forced expiratory maneuver, illustrated diagrammatically in Figure 1, is performed in all examina-

Figure 1 Lung Capacities and Volumes in the Normal State and in Three Abnormal Conditions**

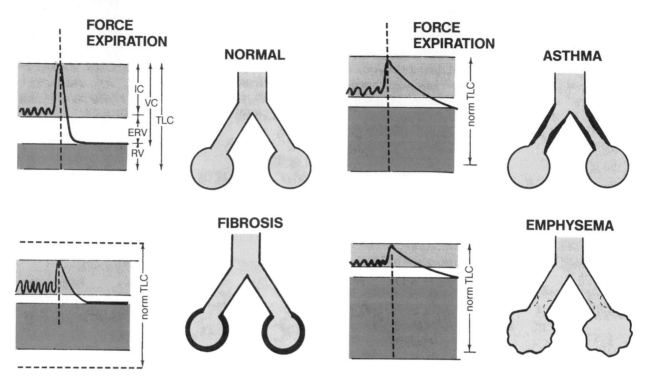

IC: Inspiratory capacity, **VC:** Vital capacity, **TLC:** Total lung capacity, **RV:** Residual volume, **ERV:** Expiratory reserve volume
**Residual volume, and therefore total lung capacity, cannot be measured by spirometry alone.

tions of permanent impairment. The maneuver measures the mechanical ventilatory capacity of the lungs. There are three component parts: forced vital capacity, or FVC; forced expiratory volume in the first second, or FEV_1; and the ratio of these measurements expressed as a percentage, or the FEV_1/FVC ratio. Correlation between work status and FEV_1 values is usually good, and most patients with an FEV_1 of less than one liter are not working. Generally, individuals with an FEV_1/FVC ratio of less than 40% have a shortened life span. For interstitial lung disease, the FVC has proved to be a reliable and valid index of significant impairment.

The spirometric tests should be performed as described in the 1978 ATS Epidemiology Standardization Project. The equipment, methods of calibration, and techniques should meet the ATS criteria. The spirogram that is technically acceptable and demonstrates the best efforts by the patient should be used to calculate the FEV_1 and FVC.

Height should be measured in centimeters with the patient standing in his or her stocking feet. If a patient cannot stand or suffers from spinal

deformities, his or her height should be considered as equal to the arm span, which is the distance between the tips of the middle fingers when the arms are stretched horizontally against the wall.

The patient should be evaluated after he or she has received optimum therapy or is in optimum health. If wheezing or other evidence of bronchospasm is evident at the time of examination, the ventilatory studies should be done before and after the administration of a bronchodilator. The bronchodilator most frequently used as an aerosol is isoproterenol; the test should be performed 10 minutes after administration of two inhalations or after a total dose of 250 μg. If either metaproterenol or isoetharine is used, one should wait 15 to 20 minutes. The spirogram indicating the best effort, either before or after administration of the bronchodilator, should be used to calculate the FVC and FEV_1.

The patient's spirometry results should be compared to predicted "normal" values for FVC, FEV_1 and FEV_1/FVC ratio. Such values for both adult males and females are presented in Tables 2 through 7. To find the "normal" value, find the patient's age in the left hand column and the height along the top row, and locate the predicted value at the intersection of the respective row and column. Since for each age-height combination there is actually a distribution of normal values, one must determine the lower limit of normal by subtracting from the table the value called the "95% Confidence Interval" that is provided for each table.

For example, a 30-year-old man, who is 160 cm tall, is found to have an FVC of 3.32 liters. The lower limit of normal is $4.31-1.12=3.19$ liters. Thus, his FVC is within normal limits.

The spirometry results for black patients should be divided by 0.9 before they are compared to the predicted values. To date no other ethnic groups have been studied sufficiently to determine if there are differences from the predicted values, which are based on a white population.

Interpretation of FVC, FEV_1 and the FEV_1/FVC ratio is given in Table 1. At least one of these measures of ventilatory function should be abnormal to the degree described in a given class definition if an impairment is to be rated in that class.

TABLE 2
PREDICTED NORMAL FVC VALUES (LITERS) FOR MEN (BTPS)

AGE	146	148	150	152	154	156	158	160	162	164	166	168	170	172	174	176	178	180	182	184	186	188	190	192	194
18	3.72	3.84	3.96	4.08	4.20	4.32	4.44	4.56	4.68	4.80	4.92	5.04	5.16	5.28	5.40	5.52	5.64	5.76	5.88	6.00	6.12	6.24	6.36	6.48	6.60
20	3.68	3.80	3.92	4.04	4.16	4.28	4.40	4.52	4.64	4.76	4.88	5.00	5.12	5.24	5.36	5.48	5.60	5.72	5.84	5.96	6.08	6.20	6.32	6.44	6.56
22	3.64	3.76	3.88	4.00	4.12	4.24	4.36	4.48	4.60	4.72	4.84	4.96	5.08	5.20	5.32	5.44	5.56	5.68	5.80	5.92	6.04	6.16	6.28	6.40	6.52
24	3.60	3.72	3.84	3.95	4.08	4.20	4.32	4.44	4.56	4.68	4.80	4.92	5.04	5.16	5.28	5.40	5.52	5.64	5.76	5.88	6.00	6.12	6.24	6.36	6.48
26	3.55	3.67	3.79	3.91	4.03	4.15	4.27	4.39	4.51	4.63	4.75	4.87	4.99	5.11	5.23	5.35	5.47	5.59	5.71	5.83	5.95	6.07	6.19	6.31	6.43
28	3.51	3.63	3.75	3.87	3.99	4.11	4.23	4.35	4.47	4.59	4.71	4.83	4.95	5.07	5.19	5.31	5.43	5.55	5.67	5.79	5.91	6.03	6.15	6.27	6.39
30	3.47	3.59	3.71	3.83	3.95	4.07	4.19	4.31	4.43	4.55	4.67	4.79	4.91	5.03	5.15	5.27	5.39	5.51	5.63	5.75	5.87	5.99	6.11	6.23	6.35
32	3.43	3.55	3.67	3.79	3.91	4.03	4.15	4.27	4.39	4.51	4.63	4.75	4.87	4.99	5.11	5.23	5.35	5.47	5.59	5.71	5.83	5.95	6.07	6.19	6.31
34	3.38	3.50	3.62	3.74	3.86	3.98	4.10	4.22	4.34	4.46	4.58	4.70	4.82	4.94	5.06	5.18	5.30	5.42	5.54	5.66	5.78	5.90	6.02	6.14	6.26
36	3.34	3.46	3.58	3.70	3.82	3.94	4.06	4.18	4.30	4.42	4.54	4.66	4.78	4.90	5.02	5.14	5.26	5.38	5.50	5.62	5.74	5.86	5.98	6.10	6.22
38	3.30	3.42	3.54	3.66	3.78	3.90	4.02	4.14	4.26	4.38	4.50	4.62	4.74	4.86	4.98	5.10	5.22	5.34	5.46	5.58	5.70	5.82	5.94	6.06	6.18
40	3.25	3.37	3.49	3.61	3.73	3.85	3.97	4.09	4.21	4.33	4.45	4.57	4.69	4.81	4.93	5.05	5.17	5.29	5.41	5.53	5.65	5.77	5.89	6.01	6.13
42	3.21	3.33	3.45	3.57	3.69	3.81	3.93	4.05	4.17	4.29	4.41	4.53	4.65	4.77	4.89	5.01	5.13	5.25	5.37	5.49	5.61	5.73	5.85	5.97	6.09
44	3.17	3.29	3.41	3.53	3.65	3.77	3.89	4.01	4.13	4.25	4.37	4.49	4.61	4.73	4.85	4.97	5.09	5.21	5.33	5.45	5.57	5.69	5.81	5.93	6.05
46	3.13	3.25	3.37	3.49	3.61	3.73	3.85	3.97	4.09	4.21	4.33	4.45	4.57	4.69	4.81	4.93	5.05	5.17	5.29	5.41	5.53	5.65	5.77	5.89	6.01
48	3.08	3.20	3.32	3.44	3.56	3.68	3.80	3.92	4.04	4.16	4.28	4.40	4.52	4.64	4.76	4.88	5.00	5.12	5.24	5.36	5.48	5.60	5.72	5.84	5.96
50	3.04	3.16	3.28	3.40	3.52	3.64	3.76	3.88	4.00	4.12	4.24	4.36	4.48	4.60	4.72	4.84	4.96	5.08	5.20	5.32	5.44	5.56	5.68	5.80	5.92
52	3.00	3.12	3.24	3.36	3.48	3.60	3.72	3.84	3.96	4.08	4.20	4.32	4.44	4.56	4.68	4.80	4.92	5.04	5.16	5.28	5.40	5.52	5.64	5.76	5.88
54	2.95	3.07	3.19	3.31	3.43	3.55	3.67	3.79	3.91	4.03	4.15	4.27	4.39	4.51	4.63	4.75	4.87	4.99	5.11	5.23	5.35	5.47	5.59	5.71	5.83
56	2.91	3.03	3.15	3.27	3.39	3.51	3.63	3.75	3.87	3.99	4.11	4.23	4.35	4.47	4.59	4.71	4.83	4.95	5.07	5.19	5.31	5.43	5.55	5.67	5.79
58	2.87	2.99	3.11	3.23	3.35	3.47	3.59	3.71	3.83	3.95	4.07	4.19	4.31	4.43	4.55	4.67	4.79	4.91	5.03	5.15	5.27	5.39	5.51	5.63	5.75
60	2.83	2.95	3.07	3.19	3.31	3.43	3.55	3.67	3.79	3.91	4.03	4.15	4.27	4.39	4.51	4.63	4.75	4.87	4.99	5.11	5.23	5.35	5.47	5.59	5.71
62	2.78	2.90	3.02	3.14	3.26	3.38	3.50	3.62	3.74	3.86	3.98	4.10	4.22	4.34	4.46	4.58	4.70	4.82	4.94	5.06	5.18	5.30	5.42	5.54	5.66
64	2.74	2.86	2.98	3.10	3.22	3.34	3.46	3.58	3.70	3.82	3.94	4.06	4.18	4.30	4.42	4.54	4.66	4.78	4.90	5.02	5.14	5.26	5.38	5.50	5.62
66	2.70	2.82	2.94	3.06	3.18	3.30	3.42	3.54	3.66	3.78	3.90	4.02	4.14	4.26	4.38	4.50	4.62	4.74	4.86	4.98	5.10	5.22	5.34	5.46	5.58
68	2.65	2.77	2.89	3.01	3.13	3.25	3.37	3.49	3.61	3.73	3.85	3.97	4.09	4.21	4.33	4.45	4.57	4.69	4.81	4.93	5.05	5.17	5.29	5.41	5.53
70	2.61	2.73	2.85	2.97	3.09	3.21	3.33	3.45	3.57	3.69	3.81	3.93	4.05	4.17	4.29	4.41	4.53	4.65	4.77	4.89	5.01	5.13	5.25	5.37	5.49
72	2.57	2.69	2.81	2.93	3.05	3.17	3.29	3.41	3.53	3.65	3.77	3.89	4.01	4.13	4.25	4.37	4.49	4.61	4.73	4.85	4.97	5.09	5.21	5.33	5.45
74	2.53	2.65	2.77	2.89	3.01	3.13	3.25	3.37	3.49	3.61	3.73	3.85	3.97	4.09	4.21	4.33	4.45	4.57	4.69	4.81	4.93	5.05	5.17	5.29	5.41

FVC in liters = 0.0600 H − 0.0214 A − 4.650. R^2 = 0.54, SEE = 0.644, 95% Confidence Interval = 1.115.

Definitions of abbreviations: R^2 = coefficient of determination, SEE = standard error of estimate, H = height in cm, and A = age in years. BTPS = body temperature, ambient pressure and saturated with water vapor at these conditions. The 95% confidence interval is calculated from a one-tailed "t" test. It is a single value recommended for all heights and ages in this study. When subtracted from the predicted values, it yields the lower limit of normal.

The axes of the table are age (in years) at the side, and height (in cm) at the top. The predicted normal FVC in liters for the male patient is found at the intersection of the row for his age, and the column for his height, adapted from Crapo RO, Morris AH, Gardner RM: Reference spirometric values using techniques and equipment that meet ATS recommendations. *Am Rev Respir Dis* 1981; 123:659-664.

TABLE 3
PREDICTED NORMAL FVC VALUES FOR WOMEN (BTPS)

AGE	146	148	150	152	154	156	158	160	162	164	166	168	170	172	174	176	178	180	182	184	186	188	190	192	194
18	3.19	3.29	3.39	3.48	3.58	3.68	3.78	3.88	3.98	4.07	4.17	4.27	4.37	4.47	4.56	4.66	4.76	4.86	4.96	5.06	5.15	5.25	5.35	5.45	5.55
20	3.15	3.24	3.34	3.44	3.54	3.64	3.74	3.83	3.93	4.03	4.13	4.23	4.32	4.42	4.52	4.62	4.72	4.82	4.91	5.01	5.11	5.21	5.31	5.41	5.50
22	3.10	3.20	3.30	3.40	3.50	3.59	3.69	3.79	3.89	3.99	4.09	4.18	4.28	4.38	4.48	4.58	4.67	4.77	4.87	4.97	5.07	5.17	5.26	5.36	5.46
24	3.06	3.16	3.26	3.35	3.45	3.55	3.65	3.75	3.85	3.94	4.04	4.14	4.24	4.34	4.43	4.53	4.63	4.73	4.83	4.93	5.02	5.12	5.22	5.32	5.42
26	3.02	3.12	3.21	3.31	3.41	3.51	3.61	3.70	3.80	3.90	4.00	4.10	4.20	4.29	4.39	4.49	4.59	4.69	4.78	4.88	4.98	5.08	5.18	5.28	5.37
28	2.97	3.07	3.17	3.27	3.37	3.46	3.56	3.66	3.76	3.86	3.96	4.05	4.15	4.25	4.35	4.45	4.54	4.64	4.74	4.84	4.94	5.04	5.13	5.23	5.33
30	2.93	3.03	3.13	3.23	3.32	3.42	3.52	3.62	3.72	3.81	3.91	4.01	4.11	4.21	4.31	4.40	4.50	4.60	4.70	4.80	4.89	4.99	5.09	5.19	5.29
32	2.89	2.99	3.08	3.18	3.28	3.38	3.48	3.57	3.67	3.77	3.87	3.97	4.07	4.16	4.26	4.36	4.46	4.56	4.65	4.75	4.85	4.95	5.05	5.15	5.24
34	2.84	2.94	3.04	3.14	3.24	3.34	3.43	3.53	3.63	3.73	3.83	3.92	4.02	4.12	4.22	4.32	4.42	4.51	4.61	4.71	4.81	4.91	5.00	5.10	5.20
36	2.80	2.90	3.00	3.10	3.19	3.29	3.39	3.49	3.59	3.68	3.78	3.88	3.98	4.08	4.18	4.27	4.37	4.47	4.57	4.67	4.76	4.86	4.96	5.06	5.16
38	2.76	2.86	2.95	3.05	3.15	3.25	3.35	3.45	3.54	3.64	3.74	3.84	3.94	4.03	4.13	4.23	4.33	4.43	4.53	4.62	4.72	4.82	4.92	5.02	5.11
40	2.71	2.81	2.91	3.01	3.11	3.21	3.30	3.40	3.50	3.60	3.70	3.79	3.89	3.99	4.09	4.19	4.29	4.38	4.48	4.58	4.68	4.78	4.87	4.97	5.07
42	2.67	2.77	2.87	2.97	3.06	3.16	3.26	3.36	3.46	3.56	3.65	3.75	3.85	3.95	4.05	4.14	4.24	4.34	4.44	4.54	4.64	4.73	4.83	4.93	5.03
44	2.63	2.73	2.82	2.92	3.02	3.12	3.22	3.32	3.41	3.51	3.61	3.71	3.81	3.90	4.00	4.10	4.20	4.30	4.40	4.49	4.59	4.69	4.79	4.89	4.98
46	2.58	2.68	2.78	2.88	2.98	3.08	3.17	3.27	3.37	3.47	3.57	3.67	3.76	3.86	3.96	4.06	4.16	4.25	4.35	4.45	4.55	4.65	4.75	4.84	4.94
48	2.54	2.64	2.74	2.84	2.93	3.03	3.13	3.23	3.33	3.43	3.52	3.62	3.72	3.82	3.92	4.01	4.11	4.21	4.31	4.41	4.51	4.60	4.70	4.80	4.90
50	2.50	2.60	2.69	2.79	2.89	2.99	3.09	3.19	3.28	3.38	3.48	3.58	3.68	3.78	3.87	3.97	4.07	4.17	4.27	4.36	4.46	4.56	4.66	4.76	4.86
52	2.46	2.55	2.65	2.75	2.85	2.95	3.04	3.14	3.24	3.34	3.44	3.54	3.63	3.73	3.83	3.93	4.03	4.12	4.22	4.32	4.42	4.52	4.62	4.71	4.81
54	2.41	2.51	2.61	2.71	2.80	2.90	3.00	3.10	3.20	3.30	3.39	3.49	3.59	3.69	3.79	3.89	3.98	4.08	4.18	4.28	4.38	4.47	4.57	4.67	4.77
56	2.37	2.47	2.57	2.66	2.76	2.86	2.96	3.06	3.15	3.25	3.35	3.45	3.55	3.65	3.74	3.84	3.94	4.04	4.14	4.23	4.33	4.43	4.53	4.63	4.73
58	2.33	2.42	2.52	2.62	2.72	2.82	2.91	3.01	3.11	3.21	3.31	3.41	3.50	3.60	3.70	3.80	3.90	4.00	4.09	4.19	4.29	4.39	4.49	4.58	4.68
60	2.28	2.38	2.48	2.58	2.68	2.77	2.87	2.97	3.07	3.17	3.26	3.36	3.46	3.56	3.66	2.76	3.85	3.95	4.05	4.15	4.25	4.34	4.44	4.54	4.64
62	2.24	2.34	2.44	2.53	2.63	2.73	2.83	2.93	3.02	3.12	3.22	3.32	3.42	3.52	3.61	3.71	3.81	3.91	4.01	4.11	4.20	4.30	4.40	4.50	4.60
64	2.20	2.29	2.39	2.49	2.59	2.69	2.79	2.88	2.98	3.08	3.18	3.28	3.37	3.47	3.57	3.67	3.77	2.87	3.96	4.06	4.16	4.26	4.36	4.45	4.55
66	2.15	2.25	2.35	2.45	2.55	2.64	2.74	2.84	2.94	3.04	3.14	3.23	3.33	3.43	3.53	3.63	3.72	3.82	3.92	4.02	4.12	4.22	4.31	4.41	4.51
68	2.11	2.21	2.31	2.40	2.50	2.60	2.70	2.80	2.90	2.99	3.09	3.19	3.29	3.39	3.48	3.58	3.68	3.78	3.88	3.98	4.07	4.17	4.27	4.37	4.47
70	2.07	2.16	2.26	2.36	2.46	2.56	2.66	2.75	2.85	2.95	3.05	3.15	3.24	3.34	3.44	3.54	3.64	3.74	3.83	3.93	4.03	4.13	4.23	4.33	4.42
72	2.02	2.12	2.22	2.32	2.42	2.51	2.61	2.71	2.81	2.91	3.01	3.10	3.20	3.30	3.40	3.50	3.59	3.69	3.79	3.89	3.99	4.09	4.18	4.28	4.38
74	1.98	2.08	2.18	2.27	2.37	2.47	2.57	2.67	2.77	2.86	2.96	3.06	3.16	3.26	3.36	3.45	3.55	3.65	3.75	3.85	3.94	4.04	4.14	4.24	4.34

FVC in liters = 0.0491 H − 0.0216 A − 3.590. R^2 = 0.74, SEE = 0.393, 95% Confidence Interval = 0.676.

Definitions of abbreviations: R^2 = coefficient of determination, SEE = standard error of estimate, H = height in cm, and A = age in years. BTPS = body temperature, ambient pressure and saturated with water vapor at these conditions. The 95% confidence interval is calculated from a one-tailed "t" test. It is a single value recommended for all heights and ages in this study. When subtracted from the predicted values, it yields the lower limit of normal.

The axes of the table are age (in years) at the side, and height (in cm) at the top. The predicted normal FVC in liters for the female patient is found at the intersection of the row for her age, and the column for her height. Adapted from Crapo RO, Morris AH, Gardner RM: Reference spirometric values using techniques and equipment that meet ATS recommendations. *Am Rev Respir Dis* 1981; 123:659-664.

TABLE 4
PREDICTED NORMAL FEV₁ VALUES FOR MEN

AGE	146	148	150	152	154	156	158	160	162	164	166	168	170	172	174	176	178	180	182	184	186	188	190	192	194
18	3.42	3.50	3.58	3.66	3.75	3.83	3.91	3.99	4.08	4.16	4.24	4.33	4.41	4.49	4.57	4.66	4.74	4.82	4.91	4.99	5.07	5.15	5.24	5.32	5.40
20	3.37	3.45	3.53	3.61	3.70	3.78	3.86	3.95	4.03	4.11	4.19	4.28	4.36	4.44	4.53	4.61	4.69	4.77	4.86	4.94	5.02	5.11	5.19	5.27	5.35
22	3.32	3.40	3.48	3.57	3.65	3.73	3.81	3.90	3.98	4.06	4.15	4.23	4.31	4.39	4.48	4.56	4.64	4.73	4.81	4.89	4.97	5.05	5.14	5.22	5.30
24	3.27	3.35	3.43	3.52	3.60	3.68	3.77	3.85	3.93	4.01	4.10	4.18	4.26	4.35	4.43	4.51	4.59	4.68	4.76	4.84	4.92	5.01	5.09	5.17	5.26
26	3.22	3.30	3.39	3.47	3.55	3.63	3.72	3.80	3.88	3.97	4.05	4.13	4.21	4.30	4.38	4.46	4.54	4.63	4.71	4.79	4.88	4.90	5.04	5.12	5.21
28	3.17	3.25	3.34	3.42	3.50	3.59	3.67	3.75	3.83	3.92	4.00	4.08	4.16	4.25	4.33	4.41	4.50	4.58	4.66	4.74	4.83	4.91	4.99	5.08	5.16
30	3.12	3.21	3.29	3.37	3.45	3.54	3.62	3.70	3.78	3.87	3.95	4.03	4.12	4.20	4.28	4.36	4.45	4.53	4.61	4.70	4.78	4.86	4.94	5.03	5.11
32	3.07	3.16	3.24	3.32	3.40	3.49	3.57	3.65	3.74	3.82	3.90	3.98	4.07	4.15	4.23	4.32	4.40	4.48	4.56	4.65	4.73	4.81	4.90	4.98	5.06
34	3.02	3.11	3.19	3.27	3.36	3.44	3.52	3.60	3.69	3.77	3.85	3.94	4.02	4.10	4.18	4.27	4.35	4.43	4.52	4.60	4.68	4.76	4.85	4.93	5.01
36	2.98	3.06	3.14	3.22	3.31	3.39	3.47	3.56	3.64	3.72	3.80	3.89	3.97	4.05	4.14	4.22	4.30	4.38	4.47	4.55	4.63	4.71	4.80	4.88	4.96
38	2.93	3.01	3.09	3.18	3.26	3.34	3.42	3.51	3.59	3.67	3.76	3.84	3.92	4.00	4.09	4.17	4.25	4.33	4.42	4.50	4.58	4.67	4.75	4.83	4.91
40	2.88	2.96	3.04	3.13	3.21	3.29	3.38	3.46	3.54	3.62	3.71	3.79	3.87	3.95	4.04	4.12	4.20	4.29	4.37	4.45	4.53	4.62	4.70	4.78	4.87
42	2.83	2.91	3.00	3.08	3.16	3.24	3.33	3.41	3.49	3.57	3.66	3.74	3.82	3.91	3.99	4.07	4.15	4.24	4.32	4.40	4.49	4.57	4.65	4.73	4.82
44	2.78	2.86	2.95	3.03	3.11	3.19	3.28	3.36	3.44	3.53	3.61	3.69	3.77	3.86	3.94	4.02	4.11	4.19	4.27	4.35	4.44	4.52	4.60	4.69	4.77
46	2.73	2.81	2.90	2.98	3.06	3.15	3.23	3.31	3.39	3.48	3.56	3.64	3.73	3.81	3.89	3.97	4.06	4.14	4.22	4.31	4.39	4.47	4.55	4.64	4.72
48	2.68	2.77	2.85	2.93	3.01	3.10	3.18	3.26	3.35	3.43	3.51	3.59	3.68	3.76	3.84	3.93	4.01	4.09	4.17	4.25	4.34	4.42	4.50	4.59	4.67
50	2.63	2.72	2.80	2.88	2.97	3.05	3.13	3.21	3.30	3.38	3.46	3.55	3.63	3.71	3.79	3.88	3.96	4.04	4.12	4.21	4.29	4.37	4.46	4.54	4.62
52	2.59	2.67	2.75	2.83	2.92	3.00	3.08	3.17	3.25	3.33	3.41	3.50	3.58	3.66	3.74	3.83	3.91	3.99	4.08	4.16	4.24	4.32	4.41	4.49	4.57
54	2.54	2.62	2.70	2.79	2.87	2.95	3.03	3.12	3.20	3.28	3.36	3.45	3.53	3.61	3.70	3.78	3.86	3.94	4.03	4.11	4.19	4.28	4.36	4.44	4.52
56	2.49	2.57	2.65	2.74	2.82	2.90	2.98	3.07	3.15	3.23	3.32	3.40	3.48	3.56	3.65	3.73	3.81	3.90	3.98	4.06	4.14	4.23	4.31	4.39	4.48
58	2.44	2.52	2.60	2.69	2.77	2.85	2.94	3.02	3.10	3.18	3.27	3.35	3.43	3.52	3.60	3.68	3.76	3.85	3.93	4.01	4.10	4.18	4.26	4.34	4.43
60	2.39	2.47	2.55	2.64	2.72	2.80	2.89	2.97	3.05	3.14	3.22	3.30	3.38	3.47	3.55	3.63	3.72	3.80	3.88	3.96	4.05	4.13	4.21	4.29	4.38
62	2.34	2.42	2.51	2.59	2.67	2.76	2.84	2.92	3.00	3.09	3.17	3.25	3.34	3.42	3.50	3.58	3.67	3.75	3.83	3.91	4.00	4.08	4.16	4.25	4.33
64	2.29	2.38	2.46	2.54	2.62	2.71	2.79	2.87	2.96	3.04	3.12	3.20	3.29	3.37	3.45	3.53	3.62	3.70	3.78	3.87	3.95	4.03	4.11	4.20	4.28
66	2.24	2.33	2.41	2.49	2.58	2.66	2.74	2.82	2.91	2.99	3.07	3.15	3.24	3.32	3.40	3.49	3.57	3.65	3.73	3.82	3.90	3.98	4.07	4.15	4.23
68	2.20	2.28	2.36	2.44	2.53	2.61	2.69	2.77	2.86	2.94	3.02	3.11	3.19	3.27	3.35	3.44	3.52	3.60	3.69	3.77	3.85	3.93	4.02	4.10	4.18
70	2.15	2.23	2.31	2.39	2.48	2.56	2.64	2.73	2.81	2.89	2.97	3.06	3.14	3.22	3.31	3.39	3.47	3.55	3.64	3.72	3.80	3.89	3.97	4.05	4.13
72	2.10	2.18	2.26	2.35	2.43	2.51	2.59	2.68	2.76	2.84	2.93	3.01	3.09	3.17	3.26	3.34	3.42	3.51	3.59	3.67	3.75	3.84	3.92	4.00	4.08
74	2.05	2.13	2.21	2.30	2.38	2.46	2.55	2.63	2.71	2.79	2.88	2.96	3.04	3.13	3.21	3.29	3.37	3.46	3.54	3.62	3.70	3.79	3.87	3.95	4.04

FEV₁ in liters = 0.0414H−0.0244 A−2.190. R² = 0.64, SEE = 0.486, 95% Confidence Interval = 0.842.

Definitions of abbreviations: R² = coefficient of determination, SEE = standard error of estimate, H = height in cm, and A = age in years.
BTPS = body temperature, ambient pressure and saturated with water vapor at these conditions. The 95% confidence interval is calculated from a one-tailed "t" test. It is a single value recommended for all heights and ages in this study. When subtracted from the predicted values, it yields the lower limit of normal.

The axes of the table are age (in years) at the side, and height (in cm) at the top. The predicted normal FFV₁ in liters for the male patient is found at the intersection of the row for his age, and the column for his height. Adapted from Crapo RO, Morris AH, Gardner RM: Reference spirometric values using techniques and equipment that meet ATS recommendations. *Am Rev Respir Dis* 1981; 123:659-664.

TABLE 5
PREDICTED NORMAL FEV$_1$ VALUES FOR WOMEN

AGE	HEIGHT (CM)																								
	146	148	150	152	154	156	158	160	162	164	166	168	170	172	174	176	178	180	182	184	186	188	190	192	194
18	2.96	3.02	3.09	3.16	3.23	3.30	3.37	3.43	3.50	3.57	3.64	3.71	3.78	3.85	3.91	3.98	4.05	4.12	4.19	4.26	4.32	4.39	4.46	4.53	4.60
20	2.91	2.97	3.04	3.11	3.18	3.25	3.32	3.38	3.45	3.52	3.59	3.66	3.73	3.79	3.86	3.93	4.00	4.07	4.14	4.20	4.27	4.34	4.41	4.48	4.55
22	2.85	2.92	2.99	3.06	3.13	3.20	3.26	3.33	3.40	3.47	3.54	3.61	3.67	3.74	3.81	3.88	3.95	4.02	4.09	4.15	4.22	4.29	4.36	4.43	4.50
24	2.80	2.87	2.94	3.01	3.08	3.15	3.21	3.28	3.35	3.42	3.49	3.56	3.62	3.69	3.76	3.83	3.90	3.97	4.03	4.10	4.17	4.24	4.31	4.38	4.44
26	2.75	2.82	2.89	2.96	3.03	3.09	3.16	3.23	3.30	3.37	3.44	3.50	3.57	3.64	3.71	3.78	3.85	3.91	3.98	4.05	4.12	4.19	4.26	4.33	4.39
28	2.70	2.77	2.84	2.91	2.97	3.04	3.11	3.18	3.25	3.32	3.39	3.45	3.52	3.59	3.66	3.73	3.80	3.86	3.93	4.00	4.07	4.14	4.21	4.27	4.34
30	2.65	2.72	2.79	2.86	2.92	2.99	3.06	3.13	3.20	3.27	3.33	3.40	3.47	3.54	3.61	3.68	3.74	3.81	3.88	3.95	4.02	4.09	4.15	4.22	4.29
32	2.60	2.67	2.74	2.80	2.87	2.94	3.01	3.08	3.15	3.21	3.28	3.35	3.42	3.49	3.56	3.63	3.69	3.76	3.83	3.90	3.97	4.04	4.10	4.17	4.24
34	2.55	2.62	2.68	2.75	2.82	2.89	2.96	3.03	3.10	3.16	3.23	3.30	3.37	3.44	3.51	3.57	3.64	3.71	3.78	3.85	3.92	3.98	4.05	4.12	4.19
36	2.50	2.57	2.63	2.70	2.77	2.84	2.91	2.98	3.04	3.11	3.18	3.25	3.32	3.39	3.45	3.52	3.59	3.66	3.73	3.80	3.87	3.93	4.00	4.07	4.14
38	2.45	2.51	2.58	2.65	2.72	2.79	2.86	2.92	2.99	3.06	3.13	3.20	3.27	3.34	3.40	3.47	3.54	3.61	3.68	3.75	3.81	3.88	3.95	4.02	4.09
40	2.40	2.46	2.53	2.60	2.67	2.74	2.81	2.87	2.94	3.01	3.08	3.15	3.22	3.28	3.35	3.42	3.49	3.56	3.63	3.69	3.76	3.83	3.90	3.97	4.04
42	2.34	2.41	2.48	2.55	2.62	2.69	2.75	2.82	2.89	2.96	3.03	3.10	3.17	3.23	3.30	3.37	3.44	3.51	3.58	3.64	3.71	3.78	3.85	3.92	3.99
44	2.29	2.36	2.43	2.50	2.57	2.64	2.70	2.77	2.84	2.91	2.98	3.05	3.11	3.18	3.25	3.32	3.39	3.46	3.52	3.59	3.66	3.73	3.80	3.87	3.93
46	2.24	2.31	2.38	2.45	2.52	2.58	2.65	2.72	2.79	2.86	2.93	2.99	3.06	3.13	3.20	3.27	3.34	3.41	3.47	3.54	3.61	3.68	3.75	3.82	3.88
48	2.19	2.26	2.33	2.40	2.46	2.53	2.60	2.67	2.74	2.81	2.88	2.94	3.01	3.08	3.15	3.22	3.29	3.35	3.42	3.49	3.56	3.63	3.70	3.76	3.83
50	2.14	2.21	2.28	2.35	2.41	2.48	2.55	2.62	2.69	2.76	2.82	2.89	2.96	3.03	3.10	3.17	3.23	3.30	3.37	3.44	3.51	3.58	3.65	3.71	3.78
52	2.09	2.16	2.23	2.29	2.36	2.43	2.50	2.57	2.64	2.70	2.77	2.84	2.91	2.98	3.05	3.12	3.18	3.25	3.32	3.39	3.46	3.53	3.59	3.66	3.73
54	2.04	2.11	2.18	2.24	2.31	2.38	2.45	2.52	2.59	2.65	2.72	2.79	3.86	2.93	3.00	3.06	3.13	3.20	3.27	3.34	3.41	3.47	3.54	3.61	3.68
56	1.99	2.06	2.12	2.19	2.26	2.33	2.40	2.47	2.53	2.60	2.67	2.74	2.81	2.88	2.94	3.01	3.08	3.15	3.22	3.29	3.36	3.42	3.49	3.56	3.63
58	1.94	2.00	2.07	2.14	2.21	2.28	2.35	2.42	2.48	2.55	2.62	2.69	2.76	2.83	2.89	2.96	3.03	3.10	3.17	3.24	3.30	3.37	3.44	3.51	3.58
60	1.89	1.95	2.02	2.09	2.16	2.23	2.30	2.36	2.43	2.50	2.57	2.64	2.71	2.77	2.84	2.91	2.98	3.05	3.12	3.18	3.25	3.32	3.39	3.46	3.53
62	1.83	1.90	1.97	2.04	2.11	2.18	2.24	2.31	2.38	2.45	2.52	2.59	2.66	2.72	2.79	2.86	2.93	3.00	3.07	3.13	3.20	3.27	3.34	3.41	3.48
64	1.78	1.85	1.92	1.99	2.06	2.13	2.19	2.26	2.33	2.40	2.47	2.54	2.60	2.67	2.74	2.81	2.88	2.95	3.01	3.08	3.15	3.22	3.29	3.36	3.42
66	1.73	1.80	1.87	1.94	2.01	2.07	2.14	2.21	2.28	2.35	2.42	2.48	2.55	2.62	2.69	2.76	2.83	2.90	2.96	3.03	3.10	3.17	3.24	3.31	3.37
68	1.68	1.75	1.82	1.89	1.95	2.02	2.09	2.16	2.23	2.30	2.37	2.43	2.50	2.57	2.64	2.71	2.78	2.84	2.91	2.98	3.05	3.12	3.19	3.25	3.32
70	1.63	1.70	1.77	1.84	1.90	1.97	2.04	2.11	2.18	2.25	2.31	2.38	2.45	2.52	2.59	2.66	2.72	2.79	2.86	2.93	3.00	3.07	3.14	3.20	3.27
72	1.58	1.65	1.72	1.78	1.85	1.92	1.99	2.06	2.13	2.19	2.26	2.33	2.40	2.47	2.54	2.61	2.67	2.74	2.81	2.88	2.95	3.02	3.08	3.15	3.22
74	1.53	1.60	1.67	1.73	1.80	1.87	1.94	2.01	2.08	2.14	2.21	2.28	2.35	2.42	2.49	2.55	2.62	2.69	2.76	2.83	2.90	2.96	3.03	3.10	3.17

FEV$_1$ in liters = 0.0342 H − 0.0255 A − 1.578. R^2 = 0.80, SEE = 0.326, 95% Confidence Interval = 0.561.

Definitions of abbreviations: R^2 = coefficient of determination, SEE = standard error of estimate, H = height in cm, and A = age in years. BTPS = body temperature, ambient pressure and saturated with water vapor at these conditions. The 95% confidence interval is calculated from a one-tailed "t" test. It is a single value recommended for all heights and ages in this study. When subtracted from the predicted values, it yields the lower limit of normal.

The axes of the table are age (in years) at the side, and height (in cm) at the top. The predicted normal FEV$_1$ in liters for the female patient is found at the intersection of the row for her age, and the column for her height. Adapted from Crapo RO, Morris AH, Gardner RM: Reference spirometric values using techniques and equipment that meet ATS recommendations. *Am Rev Respir Dis* 1981; 123:659-664.

TABLE 6
PREDICTED NORMAL FEV$_1$/FVC RATIOS FOR MEN

AGE	146	148	150	152	154	156	158	160	162	164	166	168	170	172	174	176	178	180	182	184	186	188	190	192	194
18	88.8	88.5	88.3	88.0	87.7	87.5	87.2	87.0	86.7	86.4	86.2	85.9	85.7	85.4	85.1	84.9	84.6	84.4	84.1	83.8	83.6	83.3	83.1	82.8	82.5
20	88.5	88.2	88.0	87.7	87.4	87.2	86.9	86.7	86.4	86.1	85.9	85.6	85.4	85.1	84.8	84.6	84.3	84.1	83.8	83.5	83.3	83.0	82.8	82.5	82.3
22	88.2	87.9	87.6	87.4	87.1	86.9	86.6	86.3	86.1	85.8	85.6	85.3	85.0	84.8	84.5	84.3	84.0	83.7	83.5	83.2	83.0	82.7	82.4	82.2	81.9
24	87.9	87.6	87.3	87.1	86.8	86.6	86.3	86.0	85.8	85.5	85.3	85.0	84.7	84.5	84.2	84.0	83.7	83.4	83.2	82.9	82.7	82.4	82.1	81.9	81.6
26	87.6	87.3	87.0	86.8	86.5	86.3	86.0	85.7	85.5	85.2	85.0	84.7	84.4	84.2	83.9	83.7	83.4	83.1	82.9	82.6	82.4	82.1	81.8	81.6	81.3
28	87.3	87.0	86.7	86.5	86.2	86.0	85.7	85.4	85.2	84.9	84.7	84.4	84.1	83.9	83.6	83.4	83.1	82.8	82.6	82.3	82.1	81.8	81.5	81.2	81.0
30	87.0	86.7	86.4	86.2	85.9	85.7	85.4	85.1	84.9	84.6	84.4	84.1	83.8	83.6	83.3	83.1	82.8	82.5	82.3	82.0	81.8	81.5	81.2	81.0	80.7
32	86.6	86.4	86.1	85.9	85.6	85.3	85.1	84.8	84.6	84.3	84.0	83.8	83.5	83.3	83.0	82.7	82.5	82.2	82.0	81.7	81.4	81.2	80.9	80.7	80.4
34	86.3	86.1	85.8	85.6	85.3	85.0	84.8	84.5	84.3	84.0	83.7	83.5	83.2	83.0	82.7	82.4	82.2	81.9	81.7	81.4	81.1	80.9	80.6	80.4	80.1
36	86.0	85.8	85.5	85.3	85.0	84.7	84.5	84.2	84.0	83.7	83.4	83.2	82.9	82.7	82.4	82.1	81.9	81.6	81.4	81.1	80.8	80.6	80.3	80.1	79.8
38	85.7	85.5	85.2	85.0	84.7	84.4	84.2	83.9	83.7	83.4	83.1	82.9	82.6	82.4	82.1	81.8	81.6	81.3	81.1	80.8	80.5	80.3	80.0	79.8	79.5
40	85.4	85.2	84.9	84.7	84.4	84.1	83.9	83.6	83.4	83.1	82.8	82.6	82.3	82.1	81.8	81.5	81.3	81.0	80.8	80.5	80.2	80.0	79.7	79.5	79.2
42	85.1	84.9	84.6	84.3	84.1	83.8	83.6	83.3	83.0	82.8	82.5	82.3	82.0	81.7	81.5	81.2	81.0	80.7	80.4	80.2	79.9	79.7	79.4	79.1	78.9
44	84.8	84.6	84.3	84.0	83.8	83.5	83.3	83.0	82.7	82.5	82.2	82.0	81.7	81.4	81.2	80.9	80.7	80.4	80.1	79.9	79.6	79.4	79.1	78.8	78.6
46	84.5	84.3	84.0	83.7	83.5	83.2	83.0	82.7	82.4	82.2	81.9	81.7	81.4	81.1	80.9	80.6	80.4	80.1	79.8	79.6	79.3	79.1	78.8	78.5	78.3
48	84.2	84.0	83.7	83.4	83.2	82.9	82.7	82.4	82.1	81.9	81.6	81.4	81.1	80.8	80.6	80.3	80.1	79.8	79.5	79.3	79.0	78.8	78.5	78.2	78.0
50	83.9	83.7	83.4	83.1	82.9	82.6	82.4	82.1	81.8	81.6	81.3	81.1	80.8	80.5	80.3	80.0	79.8	79.5	79.2	79.0	78.7	78.5	78.2	77.9	77.7
52	83.6	83.3	83.1	82.8	82.6	82.3	82.0	81.8	81.5	81.3	81.0	80.7	80.5	80.2	80.0	79.7	79.4	79.2	78.9	78.7	78.4	78.1	77.9	77.6	77.4
54	83.3	83.0	82.8	82.5	82.3	82.0	81.7	81.5	81.2	81.0	80.7	80.4	80.2	79.9	79.7	79.4	79.1	78.9	78.6	78.4	78.1	77.8	77.6	77.3	77.1
56	83.0	82.7	82.5	82.2	82.0	81.7	81.4	81.2	80.9	80.7	80.4	80.1	79.9	79.6	79.4	79.1	78.8	78.6	78.3	78.1	77.8	77.5	77.3	77.0	76.8
58	82.7	82.4	82.2	81.9	81.7	81.4	81.1	80.9	80.6	80.4	80.1	79.8	79.6	79.3	79.1	78.8	78.5	78.3	78.0	77.8	77.5	77.2	77.0	76.7	76.5
60	82.4	82.1	81.9	81.6	81.4	81.1	80.8	80.6	80.3	80.1	79.8	79.5	79.3	79.0	78.8	78.5	78.2	78.0	77.7	77.5	77.2	76.9	76.7	76.4	76.2
62	82.1	81.8	81.6	81.3	81.0	80.8	80.5	80.3	80.0	79.7	79.5	79.2	79.0	78.7	78.4	78.2	77.9	77.7	77.4	77.1	76.9	76.6	76.4	76.1	75.8
64	81.8	81.5	81.3	81.0	80.7	80.5	80.2	80.0	79.7	79.4	79.2	78.9	78.7	78.4	78.1	77.9	77.6	77.4	77.1	76.8	76.6	76.3	76.1	75.8	75.5
66	81.5	81.2	81.0	80.7	80.4	80.2	79.9	79.7	79.4	79.1	78.9	78.6	78.4	78.1	77.8	77.6	77.3	77.1	76.8	76.5	76.3	76.0	75.8	75.5	75.2
68	81.2	80.9	80.7	80.4	80.1	79.9	79.6	79.4	79.1	78.8	78.6	78.3	78.1	77.8	77.5	77.3	77.0	76.8	76.5	76.2	76.0	75.7	75.5	75.2	74.9
70	80.9	80.6	80.4	80.1	79.8	79.6	79.3	79.1	78.8	78.5	78.3	78.0	77.8	77.5	77.2	77.0	76.7	76.5	76.2	75.9	75.7	75.4	75.2	74.9	74.6
72	80.6	80.3	80.0	79.8	79.5	79.3	79.0	78.7	78.5	78.2	78.0	77.7	77.4	77.2	76.9	76.7	76.4	76.1	75.9	75.6	75.4	75.1	74.8	74.6	74.3
74	80.3	80.0	79.7	79.5	79.2	79.0	78.7	78.4	78.2	77.9	77.7	77.4	77.1	76.9	76.6	76.4	76.1	75.8	75.6	75.3	75.1	74.8	74.5	74.3	74.0

FEV$_1$/FVC ratio in percent $= -0.1300\,H - 0.152\,A + 110.49$. $R^2 = 0.26$, SEE $= 4.78$, 95% Confidence Interval $= 8.28$.

Definitions of abbreviations: R^2 = coefficient of determination, SEE = standard error of estimate, H = height in cm, and A = age in years. BTPS = body temperature, ambient pressure and saturated with water vapor at these conditions. The 95% confidence interval is calculated from a one-tailed "t" test. It is a single value recommended for all heights and ages in this study. When subtracted from the predicted values, it yields the lower limit of normal.

The axes of the table are age (in years) at the side, and height (in cm) at the top. The predicted normal FEV$_1$/FVC ratio for the male patient is found at the intersection of the row for his age, and the column for his height. Adapted from Crapo RO, Morris AH, Gardner RM: Reference spirometric values using techniques and equipment that meet ATS recommendations. *Am Rev Respir Dis* 1981; 123:659-664.

TABLE 7
PREDICTED NORMAL FEV$_1$/FVC RATIOS FOR WOMEN

HEIGHT (CM)

AGE	146	148	150	152	154	156	158	160	162	164	166	168	170	172	174	176	178	180	182	184	186	188	190	192	194
18	92.6	92.1	91.7	91.3	90.9	90.5	90.1	89.7	89.3	88.9	88.5	88.1	87.7	87.3	86.9	86.5	86.1	85.7	85.3	84.9	84.5	84.1	83.7	83.3	82.9
20	92.0	91.6	91.2	90.8	90.4	90.0	89.6	89.2	88.8	88.4	88.0	87.6	87.2	86.8	86.4	86.0	85.6	85.2	84.8	84.4	84.0	83.6	83.2	82.8	82.4
22	91.5	91.1	90.7	90.3	89.9	89.5	89.1	88.7	88.3	87.9	87.5	87.1	86.7	86.3	85.9	85.5	85.1	84.7	84.3	83.9	83.5	83.1	82.7	82.3	81.8
24	91.0	90.6	90.2	89.8	89.4	89.0	88.6	88.2	87.8	87.4	87.0	86.6	86.2	85.8	85.4	85.0	84.6	84.2	83.8	83.4	83.0	82.6	82.2	81.7	81.3
26	90.5	90.1	89.7	89.3	88.9	88.5	88.1	87.7	87.3	86.9	86.5	86.1	85.7	85.3	84.9	84.5	84.1	83.7	83.3	82.9	82.5	82.1	81.6	81.2	80.8
28	90.0	89.6	89.2	88.8	88.4	88.0	87.6	87.2	86.8	86.4	86.0	85.6	85.2	84.8	84.4	84.0	83.6	83.2	82.8	82.4	82.0	81.5	81.1	80.7	80.3
30	89.5	89.1	88.7	88.3	87.9	87.5	87.1	86.7	86.3	85.9	85.5	85.1	84.7	84.3	83.9	83.5	83.1	82.7	82.3	81.9	81.4	81.0	80.6	80.2	79.8
32	89.0	88.6	88.2	87.8	87.4	87.0	86.6	86.2	85.8	85.4	85.0	84.6	84.2	83.8	83.4	83.0	82.6	82.2	81.8	81.3	80.9	80.5	80.1	79.7	79.3
34	88.5	88.1	87.7	87.3	86.9	86.5	86.1	85.7	85.3	84.9	84.5	84.1	83.7	83.3	82.9	82.5	82.1	81.7	81.2	80.8	80.4	80.0	79.6	79.2	78.8
36	88.0	87.6	87.2	86.8	86.4	86.0	85.6	85.2	84.8	84.4	84.0	83.6	83.2	82.8	82.4	82.0	81.6	81.1	80.7	80.3	79.9	79.5	79.1	78.7	78.3
38	87.5	87.1	86.7	86.3	85.9	85.5	85.1	84.7	84.3	83.9	83.5	83.1	82.7	82.3	81.9	81.5	81.0	80.6	80.2	79.8	79.4	79.0	78.6	78.2	77.8
40	87.0	86.6	86.2	85.8	85.4	85.0	84.6	84.2	83.8	83.4	83.0	82.6	82.2	81.8	81.4	80.9	80.5	80.1	79.7	79.3	78.9	78.5	78.1	77.7	77.3
42	86.5	86.1	85.7	85.3	84.9	84.5	84.1	83.7	83.3	82.9	82.5	82.1	81.7	81.3	80.8	80.4	80.0	79.6	79.2	78.8	78.4	78.0	77.6	77.2	76.8
44	86.0	85.6	85.2	84.8	84.4	84.0	83.6	83.2	82.8	82.4	82.0	81.6	81.2	80.7	80.3	79.9	79.5	79.1	78.7	78.3	77.9	77.5	77.1	76.7	76.3
46	85.5	85.1	84.7	84.3	83.9	83.5	83.1	82.7	82.3	81.9	81.5	81.1	80.6	80.2	79.8	79.4	79.0	78.6	78.2	77.8	77.4	77.0	76.6	76.2	75.3
48	85.0	84.6	84.2	83.8	83.4	83.0	82.6	82.2	81.8	81.4	81.0	80.6	80.1	79.7	79.3	78.9	78.5	78.1	77.7	77.3	76.9	76.5	76.1	75.7	75.3
50	84.5	84.1	83.7	83.3	82.9	82.5	82.1	81.7	81.3	80.9	80.4	80.0	79.6	79.2	78.8	78.4	78.0	77.6	77.2	76.8	76.4	76.0	75.6	75.2	74.8
52	84.0	83.6	83.2	82.8	82.4	82.0	81.6	81.2	80.8	80.3	79.9	79.5	79.1	78.7	78.3	77.9	77.5	77.1	76.7	76.3	75.9	75.5	75.1	74.7	74.3
54	83.5	83.1	82.7	82.3	81.9	81.5	81.1	80.7	80.2	79.8	79.4	79.0	78.6	78.2	77.8	77.4	77.0	76.6	76.2	75.8	75.4	75.0	74.6	74.2	73.8
56	83.0	82.6	82.2	81.8	81.4	81.0	80.6	80.1	79.7	79.3	78.9	78.5	78.1	77.7	77.3	76.9	76.5	76.1	75.7	75.3	74.9	74.5	74.1	73.7	73.3
58	82.5	82.1	81.7	81.3	80.9	80.5	80.0	79.6	79.2	78.8	78.4	78.0	77.6	77.2	76.8	76.4	76.0	75.6	75.2	74.8	74.4	74.0	73.6	73.2	72.8
60	82.0	81.6	81.2	80.8	80.4	79.9	79.5	79.1	78.7	78.3	77.9	77.5	77.1	76.7	76.3	75.9	75.5	75.1	74.7	74.3	73.9	73.5	73.1	72.7	72.3
62	81.5	81.1	80.7	80.3	79.8	79.4	79.0	78.6	78.2	77.8	77.4	77.0	76.6	76.2	75.8	75.4	75.0	74.6	74.2	73.8	73.4	73.0	72.6	72.2	71.8
64	81.0	80.6	80.2	79.7	79.3	78.9	78.5	78.1	77.7	77.3	76.9	76.5	76.1	75.7	75.3	74.9	74.5	74.1	73.7	73.3	72.9	72.5	72.1	71.7	71.3
66	80.5	80.1	79.6	79.2	78.8	78.4	78.0	77.6	77.2	76.8	76.4	76.0	75.6	75.2	74.8	74.4	74.0	73.6	73.2	72.8	72.4	72.0	71.6	71.2	70.8
68	80.0	79.5	79.1	78.7	78.3	77.9	77.5	77.1	76.7	76.3	75.9	75.5	75.1	74.7	74.3	73.9	73.5	73.1	72.7	72.3	71.9	71.5	71.1	70.7	70.3
70	79.4	79.0	78.6	78.2	77.8	77.4	77.0	76.6	76.2	75.8	75.4	75.0	74.6	74.2	73.8	73.4	73.0	72.6	72.2	71.8	71.4	71.0	70.6	70.2	69.8
72	78.9	78.5	78.1	77.7	77.3	76.9	76.5	76.1	75.7	75.3	74.9	74.5	74.1	73.7	73.3	72.9	72.5	72.1	71.7	71.3	70.9	70.5	70.1	69.7	69.2
74	78.4	78.0	77.6	77.2	76.8	76.4	76.0	75.6	75.2	74.8	74.4	74.0	73.6	73.2	72.8	72.4	72.0	71.6	71.2	70.8	70.4	70.0	69.6	69.1	68.7

FEV$_1$/FVC ratio in percent $= -0.2020\,H - 0.252\,A + 126.58$. $R^2 = 0.43$, SEE = 5.26, 95% Confidence Interval = 9.06.

Definitions of abbreviations: R^2 = coefficient of determination, SEE = standard error of estimate, H = height in cm, and A = age in years. BTPS = body temperature, ambient pressure and saturated with water vapor at these conditions. The 95% confidence interval is calculated from a one-tailed "t" test. It is a single value recommended for all heights and ages in this study. When subtracted from the predicted values, it yields the lower limit of normal.

The axes of the table are age (in years) at the side, and height (in cm) at the top. The predicted normal FEV$_1$/FVC ratio for the female patient is found at the intersection of the row for her age, and the column for her height. Adapted from Crapo RO, Morris AH, Gardner RM: Reference spirometric values using techniques and equipment that meet ATS recommendations. *Am Rev Respir Dis* 1981; 123:659-664.

TABLE 8
PREDICTED NORMAL SINGLE BREATH D$_{CO}$ VALUES FOR MEN (STPD)

AGE	146	148	150	152	154	156	158	160	162	164	166	168	170	172	174	176	178	180	182	184	186	188	190	192	194
18	29.8	30.6	31.4	32.2	33.1	33.9	34.7	35.5	36.3	37.1	38.0	38.8	39.6	40.4	41.2	42.1	42.9	43.7	44.5	45.4	46.2	47.0	47.8	48.6	49.4
20	29.3	30.2	31.0	31.8	32.6	33.4	34.3	35.1	35.9	36.7	37.5	38.4	39.2	40.0	40.8	41.6	42.5	43.3	44.1	44.9	45.7	46.6	47.4	48.2	49.0
22	28.9	29.7	30.6	31.4	32.2	33.0	33.8	34.7	35.5	36.3	37.1	37.9	38.8	39.6	40.4	41.2	42.0	42.9	43.7	44.5	45.3	46.1	47.0	47.8	48.6
24	28.5	29.3	30.1	31.0	31.8	32.6	33.4	34.2	35.1	35.9	36.7	37.5	38.3	39.2	40.0	40.8	41.6	42.4	43.3	44.1	44.9	45.7	46.5	47.4	48.2
26	28.1	28.9	29.7	30.5	31.4	32.2	33.0	33.8	34.6	35.5	36.3	37.1	37.9	38.7	39.6	40.4	41.2	42.0	42.8	43.7	44.5	45.3	46.1	46.9	47.8
28	27.7	28.5	29.3	30.1	30.9	31.8	32.6	33.4	34.2	35.0	35.9	36.7	37.5	38.3	39.1	40.0	40.8	41.6	42.4	43.2	44.1	44.9	45.7	46.5	47.3
30	27.2	28.1	28.9	29.7	30.5	31.3	32.2	33.0	33.8	34.6	35.4	36.3	37.1	37.9	38.7	39.6	40.4	41.2	42.0	42.8	43.6	44.5	45.3	46.1	46.9
32	26.8	27.6	28.5	29.3	30.1	30.9	31.7	32.6	33.4	34.2	35.0	35.8	36.7	37.5	38.3	39.1	39.9	40.8	41.6	42.4	43.2	44.1	44.9	45.7	46.5
34	26.4	27.2	28.1	28.9	29.7	30.5	31.3	32.1	33.0	33.8	34.6	35.4	36.2	37.1	37.9	38.7	39.5	40.4	41.2	42.0	42.8	43.6	44.4	45.3	46.1
36	26.0	26.8	27.6	28.4	29.3	30.1	30.9	31.7	32.5	33.4	34.2	35.0	35.8	36.6	37.5	38.3	39.1	39.9	40.7	41.6	42.4	43.2	44.0	44.8	45.7
38	25.6	26.4	27.2	28.0	28.8	29.7	30.5	31.3	32.1	32.9	33.8	34.6	35.4	36.2	37.0	37.9	38.7	39.5	40.3	41.1	42.0	42.8	43.6	44.4	45.2
40	25.1	26.0	26.8	27.6	28.4	29.2	30.1	30.9	31.7	32.5	33.3	34.2	35.0	35.8	36.6	37.4	38.3	39.1	39.9	40.7	41.5	42.4	43.2	44.0	44.8
42	24.7	25.5	26.4	27.2	28.0	28.8	29.6	30.5	31.3	32.1	32.9	33.7	34.6	35.4	36.2	37.0	37.8	38.7	39.5	40.3	41.1	41.9	42.8	43.6	44.4
44	24.3	25.1	25.9	26.8	27.6	28.4	29.2	30.0	30.9	31.7	32.5	33.3	34.1	35.0	35.8	36.6	37.4	38.2	39.1	39.9	40.7	41.5	42.3	43.2	44.0
46	23.9	24.7	25.5	26.3	27.2	28.0	28.8	29.6	30.4	31.3	32.1	32.9	33.7	34.6	35.4	36.2	37.0	37.8	38.6	39.5	40.3	41.1	41.9	42.7	43.6
48	23.5	24.3	25.1	25.9	26.7	27.6	28.4	29.2	30.0	30.8	31.7	32.5	33.3	34.1	34.9	35.8	36.6	37.4	38.2	39.1	39.9	40.7	41.5	42.3	43.1
50	23.1	23.9	24.7	25.5	26.3	27.1	28.0	28.8	29.6	30.4	31.2	32.1	32.9	33.7	34.5	35.4	36.2	37.0	37.8	38.6	39.4	40.3	41.1	41.9	42.7
52	22.6	23.4	24.3	25.1	25.9	26.7	27.6	28.4	29.2	30.0	30.8	31.6	32.5	33.3	34.1	34.9	35.7	36.6	37.4	38.2	39.0	39.9	40.7	41.6	42.3
54	22.2	23.0	23.8	24.7	25.5	26.3	27.1	27.9	28.8	29.6	30.4	31.2	32.0	32.9	33.7	34.5	35.3	36.1	37.0	37.8	38.6	39.4	40.2	41.1	41.9
56	21.8	22.6	23.4	24.2	25.1	25.9	26.7	27.5	28.3	29.2	30.0	30.8	31.6	32.4	33.3	34.1	34.9	35.7	36.5	37.4	38.2	39.0	39.8	40.6	41.5
58	21.4	22.2	23.0	23.8	24.6	25.5	26.3	27.1	27.9	28.7	29.6	30.4	31.2	32.0	32.8	33.7	34.5	35.3	36.1	36.9	37.8	38.6	39.4	40.2	41.0
60	20.9	21.8	22.6	23.4	24.2	25.0	25.9	26.7	27.5	28.3	29.1	30.0	30.8	31.6	32.4	33.2	34.1	34.9	35.7	36.5	37.3	38.2	39.0	39.8	40.6
62	20.5	21.3	22.2	23.0	23.8	24.6	25.4	26.3	27.1	27.9	28.7	29.5	30.4	31.2	32.0	32.8	33.6	34.5	35.3	36.1	36.9	37.7	38.6	39.4	40.2
64	20.1	20.9	21.7	22.6	23.4	24.2	25.0	25.8	26.7	27.5	28.3	29.1	29.9	30.8	31.6	32.4	33.2	34.1	34.9	35.7	36.5	37.3	38.1	39.0	39.8
66	19.7	20.5	21.3	22.1	23.0	23.8	24.6	25.4	26.2	27.1	27.9	28.7	29.5	30.4	31.2	32.0	32.8	33.6	34.4	35.3	36.1	36.9	37.7	38.6	39.4
68	19.3	20.1	20.9	21.7	22.6	23.4	24.2	25.0	25.8	26.6	27.5	28.3	29.1	29.9	30.7	31.6	32.4	33.2	34.0	34.9	35.7	36.5	37.3	38.1	38.9
70	18.8	19.7	20.5	21.3	22.1	22.9	23.8	24.6	25.4	26.2	27.0	27.9	28.7	29.5	30.3	31.1	32.0	32.8	33.6	34.4	35.2	36.1	36.9	37.7	38.5
72	18.4	19.2	20.1	20.9	21.7	22.5	23.3	24.2	25.0	25.8	26.6	27.4	28.3	29.1	29.9	30.7	31.5	32.4	33.2	34.0	34.8	35.6	36.5	37.3	38.1
74	18.0	18.8	19.6	20.5	21.3	22.1	22.9	23.7	24.6	25.4	26.2	27.0	27.8	28.7	29.5	30.3	31.1	31.9	32.8	33.6	34.4	35.2	36.0	36.9	37.7

D_{CO} in ml/min/mm Hg = 0.410 H − 0.210 A − 26.31. R^2 = 0.60, SEE = 4.82, 95% Confidence Interval = 8.2.

Definitions of abbreviations: R^2 = coefficient of determination, SEE = standard error of estimate, H = height in cm, and A = age in years. STPD = temperature 0°C, pressure 760 mm Hg and dry (0 water vapor). The 95% confidence interval is calculated from a one-tailed "t" test. It is a single value recommended for all heights and ages in this study. When subtracted from the predicted values, it yields the lower limit of normal.

The regression analysis has been normalized to a standard hemoglobin using Cotes' modification of the relationship described by Roughton and Forster.

The axes of the table are age (in years) at the side, and height (in cm) at the top. The predicted normal D_{CO} in ml/min/mm Hg for the male patient is found at the intersection of the row for his age, and the column for his height. Adapted from Crapo RO, Morris AH: Standardized single breath normal values for carbon monoxide diffusing capacity. *Am Rev Respir Dis* 1981; 123: 185-190.

TABLE 9
PREDICTED NORMAL SINGLE BREATH D$_{CO}$ VALUES FOR WOMEN (STPD)

HEIGHT (CM)

AGE	146	148	150	152	154	156	158	160	162	164	166	168	170	172	174	176	178	180	182	184	186	188	190	192	194
18	26.0	26.5	27.0	27.6	28.1	28.6	29.2	29.7	30.2	30.8	31.3	31.9	32.4	32.9	33.5	34.0	34.5	35.1	35.6	36.1	36.7	37.2	37.7	38.3	38.8
20	25.7	26.2	26.7	27.3	27.8	28.4	28.9	29.4	30.0	30.5	31.0	31.6	32.1	32.6	33.2	33.7	34.2	34.8	35.3	35.8	36.4	36.9	37.4	38.0	38.5
22	25.4	25.9	26.5	27.0	27.5	28.1	28.6	29.1	29.7	30.2	30.7	31.3	31.8	32.3	32.9	33.4	33.9	34.5	35.0	35.5	36.1	36.6	37.1	37.7	38.2
24	25.1	25.6	26.2	26.7	27.2	27.8	28.3	28.8	29.4	29.9	30.4	31.0	31.5	32.0	32.6	33.1	33.6	34.2	34.7	35.2	35.8	36.3	36.8	37.4	37.9
26	24.8	25.3	25.9	26.4	26.9	27.5	28.0	28.5	29.1	29.6	30.1	30.7	31.2	31.7	32.3	32.8	33.3	33.9	34.4	34.9	35.5	36.0	36.5	37.1	37.6
28	24.5	25.0	25.6	26.1	26.6	27.2	27.7	28.2	28.8	29.3	29.8	30.4	30.9	31.4	32.0	32.5	33.0	33.6	34.1	34.6	35.2	35.7	36.2	36.8	37.3
30	24.2	24.7	25.3	25.8	26.3	26.9	27.4	27.9	28.5	29.0	29.5	30.1	30.6	31.1	31.7	32.2	32.7	33.3	33.8	34.3	34.9	35.4	35.9	36.5	37.0
32	23.9	24.4	25.0	25.5	26.0	26.6	27.1	27.6	28.2	28.7	29.2	29.8	30.3	30.8	31.4	31.9	32.4	33.0	33.5	34.1	34.6	35.1	35.7	36.2	36.7
34	23.6	24.1	24.7	25.2	25.7	26.3	26.8	27.3	27.9	28.4	28.9	29.5	30.0	30.6	31.1	31.6	32.2	32.7	33.2	33.8	34.3	34.8	35.4	35.9	36.4
36	23.3	23.8	24.4	24.9	25.4	26.0	26.5	27.1	27.6	28.1	28.7	29.2	29.7	30.3	30.8	31.3	31.9	32.4	32.9	33.5	34.0	34.5	35.1	35.6	36.1
38	23.0	23.6	24.1	24.6	25.2	25.7	26.2	26.8	27.3	27.8	28.4	28.9	29.4	30.0	30.5	31.0	31.6	32.1	32.6	33.2	33.7	34.2	34.8	35.3	35.8
40	22.7	23.3	23.8	24.3	24.9	25.4	25.9	26.5	27.0	27.5	28.1	28.6	29.1	29.7	30.2	30.7	31.3	31.8	32.3	32.9	33.4	33.9	34.5	35.0	35.5
42	22.4	23.0	23.5	24.0	24.6	25.1	25.6	26.2	26.7	27.2	27.8	28.3	28.8	29.4	29.9	30.4	31.0	31.5	32.0	32.6	33.1	33.6	34.2	34.7	35.2
44	22.1	22.7	23.2	23.7	24.3	24.8	25.3	25.9	26.4	26.9	27.5	28.0	28.5	29.1	29.6	30.1	30.7	31.2	31.7	32.3	32.8	33.3	33.9	34.4	34.9
46	21.8	22.4	22.9	23.4	24.0	24.5	25.0	25.6	26.1	26.6	27.2	27.7	28.2	28.8	29.3	29.8	30.4	30.9	31.4	32.0	32.5	33.0	33.6	34.1	34.6
48	21.5	22.1	22.6	23.1	23.7	24.2	24.7	25.3	25.8	26.3	26.9	27.4	27.9	28.5	29.0	29.5	30.1	30.6	31.1	31.7	32.2	32.8	33.3	33.8	34.4
50	21.2	21.8	22.3	22.8	23.4	23.9	24.4	25.0	25.5	26.0	26.6	27.1	27.6	28.2	28.7	29.3	29.8	30.3	30.9	31.4	31.9	32.5	33.0	33.5	34.1
52	20.9	21.5	22.0	22.5	23.1	23.5	24.1	24.7	25.2	25.8	26.3	26.8	27.4	27.9	28.4	29.0	29.5	30.0	30.6	31.1	31.6	32.2	32.7	33.2	33.8
54	20.6	21.2	21.7	22.3	22.8	23.3	23.9	24.4	24.9	25.5	26.0	26.5	27.1	27.6	28.1	28.7	29.2	29.7	30.3	30.8	31.3	31.9	32.4	32.9	33.5
56	20.4	20.9	21.4	22.0	22.5	23.0	23.6	24.1	24.6	25.2	25.7	26.2	26.8	27.3	27.8	28.4	28.9	29.4	30.0	30.5	31.0	31.6	32.1	32.6	33.2
58	20.1	20.6	21.1	21.7	22.2	22.7	23.3	23.8	24.3	24.9	25.4	25.9	26.5	27.0	27.5	28.1	28.6	29.1	29.7	30.2	30.7	31.3	31.8	32.3	32.9
60	19.8	20.3	20.8	21.4	21.9	22.4	23.0	23.5	24.0	24.6	25.1	25.6	26.2	26.7	27.2	27.8	28.3	28.8	29.4	29.9	30.4	31.0	31.5	32.0	32.6
62	19.5	20.0	20.5	21.1	21.6	22.1	22.7	23.2	23.7	24.3	24.8	25.3	25.9	26.4	26.9	27.5	28.0	28.5	29.1	29.6	30.1	30.7	31.2	31.7	32.3
64	19.2	19.7	20.2	20.8	21.3	21.8	22.4	22.9	23.4	24.0	24.5	25.0	25.6	26.1	26.6	27.2	27.7	28.2	28.8	29.3	29.8	30.4	30.9	31.5	32.0
66	18.9	19.4	19.9	20.5	21.0	21.5	22.1	22.6	23.1	23.7	24.2	24.1	25.3	25.8	26.3	26.9	27.4	28.0	28.5	29.0	29.6	30.1	30.6	31.2	31.7
68	18.6	19.1	19.6	20.2	20.7	21.2	21.8	22.3	22.8	23.4	23.9	24.5	25.0	25.5	26.1	26.6	27.1	27.7	28.2	28.7	29.3	29.8	30.3	30.9	31.4
70	18.3	18.8	19.3	19.9	20.4	21.0	21.5	22.0	22.6	23.1	23.5	24.2	24.7	25.2	25.8	26.3	26.8	27.4	27.9	28.4	29.0	29.5	30.0	30.6	31.1
72	18.0	18.5	19.1	19.6	20.1	20.7	21.2	21.1	22.3	22.8	23.3	23.9	24.4	24.9	25.5	26.0	26.5	27.1	27.6	28.1	28.7	29.2	29.7	30.3	30.8
74	17.7	18.2	18.8	19.3	19.8	20.4	20.9	21.4	22.0	22.5	23.0	23.6	24.1	24.6	25.2	25.7	26.2	26.8	27.3	27.8	28.4	28.9	29.4	30.0	30.5

D$_{CO}$ in ml/min/mm Hg = 0.267 H − 0.148 A − 10.34. R^2 = 0.60, SEE = 3.40, 95% Confidence Interval = 5.74.

Definitions of abbreviations: R^2 = coefficient of determination, SEE = standard error of estimate, H = height in cm, and A = age in years. STPD = temperature 0°C, pressure 760 mm Hg and dry (0 water vapor). The 95% confidence interval is calculated from a one-tailed "t" test. It is a single value recommended for all heights and ages in this study. When subtracted from the predicted values, it yields the lower limit of normal.

The regression analysis has been normalized to a standard hemoglobin using Cotes' modification of the relationship described by Roughton and Forster.

The axes of the table are age (in years) at the side, and height (in cm) at the top. The predicted normal D$_{CO}$ in ml/min/mm Hg for the female patient is found at the intersection of the row for her age, and the column for her height. Adapted from Crapo RO, Morris AH: Standardized single breath normal values for carbon monoxide diffusing capacity. *Am Rev Respir Dis* 1981; 123: 185-190.

Diffusing capacity of carbon monoxide (D$_{CO}$):
The single breath D$_{CO}$ should be performed when a patient has respiratory complaints that are of greater severity than the observed spirometry results would indicate. The methodology for performing single breath D$_{CO}$ is described in the 1978 ATS Epidemiology Standardization Project.

The D$_{CO}$ measures the amount of CO which diffuses across the alveolar-capillary membrane in a specified amount of time. It is especially useful in detecting abnormalities that limit gas transference, such as interstitial fibrosis of the lung parenchyma. However, measurement of diffusing capacity is affected by many factors. A decrease in hemoglobin concentration of 2.5 to 3.0 gm/100 ml will reduce the value of the diffusing capacity by approximately 10%; corrections can be made for severe anemia or polycythemia. The change in alveolar oxygen tension that occurs at moderate altitudes, such as 5,000 feet above sea level, or with alveolar hypoventilation, theoretically may affect D$_{CO}$ measurement by as much as 5%. However, these effects are usually of little significance, and in fact are smaller than the variability of the test itself, which is quite large.

Predicted "normal" values are presented in Tables 8 and 9; these tables are to be used in a manner similar to the tables on ventilatory capacity. A laboratory that performs the D$_{CO}$ under conditions or with procedures that are different from the ATS recommendations should either develop and verify its own prediction equations or use an accepted and verified equation that is appropriate to its needs.

Estimated exercise capacity: Testing to measure exercise capacity should be done: (1) when an individual's spirometry and D$_{CO}$ measurement are not within the 95% confidence interval for his or her age and height; OR (2) his or her spirometry and D$_{CO}$ measurements do not indicate severe impairment as defined below; OR (3) the individual states that he or she is physically unable to meet the demands of a specific job because of breathlessness; OR (4) the individual has not performed maximally or correctly in the spirometry or D$_{CO}$ tests.

Exercise testing is not recommended for an individual who, in the opinion of the examining physician, has medical contraindications to such tests.

In the estimated exercise capacity test, a person is placed on either a treadmill or a cycle ergometer. The $\dot{V}O_2$, or oxygen consumption per minute, is not measured directly but is determined through its relationship with power output, which is measured in kilopond meters/min (KPM/min). The power output is related to the grade and speed of the treadmill.

Measured exercise capacity: This test should be done when an examiner has doubts as to the accuracy of the estimated exercise capacity test. Such doubts may arise when there are inappropriate changes in either heart rate or minute ventilation, or when the patient is unable to complete the estimated exercise capacity test because of non-respiratory symptoms such as leg muscle fatigue. The details concerning both the measured and estimated work capacity tests can be found in the ATS Statement on the Evaluation of Impairment/Disability Secondary to Respiratory Disease.

Exercise capacity is measured by the $\dot{V}O_2$ in ml/(kg·min), or in METS, a unit equal to 3.5 ml/(kg·min) (see Chapter 4). Tables are available that equate specific work tasks with either $\dot{V}O_2$ or METS. Generally, working at his or her own pace, a person can sustain work output for an 8-hour period if the person does not exceed 40% of his or her maximum $\dot{V}O_2$ ($\dot{V}O_2$ max) as determined by exercise tests.

Arterial blood gases: Blood gas determinations are considered invasive, and the results are difficult to standardize due to the effects of factors such as hyperventilation, breathholding, altitude, obesity, and portal hypertension. Thus, this examination should be reserved for selected cases and performed under rigidly controlled laboratory conditions. Hypoxemia must be documented on two occasions at least four weeks apart. If hypoxemia is suspected, blood gas determinations can be done during an exercise capacity test. In general, for most persons with obstructive lung disease, the FEV$_1$ correlates better with exercise capacity than does the partial pressure of arterial oxygen.

Maximum voluntary ventilation (MVV): This test is not as useful as the FEV$_1$, because it is more difficult to learn and is more fatiguing; it is influenced by the physical properties of the chest wall, and the instrumentation requirements are more rigid. Furthermore, in interstitial disease the MVV may be normal even when there is a severe impairment of gas exchange. The MVV is recommended only as an optional procedure.

Miscellaneous tests of flow and volume: The forced expiratory flow during the middle half of the FVC ($FEF_{25-75\%}$), the closing volume, closing capacity, and the volume of isoflow are tests designed to detect disease in airways less than two mm internal diameter and are not recommended for the assessment of impairment.

Criteria for Evaluating Permanent Impairment

Table 1 presents the criteria for rating permanent impairment, and Figure 2 graphically displays the recommended scheme for testing for impairment.

To be placed in a specific class, an individual need not meet all the criteria of that class. Overlapping of the symptoms of dyspnea and of physiologic test results is inevitable. In determining the impairment class, the examiner should give more weight to objective findings than to subjective symptoms. The reader will note that specific criteria for the D_{CO} have not been included in the classification of impairment given in Table 1, except when the D_{CO} falls below 40% of predicted; this is due to the especially large variation of D_{CO} measurements. Similarly, the value of $\dot{V}O_2$ max less than 15 ml/(kg·min) is not a hard and fast criterion for severe impairment; a person may be considered severely impaired if 30% to 40% of his or her $\dot{V}O_2$ max is not sufficient to meet the $\dot{V}O_2$ costs of his or her occupational activity over an 8-hour period.

Arterial blood gas determination may itself indicate severe impairment. A person with a resting PaO_2 of less than 60 mm Hg in room air may be deemed severely impaired if he or she has evidence of one or more of the secondary conditions related to arterial hypoxemia, such as pulmonary hypertension, cor pulmonale, increasingly severe hypoxemia during exercise testing, and erythrocytosis.

A resting PaO_2 of less than 50 mm Hg in room air in a person who is stable and receiving optimal therapy is itself a criterion for severe impairment.

Finally, an asthmatic patient is considered to be severely impaired (Class 4) if the examiner can document attacks of bronchospasm severe enough to require treatment in an emergency room of a hospital at least once every two months or on the average of 6 times per year, despite optimum therapy from an allergist or pulmonary physician. This individual should also have prolonged expiration with wheezing or rhonchi between attacks.

Figure 2

DETERMINATION OF IMPAIRMENT BY PHYSIOLOGIC TESTING

Test Schema

The following test schema is proposed for determining whether an individual is impaired by respiratory disease. The reader should refer to the text for an explanation of the use of these tests.

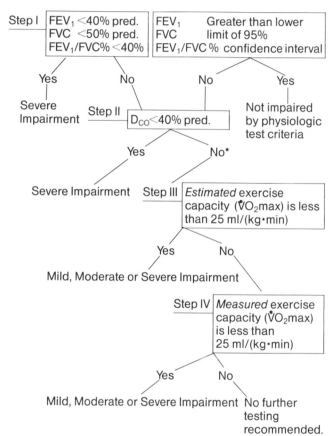

*If FEV_1, FVC, FEV_1/FVC% and D_{CO} are above the lower cut-off limits and the patient continues to have complaints of breathlessness, continue to Steps III and IV.

Adapted from American Thoracic Society: Evaluation of Impairment/disability secondary to respiratory disease. *Amer Rev Respir Dis* 1982;126(5):945-951, p 946. Copyright © 1982 American Lung Association.

Examples of Permanent Respiratory Impairment

Example 1 of Class 1 Impairment of the Whole Person: A 38-year-old non-smoking male coal miner had worked in underground mining as a cutting machine operator for 20 years. On his most recent mandatory chest radiograph examination he was found to have Category 1, simple pneumoconiosis. He requested further evaluation of his pulmonary status. He was 176 cm tall and had no positive physical findings. Pulmonary function testing gave the following results:

	Observed Values	Percent of Predicted
FVC	5.0 liters	98
FEV_1	4.13 liters	99
$FEV_1/FVC\%$	83	101
D_{CO}	38 ml/min/mm Hg	100

The $\dot{V}O_2$ max was 32 ml/(kg·min).

Diagnosis: Uncomplicated coal workers' pneumoconiosis.

Impairment: 0% impairment of the whole person.

Comment: This individual has no demonstrable functional impairment even though he has an occupational disease that is recognized by radiography.

Example 2 of Class 1 Impairment of the Whole Person: A 50-year-old male, driver of a beer delivery truck for the past 25 years, was referred for evaluation with the complaint that he had become too short of breath to carry three cases of beer up a flight of stairs. Approximately three months before referral, he had an anteroseptal myocardial infarction, and had been in the hospital for three weeks. Thereafter, he was allowed to return to work after beginning a progressive exercise program. He smoked one pack per day of unfiltered cigarettes.

Physical examination showed that the patient was 190 cm tall and had no positive physical findings. By chest radiograph the lung fields were normal, but there was an unusual prominence of the left ventricular segment of the heart. Pulmonary function results were as follows:

	Observed Values	Percent of Predicted
FVC	5.39 liters	95
FEV_1	4.0 liters	90
$FEV_1/FVC\%$	74	95
D_{CO}	37 ml/min/mm Hg	90

The $\dot{V}O_2$ max was 18 ml/(kg·min).

The patient was considered to be in Class 1 insofar as the respiratory system was concerned. But because of the cardiac abnormality, he was to receive further evaluation for impairment of the cardiovascular system.

Diagnosis: Inadequate cardiac output as a result of myocardial infarction.

Impairment: 0% impairment due to respiratory disease.

Example of Class 2 Impairment of the Whole Person: A 57-year-old man had a history of cough for 6 years' duration with slowly progressing dyspnea on exertion. Four months before examination he noticed an increase in the cough and noted also that he was becoming more dyspneic while walking one block on level ground at his own pace.

For a 5-year period ending approximately 8 years ago, the man worked for a manufacturing company, spraying asbestos insulation on the interior walls of metal buildings. For the past three years his annual chest radiographs showed diminished lung volumes, interstitial fibrosis at both lung bases, and pleural plaques suggestive of asbestosis. A transbronchial lung biopsy revealed no focal interstitial fibrosis, inflammation, and no asbestos bodies.

At examination the patient weighed 87.5 kg (193 pounds) and was 172 cm tall. Auscultation of the lungs disclosed end-respiratory crackles at both lung bases.

	Observed Values	Percent of Predicted
FVC	3.30 liters	83
FEV_1	1.99 liters	62
$FEV_1/FVC\%$	60	80
D_{CO}	17.8 ml/min/mm Hg	77

$\dot{V}O_2$ max was 22 ml/(kg·min).

Diagnosis: Asbestosis.

Impairment: 25% impairment of the whole person.

Comment: While at the time of this evaluation the man was in Class 2, the symptoms and signs of asbestosis could progress with time, impairing him further.

Example of Class 3 Impairment of the Whole Person: A 56-year-old male, a foundry worker for 22 years, complains of progressing dyspnea of 5

years' duration. He now has difficulty keeping up with other men his age. He usually has to stop on the second flight going up stairs, and he can walk only 1/2 mile on level ground at his own pace. He has had a cough for 8 years that has been productive of more than two tablespoons of whitish, non-smelling sputum per day. He has smoked a pack per day of nonfilter cigarettes since age 14 years.

In the foundry during the first 15 years of his employment, little effort was made to control dust, and there was considerable sand dust from the molds. Recently, dust control measures have been better.

Examination shows that the patient is 170 cm tall and he has bilateral, basilar, end-expiratory, fine-pitched crackles. The examination otherwise is unremarkable and chest radiograph is normal. Pulmonary function studies show the following:

	Observed Values	Percent of Predicted
FVC	3.48 liters	80
FEV_1	1.60 liters	45
$FEV_1/FVC\%$	46	——
D_{CO}	16 ml/min/mm Hg	51

The $\dot{V}O_2$ max was 16 ml/(kg·min).

Diagnosis: Chronic bronchitis and pulmonary emphysema.

Impairment: 35% impairment of the whole person.

Comment: This man has an obvious obstructive ventilatory defect with impairment of his diffusion capacity. His oxygen intake is limited, probably because of his decreased ventilatory ability.

Example of Class 4 Impairment of the Whole Person: A 60-year-old male worked as an insulator for 40 years. He had particularly heavy exposure to asbestos over a 5-year period during the construction of a steam generating plant. He had no known asbestos exposure during the past 8 years, during which time he worked with fiberglass. He smoked two packs of cigarettes per day from the age of 15 years to that of 50 years, at which time he cut down to one pack per day. During the past 10 years he noted gradually increasing fatigue and shortness of breath. While at first he was unable to keep up with others when walking up hills, during the past three years he became unable to walk as rapidly as others on level ground. Therefore he

stopped working about two months before he was examined. He denied having a productive cough.

Examination disclosed that the patient was 186 cm tall. He had digital clubbing and cyanosis of the nail beds, ear lobes and tip of the nose. He had fine respiratory crackles over the lower half of both lung bases posteriorly. No other abnormalities were noted.

Chest radiograph disclosed bilateral pleural thickening, a small linear calcification near the left side of the heart, a linear calcification in the dome of the right hemidiaphragm, and linear densities in the lower half of each lung field. Pulmonary function testing revealed:

	Observed Values	Percent of Predicted
FVC	3.13 liters	60
FEV_1	1.0 liters	25
$FEV_1/FVC\%$	31	——
D_{CO}	7.46 ml/min/mm Hg	20

The $\dot{V}O_2$ max was 11 ml/(kg·min).

Diagnosis: Asbestosis and pulmonary emphysema.

Impairment: 70% impairment of the whole person.

Comment: This patient had a severe combined restrictive and obstructive ventilatory impairment with marked reduction of his diffusing capacity and a decreased $\dot{V}O_2$ max.

Criteria for Evaluating Impairment from Lung Cancer

Lung cancer has both form and function. The form of lung cancer is the basis for most staging systems that are termed clinical but are in reality morphologic and anatomic in character. Such systems classify (1) according to cell type, as with squamous cell carcinoma, adenocarcinoma, large cell anaplastic (bronchioalveolar cell carcinoma), and small cell anaplastic (oat cell carcinoma); (2) according to anatomic location, either central or peripheral; (3) according to involvement of regional nodes, for instance, the lobar, tracheobronchial, hilar or mediastinal nodes; or (4) according to distant hematogenous spread, for example, to the liver, brain, bone, or adrenal gland.

The functional effects of lung cancer are responsible for the impairment that a person may develop. The functional assessment depends on evaluating

TABLE 10—FUNCTIONAL EVALUATION OF THE PATIENT WITH LUNG CANCER

Patient Condition	% Impairment	Functional Assessment
A. Able to carry on normal activity and to work. No special care is needed.	0	Normal, no complaints, no evidence of disease.
	10	Able to carry on normal activity, minor signs or symptoms of disease.
	20	Normal activity with effort, some signs or symptoms of disease.
B. Unable to work. Able to be at home, care for most personal needs. A varying degree of assistance is needed.	30	Cares for self. Unable to carry on normal activity or to do active work.
	40	Requires occasional assistance but is able to care for most of his or her needs.
	50	Requires considerable assistance and frequent medical care.
C. Unable to care for self. Requires equivalent of institutional or hospital care. Disease may be progressing rapidly.	60	Disabled, requires special care and assistance.
	70	Severely disabled, hospitalization indicated.
	80	Hospitalization necessary, active support treatment necessary.
	90	Moribund
	100	Death

Adapted from Karnofsky DA, Burchenal JH: The clinical evaluation of chemotherapeutic agents, in MacLeod CM (ed): *Evaluation of Chemotherapeutic Agents*. New York, Columbia University Press, 1949, p. 196. Copyright © 1949, Columbia University Press.

the clinical condition of the patient. In Table 10 is a functional classification of patients with cancer adapted from Karnofsky and Burchenal that is applicable to the patient with lung cancer.

Impairment Resulting from Breathing Abnormalities During Sleep

The major syndromes caused by breathing abnormalities during sleep are obstructive sleep apnea, central sleep apnea, and Cheyne-Stokes respiration. These syndromes may prevent progression through the normal stages of sleep, produce frequent arousals, and lead to insomnia or daytime hypersomnolence. Hypoxia during obstructive sleep apnea is generally more severe than hypoxia from central sleep apnea and Cheyne-Stokes respiration. Chronic nocturnal hypoxemia may contribute to the daytime pulmonary and systemic hypertension, cardiomegaly, arrhythmias, mental confusion, and personality changes that are often found in patients with these disorders.

The sleep apnea syndromes and methods of evaluating them are discussed in Appendix C. The permanent impairments due to hypersomnolence, hemodynamic changes, and personality changes should be rated independently according to the criteria in Chapters 2, 4 and 12, respectively, and combined using the Combined Values Chart to

arrive at impairment of the whole person due to sleep and arousal disorders.

References

1. American Thoracic Society: Evaluation of impairment/disability secondary to respiratory disease. *Am Rev Respir Dis* 1982; 126:945-951.

2. Crapo RO, Morris AH, Gardner RM: Reference spirometric values using techniques and equipment that meet ATS recommendations. *Am Rev Respir Dis* 1981; 123:659-664.

3. Crapo RO, Morris AH: Standardized single breath normal values for carbon monoxide diffusing capacity. *Am Rev Respir Dis* 1981; 123:185-190.

4. American College of Sports Medicine: *Guidelines for Graded Testing and Exercise Prescription*, ed 2. Philadelphia, Lea and Febiger, 1980, pp 29-32.

5. Karnofsky DA, Burchenal JH: The clinical evaluation of chemotherapeutic agents, in MacLeod CM (ed): *Evaluation of Chemotherapeutic Agents*. New York, Columbia University Press, 1949, p 196.

Chapter 4

The Cardiovascular System

Introduction

The purpose of this chapter is to assist the physician by providing criteria for the evaluation of permanent impairment of the cardiovascular system according to the person's ability to perform the activities of daily living. The cardiovascular system consists of the heart, the aorta, the systemic arteries and the pulmonary arteries; impairment of the system includes abnormal elevation of pressure in either the aorta, or systemic hypertension, or in the pulmonary artery, or pulmonary hypertension. The coronary and peripheral circulations are considered to be part of the cardiovascular system; however, impairment from disorders of the cerebral circulation is considered in Chapter 2.

Before using the information in this chapter, the reader is urged to consult the Preface to the Guides, which provides a general discussion of the purpose of the Guides, and of the situations in which they are useful; and discusses techniques for the evaluation of the patient and for report preparation.

Symptomatic Limitation

In this chapter reference is made to limitation of activities of daily living because of symptoms. Information about such limitation is subjective and it is open to interpretation on the part of both patient and examiner. Therefore, when it is possible, the examiner should obtain objective data about the extent of the limitation before attempting to estimate the degree of permanent impairment. When estimating the extent of a limitation due to symptoms, the physician should use the functional classification in Table 1.

Exercise Testing

In most circumstances the physician should attempt to quantitate limitations due to symptoms

TABLE 1
FUNCTIONAL CLASSIFICATIONS*

Class 1: The patient has cardiac disease but no resulting limitation of physical activity. Ordinary physical activity does not cause undue fatigue, palpitation, dyspnea, or anginal pain.

Class 2: The patient has cardiac disease resulting in slight limitation of physical activity. The patient is comfortable at rest and in the performance of ordinary, light, daily activities. Greater than ordinary physical activity, such as heavy physical exertion, results in fatigue, palpitation, dyspnea, or anginal pain.

Class 3: The patient has cardiac disease resulting in marked limitation of physical activity. The patient is comfortable at rest. Ordinary physical activity results in fatigue, palpitation, dyspnea, or anginal pain.

Class 4: The patient has cardiac disease resulting in inability to carry on any physical activity without discomfort. Symptoms of inadequate cardiac output, pulmonary congestion, systemic congestion, or of the anginal syndrome may be present, even at rest. If any physical activity is undertaken, discomfort is increased.

*Adapted from: Criteria Committee of the New York Heart Association: *Diseases of the Heart and Blood Vessels: Nomenclature and Criteria for Diagnosis*, ed 6, Boston, Little Brown and Company, 1964, pp 112-113. Copyright © 1964, Little Brown and Company. For the purposes of assessing impairment this well established classification is to be preferred over the newer classification introduced in the 7th edition in 1973.

by observing the patient during exercise. The most widely used and standardized exercise protocols involve the use of a motor-driven treadmill with varying grades and speeds. The protocols vary slightly, but they all attempt to relate the exercise to excess energy expended and to functional class. The excess energy expended usually is expressed with the "MET," a term that represents the multiples of resting metabolic energy utilized for any given activity. One MET is considered to be 3.5 ml/(kg·min). The 70 kg man who burns 1.2 kilocalories per minute sitting at rest uses approximately three METS when walking 4 kilometers per hour.

Table 2 displays the relationship of excess energy expenditures in METS to functional class according to the protocols of several investigators. With all protocols, the exercise periods last for three minutes; the periods are represented in the table by boxes with numbers giving the estimated METS involved.

If a treadmill is not available, steps may be used to attempt to quantitate the exercise capacity of a patient. Table 3 shows the relationships of exercise with steps of various heights, excess energy expenditure, and fuctional class.

Estimations of excess energy expenditure also can be made with a bicycle ergometer (Table 4).

Some laboratories are equipped to measure oxygen consumption and carbon dioxide production during exercise. Data on a patient acquired by these techniques may become the most accurate method of estimating a patient's exercise capacity.

A major problem with using any exercise testing technique to attempt to quantitate an individual's functional capacity is the marked variability in patients' abilities and willingness to cooperate. Therefore, the physician also must estimate the individual's cooperation and effort during the test; some patients will continue far beyond where they should, while others will stop after minimal effort because they feel fatigued.

TABLE 2
RELATIONSHIP OF METS AND FUNCTIONAL CLASS ACCORDING TO 5 TREADMILL PROTOCOLS

TREADMILL TESTS	METS	1.6	2	3	4	5	6	7	8	9	10	11	12	13	14	15	16
	Ellestad					1.7	3.0			4.0						5.0	
		colspan: 10 PER CENT GRADE															
	Bruce					1.7		2.5		3.4					4.2		
						10		12		14					16		
		3.4 MILES PER HOUR															
	Balke				2	4	6	8	10	12	14	16	18	20	22	24	26
		3.0 MILES PER HOUR															
	Balke				0	2.5	5	7.5	10	12.5	15	17.5	20	22.5			
	Naughton	1.0	2.0 MILES PER HOUR														
		0	0	3.5	7	10.5	14	17.5									
	METS	1.6	2	3	4	5	6	7	8	9	10	11	12	13	14	15	16
	CLINICAL STATUS		**SYMPTOMATIC PATIENTS** (METS 4–7)														
				DISEASED, RECOVERED (METS 4–8)													
						SEDENTARY HEALTHY (METS 6–11)											
								PHYSICALLY ACTIVE SUBJECTS (METS 8–16)									
	FUNCTIONAL CLASS	**IV**	**III**			**II**			**I and NORMAL**								

In the Ellestad protocol, the numbers in the boxes are miles per hour (mph); in the Bruce protocol the top numbers are mph and the bottom numbers are the percent grade. In the Balke and Naughton protocols the numbers are the percent grade.

Adapted from: Fox SM III, Naughton JP, Haskell WL: Physical activity and the prevention of coronary heart disease. *Annals of Clinical Research* 1971; 3:404-432.

TABLE 3
RELATIONSHIP OF METS AND FUNCTIONAL CLASS ACCORDING TO TWO STEP PROTOCOL

HEIGHT OF (cm) STEP		30 STEPS PER MINUTE															
		4	8	12	16	20	24	28	32	36	40						
		24 STEPS PER MINUTE															
		5	12	18	25	32	35										
METS	1.6	2	3	4	5	6	7	8	9	10	11	12	13	14	15	16
CLINICAL STATUS	SYMPTOMATIC PATIENTS / DISEASED, RECOVERED / SEDENTARY HEALTHY / PHYSICALLY ACTIVE SUBJECTS																
FUNCTIONAL CLASS	IV	III			II		I and NORMAL										

Source: Fox SM III, Naughton JP, Haskell WL: Physical activity and the prevention of coronary heart disease. *Annals of Clinical Research* 1971; 3:404-432.
Copyright © 1971 The Finnish Medical Society Duodecim

TABLE 4
ENERGY EXPENDITURE IN METS DURING BICYCLE ERGOMETRY

Body Weight		Work Rate on Bicycle Ergometer (kg m⁻¹ min⁻¹ and Watts)													
		75	150	300	450	600	750	900	1050	1200	1350	1500	1650	1800	(kg m⁻¹ min⁻¹)
(kg)	(lb)	12	25	50	75	100	125	150	175	200	225	250	275	300	(Watts)
20	44	4.0	6.0	10.0	14.0	18.0	22.0								
30	66	3.4	4.7	7.3	10.0	12.7	15.3	17.9	20.7	23.3					
40	88	3.0	4.0	6.0	8.0	10.0	12.0	14.0	16.0	18.0	20.0	22.0			
50	110	2.8	3.6	5.2	6.8	8.4	10.0	11.5	13.2	14.8	16.3	18.0	19.6	21.1	
60	132	2.7	3.3	4.7	6.0	7.3	8.7	10.0	11.3	12.7	14.0	15.3	16.7	18.0	
70	154	2.6	3.1	4.3	5.4	6.6	7.7	8.8	10.0	11.1	12.2	13.4	14.0	15.7	
80	176	2.5	3.0	4.0	5.0	6.0	7.0	8.0	9.0	10.0	11.0	12.0	13.0	14.0	
90	198	2.4	2.9	3.8	4.7	5.6	6.4	7.3	8.2	9.1	10.0	10.9	11.8	12.6	
100	220	2.4	2.8	3.6	4.4	5.2	6.0	6.8	7.6	8.4	9.2	10.0	10.8	11.6	
110	242	2.4	2.7	3.4	4.2	4.9	5.6	6.3	7.1	7.8	8.5	9.3	10.0	10.7	
120	264	2.3	2.7	3.3	4.0	4.7	5.3	6.0	6.7	7.3	8.0	8.7	9.3	10.0	

Source: American College of Sports Medicine. *Guidelines for Graded Exercise Testing and Exercise Prescription.* Philadelphia, Lea and Febiger, 1975, p. 17.
Copyright © 1975, American College of Sports Medicine.

Valvular Heart Disease

Valvular heart disease may be caused by congenital, rheumatic, infectious, or traumatic factors, or a combination. Valvular disease may result in (1) an increased work load on either the left or right ventricle, leading to hypertrophy and/or dilation of the ventricle and eventually to ventricular failure with congestion of the lungs or other organs; (2) obstruction to inflow of the ventricle as in mitral or tricuspid stenosis, causing congestion of organs even in the absence of ventricular failure; and (3) decreased cardiac output.

Valvular heart disease can be detected and its severity assessed by a thorough history and physical examination. The precision of the estimate of impairment often can be improved by obtaining appropriate laboratory studies, which may include electrocardiogram (ECG), chest radiograph, echocardiogram, exercise testing, radioisotope studies, hemodynamic measurements, or angiography.

The severity of valvular heart disease can be reduced, but not fully reversed, by operative procedures on the valves or by replacement of the valve with a prosthetic device. After such a procedure, sufficient time from the date of operation must elapse to allow maximum recovery of the heart, lungs and other organs before estimating permanent impairment due to the valvular disease.

In addition, medications may affect the severity of valvular heart disease, especially limitations due to symptoms. Therefore, sufficient time must be allowed for these medications to be introduced and adjusted, and for them to exert their effects, before an estimate of permanent impairment is made.

Criteria for Evaluating Impairment Due to Valvular Disease

Class 1—Impairment of the Whole Person, 0-10%: A patient belongs in Class 1 when (a) the patient has evidence by physical examination or laboratory test of valvular heart disease, but no symptoms in the performance of ordinary daily activities or even upon moderately heavy exertion (functional class 1); AND (b) the patient does not require continuous treatment, although prophylactic antibiotics may be recommended at the time of a surgical procedure to reduce the risk of bacterial endocarditis; AND (c) the patient remains free of signs of congestive heart failure; AND (d) there are no signs of ventricular hypertrophy or dilation, and the severity of the stenosis or regurgitation is estimated to be mild; OR (e) in the patient who has recovered from valvular heart surgery, all of the above criteria are met.

Example 1: A 22-year-old woman has a mid-systolic click and a late systolic murmur. She has no symptoms, and there are no signs of cardiac enlargement, or congestive heart failure, or cardiac rhythm disturbance. Physical examination reveals slight pectus excavatum. Chest radiograph and electrocardiogram (ECG) are normal. An echocardiogram shows prolapse of the mitral valve and normal left atrial and left ventricular size and function.

Diagnosis: Mitral valve prolapse syndrome.

Impairment: 0% impairment of the whole person.

Comment: If the ECG showed definite T wave abnormalities, or the echocardiogram showed slight enlargement of the left atrium or left ventricle, then the valve disorder would be estimated at 1% to 10% impairment, depending on the severity of the abnormality as shown by the laboratory studies.

A patient who has the murmur of aortic regurgitation or the signs of a bicuspid aortic valve, but who has no symptoms, no signs of cardiac enlargement, and no signs of congestive heart failure, might be estimated to have an impairment of 1% to 10%, depending on the estimated severity of the aortic valve disease.

The echocardiogram is not necessary to establish the diagnosis or degree of impairment.

Example 2: A 30-year-old woman has recovered from mitral commissurotomy, is asymptomatic, and has returned to an active life. She had rheumatic fever at age 8 and has had no recurrences.

Physical examination reveals a well healed surgical wound without tenderness. There are no abnormal precordial pulsations or signs of congestive heart failure. The first heart sound is loud; an opening snap is heard approximately 100 milliseconds after the second heart sound and there is a short rumble in mid-diastole. A grade 1/6 to 2/6 holosystolic murmur is heard at the apex.

Chest radiograph shows a heart of normal size and no signs of pulmonary congestion. An ECG has minimal P wave abnormalities. Echocardiogram shows slight enlargement of the left atrium and no enlargement or dysfunction of the ventricles.

Diagnosis: Mitral stenosis and post-mitral commissurotomy.

Impairment: 5% to 10% impairment of the whole person.

Comment: The estimated degree of impairment will depend on the estimated severity of mitral regurgitation, residual stenosis, etc. Echocardiogram, cardiac catheterization, and angiography are not necessary and should not be obtained solely to help estimate the impairment.

Class 2—Impairment of the Whole Person, 15-25%: A patient belongs in Class 2 when (a) the patient has evidence by physical examination or laboratory studies of valvular heart disease, and there are no symptoms in the performance of ordinary daily activities, but symptoms develop on moderately heavy physical exertion (functional class 2); OR (b) the patient requires moderate dietary adjustment or drugs to prevent symptoms or to remain free of the signs of congestive heart failure or other consequences of valvular heart disease, such as syncope, chest pain and emboli; OR (c) the patient has signs or laboratory evidence of cardiac chamber hypertrophy and/or dilation, and the severity of the stenosis or regurgitation is estimated to be moderate, and surgical correction is not feasible or advisable; OR (d) the patient has recovered from valvular heart surgery and meets the above criteria.

Example 1: A 63-year-old man was noted during a routine examination 5 years ago to have the murmur of aortic regurgitation and mild heart failure. He is an office worker, and he plays 18 holes of golf regularly, using an electric cart. The patient has been advised to restrict his salt intake and to take digoxin 0.25 mg daily.

At present, the patient's blood pressure is 160/50 mm Hg, the pulse is 70 beats per minute and regular, and the peripheral pulses are bounding. There are no signs of congestive heart failure. The apical impulse is just outside the midclavicular line, is slightly larger than normal, and is slightly prolonged. There is a grade 3/6 harsh, short, systolic ejection murmur in the aortic area, and a grade 3/6 long decrescendo diastolic murmur along the left lower sternal border. A faint mid-diastolic rumble is heard at the apex. The first and second heart sounds are normal.

An ECG shows tall R waves in V5 and V6 with low but upright T waves. Chest radiograph shows prominence of the apical portion of the cardiac silhouette and no cardiomegaly or pulmonary congestion. Echocardiogram shows a normal-sized aortic root, delicate aortic valve leaflets, fluttering of the anterior leaflet of the mitral valve, and ventricular volumes and volume indices at the upper limits of normal.

Cardiac catheterization and angiography show the following pressures: aorta 160/40 mm Hg, left ventricle 160/12 mm Hg, left atrium "a" 12 mm Hg and "v" 10 mm Hg. Aortography reveals moderate aortic regurgitation.

Diagnosis: Moderately severe aortic regurgitation of uncertain etiology.

Impairment: 20% to 25% impairment of the whole person.

Comment: Even though the patient is asymptomatic, impairment would be estimated to be greater if there were cardiomegaly, deeply inverted T waves in leads 1, L, V5 and V6, or a dilated left ventricle on the echocardiogram. The cardiac catheterization and angiography were not necessary in this case to estimate the degree of impairment.

Example 2: A 66-year-old woman had several syncopal episodes three years ago, was found to have severe calcific stenosis of the aortic valve, and underwent aortic valve replacement with a large Bjork-Shiley prosthesis. She has returned to an active life, which includes walking two miles each morning. She takes oral anticoagulants to maintain the prothrombin time in the therapeutic range, the level being tested every three weeks. She takes antibiotics before dental or operative procedures but no other medication.

Physical examination discloses normal blood pressure and pulse and no signs of heart failure. The apical impulse has a slightly sustained quality. On auscultation a grade 1/6 early systolic murmur is heard in the first right intercostal space. The first heart sound is normal and the second heart sound is very sharp.

ECG reveals a normal rhythm and QRS pattern, and low T waves in leads 1, L, V5 and V6. Chest radiograph shows slight prominence of the apex of the heart, a properly positioned prosthesis, and no evidence of pulmonary congestion. Echocardiogram discloses a properly positioned prosthesis and ventricles of normal size with thickening of the left ventricular wall.

Cardiac catheterization and angiography show normal pressure in the left ventricle and a 15 mm Hg pressure gradient between the left ventricle and aorta. Aortography shows minimal aortic regurgitation.

Diagnosis: Calcific aortic stenosis, probably related to congenital bicuspid aortic valve, valve replacement with a Bjork-Shiley prosthesis.

Impairment: 20% impairment of the whole person.

Comment: The degree of impairment in this person might be greater if a faint decrescendo diastolic murmur were heard along the left sternal border, or if the gradient across the valve were slightly higher.

Class 3—Impairment of the Whole Person, 30-50%: A patient belongs in Class 3 when (a) the patient has signs of valvular heart disease and has slight to moderate symptomatic discomfort during the performance of ordinary daily activities (functional class 3); AND (b) dietary therapy or drugs do not completely control symptoms or prevent congestive heart failure; AND (c) the patient has signs or laboratory evidence of cardiac chamber hypertrophy or dilation, the severity of the stenosis or regurgitation is estimated to be moderate or severe, and surgical correction is not feasible; OR (d) the patient has recovered from heart valve surgery but continues to have symptoms and signs of congestive heart failure including cardimegaly.

Example 1: A 71-year-old man with idiopathic thrombocytopenia that does not respond to medications has had moderate exertional dyspnea for the past two years despite the continued use of diuretics and digoxin. Presently, he is comfortable at rest, but he becomes short of breath when climbing to the second floor. He sleeps on two pillows and has not awakened short of breath since the dose of diuretics was increased one year ago.

Physical examination reveals a patient able to lie flat comfortably. Blood pressure is 110/80 mm Hg, and pulse rate is 84 beats per minute and irregular. The venous pressure is normal and there is no edema. Breath sounds are harsh at each base, but there are no rales. The apical impulse is large, hyperdynamic and displaced to the anterior axillary line. There is a slight parasternal heave. The first and second heart sounds are loud, and a grade 4/6 holosystolic murmur is heard at the lower sternal border, apex, and axilla. A third heart sound is audible.

The ECG shows atrial fibrillation with an irregular ventricular response of about 80 per minute. There are low T waves, but the QRS pattern is normal. The chest radiograph shows cardiomegaly with a large left atrium. There is prominence of the vasculature of the upper lobes. Echocardiogram shows slight enlargement of the left and right ventricles and definite enlargement of the left atrium with "hammocking" that suggests mitral valve prolapse.

Diagnosis: Severe mitral regurgitation due to mitral valve prolapse.

Impairment: 50% impairment of the whole person.

Comment: Greater exercise tolerance and less cardiomegaly would suggest a lower degree of impairment.

Example 2: A 60-year-old woman had surgery to replace the aortic and mitral valves one year ago. Despite taking oral anticoagulants, digoxin, and diuretics and restricting salt in her diet, she does not have much stamina. She tires easily and must rest each afternoon. Ankle edema sometimes

develops, but it clears promptly after she takes an extra diuretic tablet. She sleeps on one pillow and has no nocturnal dyspnea. While able to do light house work, the patient has not felt so well that she wishes to return to her work as a seamstress. Her weight remains about 15 pounds below preoperative weight.

Physical examination reveals the patient to be comfortable when lying flat. Blood pressure is 110/70 mm Hg; pulse is 80 beats per minute and irregular. Venous pressure is normal and there is no edema. The lungs are clear. The apical impulse is enlarged, is located at the anterior axillary line, and is sustained through all of systole; there is no parasternal heave. The prosthetic valve sounds are normal. A grade 1/6 early systolic murmur is heard in the first right interspace and along the left sternal border.

The ECG shows atrial fibrillation with an irregular ventricular response of about 80 per minute. Chest radiograph shows cardiomegaly with left ventricular and left atrial enlargement. There is prominence of the vasculature in the upper lobes. Echocardiogram shows no evidence of prosthetic valve malfunction or displacement. There is slight enlargement of the ventricles and left atrium. Ventricular function is good.

Diagnosis: Aortic and mitral valve disease, probably rheumatic in origin; surgical replacement of valves.

Impairment: 40% impairment of the whole person.

Class 4—Impairment of the Whole Person, 55-100%: A patient belongs in Class 4 when (a) the patient has signs by physical examination of valvular heart disease, and symptoms at rest or in the performance of less than ordinary daily activities (functional class 4); AND (b) dietary therapy and drugs cannot control symptoms or prevent signs of congestive heart failure; AND (c) the patient has signs or laboratory evidence of cardiac chamber hypertrophy and/or dilation; and the severity of the stenosis or regurgitation is estimated to be moderate or severe, and surgical correction is not feasible; OR (d) the patient has recovered from valvular heart surgery but continues to have symptoms or signs of congestive heart failure.

Example 1: A 45-year-old woman has had treatment for congestive heart failure over a 10-year period. In spite of properly using diuretics and digoxin and, for the past year, a peripheral vasodilator, the patient continues to become breathless on minimal exertion. Even going to the bathroom causes breathlessness and fatigue. She sleeps on three pillows. For years, her ankles have been swollen, and over the last year her abdomen has become protuberant.

Physical examination shows a woman who is pale and weak. Her face is thin, showing temporal depression, and jaundice is present. She is breathing 22 times per minute, and blood pressure is 110/70 mm Hg; the pulse rate is about 80 beats per minute and irregular. The patient prefers the sitting position, and in that position, the neck veins are distended to the mid-neck and show prominent V waves.

There are rales at both lung bases. There is a parasternal heave. On auscultation there is a grade 3/6 harsh systolic murmur in the second right interspace; this murmur is long but stops in late systole. After a time gap, a long, loud decrescendo diastolic murmur is heard. At the lower sternal border and at the apex, respectively, are a blowing

holosystolic murmur and a mid-diastolic rumble. The first heart sound is diminished and the second heart sound is loud in the second left interspace. The liver is large and pulsatile, and it has a span of approximately 12 cm. Ascites and 3-plus pitting edema of the thighs, sacral area, and legs are present.

The ECG shows atrial fibrillation and an irregular ventricular response of about 80 per minute. There is low voltage of the QRS and T waves. The chest radiograph shows massive cardiomegaly suggesting enlargement of all chambers. There is prominence of the vasculature in the upper lobes, and Kerley B lines are seen on both sides. The echocardiogram shows enlargement of all chambers. The left ventricular ejection fraction is 20 percent.

Diagnosis: Aortic and mitral stenosis and regurgitation, and tricuspid regurgitation, of rheumatic etiology.

Impairment: 100% impairment of the whole person.

TABLE 5—IMPAIRMENT CLASSIFICATION FOR VALVULAR HEART DISEASE

Class 1 (0-10% Impairment)	**Class 2** (15-25% Impairment)	**Class 3** (30-50% Impairment)	**Class 4** (55-100% Impairment)
The patient has evidence by physical examination or laboratory studies of valvular heart disease, but no symptoms in the performance of ordinary daily activities or even upon moderately heavy exertion (functional class 1);	The patient has evidence by physical examination or laboratory studies of valvular heart disease, and there are no symptoms in the performance of ordinary daily activities, but symptoms develop on moderately heavy physical exertion (functional class 2);	The patient has signs of valvular heart disease and has slight to moderate symptomatic discomfort during the performance of ordinary daily activities (functional class 3);	The patient has signs by physical examination of valvular heart disease, and symptoms at rest or in the performance of less than ordinary daily activities (functional class 4);
AND		**AND**	**AND**
The patient does not require continuous treatment, although prophylactic antibiotics may be recommended at the time of a surgical procedure to reduce the risk of bacterial endocarditis;	**OR** The patient requires moderate dietary adjustment or drugs to prevent symptoms or to remain free of the signs of congestive heart failure or other consequences of valvular heart disease, such as syncope, chest pain and emboli;	Dietary therapy or drugs do not completely control symptoms or prevent congestive heart failure; **AND**	Dietary therapy and drugs cannot control symptoms or prevent signs of congestive heart failure; **AND**
AND The patient remains free of signs of congestive heart failure;	**OR** The patient has signs or laboratory evidence of cardiac chamber hypertrophy and/or dilation, and the severity of the stenosis or regurgitation is estimated to be moderate, and surgical correction is not feasible or advisable;	The patient has signs or laboratory evidence of cardiac chamber hypertrophy or dilation, the severity of the stenosis or regurgitation is estimated to be moderate or severe, and surgical correction is not feasible;	The patient has signs or laboratory evidence of cardiac chamber hypertrophy and/or dilation; and the severity of the stenosis or regurgitation is estimated to be moderate or severe, and surgical correction is not feasible;
AND There are no signs of ventricular hypertrophy or dilation, and the severity of the stenosis or regurgitation is estimated to be mild;		**OR** The patient has recovered from heart valve surgery but continues to have symptoms and signs of congestive heart failure including cardiomegaly.	**OR** The patient has recovered from valvular heart surgery but continues to have symptoms or signs of congestive heart failure.
OR In the patient who has recovered from valvular heart surgery, all of the above criteria are met.	**OR** The patient has recovered from valvular heart surgery and meets the above criteria.		

Example 2: A 50-year-old male with mitral valve disease had advanced symptoms and signs of heart failure resulting in congestion of the pulmonary and systemic circulations. He underwent mitral valve replacement two years ago. Since then, despite restriction of activities and salt and the use of digoxin and diuretics, the patient's activities remained limited by dyspnea upon minimal exertion. Vigorous use of diuretics eliminated

peripheral edema but resulted in chemical evidence of pre-renal azotemia. The patient was able to walk a city block at a normal pace, drive an automobile, and sleep comfortably, but he became breathless after climbing one flight of stairs.

Physical examination reveals a comfortable patient with a blood pressure of 110/70 mm Hg; pulse is 80 beats per minute and irregular. The venous pressure is normal and there is no peripheral edema. There are rales at the left base. The apical impulse is normal, but there is a parasternal heave. The prosthetic valve sounds are normal but there is a grade 1/6 holosystolic murmur at the apex.

ECG shows atrial fibrillation with irregular ventricular response at about 80 per minute and low T waves. Chest radiograph shows cardiomegaly with enlargement of the left and right ventricles and left atrium. There is prominence of the pulmonary vasculature in all lung fields. No Kerley B lines are seen. The prosthetic valve is properly positioned. Echocardiogram shows enlargement of the ventricles and the left atrium. The prosthetic valve is properly positioned and functioning.

Cardiac catheterization and angiography reveal a left ventricular pressure of 110/18 mm Hg and a mean left atrial pressure of 20 mm Hg. The pulmonary artery pressure is 45/18 mm Hg. Left ventricular angiogram shows mild mitral regurgitation and reduction of ventricular contraction.

Diagnosis: Mitral valve replacement with a prosthesis; left ventricular dysfunction. The etiology probably is rheumatic.

Impairment: 80% impairment of the whole person.

The criteria for impairment due to valvular heart disease are shown in Table 5.

Coronary Heart Disease

Coronary heart disease is most commonly due to arteriosclerosis of the coronary arteries, a process that results in reduced coronary blood flow. Other causes of limited or reduced coronary blood flow include coronary artery spasm, emboli, congenital abnormality, and trauma. Also, inflammatory processes and arteritis can obstruct the coronary arteries, especially the coronary ostia.

Reduced coronary flow may result in injury to the myocardium, leading to infarction or diffuse fibrosis. The degree of impairment of the individual is determined by the consequences of both the reduced coronary blood flow and the reduced ventricular function. Reduced coronary blood flow also can cause angina pectoris, which itself may impair a person's ability to perform his or her usual activities. In addition, reduced coronary blood flow and myocardial damage may cause cardiac arrhythmias, which are discussed in a separate section.

The physician must obtain a detailed history in order to estimate the degree of impairment due to coronary heart disease. The physical examination may contribute to estimating the severity of the disorder and especially to estimating the degree of impairment of ventricular function. In most patients laboratory studies also will be necessary. Studies obtained at rest, during exercise, and after exercise are especially useful in evaluating patients suspected of having coronary heart disease. Coronary angiography may be necessary in some patients.

Impairment due to coronary heart disease can be reduced but not eliminated by diet, exercise training programs, cessation of cigarette smoking, use of medications, and surgical procedures. Sufficient time must be allowed for these measures to have an effect before an estimate of permanent impairment is made.

Criteria for Evaluating Permanent Impairment Due to Coronary Heart Disease

Class 1—Impairment of the Whole Person, 0-10%: Because of the serious implications of reduced coronary blood flow, it is not reasonable to classify the degree of impairment as 0% to 10% in any patient who has symptoms of coronary heart disease corroborated by physical examination or laboratory tests. This class of impairment should be reserved for the patient with an equivocal history of angina pectoris on whom coronary angiography is performed, or for a patient on whom coronary angiography is performed for other reasons and in whom is found less than 50% reduction in the cross-sectional area of a coronary artery.

Class 2—Impairment of the Whole Person, 15-25%:
A patient belongs in Class 2 when (a) the patient has history of a myocardial infarction or angina pectoris that is documented by appropriate laboratory studies, but at the time of evaluation the patient has no symptoms while performing ordinary daily activities or even moderately heavy physical exertion (functional class 1); AND (b) the patient may require moderate dietary adjustment and/or medication to prevent angina or to remain free of signs and symptoms of congestive heart failure; AND (c) the patient is able to walk on the treadmill or bicycle ergometer and obtain a heart rate of 90% of his or her predicted maximum heart rate without developing significant ST segment shift, ventricular tachycardia, or hypotension; if the patient is uncooperative or unable to exercise because of disease affecting another organ system, this requirement may be omitted; OR (d) the patient has recovered from coronary artery surgery or angioplasty, remains asymptomatic during ordinary daily activities, and is able to exercise as outlined above. If the patient is taking a beta adrenergic blocking agent, he or she should be able to exercise on the treadmill or bicycle ergometer to a level estimated to cause an energy expenditure of at least 10 METS as a substitute for the heart rate target.

Any of the exercise protocols in Figure 1 may be used. The maximum and 90% of maximum predicted heart rates by age and sex group are presented in Table 6.

TABLE 6

MAXIMAL AND 90% OF MAXIMAL ACHIEVABLE HEART RATE, BY AGE, AND SEX

Heart Rate		Age							
		30	35	40	45	50	55	60	65
Men	Maximal	193	191	189	187	184	182	180	178
	90% Maximal	173	172	170	168	166	164	162	160
Women	Maximal	190	185	181	177	172	168	163	159
	90% Maximal	171	167	163	159	155	151	147	143

Source: Sheffield LH: Exercise stress testing, in Braunwald E (ed): *Heart Disease—A Textbook of Cardiovascular Medicine*, Philadelphia, WB Saunders Company, 1980, p. 262. Copyright © 1980, WB Saunders Company.

Example 1: A 50-year-old man had an acute myocardial infarction 6 months ago. He was hospitalized for 10 days, at which time serial ECGs showed classical changes of an inferior wall infarction. After recovering, the patient returned to his work as an attendant in a service station.

At present, the man is following a diet to maintain a weight of 160 lb, which is 25 lb less than his weight one year ago. He has no symptoms and is receiving no medication.

Physical examination and chest radiographs are normal. The ECG shows Q waves in leads 2, 3, and F and flat T waves in the same leads. When he exercises, his heart rate is 152 beats per minute, and he has an adequate rise in blood pressure; there are no ECG pattern changes indicating ischemia or arrhythmias.

Diagnosis: Recent inferior wall myocardial infarction.

Impairment: 20% impairment of the whole person.

Comment: An uncomplicated recovery from an anterior wall infarction would equal 25% impairment.

Example 2: A 52-year-old woman underwent coronary artery bypass surgery 6 months ago for relief of angina. A vein graft was placed into the left anterior descending coronary artery and another into the right coronary artery. Preoperative coronary angiography had shown no significant obstruction in the circumflex coronary artery.

Since surgery the patient has done well and has returned to work as a client service specialist for an insurance firm. She has had no symptoms but has avoided heavy physical exertion. She is taking 0.3 gm aspirin daily but no other medications. An exercise test 10 days ago showed a heart rate of 144 beats per minutes after 10 minutes of exercise, and no ST segment shifts or arrhythmias.

Physical examination reveals a well healed scar and a normal heart. The resting ECG shows low T waves in leads 1, L, V4, V5 and V6 and no Q waves. The chest radiograph shows normal heart and lungs.

Diagnosis: Coronary heart disease with coronary artery bypass surgery.

Impairment: 15% impairment of the whole person.

Class 3—Impairment of the Whole Person, 30-50%:
A patient belongs in Class 3 when (a) the patient has a history of myocardial infarction that is documented by appropriate laboratory studies, or angina pectoris that is documented by changes on a resting or exercise ECG or radioisotope study that

are suggestive of ischemia; OR (b) the patient has either a fixed or dynamic focal obstruction of at least 50% of a coronary artery, demonstrated by angiography; AND (c) the patient requires moderate dietary adjustment or drugs to prevent frequent angina or to remain free of symptoms and signs of congestive heart failure, but may develop angina pectoris or symptoms of congestive heart failure after moderately heavy physical exertion (functional class 2); OR (d) the patient has recovered from coronary artery surgery or angioplasty, continues to require treatment, and has the symptoms described above.

Example 1: A 60-year-old family physician suffered from an acute anterior wall myocardial infarction 6 months ago. He had the classical history of chest pain, diaphoresis and weakness, and typical ECG and enzyme changes. After discharge from the hospital, the patient entered a rehabilitation program, but even after three months he continued to experience fatigue and some breathlessness after a brisk walk of 20 to 30 minutes. The patient returned to work but limited his practice and accepted no new patients.

An ECG three months ago recorded a heart rate of 140 beats per minute after 10 minutes of exercise and ST segment elevation in leads 1, L, and V3 through V6. After exercising, the patient was tired but experienced no chest pain. A radioisotope angiogram revealed a large anterior aneurysm of the left ventricle and good function of the inferior wall of the left ventricle. The patient was placed on a regimen of a low salt diet, digoxin 0.25 mg daily, and hydrochlorothiazide 25 mg three times per week.

On physical examination, the patient is comfortable and there are no signs of heart failure. Blood pressure is 135/85 mm Hg and pulse is regular. Examination of the precordium reveals a large sustained impulse just above and lateral to the left nipple, centered in the third intercostal space at the anterior axillary line. A fourth heart sound is present.

The ECG shows a Q wave in leads 1, L, and V1 through V4. Chest radiograph shows cardiac enlargement and clear lung fields.

Diagnosis: Anterior left ventricular aneurysm secondary to coronary heart disease.

Impairment: 45% impairment of the whole person.

Example 2: A 62-year-old woman underwent quadruple coronary artery bypass surgery 6 months ago, but she continues to experience retrosternal chest discomfort if she hurries while doing usual activities. She is especially likely to experience discomfort in the morning and when outdoors in the cold. She enjoys walking but usually experiences discomfort if she hurries up a steep hill leading to her church. She is able to care for her house, and perform other activities without symptoms if she does not rush. She is on a diet, and she takes a beta adrenergic blocking agent and oral nitrates.

At the latest physical examination, she was comfortable and had no signs of congestive heart failure. Blood pressure was 110/70 mm Hg, and pulse was regular at 62 beats per minute. The apical impulse was normal and there were no gallops or murmurs.

An ECG showed low T waves in all leads, and the chest radiograph was normal. An exercise ECG recorded a heart rate of 118 beats per minute after 10 minutes of exercise. The patient experienced retrosternal discomfort during the last minute of exercise, and there was 1.5 mm of ST segment depression in leads V4 through V6 at one and two minutes after exercise. Thallium was injected during exercise, and a definite anterior wall filling defect was demonstrated that only partially refilled during redistribution study. A multigated blood pool radioisotope angiogram revealed reduction of movement of the anterior wall, and that part was akinetic during exercise.

A coronary angiogram revealed 90% or greater obstruction of all three coronary arteries. The grafts to the right, circumflex, and left anterior descending coronary arteries were patent, but the graft to the diagonal branch of the left anterior descending coronary artery could not be visualized.

Diagnosis: Coronary heart disease and continued chest discomfort following coronary artery bypass surgery.

Impairment: 45% impairment of the whole person.

Class 4—Impairment of the Whole Person, 55-100%: A patient belongs in Class 4 when (a) the patient has history of a myocardial infarction that is documented by appropriate laboratory studies, or angina pectoris that has been documented by changes on a resting ECG or radioisotope study that are highly suggestive of myocardial ischemia; OR (b) the patient has either fixed or dynamic focal obstruction of at least 50% of one or more coronary arteries, demonstrated by angiography; AND (c) moderate dietary adjustments or drugs are required to prevent angina or to remain free of symptoms and signs of congestive heart failure, but the patient continues to develop symptoms of angina pectoris or congestive heart failure during ordinary daily activities (functional class 3 or 4), there are signs or laboratory evidence of cardiac enlargement and abnormal ventricular function; OR (d) the patient has recovered from coronary artery bypass surgery or angioplasty and continues to require treatment and have symptoms as described above.

Example 1: A 42-year-old man suffered an anteroseptal myocardial infarction 6 months ago. Two years ago he had an inferior wall myocardial infarction. During the past 6 months he has continued to have episodes of retrosternal discomfort on minimal exertion and sometimes at rest, despite the use of adequate doses of beta adrenergic blocking agents, oral and sublingual nitrates, and more recently, a calcium channel blocking agent. He rarely goes a full day without an episode of chest discomfort lasting from 1 to 10 minutes.

On examination, the patient is comfortable at rest. His blood pressure is 120/80 mm Hg and his resting pulse rate is 54 beats per minute. There are no signs of congestive heart failure. The apical impulse is enlarged, sustained, and displaced laterally to the anterior axillary line at the fifth intercostal space. The first heart sound is soft and there is a prominent fourth heart sound. A grade 2/6 holosystolic murmur is present at the apex.

The resting ECG shows Q waves in leads 2, 3 and F, a QS pattern in V1 through V3 and a QR in V4; the T waves are low in all leads. The chest radiograph shows marked cardiomegaly and prominence of the vasculature in the upper lung fields. During exercise the patient develops pain and ST depression in 1, L, V5 and V6 after two minutes. The ejection fraction falls from 30% to 25% as measured by the multigated blood pool scan.

Diagnosis: Angina pectoris and left ventricular failure due to coronary heart disease.

Impairment: 90% impairment of the whole person.

Example 2: A 46-year-old woman had quadruple coronary artery bypass surgery 6 months ago but continues to have pain each day and to be weak and breathless after minimal exertion. She sleeps on three pillows; often she awakens short of breath and must sit in a chair for the remainder of the night. These symptoms continue despite digitalis, diuretics, nitrates, calcium channel blocking agents, and hydralazine.

On examination, there is evidence of weight loss. The patient prefers the sitting position. Blood pressure is 110/70 mm Hg, and the heart rate is 92 beats per minute. The neck veins distend when hand pressure is applied to the abdomen, even when the head of the examining table is elevated 45 degrees. The apical impulse is enlarged, sustained, and displaced to the anterior axillary line, and a parasternal heave is present. There are rales at both lung bases and dullness at the right lung base. The first heart sound is soft and there is a prominent third heart sound. A grade 2/6 holosystolic murmur is present at the apex.

The ECG shows a QS pattern in V1 through V4, prominent Q waves in V5 and V6, and low R waves throughout. The T waves are inverted in 1, L and V1 through V5, and low elsewhere. Chest radiograph shows marked cardiomegaly, increased vascular markings in the upper lung fields, and a small, right-sided pleural effusion.

Coronary angiography shows total occlusion of the left anterior descending coronary artery and 90% blockage in both the right and circumflex coronary arteries. The graft to the right coronary artery and the graft to one of the branches of the circumflex artery are patent, but the graft to the other branch of the circumflex artery and the graft to the anterior descending artery are not visualized. The ventriculogram shows an ejection fraction of 20%; there is akinesis of the entire anterior wall and poor contraction elsewhere.

Diagnosis: Angina pectoris and left ventricular failure after coronary artery bypass surgery.

Impairment: 100% impairment of the whole person.

The criteria for permanent impairment due to coronary heart disease are found in Table 7.

TABLE 7—IMPAIRMENT CLASSIFICATION FOR CORONARY HEART DISEASE

Class 1 (0-10% Impairment)	Class 2 (15-25% Impairment)	Class 3 (30-50% Impairment)	Class 4 (55-100% Impairment)
Because of the serious implications of reduced coronary blood flow, it is not reasonable to classify the degree of impairment as 0% to 10% in any patient who has symptoms of coronary heart disease corraborated by physical examination or laboratory tests. This class of impairment should be reserved for the patient with an equivocal history of angina pectoris on whom coronary angiography is performed, or for a patient on whom coronary angiography is performed for other reasons and in whom is found less than 50% reduction in the cross sectional area of a coronary artery.	The patient has history of a myocardial infarction or angina pectoris that is documented by appropriate laboratory studies, but at the time of evaluation the patient has no symptoms while performing ordinary daily activities or even moderately heavy physical exertion (functional class 1); **AND** The patient may require moderate dietary adjustment and/or medication to prevent angina or to remain free of signs and symptoms of congestive heart failure; **AND** The patient is able to walk on the treadmill or bicycle ergometer and obtain a heart rate of 90% of his or her predicted maximum heart rate without developing significant ST segment shift, ventricular tachycardia, or hypotension; if the patient is uncooperative or unable to exercise because of disease affecting another organ system, this requirement may be omitted; **OR** The patient has recovered from coronary artery surgery or angioplasty, remains asymptomatic during ordinary daily activities, and is able to exercise as outlined above. If the patient is taking a beta adrenergic blocking agent, he or she should be able to walk on the treadmill to a level estimated to cause an energy expenditure of at least 10 METS as a substitute for the heart rate target.	The patient has a history of myocardial infarction that is documented by appropriate laboratory studies, and/or angina pectoris that is documented by changes on a resting or exercise ECG or radioisotope study that are suggestive of ischemia; **OR** The patient has either a fixed or dynamic focal obstruction of at least 50% of a coronary artery, demonstrated by angiography; **AND** The patient requires moderate dietary adjustment or drugs to prevent frequent angina or to remain free of symptoms and signs of congestive heart failure, but may develop angina pectoris or symptoms of congestive heart failure after moderately heavy physical exertion (functional class 2); **OR** The patient has recovered from coronary artery surgery or angioplasty, continues to require treatment, and has the symptoms described above.	The patient has history of a myocardial infarction that is documented by appropriate laboratory studies, or angina pectoris that has been documented by changes on a resting ECG or radioisotope study that are highly suggestive of myocardial ischemia; **OR** The patient has either fixed or dynamic focal obstruction of at least 50% of one or more coronary arteries, demonstrated by angiography; **AND** Moderate dietary adjustments or drugs are required to prevent angina or to remain free of symptoms and signs of congestive heart failure, but the patient continues to develop symptoms of angina pectoris or congestive heart failure during ordinary daily activities (functional class 3 or 4), or there are signs or laboratory evidence of cardiac enlargement and abnormal ventricular function; **OR** The patient has recovered from coronary artery bypass surgery or angioplasty and continues to require treatment and have symptoms as described above.

Congenital Heart Disease

In recent years, surgical procedures designed to correct or improve the circulation of infants and children with congenital cardiac disorders have allowed many of these individuals to live to adulthood. Many of these surgically treated patients continue to have less than perfect functioning of the heart and circulation and are therefore impaired.

Congenital heart disease may be recognized by history and upon physical examination, but often the exact diagnosis and the patient's functional impairment require special studies,

including ECG, chest radiograph, radioisotope studies, echocardiography, hemodynamic measurements, and angiography. A quantitation of limitations due to symptoms is found in Table 1.

Criteria for Evaluating Impairment Due to Congenital Heart Disease

Class 1—Impairment of the Whole Person, 0-10%: A patient belongs in Class 1 when (a) the patient has evidence by physical examination or laboratory studies of congenital heart disease and has no symptoms in the performance of ordinary daily activities, or even upon moderately heavy physical exertion; AND (b) continuous treatment is not required, although prophylactic antibiotics may be recommended after surgical procedures to reduce the risk of bacterial endocarditis; and the patient remains free of signs of congestive heart failure and cyanosis; AND (c) there are no signs of cardiac chamber hypertrophy or dilation; the evidence of residual valvular stenosis or regurgitation is estimated to be mild; there is no evidence of left-to-right or right-to-left shunt; and the pulmonary vascular resistance is estimated to be normal; OR (d) in the patient who has recovered from corrective heart surgery, all of the above criteria are met.

Example 1: A 22-year-old woman is known to have had a loud systolic murmur along the left sternal border since childhood. She underwent cardiac catheterization at the ages of 2 and 18 years, and on both occasions a 20 mm Hg gradient was noted between the right ventricle and the pulmonary artery. She also had normal pulmonary artery pressures, no evidence of shunts, and normal cardiac output. The patient has never had symptoms referable to the cardiovascular system.

At present, physical examination shows the patient to be comfortable without signs of heart failure or cyanosis. The precordium is without heaves, thrills, or taps. The first heart sound is normal and the second heart sound is widely split, and there is variation with respiration. There is a grade 3/6 systolic murmur that ends well short of the second heart sound; the murmur is loudest in the second left intercostal space. There are no diastolic murmurs or gallops. Chest radiograph and ECG are normal.

Diagnosis: Mild pulmonary valve stenosis.

Impairment: 10% impairment of the whole person.

Comment: If the gradient were greater than 40 mm Hg, or if the ECG were to show right ventricular hypertrophy, then the patient would be in a higher category of impairment, and should be considered for surgical treatment of the stenosis. An asymptomatic patient with a small ventricular septal defect might also be rated at the upper end of Class 1 impairment, but if bacterial endocarditis had ever been present, then the impairment rating would be higher. Also in this category might be a patient who has a small atrial septal defect with normal pressures in all cardiac chambers and great vessels, or a patient who has anomalous venous return of a small segment of the lung.

Example 2: A 25-year-old woman underwent repair of secundum atrial septal defect 10 years ago. There were no complications, and the patient remained asymptomatic and returned to a normally active life.

Physical examination at present shows a well-healed wound over the sternum without tenderness. There are no abnormal precordial pulsations or signs of congestive heart failure. The first heart sound is normal. The second heart sound is widely split and there is some variation with respiration in the degree of splitting. A grade 2/6 early systolic ejection murmur is heard along the left sternal border.

The ECG shows an incomplete right bundle branch block pattern. The chest radiograph is normal. The echocardiogram shows enlargement of the right ventricle and reduced motion of the ventricular septum. Findings of cardiac catheterization and angiography are normal.

Diagnosis: Atrial septal defect with surgical closure.

Impairment: 0% impairment of the whole person.

Comment: If a very small left-to-right shunt were demonstrated postoperatively, then the degree of impairment might be raised to 5% to 10%. Echocardiogram, cardiac catheterization, and angiography are not necessary for evaluating the degree of impairment.

Class 2—Impairment of the Whole Person, 15-25%: A patient belongs in Class 2 when (a) the patient has evidence by physical examination or laboratory studies of congenital heart disease, has no symptoms in the performance of ordinary daily activities, and has symptoms with moderately heavy physical exertion (functional class 2); OR (b) the patient requires moderate dietary adjustments or drugs to prevent symptoms or to remain free of signs of congestive heart failure or other consequences of congenital heart disease, such as syncope, chest pain, emboli, or cyanosis; OR (c) there are signs or laboratory evidence of cardiac chamber hypertrophy or dilation, or the severity of valvular stenosis or regurgitation is estimated to be moderate; or there is evidence of a small residual left-to-right or right-to-left shunt; or there is evidence of moderate elevation of the pulmonary vascular resistance, which should be less than one-half the systemic vascular resistance; OR (d) the patient has recovered from surgery for the treatment of congenital heart disease and meets the above criteria for impairment.

Example 1: A 35-year-old woman had a systolic murmur and abnormal cardiac sounds for many years. She led a relatively normal life but avoided participation in sports at the advice of physicians. During the past year she noted becoming weak and tired more easily than usual and also noticed regular pounding of the heart with minimal exertion. The palpitations were not associated with symptoms of inadequate cerebral perfusion and were never sustained. There was no history of cyanosis, breathlessness, or peripheral edema.

On examination, the patient is comfortable and has no cyanosis. There are prominent V waves in the neck veins, and the liver is enlarged to a width of 12 cm. The lungs are clear. There are no thrills, taps or heaves in the precordium. The first heart sound is loud and is followed by a very loud, sharp sound in early systole that is heard best along the left sternal border. The second heart sound is loud, and there is an early diastolic sound heard best at the midprecordium. A holosystolic murmur is heard along the left sternal border that increases in intensity with inspiration.

The ECG demonstrates a right bundle branch block pattern, and the R wave in V1 is very low. There is a broad, notched P wave in leads 3 and F, and inverted T waves in V1 and V2. There are occasional premature atrial beats. The chest radiograph shows marked enlargement of the cardiac silhouette, particularly to the right of the sternum. The pulmonary vasculature is normal. Echocardiogram shows features suggesting Ebstein's anomaly of the tricuspid valve.

Cardiac catheterization and angiography demonstrate a mean right atrial pressure of 7 mm Hg with V waves of 15 mm Hg. Right ventricular and pulmonary artery pressures are normal. There is no evidence of left-to-right or right-to-left shunt.

Intracardiac electrograms show a right ventricular ECG pattern at the time the catheter lumen is recording right atrial pressures. Angiography reveals a markedly displaced tricuspid valve, an enormous right atrium, and a small right ventricle.

Diagnosis: Ebstein's anomaly of the tricuspid valve.

Impairment: 25% impairment of the whole person.

Comment: If the patient had a right-to-left shunt, then the rated degree of impairment would be considerably higher. Also, if the patient had

cardiac arrhythmias causing symptoms, impairment would be rated according to the specific criteria for arrhythmias, and the impairment due to congenital heart disease and arrythmias would be combined using the Combined Values Chart.

Example 2: A 42-year-old male underwent open heart surgery 15 years ago for the treatment of tetralogy of Fallot. The procedure resulted in relief of pulmonary stenosis, placement of a pericardial bridge in the outflow tract of the right ventricle, and closure of the ventricular septal defect. After the operation, the patient did well without medication and achieved his present position as dispatcher for a trucking firm.

At examination, the man appears healthy. Blood pressure is 110/70 mm Hg and the pulse is regular at 70 beats per minute. There are no signs of congestive heart failure, and precordium is normal. The first heart sound is normal. The second heart sound is louder than normal and it is followed by a mid-diastolic, scratchy murmur heard in the second and third left intercostal spaces. There is also a short, grade 2/6 ejection systolic murmur heard in the same places.

The ECG shows right bundle branch block. Chest radiograph shows an apical prominence at the left side of the cardiac silhouette. Echocardiography shows thickening of the right ventricular wall and dilation of the right ventricular cavity with diminished ventricular septal motion. Cardiac catheterization and angiography demonstrate right ventricular pressure of 28 mm Hg in systole and 5 mm Hg in diastole, and a pulmonary artery pressure of 20 mm Hg in systole and 5 mm Hg in diastole. Cardiac output is normal and there is no evidence of a shunt.

Diagnosis: Tetralogy of Fallot with surgical relief of pulmonary valve stenosis and closure of the ventricular septal defect.

Impairment: 15% to 20% impairment of the whole person.

Comment: Had there been evidence of a shunt, the impairment rating would have been greater. Also, if a conduit or prosthesis had been placed in the pulmonary outflow tract, or if significant symptoms had been present, the rating would have been greater.

Class 3 — Impairment of the Whole Person, 30-50%: A patient belongs in Class 3 when (a) the patient has evidence by physical examination or laboratory studies of congenital heart disease and experiences symptoms during the performance of ordinary daily activities (functional class 3); AND (b) diet modifications and drugs do not completely control symptoms or prevent signs of congestive heart failure; AND (c) there are signs or laboratory evidence of cardiac chamber hypertrophy or dilation; or the severity of valvular stenosis or regurgitation is estimated to be moderate or severe; or there is evidence of a right-to-left shunt; or there is evidence of a left-to-right shunt with the pulmonary flow being greater than two times the systemic flow; or the pulmonary vascular resistance is elevated to greater than one-half the systemic vascular resistance; OR (d) the patient has recovered from surgery for the treatment of congenital heart disease but continues to have functional class 3 symptoms; or continues to have signs of congestive failure or cyanosis, and there is evidence of cardiomegaly and significant residual valvular stenosis or regurgitation, left-to-right shunt, right-to-left shunt, or elevated pulmonary vascular resistance.

Example 1: A 52-year-old woman has Ebstein's anomaly of the tricuspid valve, the diagnosis having been made years ago with the aid of echocardiography, cardiac catheterization and angiography. During the past several years, she has had increasing breathlessness during daily activities such as climbing stairs, mopping or cleaning. Also, she has noticed ankle edema and increased abdominal girth. With the use of diuretics the edema and ascites have diminished. The patient restricts the salt in her diet and takes digitalis.

On examination, the patient appears well, but there is duskiness of the lips and the fingernails. The V wave in the neck veins is markedly elevated, and the liver is 14 cm wide and slightly pulsatile. The lungs are clear. A very active parasternal area without a distinct heave is found in the precordium. The first heart sound is loud and is followed by a loud early systolic sound along the left sternal border. The second heart sound is widely split and is followed by an early diastolic sound. There is a holosystolic murmur that increases with inspiration heard best at the left of the sternum. There is also a diastolic murmur heard best during inspiration and along the left sternal border. There is no peripheral edema and no evidence of ascites at this time.

The ECG shows right bundle branch block with low R waves in V1 and prominent P waves.

The chest radiograph shows a greatly enlarged cardiac silhouette especially to the right of the sternum. The pulmonary vasculature is normal. Echocardiogram shows typical changes of Ebstein's anomaly of the tricuspid valve. Previous cardiac catheterization showed changes of Ebstein's anomaly and a small atrial right-to-left shunt.

Diagnosis: Ebstein's anomaly of the tricuspid valve.

Impairment: 50% impairment of the whole person.

Example 2: A 20-year-old man underwent a Mustard procedure 10 years ago for treatment of transposition of the great vessels. In infancy he had a Blalock-Hanlon procedure. After the Mustard procedure, he did moderately well, but never developed satisfactory stamina, tiring easily and being unable to participate in activities such as tennis and hiking because of dyspnea and fatigue.

On examination, the patient appears healthy but underweight, and had no cyanosis. The neck veins are distended and show a prominent A wave. The liver is not enlarged and there is no peripheral edema. The lungs are clear. There are parasternal and apical heaves at the precordium. S1 and S2 are normal. There is a holosystolic murmur at the left sternal border, and a fourth heart sound is present.

The ECG shows tall R wave voltage in all of the precordial leads. The chest radiograph shows moderate cardiomegaly and clear lungs. The echocardiogram shows signs of a properly functioning intra-atrial baffle. Both ventricular cavities are enlarged, but there is good ventricular function. Cardiac catheterization and angiography demonstrate an elevated right mean atrial pressure of 12 mm Hg with A waves of 20 mm Hg. Right ventricular and pulmonary artery systolic pressures are 30 to 35 mm Hg.

Diagnosis: Transposition of the great vessels, with Mustard procedure.

Impairment: 40% to 50% impairment of the whole person.

Comment: If significant arrhythmias were to complicate the postoperative period, they would be evaluated according to the criteria in the section on arrythmias, and the two impairment ratings would be combined using the Combined Values Chart to determine impairment of the whole person due to cardiac disease.

TABLE 8—IMPAIRMENT CLASSIFICATION FOR CONGENITAL HEART DISEASE

Class 1 (0-10% Impairment)	Class 2 (15-25% Impairment)	Class 3 (30-50% Impairment)	Class 4 (55-100% Impairment)
The patient has evidence by physical examination or laboratory studies of congenital heart disease and has no symptoms in the performance of ordinary daily activities, or even upon moderately heavy physical exertion;	The patient has evidence by physical examination or laboratory studies of congenital heart disease, has no symptoms in the performance of ordinary daily activities, and has no symptoms with moderately heavy physical exertion (functional class 2);	The patient has evidence by physical examination or laboratory studies of congenital heart disease and experiences symptoms during the performance of ordinary daily activities (functional class 3);	The patient has signs of congenital heart disease and experiences symptoms of congestive heart failure at less than ordinary daily activities (functional class 4);
AND	**OR**	**AND**	**AND**
Continuous treatment is not required, although prophylactic antibiotics may be recommended after surgical procedures to reduce the risk of bacterial endocarditis; and the patient remains free of signs of congestive heart failure and cyanosis;	The patient requires moderate dietary adjustments or drugs to prevent symptoms or to remain free of signs of congestive heart failure or other consequences of congenital heart disease, such as syncope, chest pain, emboli, or cyanosis;	Diet modification and drugs do not completely control symptoms or prevent signs of congestive heart failure;	Dietary therapy and drugs do not prevent symptoms or signs of congestive heart failure;
AND	**OR**	**AND**	**AND**
There are no signs of cardiac chamber hypertrophy or dilation; the evidence of residual valvular stenosis or regurgitation is estimated to be mild; there is no evidence of left-to-right or right-to-left shunt; and the pulmonary vascular resistance is estimated to be normal;	There are signs or laboratory evidence of cardiac chamber hypertrophy or dilation, or the severity of valvular stenosis or regurgitation is estimated to be moderate; or there is evidence of a small residual left-to-right or right-to-left shunt; or there is evidence of moderate elevation of the pulmonary vascular resistance, which should be less than one-half the systemic vascular resistance;	There are signs or laboratory evidence of cardiac chamber hypertrophy or dilation; or the severity of valvular stenosis or regurgitation is estimated to be moderate or severe; or there is evidence of a right-to-left shunt; or there is evidence of a left-to-right shunt with the pulmonary flow being greater than two times the systemic flow; or the pulmonary vascular resistance is elevated to greater than one-half the systemic vascular resistance;	There is evidence from physical examination or laboratory studies of cardiac chamber hypertrophy or dilation, or the pulmonary vascular resistance remains elevated at greater than one-half of the systemic vascular resistance; or the severity of the valvular stenosis or regurgitation is estimated to be moderate to severe; or there is a left-to-right shunt with the pulmonary flow being greater than two times the systemic flow; or there is a left-to-right shunt with the pulmonary vascular resistance being elevated to greater than one-half the systemic vascular resistance; or there is a right-to-left shunt;
OR	**OR**	**OR**	**OR**
In the patient who has recovered from corrective heart surgery, all of the above criteria are met.	The patient has recovered from surgery for the treatment of congenital heart disease and meets the above criteria for impairment.	The patient has recovered from surgery for the treatment of congenital heart disease but continues to have functional class 3 symptoms; or continues to have signs of congestive failure or cyanosis, and there is evidence of cardiomegaly and significant residual valvular stenosis or regurgitation, left-to-right shunt, right-to-left shunt, or elevated pulmonary vascular resistance.	The patient has recovered from heart surgery for the treatment of congenital heart disease and continues to have symptoms or signs of congestive heart failure causing impairment as outlined above.

Class 4—Impairment of the Whole Person, 55-100%: A patient belongs in Class 4 when (a) the patient has signs of congenital heart disease and experiences symptoms of congestive heart failure at less than ordinary daily activities (functional class 4); AND (b) dietary therapy and drugs do not prevent symptoms or signs of congestive heart failure; AND (c) there is evidence from physical examination or laboratory studies of cardiac chamber hypertrophy or dilation, or the pulmonary vascular resistance remains elevated at greater than one-half of the systemic vascular resistance; or the severity of the valvular stenosis or regurgitation is estimated to be moderate to severe; or there is a left-to-right shunt with the pulmonary flow being greater than two times the systemic flow; or there is a left-to-right shunt with the pulmonary vascular resistance being elevated to greater than one-half the systemic vascular resistance; or there is a right-to-left shunt; OR (d) the patient has recovered from heart surgery for the treatment of congenital heart disease and continues to have symptoms or signs of congestive heart failure causing impairment as outlined above.

Example 1: A 23-year-old woman with Eisenmenger's complex, with a diagnosis made 10 years ago, has been followed regularly. She had cardiac catheterization and angiography, and a ventricular septal defect and pulmonary vascular resistance equal to systemic vascular resistance were found. Recently, she became markedly limited in her activities because of fatigue on minimal exertion. Peripheral edema of recent onset responded to diuretic therapy.

On examination, the woman has mild cyanosis that intensifies with exertion. There are prominent A waves in the neck veins, but there is no jugular venous distention when the patient is at a 45 degree angle. The liver is not enlarged and there is no peripheral edema. The lungs are clear. There is a forceful, sustained parasternal heave. The first heart sound is normal and the second is narrowly split. There is a marked increase in the second component of the second sound. There is a short, early systolic ejection murmur along the left sternal border.

The ECG shows right ventricular hypertrophy and peaked P waves in leads 2, 3, and F. Chest radiograph shows evidence of right ventricular hypertrophy, marked prominence of the proximal portion of the pulmonary arteries, and greatly diminished pulmonary vascular markings in the periphery of the lung fields.

Diagnosis: Eisenmenger complex with ventricular septal defect and elevated pulmonary vascular resistance.

Impairment: 100% impairment of the whole person.

Example 2: A 35-year-old man with tetralogy of Fallot had a Blalock-Taussig systemic-to-pulmonary artery anastomosis as a child, which was ligated during a second operative procedure. At that time, pulmonary stenosis was relieved by removing muscle in the outflow area of the right ventricle, and the ventricular septal defect was closed. After the second operation the patient did not do well, continuing to tire easily. Significant peripheral edema and ascites responded to the use of diuretics. He was comfortable during light work activities about the home but became weak and breathless on more vigorous exertion.

At examination, the patient has no cyanosis. There is a prominent V wave in the neck veins. The liver is 14 cm across. There is palpable cardiac activity parasternally but no sustained heave. There is a grade 3/6 holosystolic murmur along the left sternal border and a mid-diastolic murmur in the second left interspace. The first heart sound is normal and the second heart sound is single and loud.

The ECG shows right bundle branch block. The chest radiograph shows cardiomegaly and a right pleural effusion. The echocardiogram shows a dilated, poorly-functioning right ventricle. Cardiac catheterization and angiography show severe tricuspid regurgitation and a dilated, poorly-functioning right ventricle.

Diagnosis: Tetralogy of Fallot with surgical relief of the pulmonary stenosis and closure of the ventricular septal defect, followed by development of tricuspid regurgitation and heart failure.

Impairment: 90% impairment of the whole person.

Criteria for impairment due to congenital heart disease are found in Table 8.

Hypertensive Cardiovascular Disease

Elevated pressure within the systemic arterial system is known as hypertension. A transient elevation of arterial pressure is the normal physiologic response to exercise and excitement, but a sustained elevation of pressure is not normal and can lead to damage of arterial walls and of the organs supplied by these vessels, especially the brain and the kidneys. Also, sustained increased pressure may lead to a tearing of the intima of the aorta, and possibly to a dissection of the media and rupture. Elevated pressure in the arterial system, if sustained, greatly increases the work of the left ventricle. Initially this leads to compensatory hypertrophy, but eventually it causes failure of the left ventricle with all of the attendant complications including death.

The cause of hypertension in most patients is not understood, and the disorder is therefore called "essential" or "primary" hypertension. In some patients, the hypertension can be established as being due to other disorders, in which case the disorder is termed "secondary" hypertension. An organized approach to detect secondary disorders is warranted because their correction may lead to elimination of the hypertension. Secondary hypertension may be due to coarctation of the aorta, renal artery obstruction, renal parenchymal disease, hyperaldosteronism, Cushing's disease, rare endocrine disorders such as pheochromocytoma, and chronic nocturnal hypoxia due to the sleep apnea syndromes.

In the patient in whom a diagnosable disorder causes the hypertension, estimation of permanent impairment should not be undertaken until

119

adequate time has elapsed after treatment of the disorder. If other organs are affected, as with the kidneys in chronic renal disease, then the degree of impairment due to the hypertension should be combined with that due to the other organ system, using the Combined Values Chart.

Drugs are now available with acceptable side effects that can maintain blood pressure in the normal range in most patients with primary hypertension and in most with secondary hypertension and no correctable cause. Ratings of impairment due to hypertension should be delayed until after the drugs have been prescribed and their doses have been adjusted to achieve maximum effect.

Before classifying a patient as having hypertensive cardiovascular disease, the physician should make several determinations of the arterial pressure. Hypertensive cardiovascular disease is not necessarily present when a patient exhibits transient or irregular episodes of elevated arterial pressure; these could be associated with an emotional or environmental stimulus or with signs or symptoms of cardiovascular system hyperactivity. Most authorities agree that hypertensive cardiovascular disease is present when the diastolic pressure is repeatedly in excess of 90 mm Hg.

Criteria for Evaluating Impairment Due to Hypertensive Cardiovascular Disease

Class 1—Impairment of the Whole Person, 0-10%: A patient belongs in Class 1 when (1) the patient has no symptoms and the diastolic pressures are repeatedly in excess of 90 mm Hg; AND (2) the patient is taking antihypertensive medications but has none of the following abnormalities: (a) abnormal urinalyis or renal function tests; (b) history of hypertensive cerebrovascular disease; (c) evidence of left ventricular hypertrophy; (d) hypertensive vascular abnormalities of the optic fundus, except minimal narrowing of arterioles.

Example: A 26-year-old ophthalmology resident was told when 18 years old that his blood pressure was high. This finding was confirmed by numerous determinations of blood pressure made during medical school. An employment examination at the beginning of his internship confirmed the elevated blood pressure, and he was sent for a diagnostic work-up and treatment. No cause for the elevated blood pressure was found. The patient was asymptomatic, and he was started on a regimen of restricted salt intake, weight control and regular exercise.

His blood pressure remained elevated and he was prescribed an antihypertensive medication.

At the latest series of examinations, the patient's blood pressure was 160/105 mm Hg in both arms and 170/105 mm Hg in the right leg. All arterial pulses were of good quality. A week later the pressures were the same. All other physical findings were normal.

The ECG and chest radiograph were normal. Serum electrolytes, including the BUN and serum creatinine, and urinanalysis were normal.

Diagnosis: Essential hypertension.

Impairment: 5% impairment of the whole person.

Comment: It may be necessary to alter the antihypertensive medication to effect a reduction in the blood pressure.

Class 2—Impairment of the Whole Person, 15-25%: A patient belongs in Class 2 when (1) the patient has no symptoms and the diastolic pressures are repeatedly in excess of 90 mm Hg; AND (2) the patient is taking antihypertensive medication and has any of the following abnormalities: (a) proteinuria and abnormalities of the urinary sediment, but no impairment of renal function as measured by blood urea nitrogen (BUN) and serum creatinine determinations; (b) history of hypertensive cerebrovascular damage; (c) definite hypertensive changes in the retinal arterioles, including crossing defects and/or old exudates.

Example: A 40-year-old woman had an elevated blood pressure during a pregnancy at age 32 years, but the pressure was normal three weeks and 12 months post partum. Recently she had bleeding between menstrual periods. Her gynecologist found her blood pressure to be in the range of 160/105 to 150/100 mm Hg on several occasions. Leg blood pressures were also elevated.

Findings on physical examination were normal, including the fundal vessels and the heart.

The ECG and chest radiograph were normal. Serum electrolytes were normal, including the BUN and creatinine levels. Urinalysis showed 2 + proteinuria, and the sediment showed 1 to 3 red blood cells per high power field. The proteinuria was confirmed on two occasions. A 24-hour urine collection yielded 1400 mg of protein.

Diagnosis: Essential hypertension with proteinuria.

Impairment: 15% impairment of the whole person.

Comment: If the pressure remains elevated after restricting dietary salt and beginning a regimen of weight control and exercise, an antihypertensive drug should be recommended.

Class 3 — Impairment of the Whole Person, 30-50%: A patient belongs in Class 3 when (1) the patient has no symptoms and the diastolic pressure readings are consistently in excess of 90 mm Hg; AND (2) the patient is taking antihypertensive medication and has any of the following abnormalities: (a) diastolic pressure readings usually in excess of 120 mm Hg; (b) proteinuria or abnormalities in the urinary sediment, with evidence of impaired renal function as measured by elevated BUN and serum creatinine, or by creatinine clearance below 50%; (c) hypertensive cerebrovascular damage with permanent neurological residual; (d) left ventricular hypertrophy according to findings of physical examination, ECG, or chest radiograph, but no symptoms, signs, or evidence by chest radiograph of congestive heart failure; or (e) retinopathy, with definite hypertensive changes in the arterioles, such as "copper" or "silver wiring," or A-V crossing changes, with or without hemorrhages and exudates.

Example: A 48-year-old man was admitted to the hospital 8 months ago with headaches, blurred vision, and breathlessness of two weeks' duration. His blood pressure was 260/160 mm Hg in the arms and legs. He was drowsy but he had no localizing neurological signs.

The patient's fundi showed arterial spasm, hemorrhages, and bilateral papilledema. Examination of the heart, lungs and abdomen, and chest radiograph were normal. The ECG showed low T waves in the lateral chest leads; the BUN was 40 mg/100 ml and serum creatinine 3.2 mg/100 ml. Urinalysis was abnormal, showing 3+ proteinuria, numerous red blood cells, and occasional white blood cells.

With treatment, the patient's symptoms cleared, and he remained asymptomatic. He took three antihypertensive drugs faithfully, but his diastolic blood pressures remained above 120 mm Hg.

Diagnosis: Essential hypertension with a history of hypertensive encephalopathy.

Impairment: 45% to 50% impairment of the whole person.

Comment: If any of the other findings had persisted, but the diastolic blood pressure had returned to normal, then the estimate of impairment would have been less.

Class 4 — Impairment of the Whole Person, 55-100%: A patient belongs in Class 4 when (1) the patient has a diastolic pressure consistently in excess of 90 mm Hg; AND (2) the patient is taking antihypertensive medication and has any two of the following abnormalities: (a) diastolic pressure readings usually in excess of 120 mm Hg; (b) proteinuria and abnormalities in the urinary sediment, with impaired renal function and evidence of nitrogen retention as measured by elevated BUN and serum creatinine or by creatinine clearance below 50%; (c) hypertensive cerebrovascular damage with permanent neurological deficits; (d) left ventricular hypertrophy; (e) retinopathy as manifested by hypertensive changes in the arterioles, retina, or optic nerve; (f) history of congestive heart failure; OR (3) the patient has left ventricular hypertrophy with the persistence of congestive heart failure despite digitalis and diuretics.

Example 1: A 48-year-old man had a long history of severe hypertension and took drugs intermittently. He had no symptoms until a year ago, when he developed breathlessness on exertion, orthopnea, and occasional nocturnal dyspnea. These symptoms improved after the administration of digitalis and diuretics. However, he still became breathless on heavy exertion and occasionally awakened with breathlessness.

Examination reveals a comfortable patient with blood pressure of 170/95 mm Hg and a pulse rate of 84 beats per minute. There are no signs of congestive heart failure. In the fundus there are increased light reflex from the arterioles and A-V crossing depressions, but no hemorrhages or exudates; the disc is flat. The left ventricular impulse is enlarged and sustained but in the normal position. The first heart sound is normal and the second is increased in intensity. There is a fourth heart sound and no murmurs.

The ECG shows left ventricular hypertrophy as evidenced by tall R waves in the lateral chest leads and inverted T waves in the same leads. Chest radiograph shows mild cardiomegaly and normal pulmonary vasculature. The serum electrolytes and urinalysis are normal.

Diagnosis: Essential hypertension and hypertensive heart disease with history of congestive heart failure.

Impairment: 55% impairment of the whole person.

Example 2: A 62-year-old woman has received treatment for high blood pressure for 10 years. Despite taking drugs and following a restricted salt and weight control diet, she continued to have elevation of blood pressure. Two years ago she developed congestive heart failure that initially improved with the use of digitalis and diuretics. Six months ago she began to have marked tiredness and breathlessness on daily activities. Her ankles remained swollen.

Examination reveals a comfortable woman with blood pressure of 180/100 mm Hg in the arms and legs. There is edema of the ankles and lower legs. Fundal examination reveals increased light reflex of the arterioles with A-V crossing compressions and no hemorrhages or exudates; the discs are flat. There is no elevation of the neck veins. The apical impulse is enlarged, sustained, and displaced to the anterior axillary line. The first heart sound is normal, the second heart sound is increased, and there is a fourth heart sound. Rales are heard at both lung bases. There is edema of the ankles and pretibial area.

The ECG shows a deep S wave in V2, but the height of the R waves in V5 and V6 is normal. There are low T waves in 1, L, and V4 through V6. The chest radiograph shows cardiomegaly and prominence of the pulmonary vasculature in the upper lung fields. The serum electrolytes, BUN and creatinine, and urinalysis are normal.

Diagnosis: Essential hypertension with congestive heart failure.

Impairment: 90% impairment of the whole person.

Criteria for impairment due to hypertensive cardiovascular diseases are found in Table 9.

TABLE 9—IMPAIRMENT CLASSIFICATION FOR HYPERTENSIVE CARDIOVASCULAR DISEASE

Class 1 (0-10% Impairment)	Class 2 (15-25% Impairment)	Class 3 (30-50% Impairment)	Class 4 (55-100% Impairment)
The patient has no symptoms and the diastolic pressures are repeatedly in excess of 90 mm Hg;	The patient has no symptoms and the diastolic pressures are repeatedly in excess of 90 mm Hg;	The patient has no symptoms and the diastolic pressure readings are consistently in excess of 90 mm Hg;	The patient has a diastolic pressure consistently in excess of 90 mm Hg;
AND	**AND**	**AND**	**AND**
The patient is taking antihypertensive medications but has none of the following abnormalities: (1) abnormal urinalysis or renal function tests; (2) history of hypertensive cerebrovascular disease; (3) evidence of left ventricular hypertrophy; (4) hypertensive vascular abnormalities of the optic fundus, except minimal narrowing of arterioles.	The patient is taking antihypertensive medication and has any of the following abnormalities: (1) proteinuria and abnormalities of the urinary sediment, but no impairment of renal function as measured by blood urea nitrogen (BUN) and serum creatinine determinations; (2) history of hypertensive cerebrovascular damage; (3) definite hypertensive changes in the retinal arterioles, including crossing defects and old exudates.	The patient is taking antihypertensive medication and has any of the following abnormalities: (1) diastolic pressure readings usually in excess of 120 mm Hg; (2) proteinuria or abnormalities in the urinary sediment, with evidence of impaired renal function as measured by elevated BUN and serum creatinine, or by creatinine clearance below 50%; (3) hypertensive cerebrovascular damage with permanent neurological residual; (4) left ventricular hypertrophy according to findings of physical examination, ECG, or chest radiograph, but no symptoms, signs, or evidence by chest radiograph of congestive heart failure; or (5) retinopathy, with definite hypertensive changes in the arterioles, such as "copper" or "silver wiring," or A-V crossing changes, with or without hemorrhages and exudates.	The patient is taking antihypertensive medication and has any two of the following abnormalities: (1) diastolic pressure readings usually in excess of 120 mm Hg; (2) proteinuria and abnormalities in the urinary sediment, with impaired renal function and evidence of nitrogen retention as measured by elevated BUN and serum creatinine or by creatinine clearance below 50%; (3) hypertensive cerebrovascular damage with permanent neurological deficits; (4) left ventricular hypertrophy; (5) retinopathy as manifested by hypertensive changes in the arterioles, retina, or optic nerve; (6) history of congestive heart failure; **OR** The patient has left ventricular hypertrophy with the persistence of congestive heart failure despite digitalis and diuretics.

Cardiomyopathies

Cardiomyopathies result in impairment of the whole person by causing abnormal ventricular function. Abnormal ventricular function may not result in abnormal hemodynamics, or it may result in pulmonary and/or systemic organ congestion and decreased cardiac output. Abnormal ventricular function related to coronary heart disease, valvular heart disease and hypertensive heart disease are covered in their respective sections. Cardiomyopathies may also cause arrhythmias; these are considered in a different section of this chapter. Some cardiomyopathies are reversible. Every effort should be made to identify the reversible forms and to treat them appropriately over an adequate period of time before estimating any suspected permanent impairment.

There are many mechanisms by which the cardiomyopathies arise, but they can be divided conveniently into three major types: (1) dilated or congestive; (2) hypertrophic; and (3) restrictive. These disorders can be recognized in most patients by taking careful histories and performing careful physical examinations. In most patients, it also is appropriate to supplement these procedures with selected laboratory studies.

Criteria for Evaluating Impairment Due to Cardiomyopathy

Class 1—Impairment of the Whole Person, 0-10%:
A patient belongs in Class 1 when (a) the patient is asymptomatic and there is evidence of impaired left ventricular function from clinical examination or laboratory studies; AND (b) there is no evidence of congestive heart failure or cardiomegaly from physical examination or laboratory studies.

Example: One year ago a 26-year-old woman delivered a normal child, but three days post partum she developed signs of pulmonary congestion. She was normotensive. There was no evidence of valvular heart disease, and the ECG was within normal limits except for sinus tachycardia. She was treated successfully with digitalis and diuretics. Over the next several months, the woman returned to full activities and had no symptoms. Six months ago the digitalis and diuretics were discontinued. She was advised to avoid subsequent pregnancies. She led a normal life caring for three children and her home.

At present, the woman has no signs of congestive failure. Blood pressure is 110/70 mm Hg, and pulse is regular at 70 beats per minute. The precordium is quiet without ventricular heaves. The heart sounds are normal. The ECG is normal. The chest radiograph demonstrates slight cardiomegaly without specific chamber enlargement. Echocardiography shows an ejection fraction of 55%. Exercise testing demonstrates no ECG change; echo-measured ejection fraction falls to 50%.

Diagnosis: Postpartum cardiomyopathy.

Impairment: 10% impairment of the whole person.

Comment: If the woman had symptoms, she would be rated as having considerably greater impairment. If the heart size were normal, and the ejection fraction were normal at rest and increased on exercise, then the estimate of impairment would be less than 10%.

Class 2—Impairment of the Whole Person, 15-25%:
A patient belongs in Class 2 when (a) the patient is asymptomatic and there is evidence of impaired left ventricular function from physical examination or laboratory studies; AND (b) moderate dietary adjustment or drug therapy is necessary for the patient to be free of symptoms and signs of congestive heart failure; OR (c) the patient has recovered from surgery for the treatment of hypertrophic cardiomyopathy and meets the criteria in (a) and (b) above.

Example 1: A 59-year-old man consumed excessive amounts of alcohol over a period of many years and probably had a poor diet most of that time. He was admitted to the hospital a year ago with severe pulmonary congestion. A thorough evaluation indicated that this was probably due to left ventricular failure attributable to a combination of excessive alcohol intake and poor nutrition. The man responded promptly to nutritional treatment, digitalis, and diuretics. He avoided alcohol and returned to a fully active life, working as greens keeper on a golf course. During the past year he was seen regularly by his physician, who elected to maintain him on digitalis and moderate salt restriction because of a persisting gallop rhythm.

On examination, the patient appears comfortable and has no signs of congestive heart failure. Blood pressure is 120/80 mm Hg, and pulse is regular at 70 beats per minute. At the precordium, the apical impulse is larger than normal, slightly sustained, and displaced to the anterior axillary line. There is no parasternal heave. The first and second heart sounds are normal. A third heart sound is present at the apex. There are no murmurs.

The ECG shows small R waves in the lateral chest leads and low T waves in the same leads. The chest radiograph shows moderate cardiomegaly with no specific chamber enlargement. There is no pulmonary congestion. The echocardiogram at rest has an ejection fraction of 40%, and this remains at 40% following exercise. There are no ECG changes during exercise.

Diagnosis: Cardiomyopathy, probably alcoholic and nutritional.

Impairment: 25% impairment of the whole person.

Example 2: An 18-year-old man, whose father has hypertrophic cardiomyopathy, was examined by his physician and found to have evidence of hypertrophic cardiomyopathy. The patient had no heart-related symptoms and was an active participant in sports.

On examination, the man appears healthy and has no evidence of congestive heart failure. Blood pressure is 130/70 mm Hg and the pulse is regular at 70 beats per minute. Carotid pulses are brisk and the apical impulse is normal. The first and second heart sounds are normal, and there is a grade 2/6 mid-systolic murmur heard best along the left sternal border; there is no gallop.

The ECG shows prominent Q waves and low T waves in the lateral chest leads. Chest radiograph shows a normal-sized heart and no pulmonary congestion. Echocardiogram shows marked thickening of the ventricular septum and some thickening of the posterior ventricular wall. The mitral valve motion is normal, and ejection fraction is 80%.

Diagnosis: Hypertrophic cardiomyopathy.

Impairment: 20% impairment of the whole person.

Comment: The patient was advised to avoid strenuous physical exertion, and the importance of follow-up evaluation was stressed.

Class 3—Impairment of the Whole Person, 30-50%: A patient belongs in Class 3 when (a) the patient develops symptoms of congestive heart failure on greater than ordinary daily activities (functional class 3) and there is evidence of abnormal ventricular function from physical examination or laboratory studies; AND (b) moderate dietary restriction or the use of drugs is necessary to minimize the patient's symptoms, or to prevent the appearance of signs of congestive heart failure or

evidence of it by laboratory study; OR (c) the patient has recovered from surgery for the treatment of hypertrophic cardiomyopathy and meets the criteria described above.

Example: A 54-year-old woman has been treated by her physician for the past three years for symptoms of congestive failure and inadequate cardiac output. Two years ago she underwent cardiac catheterization and cineangiography, the studies demonstrating no evidence of coronary artery or valvular disease. Ventricular function then was poor; the end diastolic pressure was elevated to 18 mm Hg and the ejection fraction was 30%. During the past year the patient's condition has been stable; and she has been able to do kitchen work, go shopping, and drive an automobile. She becomes breathless on climbing a flight of stairs and prefers to sleep on two pillows.

At examination, the patient's blood pressure is 110/70 mm Hg, and the pulse is regular at 70 beats per minute. The neck veins are not distended, there is no peripheral edema, and the lungs are clear. There is a markedly enlarged apical impulse, which is sustained and displaced laterally to the anterior axillary line. An early diastolic impulse is palpable following the systolic impulse. The first heart sound is diminished, the second heart sound is normal, and there is a prominent third heart sound. There are no murmurs.

The ECG shows low T waves in all leads. There is a QS pattern in V1 and V2. The chest radiograph shows marked cardiomegaly with some distention of the pulmonary vessels in the upper lobes. Echocardiography shows a moderately dilated left ventricle with an ejection fraction of 30% and an enlarged left atrium.

Diagnosis: Idiopathic cardiomyopathy.

Impairment: 50% impairment of the whole person.

Class 4—Impairment of the Whole Person, 55-100%: A patient belongs in Class 4 when (a) the patient is symptomatic during ordinary daily activities despite the appropriate use of dietary adjustment and drugs, and there is evidence of abnormal ventricular function from physical examination or laboratory studies; OR (b) there are persistent signs of congestive heart failure despite the use of dietary adjustment and drugs; OR (c) the patient has recovered from surgery for the treatment of hypertrophic cardiomyopathy and meets the above criteria.

Example: A 38-year-old woman had the diagnosis made of hypertrophic cardiomyopathy at age 30 years. For a number of years she frequently experienced chest pain despite the use of beta adrenergic blocking agents. Nitrates were not effective and seemed to worsen her pain. Because of the angina, the woman underwent cardiac surgery to remove a large portion of the ventricular septum. There were no postoperative complications. She continued to experience angina almost on a daily basis. Many of the episodes occurred at rest, but they could also be provoked by sexual intercourse, by running up stairs, or by other activities. She also experienced several syncopal spells in the past two months.

Examination discloses that the patient is comfortable at rest. Her blood pressure is 140/80 mm Hg, and the pulse is regular at 52 beats per minute. The carotid pulse is quick and "jerky" in quality bilaterally. The venous pressure is normal and the lungs are clear. There is no peripheral edema. There is a sustained apical impulse that is moderately enlarged and displaced laterally to the anterior axillary line. A grade 3/6 long, almost holosystolic murmur is heard best at the left mid-precordium and poorly transmitted to the left axilla. The first and second heart sounds are normal and a fourth heart sound is present.

The ECG shows a sinus rhythm with Q waves in leads 1, L, and V1 through V3, and low T waves in the lateral chest leads as well as in leads 1 and L. Chest radiograph shows moderate cardiomegaly with normal pulmonary vasculature. Exercise ECG shows ST segment depression in 1, L, and V4 through V6, at a heart rate of 75 beats per minute that is low because the patient is receiving beta adrenergic blocking agents. The resting 201 Thallium perfusion scan shows the ventricular septum to be thick. No new perfusion defect develops following exercise.

Echocardiography shows a thick ventricular septum and a reduced ventricular ejection fraction of 35%. Mitral valve motion is slightly abnormal in that there is evidence of impaired left ventricular filling. The left atrium is enlarged.

Diagnosis: Hypertrophic cardiomyopathy, with resection of a portion of the left ventricular septum.

Impairment: 100% impairment of the whole person.

The criteria for permanent impairment due to cardiomyopathies are found in Table 10.

TABLE 10—IMPAIRMENT CLASSIFICATION FOR CARDIOMYOPATHIES

Class 1 (0-10% Impairment)	Class 2 (15-25% Impairment)	Class 3 (30-50% Impairment)	Class 4 (55-100% Impairment)
The patient is asymptomatic and there is evidence of impaired left ventricular function from clinical examination or laboratory studies;	The patient is asymptomatic and there is evidence of impaired left ventricular function from physical examination or laboratory studies;	The patient develops symptoms of congestive heart failure on greater than ordinary daily activities (functional class 3) and there is evidence of abnormal ventricular function from physical examination or laboratory studies;	The patient is symptomatic during ordinary daily activities despite the appropriate use of dietary adjustment and drugs, and there is evidence of abnormal ventricular function from physical examination or laboratory studies;
AND	**AND**		
There is no evidence of congestive heart failure or cardiomegaly from physical examination or laboratory studies.	Moderate dietary adjustment or drug therapy is necessary for the patient to be free of symptoms and signs of congestive heart failure;	**AND**	**OR**
		Moderate dietary restriction or the use of drugs is necessary to minimize the patient's symptoms, or to prevent the appearance of signs of congestive heart failure or evidence of it by laboratory study;	There are persistent signs of congestive heart failure despite the use of dietary adjustment and drugs;
	OR		
	The patient has recovered from surgery for the treatment of hypertrophic cardiomyopathy and meets the criteria in (a) and (b) above.		**OR**
		OR	The patient has recovered from surgery for the treatment of hypertrophic cardiomyopathy and meets the above criteria.
		The patient has recovered from surgery for the treatment of hypertrophic cardiomyopathy and meets the criteria described above.	

Pericardial Heart Disease

Diseases of the pericardium include inflammation (1) associated with systemic illnesses such as lupus erythematosis; (2) in reaction to mechanical forces such at trauma or irradiation; (3) with no obvious cause (idiopathic pericarditis); and (4) associated with infections caused by viruses or bacteria. The pericardium may also be affected by tumors.

The most common pericardial disorder leading to permanent impairment is constrictive pericarditis. Surgical removal of the thickened pericardium may significantly reduce symptoms and improve the overall condition of the patient with constrictive pericarditis. It is imperative to allow sufficient time for the patient to recover from the surgery before assessing permanent impairment.

While pain and compromise of cardiac function because of tamponade can cause some impairment, they are rare as causes of permanent impairment, although chronic pericarditis with recurring episodes of tamponade, or pericardial disease related to tumors, may lead to permanent impairment. It is important to allow adequate time for resolution of an acute illness, and for medical or sugical therapy to be effective, before assessing permanent impairment.

Diagnosis of pericardial disease can be made by history, identifying a pericardial friction rub or early diastolic pericardial knock, by demonstrating pericardial effusion, thickening or calcification on an echocardiogram, or by hemodynamic or angiographic findings at cardiac catheterization.

Criteria for Evaluating Impairment Due to Pericardial Heart Disease

Class 1—Impairment of the Whole Person, 0-10%: A patient belongs in Class 1 when (a) the patient has no symptoms in the performance of ordinary daily activities or moderately heavy physical exertion, but does have evidence from either physical examination or laboratory studies of pericardial heart disease; AND (b) continuous treatment is not required, and there are no signs of cardiac enlargement, or of congestion of lungs or other organs; OR (c) in the patient who has had surgical removal of the pericardium, there are no adverse consequences of the surgical removal and the patient meets the criteria above.

Example: A 28-year-old male postal clerk experienced an acute, self-limited, febrile illness three months ago, associated with anterior chest pain and a pericardial friction rub, diagnosed as acute pericarditis. His echocardiogram at that time showed a small pleural effusion. The illness resolved with curtailed physical activities and the taking of aspirin over a period of three weeks. The patient returned to work and led a normal life without symptoms. Evaluation for the presence of tuberculosis and for systemic illnesses was negative.

Diagnosis: Acute benign idiopathic pericarditis.

Impairment: 0% impairment of the whole person.

Comment: Though it is possible that constrictive pericarditis might develop later, most patients such as the one described above would experience no long-term disorder that would increase the permanent impairment rating above 0%.

Class 2—Impairment of the Whole Person, 15-25%: A patient belongs in Class 2 when (a) the patient has no symptoms in the performance of ordinary daily activities, but does have evidence from either physical examination or laboratory studies of pericardial heart disease; BUT (b) moderate dietary adjustment or drugs are required to keep the patient free from symptoms and signs of congestive heart failure; OR (c) the patient has signs or laboratory evidence of cardiac chamber hypertrophy or dilation; OR (d) the patient has recovered from surgery to remove the pericardium and meets the criteria above.

Example: A 52-year-old man was treated for tuberculous pericarditis one year ago with good response to chemotherapy. The diagnosis was established by a pericardial biopsy demonstrating acid fast bacilli. After the initiation of therapy, the patient remained asymptomatic and fully active.

At present, the patient is comfortable and has no signs of congestive heart failure. The heart sounds are of good quality and there are no abnormal sounds or rubs.

The ECG shows flat T waves in leads 1, L, V5 and V6. The chest radiograph is normal. The echocardiogram shows some thickening of the pericardium posteriorly and normal ventricular and valvular function.

Diagnosis: Inactive tuberculous pericarditis.

Impairment: 15% impairment of the whole person.

Class 3—Impairment of the Whole Person, 30-50%: A patient belongs in Class 3 when (a) the patient has slight to moderate discomfort in the performance of greater than ordinary daily activities (functional class 2) despite dietary or drug therapy, and the patient has evidence from physical examination or laboratory studies of pericardial heart disease; AND (b) physical signs are present, or there is laboratory evidence of cardiac chamber enlargement or there is evidence of significant pericardial thickening and calcification; OR (c) the patient has recovered from surgery to remove the pericardium but continues to have the symptoms, signs and laboratory evidence described above.

Example: A 45-year-old real estate broker and school teacher had a pericardiectomy for constrictive pericarditis 10 years ago and had a good recovery. He continued to have some limitation of activity characterized by weakness and breathlessness on heavy physical exertion but worked regularly.

The venous pressure is normal and there is no edema. His blood pressure is normal and his pulse is regular on examination. There are no ventricular heaves, thrills, or taps. The first heart sound is normal and the second heart sound is diminished. There are no extra sounds or rubs.

The ECG demonstrates low voltage QRS and T waves in all leads. The chest radiograph shows considerable cardiomegaly and some calcification at the posterior aspect of the heart. The lung fields are clear. Echocardiography shows thickening of the pericardium and moderate diminution of right and left ventricular contraction; the left ventricular ejection fraction is 50%.

Diagnosis: Constrictive pericarditis with pericardiectomy.

Impairment: 30% impairment of the whole person.

Comment: If the patient had even more limitation of activities, a level of impairment beyond the 30% might be assigned.

Class 4—Impairment of the Whole Person, 55-100%: A patient belongs in Class 4 when (a) the patient has symptoms on performance of ordinary daily activities (functional class 3 or 4) in spite of using appropriate dietary restriction or drugs, and evidence from physical examination or laboratory studies of pericardial heart disease; AND (b) the patient has signs or laboratory evidence of congestion of the lungs or other organs; OR (c) the patient has recovered from surgery to remove the pericardium and continues to have the symptoms, signs, and laboratory evidence described above.

TABLE 11—IMPAIRMENT CLASSIFICATION FOR PERICARDIAL DISEASE

Class 1 (0-10% Impairment)	Class 2 (15-25% Impairment)	Class 3 (30-50% Impairment)	Class 4 (55-100% Impairment)
The patient has no symptoms in the performance of ordinary daily activities or moderately heavy physical exertion, but does have evidence from either physical examination or laboratory studies of pericardial heart disease;	The patient has no symptoms in the performance of ordinary daily activities, but does have evidence from either physical examination or laboratory studies of pericardial heart disease;	The patient has slight to moderate discomfort in the performance of greater than ordinary daily activities (functional class 2) despite dietary or drug therapy, and the patient has evidence from physical examination or laboratory studies of pericardial heart disease;	The patient has symptoms on performance of ordinary daily activities (functional class 3 or 4) in spite of using appropriate dietary restrictions or drugs, and evidence from physical examination or laboratory studies of pericardial heart disease;
AND	**BUT**	**AND**	**AND**
Continuous treatment is not required, and there are no signs of cardiac enlargement, or of congestion of lungs or other organs;	Moderate dietary adjustment or drugs are required to keep the patient free from symptoms and signs of congestive heart failure;	Physical signs are present, or there is laboratory evidence of cardiac chamber enlargement or there is evidence of significant pericardial thickening and calcification;	The patient has signs or laboratory evidence of congestion of the lungs or other organs;
OR	**OR**		**OR**
In the patient who has had surgical removal of the pericardium, there are no adverse consequences of the surgical removal and the patient meets the criteria above.	The patient has signs or laboratory evidence of cardiac chamber hypertrophy or dilation;	**OR**	The patient has recovered from surgery to remove the pericardium and continues to have symptoms, signs, and laboratory evidence described above.
	OR	The patient has recovered from surgery to remove the pericardium but continues to have the symptoms, signs and laboratory evidence described above.	
	The patient has recovered from surgery to remove the pericardium and meets the criteria above.		

Example: One year ago a 62-year-old man had profound ascites, peripheral edema, weight loss, and signs of pulmonary congestion that were attributed to constrictive pericarditis. Pericardiectomy relieved the severe ascites and peripheral edema. However, the man continued to have fatigue and breathlessness on ordinary daily activities and was unable because of weakness to climb a flight of stairs without resting. He was relatively comfortable when walking on the level and doing light household activities.

On examination, the man is comfortable. The neck veins are normal and there is no peripheral edema or ascites. Evidence of marked weight loss remains. There are no ventricular heaves, thrills, or taps in the precordium. The heart sounds are diminished, and there are no murmurs or extra sounds.

An ECG shows low voltage of the QRS and the T waves. The chest radiograph shows marked cardiomegaly and some distention of pulmonary vasculature in the upper lobes. The echocardiogram demonstrates reduction of ventricular function and left ventricular ejection fraction of 40%.

Diagnosis: Constrictive pericarditis with pericardiectomy.

Impairment: 75% impairment of the whole person.

Comment: If the patient had symptoms with minimal daily activities, or if he had signs of overt congestion at the time of evaluation, then the degree of impairment might be as high as 100%.

The criteria for impairment due to pericardial disease are found in Table 11.

Arrhythmias

Arrhythmias may occur in patients with structurally and functionally normal hearts or in patients with any type of organic heart disease. An arrhythmia is defined as one or more heart beats generated at a site other than the sinus node. An impulse that is generated in the sinus node but is not transmitted normally through the conducting system is considered an arrhythmia of the conduction defect type.

Arrhythmias tend to fluctuate remarkably in the frequency with which they occur. Thus, adequate documentation of the arrhythmia and estimation of the frequency with which it occurs must be made. The associated symptoms may be considerably different from the symptoms of other forms of heart disease. Arrhythmias may cause syncope, palpitation, dizziness, light headedness, chest heaviness, or shortness of breath, or combinations of these symptoms.

The degree of impairment from cardiac arrhythmias often will have to be combined with the degree of impairment due to an underlying heart disease; this combining should be done according to the Combined Values Chart. After instituting therapy for the arrhythmias, one should allow an appropriate amount of time to pass before estimating the extent of the permanent impairment.

Criteria for Evaluating Impairment Due to Arrhythmias

Class 1—Impairment of the Whole Person, 0-10%: A patient belongs in Class 1 when (a) the patient is asymptomatic during ordinary activities and a cardiac arrhythmia is documented by ECG; AND (b) there is no documentation of three or more consecutive ectopic beats or periods of asytole greater than 1.5 seconds, and both the atrial and ventricular rates are maintained between 50 and 100 beats per minute; AND (c) there is no evidence of organic heart disease.

Example: A 56-year-old man without symptoms had frequent premature beats during an annual physical examination. The remainder of the examination was normal. An ECG showed frequent premature complexes. Chest radiograph was normal.

Diagnosis: Atrial premature complexes.

Impairment: 0% impairment of the whole person.

Class 2—Impairment of the Whole Person, 15-25%: A patient belongs in Class 2 when (a) the patient is asymptomatic during ordinary daily activities and a cardiac arrhythmia is documented by ECG; AND (b) moderate dietary adjustment, or the use of drugs, or an artificial pacemaker, is required to prevent symptoms related to the cardiac arrhythmia; OR (c) the arrhythmia persists and there is organic heart disease.

Example 1: A 62-year-old man without symptoms during an annual examination had atrial fibrillation with an irregular ventricular response of about 85 beats per minute. The remainder of the examination was normal, including ECG, chest radiograph and echocardiogram.

Diagnosis: Atrial fibrillation.

Impairment: 15% impairment of the whole person.

Comment: If it were necessary for the patient to take digitalis to maintain the ventricular response between 50 and 100 per minute, the estimated impairment would be slightly greater.

Example 2: A 52-year-old plumber had recurring syncope a year ago and was treated with insertion of a permanent artificial pacemaker. After treatment, the patient felt well and continued to work.

On examination, the man appears well and shows no signs of congestive heart failure. His pulse is regular at 72 beats per minute, and blood pressure is 120/80 mm Hg. There are no ventricular heaves, thrills, or taps in the precordium. The heart sounds are of good quality and there are no murmurs.

The ECG shows complete capture of the heart by the artificial pacemaker running at 72 beats per minute. A rare premature ventricular beat is sensed by the pacemaker, and the pacemaker is properly inhibited.

Diagnosis: Adams-Stokes attacks in a patient with complete heart block, managed with a properly functioning artificial pacemaker.

Impairment: 20% impairment of the whole person.

Class 3—Impairment of the Whole Person, 30-50%: A patient belongs in Class 3 when (a) the patient has symptoms despite the use of dietary therapy or drugs or of an artificial pacemaker and a cardiac arrhythmia is documented with ECG; BUT (b) the patient is able to lead an active life and the symptoms due to the arrhythmia are limited to infrequent palpitations and episodes of light-headedness, or other symptoms of temporarily inadequate cardiac output.

Example: A 44-year-old airline ground crew member experienced recurrent episodes of a sensation of rapid heart action accompanied by light-headedness or "swimming" in the head. The episodes lasted five to fifteen minutes. While vagal-type maneuvers occasionally terminated an episode, usually they stopped for no obvious reason. During the episodes the patient felt weak and could not perform any type of physical activity. Usually he would lie down and try breathholding and other maneuvers. He never experienced frank syncope.

The patient underwent Holter monitoring and

was found to have atrial tachycardia of 155 beats per minute during one of the symptomatic episodes. The ECG showed typical patterns of the Wolff-Parkinson-White syndrome. The patient was started on quinidine sulfate 300 mg every 6 hours, but he continued to have an occasional episode. After the dose was increased to 400 mg, the patient became symptom-free. He was on that regimen for 8 months. His stools were loose, he had no severe diarrhea and he has experienced no abdominal pain.

Diagnosis: Wolff-Parkinson-White syndrome with atrial tachycardia, adequately controlled by quinidine.

Impairment: 30% impairment of the whole person.

Comment: If the patient were to continue to have palpitations, or even a rare episode associated with symptoms of inadequate cerebral perfusion, then the degree of estimated impairment might be as high as 50%.

Class 4—Impairment of the Whole Person, 55-100%: A patient belongs in Class 4 when (a) the patient has symptoms due to documented cardiac arrhythmia that are constant and interfere with ordinary daily activities (functional class 3 or 4); OR (b) the patient has frequent symptoms of inadequate cardiac output documented by ECG to be due to frequent episodes of cardiac arrhythmia; OR (c) the patient continues to have episodes of syncope that are either due to, or have a high probability of being related to, the arrhythmia. To fit into this category of impairment, the symptoms must be present despite the use of dietary therapy, drugs, or artificial pacemakers.

Example: A 28-year-old mother of three has experienced episodes of rapid heart action for over 10 years. These are associated with an uncomfortable retrosternal pressure, a fainting sensation, and general weakness. She has had several spells of unconsciousness, during which her husband has had to use cardiopulmonary resuscitation. During all episodes the tachyarrhythmia has ended spontaneously within 30 minutes, and external electrical conversion has not been necessary.

The patient has had a number of antiarrhythmic medications, and for the past 6 months she has been taking quinidine sulfate 300 mg every 6 hours, procainamide 750 mg every 4 hours, and propranalol 160 mg twice daily. This program had controlled the arrhythmia fairly well. However, the patient continues to have episodes about once a month, none associated with loss of consciousness. She has developed serological abnormalities characteristic of lupus erythematosis and has had occasional swelling of the small joints in the hands, which has responded to low doses of corticosteroids.

A thorough evaluation of the patient's cardiovascular system has revealed no evidence of valvular or myocardial disease. An interval ECG shows a normal pattern and rhythm; ECGs taken during the episodes of the palpitations have shown a rapid regular rhythm at about 220 to 250 beats per minute. Electrophysiological studies have demonstrated no abnormal conduction problems. Ventricular tachycardia has been easily induced, its pattern being similar to that recorded during one of her spontaneous episodes.

Diagnosis: Recurrent ventricular tachycardia.

Impairment: 90% impairment of the whole person.

Comment: The degree of impairment would depend upon how often the patient has episodes and the nature of the systemic symptoms that these episodes produced.

The criteria for permanent impairment due to arrhythmias are found in Table 12.

Vascular Diseases Affecting the Extremities

Permanent impairment due to peripheral vascular disorders most commonly results from (1) diseases of the arteries that reduce blood flow and lead to one or more of the following: intermittent claudication, pain at rest, minor trophic changes, ulceration, gangrene, loss of extremity, Raynaud's phenomenon; (2) diseases of the veins resulting in one or more of the following: pain, edema, induration, stasis dermatitis, ulceration; or (3) disorders of the lymphatics, leading to chronic lymphedema that may be complicated by recurrent acute infection.

The etiological factors most commonly encountered in patients with arterial disorders are arteriosclerosis, trauma, and inflammatory processes as with thromboangiitis obliterans. The venous system is most frequently affected by varicose veins, thrombosis and chronic deep venous insufficiency. Diseases of the lymphatic system that most frequently cause impairment are obstructive lesions of an inflammatory or neoplastic origin.

Prior to evaluation of impairment, a specific diagnosis of vascular disease should be established. The estimated amount of the impairment depends on the severity and extent of the lesions, rather than on the specific diagnosis.

TABLE 12—IMPAIRMENT CLASSIFICATION FOR CARDIAC ARRHYTHMIAS*

Class 1 (0-10% Impairment)	Class 2 (15-25% Impairment)	Class 3 (30-50% Impairment)	Class 4 (55-100% Impairment)
The patient is asymptomatic during ordinary activities and a cardiac arrhythmia is documented by ECG;	The patient is asymptomatic during ordinary daily activities and a cardiac arrhythmia is documented by ECG;	The patient has symptoms despite the use of dietary therapy or drugs or of an artificial pacemaker and a cardiac arrhythmia is documented with ECG;	The patient has symptoms due to documented cardiac arrhythmia that are constant and interfere with ordinary daily activities (functional class 3 or 4);
AND	**AND**	**BUT**	**OR**
There is no documentation of three or more consecutive ectopic beats or periods of asystole greater than 1.5 seconds, and both the atrial and ventricular rates are maintained between 50 and 100 beats per minute;	Moderate dietary adjustment, or the use of drugs, or an artificial pacemaker, is required to prevent symptoms related to the cardiac arrhythmia;	The patient is able to lead an active life and the symptoms due to the arrhythmia are limited to infrequent palpitations and episodes of light-headedness, or other symptoms of temporarily inadequate cardiac output.	The patient has frequent symptoms of inadequate cardiac output documented by ECG to be due to frequent episodes of cardiac arrhythmia;
AND	**OR**		**OR**
There is no evidence of organic heart disease.	The arrhythmia persists and there is organic heart disease.		The patient continues to have episodes of syncope that are either due to, or have a high probability of being related to, the arrhythmia. To fit into this category of impairment, the symptoms must be present despite the use of dietary therapy, drugs, or artificial pacemakers.

* If an arrhythmia is a result of organic heart disease, the arrhythmia should be evaluated separately and its impairment rating should be combined with the impairment rating for the organic heart disease using the Combined Values Chart.

When amputation due to peripheral vascular disease is involved, the percentage of permanent impairment due to the amputation is determined in accordance with the criteria discussed in Chapter 1. The percentage value due to amputation and that due to the peripheral vascular disease then are combined using the Combined Values Chart.

Criteria for Evaluating Impairment

Class 1—Impairment of the Whole Person, 0%: A patient belongs in Class 1 when (a) the patient experiences neither intermittent claudication nor pain at rest; AND (b) the patient experiences only transient edema; AND (c) on physical examination, not more than the following findings are present: loss of pulses; minimal loss of subcutaneous tissue of fingertips; calcification of arteries as detected by x-ray examination; asymptomatic dilation of arteries or of veins, not requiring surgery and not resulting in curtailment of activity; Raynaud's phenomenon that occurs with exposure to temperatures lower than 0°C (32°F) but is readily controlled by medication.

Example: A 27-year-old woman had ileofemoral phlebitis after childbirth. The pain in the leg subsided on medication that included anticoagulants, but for several months afterward the woman had to wear an elastic stocking to prevent moderate edema. At present the woman has a mild swelling of the ankles at the end of the day, which disappears by morning. She no longer uses the elastic support.

Diagnosis: Ileofemoral phlebitis.

Impairment: 0% impairment of the whole person.

Class 2—Impairment of the Whole Person, 5-20%: A patient belongs in Class 2 when (a) the patient experiences intermittent claudication on walking at least 100 yards at an average pace; OR (b) there is persistent edema of a moderate degree, incompletely controlled by elastic supports; OR (c) there is vascular damage as evidenced by a sign, such as that of a healed, painless stump of an amputated digit showing evidence of persistent vascular disease or of a healed ulcer; OR (d) Raynaud's phenomenon occurs on exposure to temperatures lower than 4°C (39°F), but is controlled by medication.

Example 1: Two years ago a 53-year-old man experienced sudden pain in the calf of his left leg while walking. For several months thereafter the left leg felt cooler than the right. The left superficial femoral artery was found to be occluded. During the past year he could walk only 200 yards before having pain, and stopping the walking gave relief. He had no other symptoms.

Diagnosis: Arteriosclerosis obliterans.

Impairment: 15% impairment of the whole person.

Example 2: Several years ago, three fingers of a woman's left hand became painful, cool, and alternately white and cyanotic. A while later, the woman's middle finger was injured and became infected and painful. The tip of the finger became necrotic, and therefore the distal phalanx was amputated. Recovery was uneventful, and the patient has experienced no progression of symptoms.

Diagnosis: Raynaud's phenomenon.

Impairment: 15% impairment due to Raynaud's phenomenon, and 5% impairment due to amputation of distal phalanx of middle finger, which combine to 19% impairment of the whole person.

Class 3—Impairment of the Whole Person, 25-45%: A patient belongs in Class 3 when (a) the patient experiences intermittent claudication on walking as few as 25 yards and no more than 100 yards at an average pace; OR (b) there is marked edema that is only partially controlled by elastic supports; OR (c) there is vascular damage as evidenced by a sign such as a healed amputation of two or more digits of one extremity, with evidence of persisting vascular disease or superficial ulceration; OR (d) Raynaud's phenomenon occurs on exposure to temperatures lower than 10°C (50°F), and it is only partially controlled by medication.

Example: A 45-year-old lumberjack, who had used a chain saw daily for more than 10 years, three to four years ago had symptoms of Raynaud's phenomenon of the right hand and fingers on exposure to temperatures lower than 10°C; he also had onset of a painful, nonhealing ulcer of the right index finger three months ago. Examination revealed normal wrist pulses but delayed return of color to the fingers of the right hand on releasing the clenched fist, while either radial or ulnar pulse was occluded manually at the wrist (Allen Test). Occlusion of the superficial and deep palmar arches of the right hand was confirmed by Doppler ultrasonic flow velocity testing and by plethysmography. The distal phalanx of the index finger was gangrenous and was amputated.

Diagnosis: Chronic occupational occlusive arterial disease of the hand.

TABLE 13—IMPAIRMENT CLASSIFICATION FOR PERIPHERAL VASCULAR DISEASE

Class 1 (0% Impairment)	Class 2 (5-20% Impairment)	Class 3 (25-45% Impairment)	Class 4 (50-75% Impairment)	Class 5 (80-95% Impairment)
The patient experiences neither intermittent claudication nor pain at rest; **AND** The patient experiences only transient edema; **AND** On physical examination, not more than the following findings are present: loss of pulses; minimal loss of subcutaneous tissue of fingertips; calcification of arteries as detected by radiographic examination; asymptomatic dilation of arteries or of veins, not requiring surgery and not resulting in curtailment of activity; Raynaud's phenomenon that occurs with exposure to temperatures lower than 0°C (32°F) but is readily controlled by medication.	The patient experiences intermittent claudication on walking at least 100 yards at an average pace; **OR** There is persistent edema of a moderate degree, incompletely controlled by elastic supports; **OR** There is vascular damage as evidenced by a sign, such as that of a healed, painless stump of an amputated digit showing evidence of persistent vascular disease, or of a healed ulcer; **OR** Raynaud's phenomenon occurs on exposure to temperatures lower than 4°C (39°F), but is controlled by medication.	The patient experiences intermittent claudication on walking as few as 25 yards and no more than 100 yards at an average pace; **OR** There is marked edema that is only partially controlled by elastic supports; **OR** There is vascular damage as evidenced by a sign such as a healed amputation of two or more digits of one extremity, with evidence of persisting vascular disease or superficial ulceration; **OR** Raynaud's phenomenon occurs on exposure to temperatures lower than 10°C (50°F), and it is only partially controlled by medication.	The patient experiences intermittent claudication on walking less than 25 yards, or the patient experiences intermittent pain at rest; **OR** The patient has marked edema that cannot be controlled by elastic supports; **OR** There is vascular damage as evidenced by signs such as an amputation at or above a wrist or an ankle, or amputation of two or more digits of two extremities with evidence of persistent vascular disease, or persistent widespread or deep ulceration involving one extremity; **OR** Raynaud's phenomenon occurs on exposure to temperatures lower than 15°C (59°F), and it is only partially controlled by medication.	The patient experiences severe and constant pain at rest; **OR** There is vascular damage as evidenced by signs such as amputations at or above the wrists or ankles of two extremities, or amputation of all digits of two or more extremities, with evidence of persistent vascular disease or of persistent, widespread, or deep ulceration involving two or more extremities; **OR** Raynaud's phenomenon occurs on exposure to temperatures lower than 20°C (68°F) and is poorly controlled by medication.

Impairment: 30% impairment due to occlusive arterial disease of the hand and Raynaud's phenomenon on exposure to temperatures lower than 10°C (50°F) and 6% impairment due to the amputation, which combine to give 34% impairment of the whole person.

Class 4—Impairment of the Whole Person, 50-75%: A patient belongs in Class 4 when (a) the patient experiences intermittent claudication on walking less than 25 yards, or the patient experiences intermittent pain at rest; OR (b) the patient has marked edema that cannot be controlled by elastic supports; OR (c) there is vascular damage as evidenced by signs such as an amputation at or above a wrist or an ankle, or amputation of two or more digits of two extremities with evidence of persistent vascular disease, or persistent widespread or deep ulceration involving one extremity; OR (d) Raynaud's phenomenon occurs on exposure to temperatures lower than 15°C (59°F), and it is only partially controlled by medication.

Example: A 48-year-old man had recurrent thrombophlebitis in both legs for several years. The left leg especially was affected. A year ago he had to reduce the length of time he could stand up in order to lessen the swelling and pain of a persisting deep ulcer. When on his feet, he needed full length elastic stockings, but extensive edema of the ankles and calves remained. He required long-term oral anticoagulant therapy to prevent recurrent thrombophlebitis.

Diagnosis: Recurrent thrombophlebitis with chronic, deep postphlebitic venous insufficiency.

Impairment: 50% impairment of the whole person.

Class 5—Impairment of the Whole Person, 80-95%: A patient belongs in Class 5 when (a) the patient experiences severe and constant pain at rest; OR (b) there is vascular damage as evidenced by signs such as amputations at or above the wrists or ankles of two extremities, or amputation of all digits of two or more extremities, with evidence of persistent vascular disease or of persistent, widespread, or deep ulceration involving two or more extremities; OR (c) Raynaud's phenomenon occurs on exposure to temperatures lower than 20°C (68°F) and is poorly controlled by medication. Edema alone should not be the basis for classification in Class 5.

Example: A 54-year-old man was shown to have thromboangiitis obliterans when he lost the great and second toes of the left foot, 10 years ago. At that time he underwent bilateral lumbar sympathectomy. He continued to smoke cigarettes against advice, and two years ago the left leg was amputated 3 inches below the knee.

Since then, the man's index and middle fingers on the right hand have been amputated. All sites of amputation have healed. There is an infection deep in the right foot, and there are signs of severe ischemia nearly to the knee. Further surgery is not deemed necessary at this time.

Diagnosis: Thromboangiitis obliterans.

Impairment: 85% impairment due to thromboangiitis obliterans, and 52% impairment due to past amputations, which combine to give 93% impairment of the whole person.

The criteria for permanent impairment due to peripheral vascular disease are found in Table 13.

References

1. American Heart Association Committee on Exercise: *Exercise Testing and Training of Individuals with Heart Disease or at High Risk for its Development.* Dallas, American Heart Association, 1973.

2. Sheffield LT, Roitman D: Stress testing methodology. *Progress in Cardiovascular Diseases* 1976; 19:33-49.

3. Fox SM III, Naughton JP, Haskell WL: Physical activity and the prevention of coronary heart disease. *Annals of Clinical Research* 1971; 3:404-432.

4. Bruce RA: Exercise testing for evaluation of ventricular functions. *N Engl J Med* 1977; 296:671-675.

Chapter 5

The Hematopoietic System

Introduction

The hematopoietic system deals with red cells, white cells, platelets and coagulation factors, and it includes the immune defense system. Cellular elements and proteins are manufactured in the bone marrow, lymph nodes, spleen and liver. Abnormalities may be quantitative, with too few or too many elements being produced, as in aplastic anemia and polycythemia, or they may be qualitative, with faulty production, as in congenital hemolytic anemia and hemophilia.

Hereditary defects frequently involve only a single cell line, as with the red cells in hereditary spherocytosis, or a single protein, as with factor VIII in hemophilia; acquired disorders are more likely to involve several cell lines, as with leukemia, or several proteins, as with disseminated intravascular coagulation. Neither quantitative nor qualitative disorders necessarily imply impairment, which depends on the severity of the defect and the mode of clinical expression.

Within this chapter, general reference is made to symptomatology and to limitations of the patient's daily activities. The physician should determine whether these are: (a) NONE—there are no complaints or evidence of disease, and usual activities of daily living can be performed; (b) MINIMAL—some signs or symptoms of disease are present, and there is some difficulty in performing the usual activities of daily living; (c) MODERATE—signs and symptoms of disease are present, and difficulty is experienced in performing the usual activities of daily living that require varying amounts of assistance from others; or (d) MARKED—signs and symptoms of disease are present, and assistance is needed in performing most to all activities of daily living.

Before using the information in this chapter, the reader is urged to consult the Preface to the Guides, which provides a general discussion of the purpose of the Guides, and of the situations in which they are useful; and discusses techniques for the evaluation of the patient and for report preparation.

Permanent Impairment Related to Anemia

The effects of chronic anemia on function depend upon the degree of compensatory response by the cardiovascular system. Regardless of the pathogenesis of the anemia, impairment is related to inability to deliver adequate oxygen to tissues. The heart compensates for the anemia by increasing cardiac output through an increase in heart rate, and there is further compensation through increased extraction of O_2 by the tissues, that is, an increased arteriovenous difference. Therefore, mild anemia with a hemoglobin level of about 10 gm/100 ml is associated with little impairment in a patient who has a normal cardiovascular system.

Greater degrees of anemia may be associated with increasing impairment that leads, in succession, to lack of stamina, fatigue on exertion, fatigue at rest, and finally, dyspnea at rest. Thus, there are no specific concentrations of hemoglobin that determine impairment in a given patient. Impairment is measured instead in terms of the limitations of cardiovascular response. Because anemia can be treated by transfusion, impairment may be lessened by that therapy.

Iron deficiency anemia and the megaloblastic anemias are usually reversible with proper management, and they would not feature impairment upon recovery. The same is true for many hemolytic anemias. An important exception is the patient with combined system disease, who has neurologic symptoms that become irreversible because proper therapy was given too late. Gait disturbance may render such an individual severely impaired. Persistent refractory anemia may cause impairment, regardless of etiology; the degree of impairment is related to the severity of the anemia and the need for transfusions.

Under the best of circumstances, with normal survival of tranfused red cells, the beneficial effects of transfusions last 6 to 8 weeks. In patients with hemolytic anemias due to serum factors, and in some patients who have been transfused many times, survival of transfused cells becomes shortened and transfusions must be repeated at shorter intervals of 1 to 5 weeks. As hemolysis becomes more severe, impairment increases.

Table 1 provides criteria for rating permanent impairment due to anemia.

Table 1
CRITERIA FOR EVALUATING PERMANENT IMPAIRMENT RELATED TO ANEMIA

Symptoms	Hemoglobin Level (gm/100 ml)	Transfusion Requirement	Impairment (%)
None	10-12	none	0
Minimal	8-10	none	30
Moderate-Marked	5-8*	2-3 units every 4-6 weeks	70
Moderate-Marked	5-8*	2-3 units every 2 weeks**	70-100

*Level before transfusion
**Implies hemolysis of transfused blood

Permanent Impairment Related to Polycythemia

Polycythemia vera is manifested by elevated hematocrit values above 52% in men and above 49% in women, and by red cell volumes above 36 ml/kg in men and above 32 ml/kg in women. Normal arterial oxygen tension, an enlarged spleen, slight elevation of the white cell and platelet counts, and increased leukocyte alkaline phosphatase are frequently seen. Erythrocytosis and increased red cell volume may be seen in subjects who do not have true polycythemia but who smoke more than two packs of cigarettes a day; increased carbon monoxide levels are characteristic of this so-called "smoker's polycythemia."

Polycythemia vera is usually well controlled by phlebotomy and/or the administration of radioactive phosphorus. Patients in remission on appropriate therapy have no impairment and may remain this way for many years. Eventually, myelofibrosis may develop. This is manifested by the gradual development of anemia in patients who are no longer being treated with phlebotomy or radioactive phosphorus; the spleen enlarges, the peripheral blood smear shows "tear-shaped" red cells, nucleated red cells and giant platelets, and there is a slight "shift to the left" in the white cell population.

Many patients with myelofibrosis complain of fatigue, lack of energy, low grade fever, and bone pain. Impairment may vary from *moderate* to *marked*, even in the absence of severe anemia. Most of these clinical findings are subjective, and it may be very difficult to assess objectively the degree of impairment. Weight loss, fever, perspiration, increasing serum lactic dehydrogenase (LDH), and increased reticulin and fibroblasts seen upon bone marrow biopsy may be of help in evaluation.

Currently, no therapy exists to relieve the symptoms of myelofibrosis. Transfusions may be needed for severe anemia. Patients who develop acute leukemia after years of polycythemia are, of course, totally impaired. This particular leukemia tends to be resistant to chemotherapy.

Permanent Impairment Related to White Blood Cell Diseases or Abnormalities

The primary function of the white blood cells (leukocytes) is to provide protection against invading organisms, foreign proteins and particles. Three separate white cell "families" interact to provide this protection. In addition to the cells in the circulation, each family has a fixed tissue component that not only provides the renewal or precursor pool, but also functions at fixed sites, such as the bone marrow, spleen, and lymph nodes. The white cell families are the granulocytes, lymphocytes, and monocytes-macrophages. Abnormalities in the white cell families are expressed both in terms of numbers and of alterations in function.

Granulocytes: The major function of the granulocytes is to protect against infection through the phagocytosis of invading organisms. Thus, granulocytes function primarily at the site of tissue invasion, and the observation or enumeration of granulocytes in the circulation is in reality a view of traffic to tissues. Survival of granulocytes in the circulation is brief, the half-life being approximately 6 hours. When granulocytes leave the circulation, they generally do not return. The granulocyte precursor pool is in the bone marrow, where a very large production capacity exists.

Granulocyte abnormalities of function are most commonly congenital, although acquired functional abnormalities may result from drugs and toxins. Defective granulocyte function is recognized by the occurrence of frequent infections. The evaluation of impairment under such circumstances is based on the type, frequency, and severity of the recurring infections. These may vary from furunculosis, which has no impact on functional capacity, to recurring septicemias with death. The variety of potential lesions makes a tight formula for impairment unworkable. In general, an affected individual will have a reasonably consistent pattern of infection that makes characterization on clinical grounds reliable.

Quantitative granulocyte abnormalities are of two different forms. The first is agranulocytosis, in which a loss of the granulocyte precursor pool or a markedly accelerated destruction of the granulocytes results in a reduction in circulating granulocytes. Since granulocytes in the circulation are really in transit to the tissues, there is normally a large excess or reserve of available granulocytes. Indeed, significant infections due to low numbers are uncommon, unless the circulating granulocytes are less than $500/\mu l$. Such decreases may be seen with anti-inflammatory and anti-thyroid drugs, anticonvulsants, toxins, Felty's syndrome, cancer therapy with ionizing radiation or drugs, and occasionally without recognizable cause. In the absence of reversibility, chronic neutropenia with counts below $500/\mu l$ is associated with substantially increased risk of infection, and impairment is defined in terms of the infections.

A second type of granulocyte impairment due to altered numbers is leukemic transformation. Both acute granulocytic leukemia and chronic granulocytic leukemia result in impaired function and limited life expectancy, even with currently available therapy. The evaluation of the degree of impairment is based upon the presence of symptoms and physical findings, the requirement for, and frequency of, therapy, and the ability to carry out the activities of daily living. In general, the granulocytic leukemias are less amenable to successful therapy than are the other forms of leukemia.

Lymphocytes: The major function of the lymphocytes is to provide humoral and cellular defense mechanisms. The circulating lymphocytes have their origin in lymphoid tissues, that is, the bone marrow, spleen, lymph nodes and thymus, and two-way traffic between the circulation and these tissues is known. Lymphocytes are cell types with heterogeneous functions.

Of the two major subgroups, the "T," or thymus-derived, lymphocytes, are primarily responsible for cellular immunity and are involved in delayed hypersensitivity reactions, tissue grafts, etc; the "B," or bursal-derived, lymphocytes, are primarily responsible for humoral immunity related to their production of immunoglobulins and biologically active kinins. Each of these subgroups is heterogeneous,

but the exact extent of the functional heterogeneity is not yet clear. Methods have not yet been developed to identify completely all subsets of these cells, such as memory cells, natural killer cells, and helper cells.

Lymphocyte abnormalities of function and number occur. In general, congenital abnormalities of function have been seen in the formation of parts of the lymphoid system. Acquired defects in function have been identified in Hodgkin's disease, and in connective tissue diseases, and following exposure to ionizing radiation. In general, the clinical clue to altered function is the presence of recurrent infections. Since the lymphoid precursor mass is large and extensive, and since there are not yet good methods of quantifying the subsets of lymphocytes, simple enumeration in the circulation has not been effective.

Determining failure of end-functions, such as generalized deficiencies of immunoglobulins or failure of delayed hypersensitivity reactions, has provided the best documentation of defective lymphocyte function or numbers. The evaluation of impaired function due to lymphopenia must be based upon the severity of the impairment because of recurrent infections. Finally, it should be emphasized that some diseases that are called "auto-immune" may be due to functionally altered or numerically predominant subsets of lymphocytes.

Abnormalities of lymphocyte numbers are associated with two forms of neoplastic transformation. The first form is the leukemias, either acute lymphocytic leukemia or chronic lymphocytic leukemia. The second form is the malignant lymphoid lesions that include Hodgkin's disease, malignant lymphoma, and mycosis fungoides. Evaluation of impairment due to these neoplasms follows the same parameters as expressed above.

Monocytes-Macrophages: The major function of the monocyte-macrophage family is to ingest foreign proteins, remove cellular debris and particulate material, and modulate immune responses. This functional unit of circulating monocytes and fixed macrophages, or "histiocytes," is structurally associated with endothelial cells and fibroblasts in the reticuloendothelial system. Recognition of this system is based primarily upon the phagocytic capacity of monocytes and macrophages.

Although these cells have their origin in bone marrow precursors, their traffic, potential for circulation and re-circulation, and mode of activation are not yet clearly understood. It appears that a true "reserve pool" does not exist, and that mature monocytes are released randomly to circulate for an approximate survival of 72 hours, at which time they enter the tissues to become part of the macrophage pool; however, their subsequent history is not known. This system is known to require a state of "enhanced cellular metabolism," which is called "activation," in order to function. Thus, impairment could result from either a functional defect or from altered numbers.

At present, knowledge of functional defects in the monocyte-macrophage system is limited, and the degree of impairment of the system can be correlated with the nature, type, and extent of infection.

A second abnormality of the system is seen in the lipid storage diseases (Niemann-Pick's, Fabry's, and Gaucher's diseases, and gangliosidosis type I or sea-blue histiocytosis), in which the macrophages become repositories for lipids, and cellular and organ hyperplasia occurs in the spleen, lymph nodes, bone marrow, and elsewhere. Impairment from these disorders depends upon the nature of the lipid and the rate of deposition.

Neoplastic transformation of the family occurs primarily as acute monocytic leukemia, a relatively rare form of acute leukemia. A more chronic variant, leukemic reticuloendotheliosis, is a recently recognized variant. The exact cell of origin is not clear, but the condition behaves as a form of chronic neoplastic transformation.

Criteria for Evaluating Permanent Impairment of the White Cell Systems

Class 1—Impairment of the Whole Person, 0-10%: A patient belongs in Class 1 when (a) there are symptoms or signs of leukocyte abnormality; AND (b) no or infrequent treatment is needed; AND (c) all or most of the activities of daily living can be performed.

Example 1: A 50-year-old man with no previous symptoms was admitted to the hospital after a work injury. Routine examination of the blood disclosed a leukocyte count of 18,000/cu mm, of which 82% were lymphocytes. Erythrocyte and platelet counts were within normal limits. Diagnosis was leukemia, but treatment was not given. The patient recovered from the injury and resumed normal activities.

Diagnosis—Chronic lymphocytic leukemia, stage O-I.

Impairment—0% impairment of the whole person.

Example 2: A healthy 21-year-old man suffered a ruptured spleen in an automobile crash. A splenectomy was performed. The postoperative course was uneventful. The patient returned to his normal activities of living.

Diagnosis—Splenectomy for splenic rupture.

Impairment—0% impairment of the whole person.

Class 2—Impairment of the Whole Person, 15-25%: A patient belongs in Class 2 when (a) there are symptoms and signs of leukocyte abnormality; AND (b) although continuous treatment is required, most of the activities of daily living can be performed.

Example: A 40-year-old man complained of pain and tightness in the left upper abdominal quadrant, and of an 8 lb weight loss. He was found to have splenomegaly, the spleen extending 12 cm below the costal margin, and a leukocyte count of 150,000/cu mm, with many myelocytes and progranulocytes. With treatment, the spleen regressed to 4 cm, and the leukocyte count fell to the normal range. On daily medication, the patient remains in remission. Periodic adjustment of the dosage, based on laboratory values, is required.

Diagnosis—Chronic granulocytic leukemia.

Impairment—15% impairment of the whole person.

Class 3—Impairment of the Whole Person, 30-50%: A patient belongs in Class 3 when (a) there are symptoms and signs of leukocyte abnormality; AND (b) continuous treatment is required; AND (c) there is interference with the performance of daily activities that requires occasional assistance from others.

Example 1: A boy, aged 6, was admitted to the hospital with bacterial pneumonia. He first had suffered from pneumonia at 6 months of age. Since then, he has had repeated hospitalizations for three episodes of bacterial meningitis, and several episodes of septicemia, purulent sinusitis, exudative pharyngitis, and otitis media. Between episodes of infections, he was asymptomatic and experienced few limitations in his daily activities; however, there was need for regular medical supervision, and intercurrent infections occurred frequently.

At present, there is absence of gamma globulin in the patient's electrophoretic pattern. He has a younger brother with decreased gamma globulin levels.

Diagnosis—Agammaglobulinemia.

Impairment—50% impairment of the whole person.

Example 2: A 55-year-old woman complained of weakness and dyspnea. The patient was found to have a hemoglobin of 7 gm/100 ml of blood, a hematocrit of 21%, leukocyte count of 82,000/cu mm, reticulocytes of 13%, and a positive Coombs' antiglobulin test. Although the anemia responded well to treatment, the patient developed progressive cachexia, extreme weight loss, profound weakness, and fever.

Diagnosis—Chronic lymphocytic leukemia with autoimmune hemolytic anemia.

Impairment—40% impairment due to the leukemia and 0% impairment due to the anemia controlled by therapy, which combine to give 40% impairment of the whole person.

Example 3: A 28-year-old man was found by lymph node biopsy to have Hodgkin's disease. Although he responded at first to treatment with ionizing radiation, recurrence of generalized lymphadenopathy below and above the diaphragm, pruritus, chills, and fever made necessary the employment of continuous chemotherapy. He became profoundly weak due to anemia that responded temporarily to drug treatment and transfusions.

Diagnosis—Hodgkin's disease, recurrent, active.

Impairment—50% impairment from the advanced Hodgkin's disease, which is to be combined with an appropriate value for impairment from anemia, to determine impairment of the whole person.

Class 4—Impairment of the Whole Person, 55-90%: A patient belongs in Class 4 when (a) there are symptoms and signs of leukocyte abnormality; AND (b) continuous treatment is required; AND (c) difficulty is experienced in the performance of the activities of daily living that requires continuous care from others.

Example: A 55-year-old man developed profound weakness, chills, night sweats, and fever. He had gingival hypertrophy, nosebleeds, splenomegaly such that the spleen extended 4 cm below the costal margin, and ecchymoses. Hematologic values included hemoglobin, 4 gm/100 ml; white blood cell count, 12,000/cu mm, with 80% blast forms; and platelet count, 18,000/cu mm. He responded partially to treatment but required continuous observation, frequent blood transfusions, and continuing assistance with the activities of daily living.

Diagnosis—Acute leukemia.

Impairment—90% impairment of the whole person.

Hemorrhagic Disorders and Platelets

There are several different types of bleeding disorders; in general, they may be categorized as hereditary or acquired, and as caused primarily by defects affecting platelets or blood clotting protein. Occasionally, inherited or acquired disorders, such as von Willebrand's disease and disseminated intravascular coagulation, may have both types of defects.

The initial tests useful for the diagnosis of platelet defects are the platelet count and the template bleeding time. A specific diagnosis requires further testing that involves platelet aggregation studies and various tests for the factor VIII complex.

The laboratory tests that are useful for the diagnosis of blood clotting disorders are the partial thromboplastin time, prothrombin time, thrombin time and fibrinogen level, and plasma protamine paracoagulation tests and tests for fibrin degradation products. Making a specific diagnosis frequently requires specific functional assays for clotting factor activity, and occasionally measurement of the protein level in the blood, usually by immunologic assay.

In the great majority of hereditary disorders, with the notable exception of von Willebrand's disease, the basic hemostatic defect remains unchanged throughout the patient's life. The latter disorder may be mild, with bleeding occurring only after trauma or surgery, or may be severe, with bleeding occurring spontaneously. The patients with severe hereditary blood coagulation disorders may require prophylactic therapy; this may help them participate in activities such as bicycling, that they might otherwise have to avoid because of the threat of trauma. Moreover, there are many patients who require frequent home treatment to control bleeding that interferes with their daily activities. Patients with such severe hereditary blood coagulation disorders would have 15% to 50% impairment of the whole person, depending on the frequency of treatment and the extent of interference with their normal activities.

Patients with an inherited bleeding disorder may develop complications from recurrent hemorrhage, such as joint dysfunction, and impairment from such a complication should be evaluated in accordance with criteria in the appropriate chapter of the Guides. Percentage values of several impairments should be combined using the Combined Values Chart.

Example: A 21-year-old man has severe factor VIII deficiency, or hemophilia A. He frequently has spontaneous bleeding into large joints and muscles that requires home therapy with intravenous factor VIII concentrate 2 times per week. In addition, because of past joint hemorrhages, he has significant chronic dysfunction of his left knee, right ankle and both elbows. The frequent joint and muscle hemorrhages and the need for continuous medical treatment interfere with his usual daily activities.

Diagnosis: Severe hemophilia A with permanent joint dysfunction secondary to recurrent bleeding.

Impairment: 40% impairment for the underlying bleeding disorder, combined using the Combined Values Chart with whatever percentages of impairment deemed appropriate for the joint dysfunction.

Acquired bleeding disorders may be due to platelet defects, blood clotting protein disorders, or a combination of both. Platelet defects may be due to either a decrease in the number of platelets or to an abnormality in their function. Since patients with these disorders need to avoid activities that may lead to trauma, or may need constant endocrine therapy to avoid heavy menstrual flow, a patient with a platelet disorder would have 0% to 10% impairment of the whole person. Complications that may ensue as a result of the blood platelet disorders, such as hemorrhage or thrombosis, should be evaluated in accordance with the criteria for evaluating impairment of the particular body system or organ affected, and should be combined using the Combined Values Chart with the rating for the blood platelet disorders.

Similarly, persons with autoimmune thrombocytopenia may require long-term immunosuppressive therapy, which in itself can lead to a variety of organ dysfunctions that hamper the activities of daily living. Complications resulting from therapy should be evaluated according to the criteria for evaluating impairment of the particular body system or organ affected, and combined with the rating for the appropriate blood platelet disorder, using the Combined Values Chart.

Acquired blood clotting defects are usually secondary to severe underlying conditions, such as chronic liver disease. But many patients with venous or arterial thromboembolic disease receive anticoagulant therapy with a vitamin K antagonist such as warfarin, and they need to avoid activities that might lead to trauma. In these patients there is a 0% to 10% impairment of the whole person.

Example: A 49-year-old woman has chronic idiopathic autoimmune thrombocytopenia of five years duration. She had a splenectomy, and during four of the past five years, she received corticosteroids and other immunosuppressive drugs. She is not on any medication, and her platelet count is 30,000/μl. Except for bruising easily, she has no significant bleeding problem. The patient also has severe osteoporosis and compression fractures of T12 and L1 vertebrae, and these cause her to have chronic low back pain that interferes significantly with her daily activities.

Diagnosis: Chronic idiopathic autoimmune thrombocytopenic purpura.

Impairment: 0% impairment for the underlying bleeding disorder, combined with whatever percentage of impairment is deemed appropriate for her back problem, to arrive at the estimated impairment of the whole person.

References

1. Cecil R: Hematology and hematopoietic disease, in Wyngaarden JB, Smith LH, Jr (eds): *Cecil's Textbook of Medicine*, ed 16. Philadelphia, WB Saunders Co, 1982, pp 824-1003.

2. Harrison TR: Disorders of the hematopoietic system, in Isselbacher KJ, Adams RD, Braunwald E, et al (eds): *Harrison's Principles of Internal Medicine*, ed 9. New York, McGraw Hill Book Co, 1980, pp 1514-1583.

3. Fishman MC, Hoffman AR, Klausner RD, et al: *Medicine*. Philadelphia, JB Lippencott, 1981, pp 333-378.

4. Wallerstein RO: Blood, in Krupp MA, Chatton MJ (ed): *Current Medical Diagnosis and Treatment*. Los Altos, California, Lange Medical Publication, 1982, pp 286-333.

Chapter 6

The Visual System

Introduction

The purpose of this chapter is to provide criteria for use in evaluating permanent impairment resulting from dysfunction of the visual system, which consists of the eyes, ocular adnexa and the visual pathways. A simplified method is provided for quantitating visual impairment, which can then be translated into impairment of the whole person.

Visual impairment in varying degrees occurs in the presence of a deviation from normal in one or more functions of the eye, including (1.) corrected visual acuity for objects at distance and near; (2.) visual fields; and (3.) ocular motility without diplopia. Evaluation of visual impairment is based on these three functions. Although they are not equally important, vision is imperfect without the coordinated function of all three.

Other ocular functions and disturbances are considered to the extent that they are reflected in one or more of the three coordinated functions. These other functions include color perception, adaptation to light and dark, accommodation, metamorphopsia, and binocular vision. Ocular disturbances include paresis of accommodation, iridoplegia, entropion, ectropion, epiphora, lagophthalmos and scarring. To the extent that any ocular disturbance causes impairment not reflected in visual acuity, visual fields, or ocular motility without diplopia, the impairment must be evaluated by the physician and be added to the impairment of the visual system.

One or more other ocular impairments, such as vitreous opacities, a non-reactive pupil, and light scattering disturbances of the cornea or other media, may be calculated as an additional 5% to 10% impairment of the involved eye. Permanent deformities of the orbit, scars, and cosmetic defects that may not alter ocular function should be considered individually as an additional factor that can cause up to 10% impairment of the whole person. If facial disfigurement due to scarring above the upper lip is evaluated using criteria in Chapter 7, then any overlapping percentage of impairment due to ocular scarring should be subtracted from the larger percentage.

The following equipment is necessary to test the functions of the eyes:

1. Visual acuity test charts for distance and near vision. For distance vision, the Snellen test chart with non-serif block letters* or numbers, or the illiterate E chart, or Landolt's broken-ring chart is desirable. For near vision, many charts are available, such as those with print similar to that of the Snellen chart, with Revised Jaeger Standard print, or with American point type notation for use at 35 cm or 14 inches.

2. A tangent screen, and a perimeter with standard radius of 30 cm to 33 cm, or with a larger radius, if an appropriately larger target is used.

3. Refraction equipment.

Before using the information in this chapter, the reader is urged to consult the Preface to the Guides, which provides a general discussion of the purpose of the Guides, and of the situations in which they are useful; and discusses techniques for the evaluation of the patient and for report preparation.

Criteria and Methods for Evaluating Permanent Impairment

Central Visual Acuity

Test chart illumination of at least 5 foot-candles is recommended to attain a distinct contrast of .85 or greater and a comfortable luminance of approximately 85 ± 5 candelas per square meter. The chart or reflecting surface should not be dirty or discolored. The far test distance simulates infinity at 6 m (20 ft) or at no less than 4 m (13 ft 1 in). The near test distance should be fixed at 35 cm (14 in) in keeping

---

*The 10 equally difficult letters (D, K, R, H, V, C, N, Z, S, O) of Louise Sloan are recommended for uniformity. Each letter subtends a visual angle of 5 minutes and a stroke width of 1 minute.

with the Revised Jaeger Standard. Adequate and comfortable illumination must be diffused onto the test card at a level about three times greater than that of usual room illumination. Measurements of visual acuity at near have less intertest reproducibility than those made of visual acuity at distance. Many occupational needs depend disproportionately on acuity of near vision.

Central vision should be measured and recorded for distance and for near objects, with and without wearing conventional spectacles. The use of contact lenses may further improve vision reduced by irregular astigmatism due to corneal injury or disease. However, practical problems related to fitting, expense, development of tolerance, and the fact that contact lenses are at times medically contraindicated, are sufficient at present to justify the recommendation that conventional ophthalmic lenses be used to obtain best corrected vision. In the absence of contraindications, if the patient is well adapted to contact lenses and wishes to wear them, correction by contact lenses is acceptable.

Visual acuity for distance should be recorded in the Snellen notation, using a fraction, in which the numerator is the test distance in feet or meters, and the denominator is the distance at which the smallest letter discriminated by the patient would subtend 5 minutes of arc, that is, the distance at which an eye with 20/20 vision would see that letter. The fraction notation is one of convenience that does not imply percentage of visual acuity. A similar Snellen notation using centimeters or inches, or a comparable Revised Jaeger Standard or American point-type notation, may be used in designating near visual acuity.

The notations for acuity of distance and near vision that appear in Table 1, with corresponding percentages of loss of central vision, are included only to indicate the basic values used in developing Table 2. Simply adding two percentages of loss, corresponding to appropriate notations for distance and near vision, does not provide the true percentage of loss of central vision. Rather, the functional loss of central vision is the mean of the two percentages.

Aphakia or pseudophakia is considered to be an additional visual impairment, and if it is present it is weighted by an additional 50% decrease in the value for remaining corrected central vision.

The procedure for determining loss of central vision in one eye is as follows:
1. Measure and record best central visual acuity for

distance and for near, with and without conventional corrective spectacles or contact lenses.

2. Consult Table 2 to calculate the additional loss of central vision that results from the presence of aphakia or pseudophakia.

Example: Without allowance for monocular aphakia, 14/70 for near vision and 20/200 for distance produce 83% loss of central vision. With allowance for monocular aphakia, which is applicable to corrected vision only, 14/70 for near vision and 20/200 for distance produce 91% loss of cental vision.

Table 1
VISUAL ACUITY NOTATIONS WITH CORRESPONDING PERCENTAGES OF LOSS OF CENTRAL VISION
FOR DISTANCE

English	Metric 6	Metric 4	% Loss
20/15	6/5	4/3	0
20/20	6/6	4/4	0
20/25	6/7.5	4/5	5
20/30	6/10	4/6	10
20/40	6/12	4/8	15
20/50	6/15	4/10	25
20/60	6/20	4/12	35
20/70	6/22	4/14	40
20/80	6/24	4/16	45
20/100	6/30	4/20	50
20/125	6/38	4/25	60
20/150	6/50	4/30	70
20/200	6/60	4/40	80
20/300	6/90	4/60	85
20/400	6/120	4/80	90
20/800	6/240	4/160	95

Snellen Notations span English, Metric 6, Metric 4.

FOR NEAR

Near Snellen Inches	Centimeters	Revised Jaeger Standard	American point-type	% Loss
14/14	35/35	1	3	0
14/18	35/45	2	4	0
14/21	35/53	3	5	5
14/24	35/60	4	6	7
14/28	35/70	5	7	10
14/35	35/88	6	8	50
14/40	35/100	7	9	55
14/45	35/113	8	10	60
14/60	35/150	9	11	80
14/70	35/175	10	12	85
14/80	35/200	11	13	87
14/88	35/220	12	14	90
14/112	35/280	13	21	95
14/140	35/350	14	23	98

TABLE 2—LOSS OF CENTRAL VISION* IN PERCENTAGE

Snellen Rating for Distance in Feet	14/14	14/18	14/21	14/24	14/28	14/35	14/40	14/45	14/60	14/70	14/80	14/88	14/112	14/140
20/15	0 / 50	0 / 50	3 / 52	4 / 52	5 / 53	25 / 63	27 / 64	30 / 65	40 / 70	43 / 72	44 / 72	45 / 73	48 / 74	49 / 75
20/20	0 / 50	0 / 50	3 / 52	4 / 52	5 / 53	25 / 63	27 / 64	30 / 65	40 / 70	43 / 72	44 / 72	46 / 73	48 / 74	49 / 75
20/25	3 / 52	3 / 52	5 / 53	6 / 53	8 / 54	28 / 64	30 / 65	33 / 67	43 / 72	45 / 73	46 / 73	48 / 74	50 / 75	52 / 76
20/30	5 / 53	5 / 53	8 / 54	9 / 54	10 / 55	30 / 65	32 / 66	35 / 68	45 / 73	48 / 74	49 / 74	50 / 75	53 / 76	54 / 77
20/40	8 / 54	8 / 54	10 / 55	11 / 56	13 / 57	33 / 67	35 / 68	38 / 69	48 / 74	50 / 75	51 / 76	53 / 77	55 / 78	57 / 79
20/50	13 / 57	13 / 57	15 / 58	16 / 58	18 / 59	38 / 69	40 / 70	43 / 72	53 / 77	55 / 78	56 / 78	58 / 79	60 / 80	62 / 81
20/60	16 / 58	16 / 58	18 / 59	20 / 60	22 / 61	41 / 70	44 / 72	46 / 73	56 / 78	59 / 79	60 / 80	61 / 81	64 / 82	65 / 83
20/80	20 / 60	20 / 60	23 / 62	24 / 62	25 / 63	45 / 73	47 / 74	50 / 75	60 / 80	63 / 82	64 / 82	65 / 83	68 / 84	69 / 85
20/100	25 / 63	25 / 63	28 / 64	29 / 64	30 / 65	50 / 75	52 / 76	55 / 78	65 / 83	68 / 84	69 / 84	70 / 85	73 / 87	74 / 87
20/125	30 / 65	30 / 65	33 / 67	34 / 67	35 / 68	55 / 78	57 / 79	60 / 80	70 / 85	73 / 87	74 / 87	75 / 88	78 / 89	79 / 90
20/150	34 / 67	34 / 67	37 / 68	38 / 69	39 / 70	59 / 80	61 / 81	64 / 82	74 / 87	77 / 88	78 / 89	79 / 90	82 / 91	83 / 92
20/200	40 / 70	40 / 70	43 / 72	44 / 72	45 / 73	65 / 83	67 / 84	70 / 85	80 / 90	83 / 91	84 / 92	85 / 93	88 / 94	89 / 95
20/300	43 / 72	43 / 72	45 / 73	46 / 73	48 / 74	68 / 84	70 / 85	73 / 87	83 / 91	85 / 93	86 / 93	88 / 94	90 / 95	92 / 96
20/400	45 / 73	45 / 73	48 / 74	49 / 74	50 / 75	70 / 85	72 / 86	75 / 88	85 / 93	88 / 94	89 / 94	90 / 95	93 / 97	94 / 97
20/800	48 / 74	48 / 74	50 / 75	51 / 76	53 / 77	73 / 87	75 / 88	78 / 89	88 / 94	90 / 95	91 / 96	93 / 97	95 / 98	97 / 99

*Upper figure = % loss of central vision without allowance for monocular aphakia; lower figure = % loss of central vision with allowance for monocular aphakia.

Visual Fields

The extent of the visual field is determined by using a perimetric method with a white target that subtends a 0.5 degree angle under illumination of 7 foot-candles. Such a target would be a white disc with a diameter of 3 mm, viewed at a distance of 33 cm. If the Goldmann 30 cm radius bowl perimeter is used, the III/4 e target in the kinetic mode should be employed.

The examiner should use a white disc that is 6 mm in diameter, at a distance of 33 cm, to test an aphakic patient whose eye is uncorrected, that is, not adapted to a contact lens or to an intraocular (pseudophake) implant or whose eye is fitted with aphakic spectacles. If in these instances a Goldmann bowl perimeter is used, the target should be IV/4 e in the kinetic mode. If the aphakic patient is well adapted to a contact lens or an

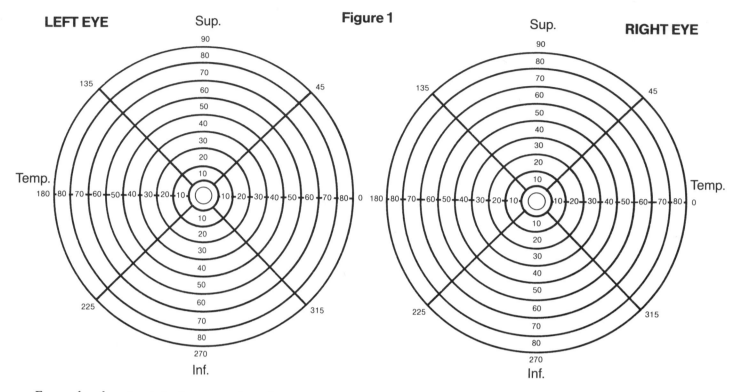

Example of perimetric charts used to plot extent or outline of visual field along the eight principal meridians that are separated by 45° intervals.

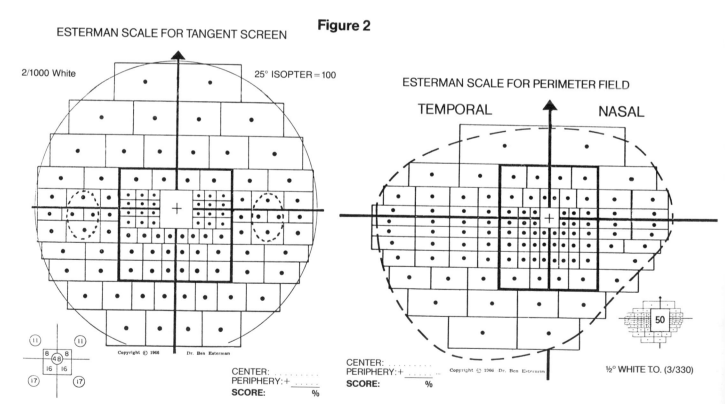

Esterman 100-unit scoring grids for (A) 1 meter tangent screen or auto plot (central 25° field) and for (B) standard arc or bowl perimeters; also for automated perimeters (full monocular field) (courtesy Dr. Benjamin Esterman).

intraocular lens, then the examiner should use the 3 mm diameter white target at 33 cm, or the Goldmann III/4 e target.

In testing, the object is brought from the periphery to the seeing area. At least two peripheral fields should be obtained that agree within 15 degrees in each meridian. The reliability of the patient's responses should be noted. The result is plotted on a visual field chart for each of the 8 principal meridians that are separated by 45 degree intervals (Figure 1).

Alternatively, the Esterman 100-unit Functional Relative Value Scale (Figure 2) may be used. A simple count of the dots printed within each of the 100 grid squares and falling within, but not touching, the field outline provides an immediate score in terms of percent of visual field present. Conversely, a simple count of the dots in each grid square falling on or outside the field outline gives the percentage of visual field loss for that eye.

The minimal normal extent of the visual field from the point of fixation is indicated in Table 3 below. The figures represent somewhat less than average normal performance, which allows for poor or delayed subjective responses or for unusual prominence of brow or nose.

The percentage of retained visual field in one eye is obtained by adding the number of degrees remaining along the 8 principal meridians given in Table 3 for the 3/330 white isopter, which normally sum to 500 degrees, and dividing the total by 5. Conversely, the percentage loss of visual field is obtained by adding the number of degrees lost along each of the 8 meridians, and dividing the total by 5. Where there is loss of a quadrant or of half a field, one-half of the value of each of the two

Table 3
MINIMAL NORMAL EXTENT OF VISUAL FIELD FROM POINT OF FIXATION

Direction of Vision	Degrees of Field
Temporally	85
Down temporally	85
Direct down	65
Down nasally	50
Nasally	60
Up nasally	55
Direct up	45
Up temporally	55
Total	500

boundary meridians should be added to the calculated loss. Visual field losses of other amounts and from other conditions can be calculated in a similar manner.

Although the extent of loss of visual fields cannot be determined accurately for a scotoma, an approximation can be obtained by subtracting the width of the scotoma from the peripheral visual field value at the same meridians. A similar estimation of visual field loss can be applied to enlargement of the blind spot, with the use of a 2 mm test object at a distance of 1 m from a tangent screen while the patient is wearing corrective lenses. For example, a general enlargement of the blind spot of 5 degrees would result in a visual field loss of $8x5\div5=8\%$ loss. Because a central scotoma directly affects central visual acuity, which is evaluated first, such visual field loss is not used again in the final calculation of visual loss.

Determining Loss of Visual Field
The following steps are taken to determine the loss of visual field:

1. Plot the extent of the visual fields on each of the eight principal meridians of a visual field chart (Figure 1).

2. (a) Determine the degrees lost by adding the degrees of visual field lost in each of the principal meridians (See Table 3).

(b) If half of a field is lost, include the two boundary meridians at a value equal to one half their total degrees value (Table 3).

3. Consult Table 4 to ascertain corresponding percentage of visual field loss.

4. Because the inferior visual field is occupationally more significant than the superior visual field, lower quadrant defects are weighted by an additional 5% loss of the visual field. Correspondingly, an inferior hemianopic loss is weighted by an additional 10% loss of the visual field.

5. When the Esterman scale is used, count the dots in each grid square that fall on or outside the field outline. This number is the final percent of visual field lost for that eye and automatically takes into account the additional weighting for lower visual field defects.

TABLE 4—LOSS OF VISUAL FIELD

Lost	Retained	% of Loss	Lost	Retained	% of Loss	Lost	Retained	% of Loss
0	500*	0	170	330	34	340	160	68
5	495	1	175	325	35	345	155	69
10	490	2	180	320	36	350	150	70
15	485	3	185	315	37	355	145	71
20	480	4	190	310	38	360	140	72
25	475	5	195	305	39	365	135	73
30	470	6	200	300	40	370	130	74
35	465	7	205	295	41	375	125	75
40	460	8	210	290	42	380	120	76
45	455	9	215	285	43	385	115	77
50	450	10	220	280	44	390	110	78
55	445	11	225	275	45	395	105	79
60	440	12	230	270	46	400	100	80
65	435	13	235	265	47	405	95	81
70	430	14	240	260	48	410	90	82
75	425	15	245	255	49	415	85	83
80	420	16	250	250	50	420	80	84
85	415	17	255	245	51	425	75	85
90	410	18	260	240	52	430	70	86
95	405	19	265	235	53	435	65	87
100	400	20	270	230	54	440	60	88
105	395	21	275	225	55	445	55	89
110	390	22	280	220	56	450	50	90
115	385	23	285	215	57	455	45	91
120	380	24	290	210	58	460	40	92
125	375	25	295	205	59	465	35	93
130	370	26	300	200	60	470	30	94
135	365	27	305	195	61	475	25	95
140	360	28	310	190	62	480	20	96
145	355	29	315	185	63	485	15	97
150	350	30	320	180	64	490	10	98
155	345	31	325	175	65	495	5	99
160	340	32	330	170	66	500	0	100
165	335	33	335	165	67			

*Or more.

Example 1: A patient has a concentric contraction to 30 degrees:

Loss	Degrees
Temporally	55
Down temporally	55
Direct down	35
Down nasally	20
Nasally	30
Up nasally	25
Direct up	15
Up temporally	25
Total loss	260

The loss of 260 degrees is equivalent to 52% loss of visual field.

Example 2: A patient has an entire temporal field loss.

Loss	Degrees
Up temporally	55
Temporally	85
Down temporally	85
Half of direct up and direct down (45 & 65)	55
Total loss	280

The loss of 280 degrees is equivalent to 56% loss of visual field.

Ocular Motility and Binocular Diplopia

Unless a patient has diplopia within 30 degrees of the center of fixation, the diplopia rarely causes significant visual impairment. An exception is diplopia upon looking downward. The extent of diplopia in the various directions of gaze is determined on an arc perimeter at 33 cm, or on a bowl perimeter at 30 cm, from the patient's eyes. Examination is made in each of the 8 major meridians by using a small test light, without adding colored lenses or correcting prisms.

To determine the impairment of ocular motility:

1. Plot the presence of diplopia along the meridians of a visual field chart.

2. Add the percentages for loss of ocular motility due to diplopia in the meridian of maximum impairment as indicated in Figure 3.

3. In the patient with one eye, individual evaluation of motility will be made by the examiner.

Example: Diplopia within the central 20 degrees is equivalent to 100% impairment of ocular motility.

Example: Diplopia on looking off center from 20 to 30 degrees is equivalent to 20% loss of ocular motility; 30 to 40 degrees is equivalent to 10% loss of ocular motility; for a total of 30% loss of ocular motility.

Figure 3

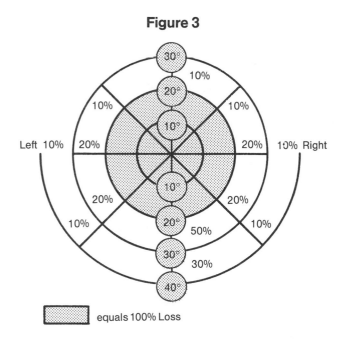

☐ equals 100% Loss

Percentage loss of ocular motility of one eye in diplopia fields.

Steps to Determine Impairment of the Whole Person Contributed by the Visual System

1. Calculate and record:
(a) percentage loss of central vision (CV) for each eye,
(b) percentage loss of visual field (VF) for each eye, and
(c) percentage loss of ocular motility (OM).

2. Using the Combined Values Chart combine the percentage loss of central vision with the percentage loss of visual field in each eye and record these values.

Example:
Right eye—
loss of central vision .56%
loss of visual field 32%
56% combined with 32% 70%

Left eye—
loss of central vision .46%
loss of visual field 32%
46% combined with 32% 63%

3. Again using the Combined Values Chart, combine the percentage loss of ocular motility with the combined value for central vision and visual field in the eye manifesting greater impairment. Disregard loss of ocular motility in other eye.

Example:
Right eye—
combined value of CV and VF 70%
loss of ocular motility 25%
70% combined with 25% 78%

4. Consult Table 5 to ascertain impairment of the visual system.

Example:
Impairment of right (worse) eye 78%
Impairment of left (better) eye 63%
Impairment of visual system 67%

Example:
Impairment of right (worse) eye 90-100%
Impairment of left (better) eye 0%
Impairment of visual system 25%

5. Consult Table 6 to ascertain the impairment of the whole person that is contributed by impairment of the visual system.

Example: 67% impairment of visual system is equivalent to 63% impairment of the whole person.

% IMPAIRMENT WORSE EYE

0	0
1	0	1
2	1	1	2
3	1	2	2	3
4	1	2	3	3	4
5	1	2	3	4	4	5
6	2	2	3	4	5	5	6
7	2	3	3	4	5	6	6	7
8	2	3	4	4	5	6	7	7	8
9	2	3	4	5	5	6	7	8	8	9
10	3	3	4	5	6	6	7	8	9	9	10
11	3	4	4	5	6	7	7	8	9	10	10	11
12	3	4	5	5	6	7	8	8	9	10	11	11	12
13	3	4	5	6	6	7	8	9	9	10	11	12	12	13
14	4	4	5	6	7	7	8	9	10	10	11	12	13	13	14
15	4	5	5	6	7	8	8	9	10	11	11	12	13	14	14	15
16	4	5	6	6	7	8	9	9	10	11	12	12	13	14	15	15	16
17	4	5	6	7	7	8	9	10	10	11	12	13	13	14	15	16	16	17
18	5	5	6	7	8	8	9	10	11	11	12	13	14	14	15	16	17	17	18
19	5	6	6	7	8	9	9	10	11	12	12	13	14	15	15	16	17	18	18	19
20	5	6	7	7	8	9	10	10	11	12	13	13	14	15	16	16	17	18	19	19	20
21	5	6	7	8	8	9	10	11	11	12	13	14	14	15	16	17	17	18	19	20	20	21
22	6	6	7	8	9	9	10	11	12	12	13	14	15	15	16	17	18	18	19	20	21	21	22
23	6	7	7	8	9	10	10	11	12	13	13	14	15	16	16	17	18	19	19	20	21	22	22	23
24	6	7	8	8	9	10	11	11	12	13	14	14	15	16	17	17	18	19	20	20	21	22	23	23	24
25	6	7	8	9	9	10	11	12	12	13	14	15	15	16	17	18	18	19	20	21	21	22	23	24	24	25
26	7	7	8	9	10	10	11	12	13	13	14	15	16	16	17	18	19	19	20	21	22	22	23	24	25	25	26
27	7	8	8	9	10	11	11	12	13	14	14	15	16	17	17	18	19	20	20	21	22	23	23	24	25	26	26	27
28	7	8	9	9	10	11	12	12	13	14	15	15	16	17	18	18	19	20	21	21	22	23	24	24	25	26	27	27	28
29	7	8	9	10	10	11	12	13	13	14	15	16	16	17	18	19	19	20	21	22	22	23	24	25	25	26	27	28	28	29
30	8	8	9	10	11	11	12	13	14	14	15	16	17	17	18	19	20	20	21	22	23	23	24	25	26	26	27	28	29	29	30
31	8	9	9	10	11	12	12	13	14	15	15	16	17	18	18	19	20	21	21	22	23	24	24	25	26	27	27	28	29	30	30	31
32	8	9	10	10	11	12	13	13	14	15	16	16	17	18	19	19	20	21	22	22	23	24	25	25	26	27	28	28	29	30	31	31	32
33	8	9	10	11	11	12	13	14	14	15	16	17	17	18	19	20	20	21	22	23	23	24	25	26	26	27	28	29	29	30	31	32	32	33
34	9	9	10	11	12	12	13	14	15	15	16	17	18	18	19	20	21	21	22	23	24	24	25	26	27	27	28	29	30	30	31	32	33	33	34
35	9	10	10	11	12	13	13	14	15	16	16	17	18	19	19	20	21	22	22	23	24	25	25	26	27	28	28	29	30	31	31	32	33	34	34	35
36	9	10	11	11	12	13	14	14	15	16	17	17	18	19	20	20	21	22	23	23	24	25	26	26	27	28	29	29	30	31	32	32	33	34	35	35	36
37	9	10	11	12	12	13	14	15	15	16	17	18	18	19	20	21	21	22	23	24	24	25	26	27	27	28	29	30	30	31	32	33	33	34	35	36	36	37
38	10	10	11	12	13	13	14	15	16	16	17	18	19	19	20	21	22	22	23	24	25	25	26	27	28	28	29	30	31	31	32	33	34	34	35	36	37	37	38
39	10	11	11	12	13	14	14	15	16	17	17	18	19	20	20	21	22	23	23	24	25	26	26	27	28	29	29	30	31	32	32	33	34	35	35	36	37	38	38	39
40	10	11	12	12	13	14	15	15	16	17	18	18	19	20	21	21	22	23	24	24	25	26	27	27	28	29	30	30	31	32	33	33	34	35	36	36	37	38	39	39	40
41	10	11	12	13	13	14	15	16	16	17	18	19	19	20	21	22	22	23	24	25	25	26	27	28	28	29	30	31	31	32	33	34	34	35	36	37	37	38	39	40	40	41
42	11	11	12	13	14	14	15	16	17	17	18	19	20	20	21	22	23	23	24	25	26	26	27	28	29	29	30	31	32	32	33	34	35	35	36	37	38	38	39	40	41	41	42
43	11	12	12	13	14	15	15	16	17	18	18	19	20	21	21	22	23	24	24	25	26	27	27	28	29	30	30	31	32	33	33	34	35	36	36	37	38	39	39	40	41	42	42	43
44	11	12	13	13	14	15	16	16	17	18	19	19	20	21	22	22	23	24	25	25	26	27	28	28	29	30	31	31	32	33	34	34	35	36	37	37	38	39	40	40	41	42	43	43	44
45	11	12	13	14	14	15	16	17	17	18	19	20	20	21	22	23	23	24	25	26	26	27	28	29	29	30	31	32	32	33	34	35	35	36	37	38	38	39	40	41	41	42	43	44	44	45
46	12	12	13	14	15	15	16	17	18	18	19	20	21	21	22	23	24	24	25	26	27	27	28	29	30	30	31	32	33	33	34	35	36	36	37	38	39	39	40	41	42	42	43	44	45	45	46
47	12	13	13	14	15	16	16	17	18	19	19	20	21	22	22	23	24	25	25	26	27	28	28	29	30	31	31	32	33	34	34	35	36	37	37	38	39	40	40	41	42	43	43	44	45	46	46	47
48	12	13	14	14	15	16	17	17	18	19	20	20	21	22	23	23	24	25	26	26	27	28	29	29	30	31	32	32	33	34	35	35	36	37	38	38	39	40	41	41	42	43	44	44	45	46	47	47	48
49	12	13	14	15	15	16	17	18	18	19	20	21	21	22	23	24	24	25	26	27	27	28	29	30	30	31	32	33	33	34	35	36	36	37	38	39	39	40	41	42	42	43	44	45	45	46	47	48	48	49
	0	1	2	3	4	**5**	6	7	8	9	**10**	11	12	13	14	**15**	16	17	18	19	**20**	21	22	23	24	**25**	26	27	28	29	**30**	31	32	33	34	**35**	36	37	38	39	**40**	41	42	43	44	**45**	46	47	48	49

TABLE 5—VISUAL SYSTEM

The values in this table are based on the following formula:

$$\frac{3 \times \text{better eye value} + \text{worse eye value}}{4} = \text{impairment of visual system.}$$

The guides to the table are percentage impairment values for each eye. The percentage for the worse eye is read at the side of the table. The percentage for the better eye is read at the bottom of the table. At the intersection of the column for the worse eye and the column for the better eye is the impairment of visual system value.

For example, when there is 60% impairment of one eye and 30% impairment of the other eye, read down the side of the table until you come to the larger value (60%). Then follow across the row until it is intersected by the column headed by 30% at the bottom of the page. At the intersection of these two columns is printed the number 38. The number (38) represents the percentage impairment of the visual system when there is 60% impairment of one eye and 30% impairment of the other eye.

If bilateral aphakia is present and corrected central vision has been used in evaluation, impairment of visual system is increased 25%. For example, a 38% impairment would be increased to 38% + (25%) (38%) = 48%

	0	1	2	3	4	5	6	7	8	9	10	11	12	13	14	15	16	17	18	19	20	21	22	23	24	25	26	27	28	29	30	31	32	33	34	35	36	37	38	39	40	41	42	43	44	45	46	47	48	49	
50	13	13	14	15	16	16	17	18	19	19	20	21	22	22	23	24	25	25	26	27	28	28	29	30	31	31	32	33	34	34	35	36	37	37	38	39	40	40	41	42	43	43	44	45	46	46	47	48	49	49	**50**
51	13	14	14	15	16	17	17	18	19	20	20	21	22	23	23	24	25	26	26	27	28	29	29	30	31	32	32	33	34	35	35	36	37	38	38	39	40	41	41	42	43	44	44	45	46	47	47	48	49	50	51
52	13	14	15	15	16	17	18	18	19	20	21	21	22	23	24	24	25	26	27	27	28	29	30	30	31	32	33	33	34	35	36	36	37	38	39	39	40	41	42	42	43	44	45	45	46	47	48	48	49	50	52
53	13	14	15	16	16	17	18	19	19	20	21	22	22	23	24	25	25	26	27	28	28	29	30	31	31	32	33	34	34	35	36	37	37	38	39	40	40	41	42	43	43	44	45	46	46	47	48	49	49	50	53
54	14	14	15	16	17	17	18	19	20	20	21	22	23	23	24	25	26	26	27	28	29	29	30	31	32	32	33	34	35	35	36	37	38	38	39	40	41	41	42	43	44	44	45	46	47	47	48	49	50	50	54
55	14	15	15	16	17	18	18	19	20	21	21	22	23	24	24	25	26	27	27	28	29	30	30	31	32	33	33	34	35	36	36	37	38	39	39	40	41	42	42	43	44	45	45	46	47	48	48	49	50	51	**55**
56	14	15	16	16	17	18	19	19	20	21	22	22	23	24	25	25	26	27	28	28	29	30	31	31	32	33	34	34	35	36	37	37	38	39	40	40	41	42	43	43	44	45	46	46	47	48	49	49	50	51	56
57	14	15	16	17	17	18	19	20	20	21	22	23	23	24	25	26	26	27	28	29	29	30	31	32	32	33	34	35	35	36	37	38	38	39	40	41	41	42	43	44	44	45	46	47	47	48	49	50	50	51	57
58	15	15	16	17	18	18	19	20	21	21	22	23	24	24	25	26	27	27	28	29	30	30	31	32	33	33	34	35	36	36	37	38	39	39	40	41	42	42	43	44	45	45	46	47	48	48	49	50	51	51	58
59	15	16	16	17	18	19	19	20	21	22	22	23	24	25	25	26	27	28	28	29	30	31	31	32	33	34	34	35	36	37	37	38	39	40	40	41	42	43	43	44	45	46	46	47	48	49	49	50	51	52	59
60	15	16	17	17	18	19	20	20	21	22	23	23	24	25	26	26	27	28	29	29	30	31	32	32	33	34	35	35	36	37	38	38	39	40	41	41	42	43	44	44	45	46	47	47	48	49	50	50	51	52	**60**
61	15	16	17	18	18	19	20	21	21	22	23	24	24	25	26	27	27	28	29	30	30	31	32	33	33	34	35	36	36	37	38	39	39	40	41	42	42	43	44	45	45	46	47	48	48	49	50	51	51	52	61
62	16	16	17	18	19	19	20	21	22	22	23	24	25	25	26	27	28	28	29	30	31	31	32	33	34	34	35	36	37	37	38	39	40	40	41	42	43	43	44	45	46	46	47	48	49	49	50	51	52	52	62
63	16	17	17	18	19	20	20	21	22	23	23	24	25	26	26	27	28	29	29	30	31	32	32	33	34	35	35	36	37	38	38	39	40	41	41	42	43	44	44	45	46	47	47	48	49	50	50	51	52	53	63
64	16	17	18	18	19	20	21	21	22	23	24	24	25	26	27	27	28	29	30	30	31	32	33	33	34	35	36	36	37	38	39	39	40	41	42	42	43	44	45	45	46	47	48	48	49	50	51	51	52	53	64
65	16	17	18	19	19	20	21	22	22	23	24	25	25	26	27	28	28	29	30	31	31	32	33	34	34	35	36	37	37	38	39	40	40	41	42	43	43	44	45	46	46	47	48	49	49	50	51	52	52	53	**65**
66	17	17	18	19	20	20	21	22	23	23	24	25	26	26	27	28	29	29	30	31	32	32	33	34	35	35	36	37	38	38	39	40	41	41	42	43	44	44	45	46	47	47	48	49	50	50	51	52	53	53	66
67	17	18	18	19	20	21	21	22	23	24	24	25	26	27	27	28	29	30	30	31	32	33	33	34	35	36	36	37	38	39	39	40	41	42	42	43	44	45	45	46	47	48	48	49	50	51	51	52	53	54	67
68	17	18	19	19	20	21	22	22	23	24	25	25	26	27	28	28	29	30	31	31	32	33	34	34	35	36	37	37	38	39	40	40	41	42	43	43	44	45	46	46	47	48	49	49	50	51	52	52	53	54	68
69	17	18	19	20	20	21	22	23	23	24	25	26	26	27	28	29	29	30	31	32	32	33	34	35	35	36	37	38	38	39	40	41	41	42	43	44	44	45	46	47	47	48	49	50	50	51	52	53	53	54	69
70	18	18	19	20	21	21	22	23	24	24	25	26	27	27	28	29	30	30	31	32	33	33	34	35	36	36	37	38	39	39	40	41	42	42	43	44	45	45	46	47	48	48	49	50	51	51	52	53	54	54	**70**
71	18	19	19	20	21	22	22	23	24	25	25	26	27	28	28	29	30	31	31	32	33	34	34	35	36	37	37	38	39	40	40	41	42	43	43	44	45	46	46	47	48	49	49	50	51	52	52	53	54	55	71
72	18	19	20	20	21	22	23	23	24	25	26	26	27	28	29	29	30	31	32	32	33	34	35	35	36	37	38	38	39	40	41	41	42	43	44	44	45	46	47	47	48	49	50	50	51	52	53	53	54	55	72
73	18	19	20	21	21	22	23	24	24	25	26	27	27	28	29	30	30	31	32	33	33	34	35	36	36	37	38	39	39	40	41	42	42	43	44	45	45	46	47	48	48	49	50	51	51	52	53	54	54	55	73
74	19	19	20	21	22	22	23	24	25	25	26	27	28	28	29	30	31	31	32	33	34	34	35	36	37	37	38	39	40	40	41	42	43	43	44	45	46	46	47	48	49	49	50	51	52	52	53	54	55	55	74
75	19	20	20	21	22	23	23	24	25	26	26	27	28	29	29	30	31	32	32	33	34	35	35	36	37	38	38	39	40	41	41	42	43	44	44	45	46	47	47	48	49	50	50	51	52	53	53	54	55	56	**75**
76	19	20	21	21	22	23	24	24	25	26	27	27	28	29	30	30	31	32	33	33	34	35	36	36	37	38	39	39	40	41	42	42	43	44	45	45	46	47	48	48	49	50	51	51	52	53	54	54	55	56	76
77	19	20	21	22	22	23	24	25	25	26	27	28	28	29	30	31	31	32	33	34	34	35	36	37	37	38	39	40	40	41	42	43	43	44	45	46	46	47	48	49	49	50	51	52	52	53	54	55	55	56	77
78	20	20	21	22	23	23	24	25	26	26	27	28	29	29	30	31	32	32	33	34	35	35	36	37	38	38	39	40	41	41	42	43	44	44	45	46	47	47	48	49	50	50	51	52	53	53	54	55	56	56	78
79	20	21	21	22	23	24	24	25	26	27	27	28	29	30	30	31	32	33	33	34	35	36	36	37	38	39	39	40	41	42	42	43	44	45	45	46	47	48	48	49	50	51	51	52	53	54	54	55	56	57	79
80	20	21	22	22	23	24	25	25	26	27	28	28	29	30	31	31	32	33	34	34	35	36	37	37	38	39	40	40	41	42	43	43	44	45	46	46	47	48	49	49	50	51	52	52	53	54	55	55	56	57	**80**
81	20	21	22	23	23	24	25	26	26	27	28	29	29	30	31	32	32	33	34	35	35	36	37	38	38	39	40	41	41	42	43	44	44	45	46	47	47	48	49	50	50	51	52	53	53	54	55	56	56	57	81
82	21	21	22	23	24	24	25	26	27	27	28	29	30	30	31	32	33	33	34	35	36	36	37	38	39	39	40	41	42	42	43	44	45	45	46	47	48	48	49	50	51	51	52	53	54	54	55	56	57	57	82
83	21	22	22	23	24	25	25	26	27	28	28	29	30	31	31	32	33	34	34	35	36	37	37	38	39	40	40	41	42	43	43	44	45	46	46	47	48	49	49	50	51	52	52	53	54	55	55	56	57	58	83
84	21	22	23	23	24	25	26	26	27	28	29	29	30	31	32	32	33	34	35	35	36	37	38	38	39	40	41	41	42	43	44	44	45	46	47	47	48	49	50	50	51	52	53	53	54	55	56	56	57	58	84
85	21	22	23	24	24	25	26	27	27	28	29	30	30	31	32	33	33	34	35	36	36	37	38	39	39	40	41	42	42	43	44	45	45	46	47	48	48	49	50	51	51	52	53	54	54	55	56	57	57	58	**85**
86	22	22	23	24	25	25	26	27	28	28	29	30	31	31	32	33	34	34	35	36	37	37	38	39	40	40	41	42	43	43	44	45	46	46	47	48	49	49	50	51	52	52	53	54	55	55	56	57	58	58	86
87	22	23	23	24	25	26	26	27	28	29	29	30	31	32	32	33	34	35	35	36	37	38	38	39	40	41	41	42	43	44	44	45	46	47	47	48	49	50	50	51	52	53	53	54	55	56	56	57	58	59	87
88	22	23	24	24	25	26	27	27	28	29	30	30	31	32	33	33	34	35	36	36	37	38	39	39	40	41	42	42	43	44	45	45	46	47	48	48	49	50	51	51	52	53	54	54	55	56	57	57	58	59	88
89	22	23	24	25	25	26	27	28	28	29	30	31	31	32	33	34	34	35	36	37	37	38	39	40	40	41	42	43	43	44	45	46	46	47	48	49	49	50	51	52	52	53	54	55	55	56	57	58	58	59	89
90	23	23	24	25	26	26	27	28	29	29	30	31	32	32	33	34	35	35	36	37	38	38	39	40	41	41	42	43	44	44	45	46	47	47	48	49	50	50	51	52	53	53	54	55	56	56	57	58	59	59	**90**
91	23	24	24	25	26	27	27	28	29	30	30	31	32	33	33	34	35	36	36	37	38	39	39	40	41	42	42	43	44	45	45	46	47	48	48	49	50	51	51	52	53	54	54	55	56	57	57	58	59	60	91
92	23	24	25	25	26	27	28	28	29	30	31	31	32	33	34	34	35	36	37	37	38	39	40	40	41	42	43	43	44	45	46	46	47	48	49	49	50	51	52	52	53	54	55	55	56	57	58	58	59	60	92
93	23	24	25	26	26	27	28	29	29	30	31	32	32	33	34	35	35	36	37	38	38	39	40	41	41	42	43	44	44	45	46	47	47	48	49	50	50	51	52	53	53	54	55	56	56	57	58	59	59	60	93
94	24	24	25	26	27	27	28	29	30	30	31	32	33	33	34	35	36	36	37	38	39	39	40	41	42	42	43	44	45	45	46	47	48	48	49	50	51	51	52	53	54	54	55	56	57	57	58	59	60	60	94
95	24	25	25	26	27	28	28	29	30	31	31	32	33	34	34	35	36	37	37	38	39	40	40	41	42	43	43	44	45	46	46	47	48	49	49	50	51	52	52	53	54	55	55	56	57	58	58	59	60	61	**95**
96	24	25	26	26	27	28	29	29	30	31	32	32	33	34	35	35	36	37	38	38	39	40	41	41	42	43	44	44	45	46	47	47	48	49	50	50	51	52	53	53	54	55	56	56	57	58	59	59	60	61	96
97	24	25	26	27	27	28	29	30	30	31	32	33	33	34	35	36	36	37	38	39	39	40	41	42	42	43	44	45	45	46	47	48	48	49	50	51	51	52	53	54	54	55	56	57	57	58	59	60	60	61	97
98	25	25	26	27	28	28	29	30	31	31	32	33	34	34	35	36	37	37	38	39	40	40	41	42	43	43	44	45	46	46	47	48	49.49		50	51	52	52	53	54	55	55	56	57	58	58	59	60	61	61	98
99	25	26	26	27	28	29	29	30	31	32	32	33	34	35	35	36	37	38	38	39	40	41	41	42	43	44	44	45	46	47	47	48	49	50	50	51	52	53	53	54	55	56	56	57	58	59	59	60	61	62	99
100	25	26	27	27	28	29	30	30	31	32	33	33	34	35	36	36	37	38	39	39	40	41	42	42	43	44	45	45	46	47	48	48	49	50	51	51	52	53	54	54	55	56	57	57	58	59	60	60	61	62	**100**
	0	1	2	3	4	**5**	6	7	8	9	**10**	11	12	13	14	**15**	16	17	18	19	**20**	21	22	23	24	**25**	26	27	28	29	**30**	31	32	33	34	**35**	36	37	38	39	**40**	41	42	43	44	**45**	46	47	48	49	

% IMPAIRMENT BETTER EYE

% IMPAIRMENT WORSE EYE

50	50																																																		
51	50	51																																																	
52	51	51	52																																																
53	51	52	52	53																																														
54	51	52	53	53	54																																													
55	51	52	53	54	54	55																																												
56	52	52	53	54	55	55	56																																											
57	52	53	53	54	55	56	56	57																																										
58	52	53	54	54	55	56	57	57	58																																									
59	52	53	54	55	55	56	57	58	58	59																																								
60	53	53	54	55	56	56	57	58	59	59	60																																							
61	53	54	54	55	56	57	57	58	59	60	60	61																																						
62	53	54	55	55	56	57	58	58	59	60	61	61	62																																					
63	53	54	55	56	56	57	58	59	59	60	61	62	62	63																																				
64	54	54	55	56	57	57	58	59	60	60	61	62	63	63	64																																			
65	54	55	55	56	57	58	58	59	60	61	61	62	63	64	64	65																																		
66	54	55	56	56	57	58	59	59	60	61	62	62	63	64	65	65	66																																	
67	54	55	56	57	57	58	59	60	60	61	62	63	63	64	65	66	66	67																																
68	55	55	56	57	58	58	59	60	61	61	62	63	64	64	65	66	67	67	68																															
69	55	56	56	57	58	59	59	60	61	62	62	63	64	65	65	66	67	68	68	69																														
70	55	56	57	57	58	59	60	60	61	62	63	63	64	65	66	66	67	68	69	69	70																													
71	55	56	57	58	58	59	60	61	61	62	63	64	64	65	66	67	67	68	69	70	70	71																												
72	56	56	57	58	59	59	60	61	62	62	63	64	65	65	66	67	68	68	69	70	71	71	72																											
73	56	57	57	58	59	60	60	61	62	63	63	64	65	66	66	67	68	69	69	70	71	72	72	73																										
74	56	57	58	58	59	60	61	61	62	63	64	64	65	66	67	67	68	69	70	70	71	72	73	73	74																									
75	56	57	58	59	59	60	61	62	62	63	64	65	65	66	67	68	68	69	70	71	71	72	73	74	74	75																								
76	57	57	58	59	60	60	61	62	63	63	64	65	66	66	67	68	69	69	70	71	72	72	73	74	75	75	76																							
77	57	58	58	59	60	61	61	62	63	64	64	65	66	67	67	68	69	70	70	71	72	73	73	74	75	76	76	77																						
78	57	58	59	59	60	61	62	62	63	64	65	65	66	67	68	68	69	70	71	71	72	73	74	74	75	76	77	77	78																					
79	57	58	59	60	60	61	62	63	63	64	65	66	66	67	68	69	69	70	71	72	72	73	74	75	75	76	77	78	78	79																				
80	58	58	59	60	61	61	62	63	64	64	65	66	67	67	68	69	70	70	71	72	73	73	74	75	76	76	77	78	79	79	80																			
81	58	59	59	60	61	62	62	63	64	65	65	66	67	68	68	69	70	71	71	72	73	74	74	75	76	77	77	78	79	80	80	81																		
82	58	59	60	60	61	62	63	63	64	65	66	66	67	68	69	69	70	71	72	72	73	74	75	75	76	77	78	78	79	80	81	81	82																	
83	58	59	60	61	61	62	63	64	64	65	66	67	67	68	69	70	70	71	72	73	73	74	75	76	76	77	78	79	79	80	81	82	82	83																
84	59	59	60	61	62	62	63	64	65	65	66	67	68	68	69	70	71	71	72	73	74	74	75	76	77	77	78	79	80	80	81	82	83	83	84															
85	59	60	60	61	62	63	63	64	65	66	66	67	68	69	69	70	71	72	72	73	74	75	75	76	77	78	78	79	80	81	81	82	83	84	84	85														
86	59	60	61	61	62	63	64	64	65	66	67	67	68	69	70	70	71	72	73	73	74	75	76	76	77	78	79	79	80	81	82	82	83	84	85	85	86													
87	59	60	61	62	62	63	64	65	65	66	67	68	68	69	70	71	71	72	73	74	74	75	76	77	77	78	79	80	80	81	82	83	83	84	85	86	86	87												
88	60	60	61	62	63	63	64	65	66	66	67	68	69	69	70	71	72	72	73	74	75	75	76	77	78	78	79	80	81	81	82	83	84	84	85	86	87	87	88											
89	60	61	61	62	63	64	64	65	66	67	67	68	69	70	70	71	72	73	73	74	75	76	76	77	78	79	79	80	81	82	82	83	84	85	85	86	87	88	88	89										
90	60	61	62	62	63	64	65	65	66	67	68	68	69	70	71	71	72	73	74	74	75	76	77	77	78	79	80	80	81	82	83	83	84	85	86	86	87	88	89	89	90									
91	60	61	62	63	63	64	65	66	66	67	68	69	69	70	71	72	72	73	74	75	75	76	77	78	78	79	80	81	81	82	83	84	84	85	86	87	87	88	89	90	90	91								
92	61	61	62	63	64	64	65	66	67	67	68	69	70	70	71	72	73	73	74	75	76	76	77	78	79	79	80	81	82	82	83	84	85	85	86	87	88	88	89	90	91	91	92							
93	61	62	62	63	64	65	65	66	67	68	68	69	70	71	71	72	73	74	74	75	76	77	77	78	79	80	80	81	82	83	83	84	85	86	86	87	88	89	89	90	91	92	92	93						
94	61	62	63	63	64	65	66	66	67	68	69	69	70	71	72	72	73	74	75	75	76	77	78	78	79	80	81	81	82	83	84	84	85	86	87	87	88	89	90	90	91	92	93	93	94					
95	61	62	63	64	64	65	66	67	67	68	69	70	70	71	72	73	73	74	75	76	76	77	78	79	79	80	81	82	82	83	84	85	85	86	87	88	88	89	90	91	91	92	93	94	94	95				
96	62	62	63	64	65	65	66	67	68	68	69	70	71	71	72	73	74	74	75	76	77	77	78	79	80	80	81	82	83	83	84	85	86	86	87	88	89	89	90	91	92	92	93	94	95	95	96			
97	62	63	63	64	65	66	66	67	68	69	69	70	71	72	72	73	74	75	75	76	77	78	78	79	80	81	81	82	83	84	84	85	86	87	87	88	89	90	90	91	92	93	93	94	95	96	96	97		
98	62	63	64	64	65	66	67	67	68	69	70	70	71	72	73	73	74	75	76	76	77	78	79	79	80	81	82	82	83	84	85	85	86	87	88	88	89	90	91	91	92	93	94	94	95	96	97	97	98	
99	62	63	64	65	65	66	67	68	68	69	70	71	71	72	73	74	74	75	76	77	77	78	79	80	80	81	82	83	83	84	85	86	86	87	88	89	89	90	91	92	92	93	94	95	95	96	97	98	98	99
100	63	63	64	65	66	66	67	68	69	69	70	71	72	72	73	74	75	75	76	77	78	78	79	80	81	81	82	83	84	84	85	86	87	87	88	89	90	90	91	92	93	93	94	95	96	96	97	98	99	99	100
	50	51	52	53	54	**55**	56	57	58	59	**60**	61	62	63	64	**65**	66	67	68	69	**70**	71	72	73	74	**75**	76	77	78	79	**80**	81	82	83	84	**85**	86	87	88	89	**90**	91	92	93	94	**95**	96	97	98	99	**100**

TABLE 6
IMPAIRMENT OF THE VISUAL SYSTEM AS IT RELATES TO IMPAIRMENT OF THE WHOLE PERSON

% Impairment of		% Impairment of		% Impairment of		% Impairment of		% Impairment of		% Impairment of	
Visual System	Whole Person	Visual System	Whole Person	Visual System	Whole Person	Visual System	Whole Person	Visual System	Whole Person	Visual System	Whole Person
0	0	15	14	30	28	45	42	60	57	75	71
1	1	16	15	31	29	46	43	61	58	76	72
2	2	17	16	32	30	47	44	62	59	77	73
3	3	18	17	33	31	48	45	63	59	78	74
4	4	19	18	34	32	49	46	64	60	79	75
5	5	20	19	35	33	50	47	65	61	80	76
6	6	21	20	36	34	51	48	66	62	81	76
7	7	22	21	37	35	52	49	67	63	82	77
8	8	23	22	38	36	53	50	68	64	83	78
9	8	24	23	39	37	54	51	69	65	84	79
10	9	25	24	40	38	55	52	70	66	85	80
11	10	26	25	41	39	56	53	71	67	86	81
12	11	27	25	42	40	57	54	72	68	87	82
13	12	28	26	43	41	58	55	73	69	88	83
14	13	29	27	44	42	59	56	74	70	89	84
										90-100	85

	% Impairment Visual System	% Impairment Whole Person
Total loss of vision one eye	25	24
Total loss of vision both eyes	100	85

References

1. Sloan LL: New test charts for the measurement of visual acuity. *Am J Ophthalmol* 1959;48:807-813.

2. Report of Working Group 39, Committee on Vision, National Academy of Sciences: Recommended Standard Procedures for the Clinical Measurement and Specification of Visual Acuity. *Adv Ophthalmol* 1980;41:103-143.

3. Esterman B: Grids for scoring visual fields, II perimeter. *Arch Ophthalmol* 1968;79:400-406.

4. Keeney AH, Duerson HL, Jr: Collated near-vision test card. *Am J Ophthalmol* 1958;46(4):592-594.

5. Keeney AH: *Ocular Examination: Basis and Technique* (ed 2). St Louis, CV Mosby Co, 1976.

6. Newell FW: *Ophthalmology: Principles and Concepts* (ed 5). St Louis, CV Mosby Co, 1982.

Chapter 7

Ear, Nose, Throat and Related Structures

Introduction

The purpose of this chapter is to provide criteria for use in evaluating permanent impairment resulting from the principal dysfunctions of the ear, nose, throat and related structures, and thereby to determine the corresponding percentage of permanent impairment of the whole person. Although the ear, nose, throat and related structures each have multiple functions, some of which are closely allied, permanent impairment usually results from a clinically established deviation from normal in one or more of the following functions: (1) hearing; (2) equilibrium; (3) respiration; (4) mastication and deglutition; (5) olfaction and taste; (6) speech; and (7) facial features and movement.

Before using the information in this chapter, the reader is urged to consult the Preface to the Guides, which provides a general discussion of the purpose of the Guides, and of the situations in which they are useful; and discusses techniques for the evaluation of the patient and for report preparation.

The Ear

The ear consists of the auricle, the external canal, the tympanum, the eustachian tube, the mastoid, the internal ear, the central pathways, and the auditory cortex.

The functions of the ear are hearing and equilibrium, which are considered separately in the following sections. The criteria for evaluating hearing impairment are relatively specific. On the other hand, it is necessary to provide rather general criteria for disturbances of equilibrium. Such disturbances of the ear as chronic otorrhea, otalgia and tinnitus are not measurable and, therefore, the physician should assign a degree of impairment that is based on severity and importance, and is consistent with established values.

Hearing

The following criteria have been adapted from information provided by the American Academy of Otolaryngology—Head and Neck Surgery, and the American Council of Otolaryngology—Head and Neck Surgery. For the purpose of this chapter, impairment of the whole person is determined from the calculation of permanent binaural hearing impairment. In using these criteria, certain abbreviations and definitions should be kept in mind:

1. Permanent hearing impairment: This is reduced hearing sensitivity that is outside the range of normal. Hearing should be evaluated after maximum rehabilitation has been achieved and when the impairment is non-progressive. The determination of impairment is basic to the evaluation of permanent handicap and disability.

2. Permanent binaural hearing impairment: This is the disadvantage caused by a binaural hearing impairment sufficient to affect the individual's efficiency in the activities of daily living.

3. Intensity: This is measured in decibels, abbreviated *dB*.

4. Frequency: This is measured in hertz, abbreviated *Hz*.

5. Hearing threshold level for pure tones: This is defined as the number of decibels (dB) above a standard audiometric zero for a given frequency at which the listener's threshold of hearing lies. It is the reading on the hearing level (HL) dial of an audiometer that is calibrated according to the American National Standards Institute (ANSI) specifications for Audiometers S3.6-1969, which were reaffirmed in 1973. This chapter provides for the rating of hearing impairment using audiometers calibrated according to the ANSI standard. Hearing levels obtained from audiometers calibrated to the older ASA-1951 standard should be corrected using the following factors:

Table 1

Frequency (Hz)	Correction Factor
500	+ 14 dB
1,000	+ 10 dB
2,000	+8.5 dB
3,000	+8.5 dB

It is common practice to add 10 dB to the average of hearing threshold levels at these four frequencies when correcting from the ASA to ANSI values.

6. Estimated hearing level for speech: This is the simple average of hearing threshold levels at the four frequencies of 500, 1,000, 2,000, and 3,000 Hz. Because of present limitations of speech audiometry, the hearing loss for speech is estimated from measurements made with a pure tone audiometer. The hearing threshold level at 3,000 Hz is included to provide an accurate assessment of hearing impairment in a variety of everyday listening conditions.

7. Evaluation of monaural hearing impairment: If the average hearing level at 500, 1,000, 2,000, and 3,000 Hz is 25 dB (ANSI-1969) or less, no impairment is presumed to exist in the ability to hear everyday sounds under everyday listening conditions. At the other extreme, however, if the average hearing level at 500, 1,000, 2,000, and 3,000 Hz is over 91.7 dB, the impairment for hearing everyday speech should be considered total, that is, 100%. For every decibel that the estimated hearing level for speech exceeds 25 dB (ANSI-1969), 1.5% of monaural impairment is assigned, to a maximum of 100%. This maximum is reached at 91.7 dB (see Table 2).

This method of computation should be applied only to adults who have acquired language. The child who has not acquired language does not benefit from the redundancy of language enjoyed by the comprehending adult. Evidence suggests that material impairment for the prelingual child may exist when the average hearing level is in the range of 15.25 dB.

8. Evaluation of binaural hearing impairment: The evaluation of binaural hearing impairment of adults is derived from the pure tone audiogram and is always based upon the functional state of both ears. The range of binaural hearing impairment is not as wide as the audiometric range of human hearing. Audiometric zero, which is presumably the average normal threshold level, is not the point at which impairment begins. Binaural hearing impairment is determined using the following formula:

$$\text{Binaural Hearing Impairment, (\%)} = \frac{5 \times \%\ \text{hearing impairment of better ear} + \%\ \text{hearing impairment of poorer ear}}{6}$$

Table 3 is derived from this formula.

Table 4 converts binaural hearing impairment to impairment of the whole person.

Objective Techniques To Determine Hearing Impairment

To determine impairment, the following steps should be taken:

1. Test each ear separately with a pure-tone audiometer and record the hearing levels at (a) 500 Hz; (b) 1,000 Hz; (c) 2,000 Hz; and (d) 3,000 Hz. It is necessary that the hearing level for each frequency be determined in every patient. The following rules apply for extreme values:

a. If the hearing level at a given frequency is greater than 100 dB or is beyond the range of the audiometer, the level shall be taken as 100 dB.

b. If the hearing level for a given frequency is better than normal, the level shall be taken as 0 dB.

2. Total these four decibel values for each ear separately. In the examples below, hearing levels are determined in dB according to ANSI-1969 standards.

Example a:

Right Ear		Left Ear
15	500 Hz	30
25	1,000 Hz	45
45	2,000 Hz	60
55	3,000 Hz	85
140		220

Example b:

Right Ear		Left Ear
80	500 Hz	75
90	1,000 Hz	80
100	2,000 Hz	90
100	3,000 Hz	95
370		340

3. Consult Table 2 for percentage of monaural hearing impairment(s). "DSHL" is the decibel sum of the hearing threshold levels at 500, 1,000, 2,000, and 3,000 Hz, and is equated to percentage of monaural hearing impairment.

Example a: Right ear: DSHL is 140, resulting in 15% hearing impairment.

Left ear: DSHL is 220, resulting in 45% hearing impairment.

Example b: Right ear: DSHL is 370, resulting in 100% hearing impairment.

Left ear: DSHL is 340, resulting in 90% hearing impairment.

4. Consult Table 3 to determine percentage of binaural hearing impairment.

Example a: 140 DSHL (better ear) + 220 DSHL (poorer ear) = 20% binaural hearing impairment.

Example b: 340 DSHL (better ear) + 370 DSHL* (poorer ear) = 92% binaural hearing impairment. *Note: Use a maximum value of 368 DSHL.

5. Consult Table 4 to determine impairment of whole person.

Example a: 20% binaural hearing impairment results in 7% impairment of the whole person.

Example b: 92% binaural hearing impairment results in 32% impairment of the whole person.

Equilibrium

Equilibrium or orientation in space is maintained by the visual, kinesthetic and vestibular mechanisms.

Vertigo, or vestibular dysequilibrium, is a sense of movement that is perceived by the patient as "subjective," in the case of movement of self, or as "objective," in the case of movement of the environment. The movements may be described as a sense of spinning, pulsion, or tilting of the visual environment with change of head position.

Disturbances of equilibrium may be classified clinically as: (1) abnormalities of gait not associated with vertigo; (2) giddiness or light-headedness that is distinguished from vertigo by the absence of feelings of movement; and (3) vertigo produced by disorders of the vestibular mechanism and its central nervous system components, including cerebral cortex, cerebellum, and brain stem, and by eye movements.

Table 2
MONAURAL HEARING IMPAIRMENT (%)*

DSHL†	%	DSHL	%	DSHL	%
100	0.0	190	33.8	285	69.3
		195	35.6	290	71.2
105	1.9	200	37.5	295	73.1
110	3.8			300	75.0
115	5.6	205	39.4		
120	7.5	210	41.2	305	76.9
		215	43.1	310	78.8
125	9.4	220	45.0	315	80.6
130	11.2			320	82.5
135	13.1	225	46.9		
140	15.0	230	48.9	325	84.4
		235	50.6	330	86.2
145	16.9	240	52.5	335	88.1
150	18.8			340	90.0
155	20.6	245	54.4		
160	22.5	250	56.2	345	90.9
		255	58.1	350	93.8
165	24.4	260	60.0	355	95.6
170	26.2			360	97.5
175	28.1	265	61.9		
180	30.0	270	63.8	365	99.4
		275	65.6	368	100.0
185	31.9	280	67.5	or greater	

*Audiometers are calibrated to ANSI-1969 standard reference levels.
†Decibel sum of the hearing threshold levels at 500, 1,000, 2,000, and 3,000 Hz.

Permanent impairment may result from any disorder causing disorientation in space or vertigo. Three regulatory systems, ocular (visual), kinesthetic (proprioceptive), and vestibular, are related to the vestibulo-ocular reflex. The evaluation of impairments of equilibrium may include consideration of one or more of these mechanisms.

This section is primarily concerned with permanent impairment resulting from defects of the vestibular (labyrinthine) mechanism and its central connections. The defects are evidenced by loss of equilibrium produced by: (1) loss of vestibular function; OR (2) disturbances of vestibular function.

Complete loss of vestibular function: This loss may be unilateral or bilateral. When the loss is unilateral, adequate central nervous system compensation may or may not occur. With total bilateral loss of vestibular function, equilibrium is totally dependent on the kinesthetic and visual systems, which are usually unable to compensate fully for movement or ambulation. Depending upon the extent of adjustment, the percentage of permanent impairment of the whole person may range from 0% to 95%.

Disturbances of vestibular function: These disorders are evidenced by vertigo (vestibular dysequilibrium)

Table 3. — Computation Of Binaural Hearing Impairment

ANSI 1969

	100	105	110	115	120	125	130	135	140	145	150	155	160	165	170	175	180	185	190	195	200	205	210	215	220	225
100	0																									
105	.3	1.9																								
110	.6	2.2	3.8																							
115	.9	2.5	4.1	5.6																						
120	1.3	2.8	4.4	5.9	7.5																					
125	1.6	3.1	4.7	6.3	7.8	9.4																				
130	1.9	3.4	5	6.6	8.1	9.7	11.3																			
135	2.2	3.8	5.3	6.9	8.4	10	11.6	13.1																		
140	2.5	4.1	5.6	7.2	8.8	10.3	11.9	13.4	15																	
145	2.8	4.4	5.9	7.5	9.1	10.6	12.2	13.8	15.3	16.9																
150	3.1	4.7	6.3	7.8	9.4	10.9	12.5	14.1	15.6	17.2	18.8															
155	3.4	5	6.6	8.1	9.7	11.3	12.8	14.4	15.9	17.5	19.1	20.6														
160	3.8	5.3	6.9	8.4	10	11.6	13.1	14.7	16.3	17.8	19.4	20.9	22.5													
165	4.1	5.6	7.2	8.8	10.3	11.9	13.4	15	16.6	18.1	19.7	21.3	22.8	24.4												
170	4.4	5.9	7.5	9.1	10.6	12.2	13.8	15.3	16.9	18.4	20	21.6	23.1	24.7	26.3											
175	4.7	6.3	7.8	9.4	10.9	12.5	14.1	15.6	17.2	18.8	20.3	21.9	23.4	25	26.6	28.1										
180	5	6.6	8.1	9.7	11.3	12.8	14.4	15.9	17.5	19.1	20.6	22.2	23.8	25.3	26.9	28.4	30									
185	5.3	6.9	8.4	10	11.6	13.1	14.7	16.3	17.8	19.4	20.9	22.5	24.1	25.6	27.2	28.8	30.3	31.9								
190	5.6	7.2	8.8	10.3	11.9	13.4	15	16.6	18.1	19.7	21.3	22.8	24.4	25.9	27.5	29.1	30.6	32.2	33.8							
195	5.9	7.5	9.1	10.6	12.2	13.8	15.3	16.9	18.4	20	21.6	23.1	24.7	26.3	27.8	29.4	30.9	32.5	34.1	35.6						
200	6.3	7.8	9.4	10.9	12.5	14.1	15.6	17.2	18.8	20.3	21.9	23.4	25	26.6	28.1	29.7	31.3	32.8	34.4	35.9	37.5					
205	6.6	8.1	9.7	11.3	12.8	14.4	15.9	17.5	19.1	20.6	22.2	23.8	25.3	26.9	28.4	30	31.6	33.1	34.7	36.3	37.8	39.4				
210	6.9	8.4	10	11.6	13.1	14.7	16.3	17.8	19.4	20.9	22.5	24.1	25.6	27.2	28.8	30.3	31.9	33.4	35	36.6	38.1	39.7	41.3			
215	7.2	8.8	10.3	11.9	13.4	15	16.6	18.1	19.7	21.3	22.8	24.4	25.9	27.5	29.1	30.6	32.2	33.8	35.3	36.9	38.4	40	41.6	43.1		
220	7.5	9.1	10.6	12.2	13.8	15.3	16.9	18.4	20	21.6	23.1	24.7	26.3	27.8	29.4	30.9	32.5	34.1	35.6	37.2	38.8	40.3	41.9	43.4	45	
225	7.8	9.4	10.9	12.5	14.1	15.6	17.2	18.8	20.3	21.9	23.4	25	26.6	28.1	29.7	31.3	32.8	34.4	35.9	37.5	39.1	40.6	42.2	43.8	45.3	46.9
230	8.1	9.7	11.3	12.8	14.4	15.9	17.5	19.1	20.6	22.2	23.8	25.3	26.9	28.4	30	31.6	33.1	34.7	36.3	37.8	39.4	40.9	42.5	44.1	45.6	47.2
235	8.4	10	11.6	13.1	14.7	16.3	17.8	19.4	20.9	22.5	24.1	25.6	27.2	28.8	30.3	31.9	33.4	35	36.6	38.1	39.7	41.3	42.8	44.4	45.9	47.5
240	8.8	10.3	11.9	13.4	15	16.6	18.1	19.7	21.3	22.8	24.4	25.9	27.5	29.1	30.6	32.2	33.8	35.3	36.9	38.4	40	41.6	43.1	44.7	46.3	47.8
245	9.1	10.6	12.2	13.8	15.3	16.9	18.4	20	21.6	23.1	24.7	26.3	27.8	29.4	30.9	32.5	34.1	35.6	37.2	38.8	40.3	41.9	43.4	45	46.6	48.1
250	9.4	10.9	12.5	14.1	15.6	17.2	18.8	20.3	21.9	23.4	25	26.6	28.1	29.7	31.3	32.8	34.4	35.9	37.5	39.1	40.6	42.2	43.8	45.3	46.9	48.4
255	9.7	11.3	12.8	14.4	15.9	17.5	19.1	20.6	22.2	23.8	25.3	26.9	28.4	30	31.6	33.1	34.7	36.3	37.8	39.4	40.9	42.5	44.1	45.6	47.2	48.8
260	10	11.6	13.1	14.7	16.3	17.8	19.4	20.9	22.5	24.1	25.6	27.2	28.8	30.3	31.9	33.4	35	36.6	38.1	39.7	41.3	42.8	44.4	45.9	47.5	49.1
265	10.3	11.9	13.4	15	16.6	18.1	19.7	21.3	22.8	24.4	25.9	27.5	29.1	30.6	32.2	33.8	35.3	36.9	38.4	40	41.6	43.1	44.7	46.3	47.8	49.4
270	10.6	12.2	13.8	15.3	16.9	18.4	20	21.6	23.1	24.7	26.3	27.8	29.4	30.9	32.5	34.1	35.6	37.2	38.8	40.3	41.9	43.4	45	46.6	48.1	49.7
275	10.9	12.5	14.1	15.6	17.2	18.8	20.3	21.9	23.4	25	26.6	28.1	29.7	31.3	32.8	34.4	35.9	37.5	39.1	40.6	42.2	43.8	45.3	46.9	48.4	50
280	11.3	12.8	14.4	15.9	17.5	19.1	20.6	22.2	23.8	25.3	26.9	28.4	30	31.6	33.1	34.7	36.3	37.8	39.4	40.9	42.5	44.1	45.6	47.2	48.8	50.3
285	11.6	13.1	14.7	16.3	17.8	19.4	20.9	22.5	24.1	25.6	27.2	28.8	30.3	31.9	33.4	35	36.6	38.1	39.7	41.3	42.8	44.4	45.9	47.5	49.1	50.6
290	11.9	13.4	15	16.6	18.1	19.7	21.3	22.8	24.4	25.9	27.5	29.1	30.6	32.2	33.8	35.3	36.9	38.4	40	41.6	43.1	44.7	46.3	47.8	49.4	50.9
295	12.2	13.8	15.3	16.9	18.4	20	21.6	23.1	24.7	26.3	27.8	29.4	30.9	32.5	34.1	35.6	37.2	38.8	40.3	41.9	43.4	45	46.6	48.1	49.7	51.3
300	12.5	14.1	15.6	17.2	18.8	20.3	21.9	23.4	25	26.6	28.1	29.7	31.3	32.8	34.4	35.9	37.5	39.1	40.6	42.2	43.8	45.3	46.9	48.4	50	51.6
305	12.8	14.4	15.9	17.5	19.1	20.6	22.2	23.8	25.3	26.9	28.4	30	31.6	33.1	34.7	36.3	37.8	39.4	40.9	42.5	44.1	45.6	47.2	48.8	50.3	51.9
310	13.1	14.7	16.3	17.8	19.4	20.9	22.5	24.1	25.6	27.2	28.8	30.3	31.9	33.4	35	36.6	38.1	39.7	41.3	42.8	44.4	45.9	47.5	49.1	50.6	52.2
315	13.4	15	16.6	18.1	19.7	21.3	22.8	24.4	25.9	27.5	29.1	30.6	32.2	33.8	35.3	36.9	38.4	40	41.6	43.1	44.7	46.3	47.8	49.4	50.9	52.5
320	13.8	15.3	16.9	18.4	20	21.6	23.1	24.7	26.3	27.8	29.4	30.9	32.5	34.1	35.6	37.2	38.8	40.3	41.9	43.4	45	46.6	48.1	49.7	51.3	52.8
325	14.1	15.6	17.2	18.8	20.3	21.9	23.4	25	26.6	28.1	29.7	31.3	32.8	34.4	35.9	37.5	39.1	40.6	42.2	43.8	45.3	46.9	48.4	50	51.6	53.1
330	14.4	15.9	17.5	19.1	20.6	22.2	23.8	25.3	26.9	28.4	30	31.6	33.1	34.7	36.3	37.8	39.4	40.9	42.5	44.1	45.6	47.2	48.8	50.3	51.9	53.4
335	14.7	16.3	17.8	19.4	20.9	22.5	24.1	25.6	27.2	28.8	30.3	31.9	33.4	35	36.6	38.1	39.7	41.3	42.8	44.4	45.9	47.5	49.1	50.6	52.2	53.8
340	15	16.6	18.1	19.7	21.3	22.8	24.4	25.9	27.5	29.1	30.6	32.2	33.8	35.3	36.9	38.4	40	41.6	43.1	44.7	46.3	47.8	49.4	50.9	52.5	54.1
345	15.3	16.9	18.4	20	21.6	23.1	24.7	26.3	27.8	29.4	30.9	32.5	34.1	35.6	37.2	38.8	40.3	41.9	43.4	45	46.6	48.1	49.7	51.3	52.8	54.4
350	15.6	17.2	18.8	20.3	21.9	23.4	25	26.6	28.1	29.7	31.3	32.8	34.4	35.9	37.5	39.1	40.6	42.2	43.8	45.3	46.9	48.4	50	51.6	53.1	54.7
355	15.9	17.5	19.1	20.6	22.2	23.8	25.3	26.9	28.4	30	31.6	33.1	34.7	36.3	37.8	39.4	40.9	42.5	44.1	45.6	47.2	48.8	50.3	51.9	53.4	55
360	16.3	17.8	19.4	20.9	22.5	24.1	25.6	27.2	28.8	30.3	31.9	33.4	35	36.6	38.1	39.7	41.3	42.8	44.4	45.9	47.5	49.1	50.6	52.2	53.8	55.3
365	16.6	18.1	19.7	21.3	22.8	24.4	25.9	27.5	29.1	30.6	32.2	33.8	35.3	36.9	38.4	40	41.6	43.1	44.7	46.3	47.8	49.4	50.9	52.5	54.1	55.6
368	16.8	18.3	19.9	21.4	23	24.6	26.2	27.7	29.3	30.8	32.4	33.9	35.5	37.1	38.6	40.2	41.8	43.3	44.9	46.4	48	49.6	51.1	52.7	54.3	55.8
ANSI 1969	100	105	110	115	120	125	130	135	140	145	150	155	160	165	170	175	180	185	190	195	200	205	210	215	220	225

Better Ear (sum 500, 1,000, 2,000, 3,000 Hz)

Values are based on the following formula:

$$\frac{5 \times \% \text{ impairment of better ear} + \% \text{ impairment of poorer ear}}{6} = \text{binaural hearing impairment, (\%)}$$

The axes are the sum of hearing levels at 500, 1,000, 2,000 and 3,000 Hz. The sum for the worse ear is read at the side; the sum for the better ear is read at the bottom. At the intersection of the column for the worse ear and the column for the better ear is the hearing handicap.

```
48.8
49.1 50.6
49.4 50.9 52.5
49.7 51.3 52.8 54.4

50    51.6 53.1 54.7 56.3
50.3 51.9 53.4 55   56.6 58.1
50.6 52.2 53.8 55.3 56.9 58.4 60
50.9 52.5 54.1 55.6 57.2 58.8 60.3 61.9
51.3 52.8 54.4 55.9 57.5 59.1 60.6 62.2 63.8

51.6 53.1 54.7 56.3 57.8 59.4 60.9 62.5 64.1 65.6
51.9 53.4 55   56.6 58.1 59.7 61.3 62.8 64.4 65.9 67.5
52.2 53.8 55.3 56.9 58.4 60   61.6 63.1 64.7 66.3 67.8 69.4
52.5 54.1 55.6 57.2 58.8 60.3 61.9 63.4 65   66.6 68.1 69.7 71.3
52.8 54.4 55.9 57.5 59.1 60.6 62.2 63.8 65.3 66.9 68.4 70   71.6 73.1

53.1 54.7 56.3 57.8 59.4 60.9 62.5 64.1 65.6 67.2 68.8 70.3 71.9 73.4 75
53.4 55   56.6 58.1 59.7 61.3 62.8 64.4 65.9 67.5 69.1 70.6 72.2 73.8 75.3 76.9
53.8 55.3 56.9 58.4 60   61.6 63.1 64.7 66.3 67.8 69.4 70.9 72.5 74.1 75.6 77.2 78.8
54.1 55.6 57.2 58.8 60.3 61.9 63.4 65   66.6 68.1 69.7 71.3 72.8 74.4 75.9 77.5 79.1 80.6
54.4 55.9 57.5 59.1 60.6 62.2 63.8 65.3 66.9 68.4 70   71.6 73.1 74.7 76.3 77.8 79.4 80.9 82.5

54.7 56.3 57.8 59.4 60.9 62.5 64.1 65.6 67.2 68.8 70.3 71.9 73.4 75   76.6 78.1 79.7 81.3 82.8 84.4
55   56.6 58.1 59.7 61.3 62.8 64.4 65.9 67.5 69.1 70.6 72.2 73.8 75.3 76.9 78.4 80   81.6 83.1 84.7 86.3
55.3 56.9 58.4 60   61.6 63.1 64.7 66.3 67.8 69.4 70.9 72.5 74.1 75.6 77.2 78.8 80.3 81.9 83.4 85   86.6 88.1
55.6 57.2 58.8 60.3 61.9 63.4 65   66.6 68.1 69.7 71.3 72.8 74.4 75.9 77.5 79.1 80.6 82.2 83.8 85.3 86.9 88.4 90
55.9 57.5 59.1 60.6 62.2 63.8 65.3 66.9 68.4 70   71.6 73.1 74.7 76.3 77.8 79.4 80.9 82.5 84.1 85.6 87.2 88.8 90.3 91.9

56.3 57.8 59.4 60.9 62.5 64.1 65.6 67.2 68.8 70.3 71.9 73.4 75   76.6 78.1 79.7 81.3 82.8 84.4 85.9 87.5 89.1 90.6 92.2 93.8
56.6 58.1 59.7 61.3 62.8 64.4 65.9 67.5 69.1 70.6 72.2 73.8 75.3 76.9 78.4 80   81.6 83.1 84.7 86.3 87.8 89.4 90.9 92.5 94.1 95.6
56.9 58.4 60   61.6 63.1 64.7 66.3 67.8 69.4 70.9 72.5 74.1 75.6 77.2 78.8 80.3 81.9 83.4 85   86.6 88.1 89.7 91.3 92.8 94.4 95.9 97.5
57.2 58.8 60.3 61.9 63.4 65   66.6 68.1 69.7 71.3 72.8 74.4 75.9 77.5 79.1 80.6 82.2 83.8 85.3 86.9 88.4 90   91.6 93.1 94.7 96.3 97.6 99.4
57.4 58.9 60.5 62.1 63.6 65.2 66.8 68.3 69.9 71.4 73   74.6 76.1 77.7 79.3 80.8 82.4 83.9 85.5 87.1 88.6 90.2 91.8 93.3 94.9 96.4 98   99.6 100

230 235 240 245 250 255 260 265 270 275 280 285 290 295 300 305 310 315 320 325 330 335 340 345 350 355 360 365 368
```

Table 4
THE RELATIONSHIP
OF BINAURAL HEARING IMPAIRMENT
TO IMPAIRMENT OF THE WHOLE PERSON

% Binaural Hearing Impairment	% Impairment of the Whole Person	% Binaural Hearing Impairment	% Impairment of the Whole Person
0 - 1.7	0	50.0- 53.1	18
1.8- 4.2	1	54.2- 55.7	19
4.3- 7.4	2	55.8- 58.8	20
7.5- 9.9	3	58.9- 61.4	21
10.0-13.1	4	61.5- 64.5	22
13.2-15.9	5	64.6- 67.1	23
16.0-18.8	6	67.2- 70.0	24
18.9-21.4	7	70.1- 72.8	25
21.5-24.5	8	72.9- 75.9	26
24.6-27.1	9	76.0- 78.5	27
27.2-30.0	10	78.6- 81.7	28
30.1-32.8	11	81.8- 84.2	29
32.9-35.9	12	84.3- 87.4	30
36.0-38.5	13	87.5- 89.9	31
38.6-41.7	14	90.0- 93.1	32
41.8-44.2	15	93.2- 95.7	33
44.3-47.4	16	95.8- 98.8	34
47.5-49.9	17	98.9-100.0	35

as defined above. In this chapter, light-headedness and abnormalities of gait not associated with vertigo are not considered.

Vertigo may be accompanied by varying degrees of nausea, vomiting, headache, immobility, ataxia, and nystagmus. Movement may increase the vertigo and these ancillary signs and symptoms. Peripheral vestibular (labyrinthine) disorders are often associated with hearing loss and tinnitus. While some vestibular disorders result in temporary impairment, others may be permanent. Evaluation of vestibular impairment should be performed when the condition is stable and maximum adjustment has been achieved.

For evaluating those patients with permanent disturbances of the vestibular mechanism, the following classification has been developed. The various classes provide a means by which a physician can correlate the patient's residual capacity for the usual activities of daily living and the extent of permanent impairment as a whole person. Use of this classification presupposes that the physician has established a firm diagnosis based on a carefully obtained history, thorough examination, and the use of appropriate objective tests, supplemented by sound clinical judgment. In that vestibular disorders cause a dynamic set of signs and symptoms, subject to peripheral changes and central nervous system

compensatory mechanisms, final conclusions should be based on the patient's condition after it is medically stable.

Class 1—Impairment of the Whole Person, 0%: A patient belongs in Class 1 when (a) signs of vestibular dysequilibrium are present without supporting objective findings; AND (b) the usual activities of daily living can be performed without assistance.

Class 2—Impairment of the Whole Person, 5-10%: A patient belongs in Class 2 when (a) signs of vestibular dysequilibrium are present with supporting objective findings; AND (b) the usual activities of daily living are performed without assistance, except for complex activities such as bike riding or certain activities related to the patient's work, such as walking on girders or scaffolds.

Class 3—Impairment of the Whole Person, 15-30%: A patient belongs in Class 3 when (a) signs of vestibular dysequilibrium are present with supportive objective findings; AND (b) the patient's usual activities of daily living cannot be performed without assistance, except such simple activities as self care, some household duties, walking on the street, and riding in a motor vehicle operated by another person.

Class 4—Impairment of the Whole Person, 35-60%: A patient belongs in Class 4 when (a) signs of vestibular dysequilibrium are present with supportive objective findings; AND (b) usual activities of daily living cannot be performed without assistance, except self care.

Class 5—Impairment of the Whole Person, 65-95%: A patient belongs in Class 5 when (a) signs of vestibular dysequilibrium are present with supportive objective findings; AND (b) the usual activities of daily living cannot be performed without assistance, except self care not requiring ambulation; AND (c) confinement to the home or premises is necessary.

The Face

The face and its structural components serve multiple functions in man.

The portal for deglutition is the mouth and lips. Disturbances in function can result in drooling or inability to contain food or liquid while eating. The lips and mouth also serve in vocal articulation, adding intelligibility to speech. The nose and mouth are the portal of entry for respiration. Impairment can be a result of neurologic disorders, such as partial or complete paralysis of the lips; scar formation and contracture of the lips; or loss of tissue.

The skin of the face has varied functions, such as body covering, resistance to trauma, sensory perception, and regulation of temperature and body fluids. Specific protective functions exist, such as coverage of the eye and its contents by the eyelid.

The face has a unique role in communication. No other part of the body serves as specific a function for personal identity and for expression of thought and emotion. Facial expressions are an integral part of normal living posture. A degree of normalcy is expected for effective verbal and nonverbal communication. Facial anatomy contributes to identity, expression, and normal functioning, and to the appearance of the forehead and cheeks; eyes, eyelids, and brows; lips and mouth; nose; and chin and neck.

In evaluating permanent impairment from a disorder of the face, functional capacity as well as structural integrity are considered. Impairment in this section is limited to abnormality in structural integrity only. (For loss of function, refer to sections regarding specific anatomical areas.) Loss of structural integrity can result from cutaneous disfigurement, such as that due to abnormal pigmentation or scars, or from loss of supporting structures, such as soft tissue, bone, or cartilage of the facial skeleton.

Class 1—Impairment of the Whole Person, 0-5%: A patient belongs in Class 1 when the facial abnormality is limited to a disorder of the cutaneous structures, such as visible scars and abnormal pigmentation. (See Chapter 11.)

Class 2—Impairment of the Whole Person, 5-10%: A patient belongs in Class 2 when there is loss of supporting structure of part of the face, with or without cutaneous disorder. Depressed cheek, nasal or frontal bones constitute a Class 2 impairment.

Class 3—Impairment of the Whole Person, 10-15%: A patient belongs in Class 3 when there is absence of a normal anatomical area of the face. Loss of an eye (see Chapter 6), or loss of part of the nose with the resulting cosmetic deformity, constitute a Class 3 impairment.

Class 4—Impairment of the Whole Person, 15-35%: A patient belongs in Class 4 when facial disfigurement is so severe that it precludes social acceptance. Massive distortion of normal facial anatomy constitutes a Class 4 impairment. (See Chapter 12.)

Facial Disfigurement

The face is such a prominent feature of a person that it plays a critical role in his physical, psychological and emotional makeup. Facial disfigurement can affect all these components and can result in social and vocational handicap.

Disfigurement of the face can result from many causes, particularly burns, accidental injury, surgery and infections. Effects upon individuals can vary tremendously. However, we recommend that "total disfigurement of the face" after treatment has been completed be deemed 15% to 35% impairment of the whole person. For assessment of impairment for associated behavioral changes, the reader is referred to Chapter 12.

Facial disfigurement can be considered total if it is severe and grossly deforming of face and features; also, it must involve at least the entire area between the brow line and the upper lip on both sides. Severe disfigurement above the brow line should be deemed, at a maximum, 1% impairment of the whole person. If it is severe below the upper lip, it may be deemed 8% impairment of the whole person. Specific prominent facial disfigurements should be deemed to have the following maximum values as impairments of the whole person:

Disfigurement	% Impairment of the Whole Person
Unilateral Total Facial Paralysis	5
Bilateral Total Facial Paralysis	8
Loss or Deformity of Outer Ear	2
Loss of the Entire Nose	25
Nasal Distortions in Physical Appearance	5

On the basis of the above guidelines, reasonable impairment values can be placed on other facial disfigurements.

The Nose, Throat, And Related Structures

For the purposes of this chapter, the nose, throat, and related structures include:

1. The nasal region: This consists of the external nose, the nasal cavity, and the nasopharynx.

2. The oral region: This consists of the mouth, teeth, tongue, hard and soft palate, region of the palatine tonsil, and oropharynx.

3. The neck and chest region: This consists of the hypopharynx, larynx, trachea, esophagus, and the bronchi.

The functions of these structures, and the order in which they will be discussed, are: (1) respiration;

(2) mastication and deglutition; (3) olfaction and taste; and (4) speech. Permanent impairment may result from a deviation from normal in any of the above functions, and, because of their close relationship, more than one structure may be involved.

Respiration

Respiration, as used in this chapter, may be defined as the act or function of breathing, that is, the act by which air is inspired and expired from the lungs.

The respiratory mechanism includes the lungs and the air passages; the latter includes the nares, nasal cavities, mouth, pharynx, larynx, trachea, and bronchi.

The scope of this chapter limits discussion of permanent impairment to that produced by defects of the air passages. The reader is referred to Chapter 3 for a discussion of impairment of the lower airways and lung parenchyma.

The most commonly encountered defect of the air passages is obstruction, which may be partial (stenosis) or complete (occlusion). Obstructions and other air passage defects are evidenced primarily by dyspnea or so-called "unusual breathlessness." The "sleep apnea syndrome" may be related to functional upper airway obstruction.

Dyspnea is a cardinal factor that contributes to a patient's diminished capacity for the activities of daily living and to permanent impairment. This subjective complaint, indicating awareness of respiratory distress, is usually noticed first, and is most severe, during exercise. When dyspnea occurs at rest, respiratory dysfunction is probably severe. Dyspnea may or may not be accompanied by other pertinent signs or symptoms.

Patients with air passage defects may be evaluated in accordance with the classification in Table 5. Permanent impairment from obstructive sleep apnea should be evaluated using the criteria in Chapter 2.

Mastication and Deglutition

The act of eating includes mastication and deglutition. Numerous conditions of nongastrointestinal origin, singly or in combination, interfere with these functions. The imposition of dietary restrictions on the patient is usually the result. Such restrictions are,

Table 5—CLASSES OF AIR PASSAGE DEFECTS

Class 1	Class 2	Class 3	Class 4
0-10% impairment of the whole person.	15-30% impairment of the whole person.†	35-50% impairment of the whole person.	Greater that 50% impairment of the whole person.
A recognized air passage defect exists.	A recognized air passage defect exists.	A recognized air passage defect exists.	A recognized air passage defect exists.
Dyspnea does NOT occur at rest.	Dyspnea does NOT occur at rest.	Dyspnea does NOT occur at rest.	Dyspnea occurs at rest, although patient is not necessarily bedridden.
Dyspnea is NOT produced by walking or climbing stairs freely, performance of other usual activities of daily living, stress, prolonged exertion, hurrying, hill-climbing, recreation* requiring intensive effort or similar activity.	Dyspnea is NOT produced by walking freely on the level, climbing at least one flight of ordinary stairs or the performance of other usual activities of daily living. Dyspnea IS produced by stress, prolonged exertion, hurrying, hill-climbing, recreation except sedentary forms, or similar activity.	Dyspnea IS produced by walking more than one or two blocks on the level or climbing one flight of ordinary stairs even with periods of rest; performance of other usual activities of daily living, stress, hurrying, hill-climbing, recreation or similar activity.	Dyspnea is aggravated by the performance of any of the usual activities of daily living beyond personal cleansing, dressing, grooming or its equivalent.
Examination reveals ONE or more of the following: partial obstruction of oropharynx, laryngogopharynx, larynx, upper trachea (to 4th ring), lower trachea, bronchi, or complete obstruction of the nose (bilateral), or nasopharynx.	Examination reveals ONE or more of the following: partial obstruction of oropharynx, laryngopharynx, larynx, upper trachea (to 4th ring), lower trachea, bronchi; or complete obstruction of the nose (bilateral), or nasopharynx.	Examination reveals ONE or more of the following: partial obstruction of oropharynx, laryngopharynx, larynx, upper trachea (to 4th ring), lower trachea or bronchi.	Examination reveals ONE or more of the following: partial obstruction of oropharynx, laryngopharynx, larynx, upper trachea (to 4th ring), lower trachea or bronchi.

* Prophylactic restriction of activity such as strenuous competitive sport does not exclude patient from Class 1.
† Patients with successful permanent tracheostomy or stoma should be rated at 25% impairment of the whole person.

therefore, the most objective criteria by which to evaluate the permanent impairment of these patients. These criteria are:

Restriction	% Impairment of the Whole Person
1. The diet is limited to semi-solid or soft foods	5-10
2. The diet is limited to liquid foods	20-30
3. Ingestion of food requires tube feeding or gastrostomy	40-60

Olfaction and Taste

Only rarely does complete loss of the closely related senses of olfaction and taste seriously affect an individual's performance of the usual activities of daily living. The rare case almost invariably involves occupational considerations that are outside the scope of a physician's responsibility in the evaluation of permanent impairment.

For this reason, a single value of 3% impairment of the whole person is suggested for use in cases involving complete bilateral loss of either sense due to peripheral lesions. This value is to be combined with any other permanent impairment value pertinent to the case, using the Combined Values Chart.

Detection by the patient of any odor or taste, even though he cannot name them, precludes a finding of permanent impairment.

Speech

In this chapter, speech means the capacity to produce vocal signals that can be heard, understood and sustained over a useful period of time. Speech ought to allow effective communication in the activities of daily living.

The causes and characteristics of abnormal speech are not considered. Consideration is given only to the degree of impairment relating to the individual's efficiency in using speech to make himself or herself understood in daily living. It is assumed that this evaluation pertains specifically to the production of voice and articulate speech, and not to the language content or structure of the patient's communication. Based on these assumptions, the primary problem is estimation of proficiency in using oral language, or measurement of the utility of speech as defined above. Esophageal speech is also included.

At this time there is no single, acceptable, proven test that will measure objectively the degrees of impairment from the many varieties of speech dis-

orders. Therefore, it is recommended that speech impairment be evaluated clinically as to audibility, intelligibility, and functional efficiency.

Audibility: This is based on the patient's ability to speak at a level sufficient to be heard.

Intelligibility: This is based on ability to articulate and to link the phonetic units of speech with sufficient accuracy to be understood.

Functional Efficiency: This is based on ability to produce a serviceably fast rate of speech output, and to sustain this output over a useful period of time.

Other definable attributes of speech, such as acceptable voice quality, pitch, and melodic variation, are not evaluated except indirectly as they affect one of the three primary capacities of speech.

A classification chart, oral reading paragraph, and examining procedures for use in estimating speech impairment are described below.

Classification Chart

Judgments as to the amount of impairment should be made with reference to the classes, percentages, and examples provided in the classification chart (Table 6). The fifteen categories of the chart suggest activities or situations with different levels of impairment. Data gathered from direct observation of the patient or from interviews should be compared with these categories, and values should be assigned considering the specific impairments that are present.

Oral Reading Paragraph

The paragraph of 100 words entitled, "The Smith House," composed of 10 sentences, provides a uniform means of comparing a speech sample of the patient with the performance of normal speakers. The phonetic elements of the paragraph are selected particularly for their relevance to intelligibility of speech.

"The Smith House"

Larry and Ruth Smith have been married nearly fourteen years. They have a small place near Long Lake. Both of them think there's nothing like the country for health. Their two boys would rather live there than any other place. Larry likes to keep some saddle horses close to the house. These make it easy to keep his sons amused. If they wish, the boys can go fishing along the shore. When it rains, they usually want to watch television. Ruth has a cherry tree on each side of the kitchen door. In June they enjoy the juice and jelly.

Table 6—SPEECH CLASSIFICATION CHART

Audibility		Intelligibility		Functional Efficiency	
Class 1 0-10% speech impair- ment	Can produce speech of intensity sufficient for MOST of the needs of everyday speech communication, although this sometimes may require effort and occasionally may be beyond the patient's capacity.	**Class 1** 0-10% speech impair- ment	Can perform MOST of the articulatory acts necessary for everyday speech communication, although listeners occasionally ask the patient to repeat and the patient may find it difficult or even impossible to produce a few phonetic units.	**Class 1** 0-10% speech impair- ment	Can meet MOST of the demands of articulation and phonation for everyday speech communication with adequate speed and ease, although occasionally the patient may hesitate or speak slowly.
Class 2 15-35% speech impair- ment	Can produce speech of intensity sufficient for MANY of the needs of everyday speech communication; is usually heard under average conditions; however, may have difficulty in automobiles, buses, trains, stations, restaurants, etc.	**Class 2** 15-35% speech impair- ment	Can perform MANY of the necessary articulatory acts for everyday speech communication. Can speak name, address, etc., and be understood by a stranger, but may have numerous inaccuracies; sometimes appears to have difficulty articulating.	**Class 2** 15-35% speech impair- ment	Can meet MANY of the demands of articulation and phonation for everyday speech communication with adequate speed and ease, but sometimes gives impression of difficulty, and speech may sometimes be discontinuous, interrupted, hesitant or slow.
Class 3 40-60% speech impair- ment	Can produce speech of intensity sufficient for SOME of the needs of everyday speech communication, such as close conversation; however, has considerable difficulty in such noisy places as listed above; the voice tires rapidly and tends to become inaudible after a few seconds.	**Class 3** 40-60% speech impair- ment	Can perform SOME of the necessary articulatory acts for everyday speech communication; can usually converse with family and friends, however, strangers may find it difficult to understand the patient; may often be asked to repeat.	**Class 3** 40-60% speech impair- ment	Can meet SOME of the demands of articulation and phonation for everyday speech communication with adequate speed and ease, but often can only sustain consecutive speech for brief periods, may give the impression of being rapidly fatigued.
Class 4 65-85% speech impair- ment	Can produce speech of intensity sufficient for a FEW of the needs of everyday speech communication; can barely be heard by a close listener or over the telephone, perhaps may be able to whisper audibly, but has no voice.	**Class 4** 65-85% speech impair- ment	Can perform a FEW of the necessary articulatory acts for everyday speech communication; can produce some phonetic units; may have approximations for a few words such as names of own family; however, unintelligible out of context.	**Class 4** 65-85% speech impair- ment	Can meet a FEW of the demands of articulation and phonation for everyday speech communication with adequate speed and ease, such as single words; or short phrases, but cannot maintain uninterrupted speech flow; speech is labored, rate is impractically slow.
Class 5 90-100% speech impair- ment	Can produce speech of intensity sufficient for NONE of the needs of everyday speech communication.	**Class 5** 90-100% speech impair- ment	Can perform NONE of the articulatory acts necessary for everyday speech communication.	**Class 5** 90-100% speech impair- ment	Can meet NONE of the demands of articulation and phonation for everyday speech communication with adequate speed and ease.

Examining Procedures

General orientation: The examining physician should have normal hearing as defined in the earlier section on Hearing.

The setting of the examination should be a reasonably quiet office that approximates the noise level conditions of everyday living.

The examiner should base judgments of impairment on two kinds of evidence: (1) direct observation of the patient's speech in the office, for example, during conversation, during the interview, and while reading and counting aloud; and (2) reports pertaining to the patient's performances in situations of everyday living. The reports or the evidence should be supplied by observers who know the patient well.

The standard of evaluation is the concept of a normal speaker's performance in average situations of everyday living. It is assumed in this context that an average speaker usually can perform as follows:

(1) Talk in a loud voice when the occasion demands it; (2) sustain phonation for at least 10 seconds in one breath; (3) complete at least a 10-word sentence in one breath; (4) form all of the phonetic units of American speech, and join them together intelligibly; and (5) maintain a rate of at least 75 to 100 words per minute, and sustain a flow of speech for a reasonable length of time.

Specific Instructions:

1. Place the patient approximately 8 ft from the examiner.

2. Interview the patient. This will permit observation of the patient's speech in ordinary conversation while obtaining information pertinent to his history.

3. Listen to the patient's speech as the patient reads aloud the short paragraph, "The Smith House." For this exercise, seat the patient with the back towards the physician, maintaining a separation of 8 ft. Instruct the patient as follows: "You are to read this passage so that I can hear you plainly. Be sure to speak so that I can understand you."

4. If additional reading procedures are required, simple prose paragraphs from a magazine may be used. A non-reader may be requested to give name, address, the days of the week, the months of the year, etc. Additional evidence regarding the patient's rate of speech and ability to sustain it may be obtained by noting the time required to count to one hundred by ones. Completion of the latter task in 60 to 75 seconds is accepted as normal.

5. Record judgment of the patient's speech capacity with regard to each of the three columns of the classification chart.

6. The degree of impairment of the speech function is equivalent to the greatest percentage of impairment recorded in any one of the three columns of the classification chart.

For example, speech capacity of a patient is judged to be:

Audibility	Intelligibility	Functional Efficiency
Class 1—10%	Class 3—50%	Class 2—30%

Then speech impairment is 50%, which on consulting Table 7 is seen to be 18% impairment of the whole person.

TABLE 7
SPEECH IMPAIRMENT AS RELATED TO IMPAIRMENT OF THE WHOLE PERSON

% Speech Impairment	% Impairment of the Whole Person	% Speech Impairment	% Impairment of the Whole Person
0	0	50	18
5	2	55	19
10	4	60	21
15	5	65	23
20	7	70	24
25	9	75	26
30	10	80	28
35	12	85	30
40	14	90	32
45	16	95	33
		100	35

Note: Impairment of the WHOLE PERSON contributed by SPEECH IMPAIRMENT may be rounded to the nearest 5% ONLY when it is the SOLE impairment involved.

References

1. Guide for the evaluation of hearing handicap. *JAMA* 1979;241:2055-2059.

2. Noble WG: *Assessment of Impaired Hearing: A critique and a new method.* New York, Academic Press, 1978.

3. ANSI Standard S3.6-1969, *Specifications for Audiometers.* American National Standards Institute, 1410 Broadway, New York, NY 10018.

4. Doty RL: A review of olfactory dysfunctions in man. *Am J Otolaryngol* 1979;1:57-59.

5. Bartoshuk LM: The psychophysics of taste. *Am J Clin Nutr* 1978; 31:1068-1077.

Chapter 8

The Digestive System

Introduction

The digestive system comprises the alimentary canal and its appendages, including the liver, biliary tract and pancreas. The oral cavity and pharynx are considered elsewhere in the Guides.

The purpose of this chapter is to provide criteria for the evaluation of permanent impairment of the digestive system according to a person's ability to perform activities of daily living. A clinically established or objectively determined deviation from normal in the transport and assimilation of ingested food, the metabolism of nutrition, or the excretion of waste products may result in permanent impairment of varying degrees.

Before using the information in this chapter, the reader is urged to consult the Preface to the Guides, which provides a general discussion of the purpose of the Guides, and the situations in which they are useful; and discusses techniques for the evaluation of the patient and for report preparation.

Desirable Weight

For the purposes of determining impairment due to disorders of the upper digestive tract (Table 1), "desirable" weight may be defined as follows:

1. If the examiner is able to determine by history or from previous medical records a weight before onset of the patient's digestive illness that he or she considers "usual," the examiner should use that weight as the "desirable" weight from which any deviations are measured.

2. If the examiner is not able to determine by history or from previous medical records a pre-illness "usual" weight, the examiner should refer to a table of "desirable" weights, and should determine deviations from the lower end of the range of the "desirable" weights for the patient's sex, height and body build. Table 2, which is based on the 1979 Body Build Study by the Society of Actuaries and Association of Life Insurance Medical Directors of America, is recommended.

For an obese patient, the pre-illness weight may not be as physiologically "desirable" as the present weight; thus, the examiner should use judgment in assessing the relative importance of weight loss in determining the impairment rating.

In most cases, the examiner should use the definition shown under part 1 above. The definition and reference in part 2 will be helpful if part 1 cannot be used.

Esophagus

Symptoms and signs of impairment include dysphagia, pyrosis or "heartburn," retrosternal pain, regurgitation, bleeding, and weight loss. One should be mindful that occasional, minor dyspepsia, "gas," and belching are within the experience of all normal persons.

Objective procedures useful in establishing esophageal impairment include, but are not limited to: (1) fluoroscopy and radiography with contrast materials; (2) peroral endoscopy; (3) cytology and/or biopsy; and (4) manometry.

Criteria for evaluating permanent impairment of esophageal function are those listed in Table 1.

Example of Class 1 Impairment of the Whole Person: A 44-year-old man complained of dysphagia six months ago after the ingestion of a broiled lobster. Now, symptoms referrable to esophageal disease cannot be elicited. Weight of 150 lb (68.1 kg) is within desirable limits for the man's height of 5 ft 10 in (1.78 meters).

Physical examination reveals a healthy-appearing man. The vital signs and the physical examination are normal. A chest radiograph and electrocardiogram are normal. Radiographic study of the upper gastrointestinal tract reveals a small sliding hiatal hernia.

Diagnosis: Hiatal hernia.

Impairment: 0% impairment of the whole person.

Comment: The symptoms are indicative of esophageal motor disorder, and a hiatal hernia is present, but these have not interfered with normal nutrition, nor have they impaired the person's ability to perform the usual activities of daily living.

Example of Class 2 Impairment of the Whole Person: A 59-year-old woman complains of having had almost daily substernal pain and dysphagia for five years. She feels better when she limits her diet to soft foods. Her symptoms are more severe when she becomes upset about the status of her invalid husband.

Physical examination reveals a woman 5 ft 7 in (1.70 meters) tall, of medium frame, appearing older than her stated age. Her blood pressure is 145/90 mm Hg. She weighs 118 lb (53.6 kg), which is less than 10% below her usual weight of 128 lb (58.0 kg). Chest radiograph and ECG are normal. Radiographic studies of the upper gastrointestinal tract reveal a corkscrew configuration or "curling," of the esophagus that is suggestive of diffuse spasm. This diagnosis is confirmed by esophageal motility studies.

Diagnosis: Diffuse spasm of the esophagus.

Impairment: 15% impairment of the whole person.

Comment: The patient's symptoms are persistent, and she is obliged to restrict her diet. Her weight is within 10% of the desirable level, and her daily activities have been impaired only slightly.

Example of Class 3 Impairment of the Whole Person: A 49-year-old man complains of intermittent substernal pain, dysphagia and nocturnal regurgitation of five years' duration. The dysphagia has been progressive. The man can swallow solid foods only by drinking large amounts of liquids. Before the onset of his illness, he weighed 180 lb (81.7 kg); now he weighs 155 lb (70.4 kg).

On physical examination, signs of weight loss are present. Height is 6 ft 2 in (1.88 meters). The vital signs are normal. Chest radiograph reveals widening of the mediastinum. An upper gastrointestinal tract study with x-rays reveals a markedly dilated and tortuous esophagus, which terminates in a filiform constrictive configuration. Dilation of the esophagus has been required about twice a year.

Diagnosis: Achalasia of the esophagus.

Impairment: 30% impairment of the whole person.

Comment: Symptoms have been persistent and progressive despite dietary limitation and esophageal dilation; weight loss has exceeded 10% of the desirable level. In this case, the impairment might be appreciably lessened if the patient could be persuaded to undergo surgical esophagomyotomy.

Example of Class 4 Impairment of the Whole Person: The patient, a 58-year-old man, 5 ft 10 in (1.78 meters) in height, has almost complete esophageal ob-

Table 1—CLASSES OF IMPAIRMENT OF THE UPPER DIGESTIVE TRACT (ESOPHAGUS, STOMACH AND DUODENUM, SMALL INTESTINE, PANCREAS)

Class 1 0-5% Impairment	Class 2 10-20% Impairment	Class 3 25-45% Impairment	Class 4 50-75% Impairment
Symptoms or signs of upper digestive tract disease are present or there is anatomic loss or alteration;	Symptoms and signs of organic upper digestive tract disease are present or there is anatomic loss or alteration;	Symptoms and signs of organic upper digestive tract disease are present or there is anatomic loss or alteration;	Symptoms and signs of organic upper digestive tract disease are present or there is anatomic loss or alteration;
and	**and**	**and**	**and**
Continuous treatment is not required;	Appropriate dietary restrictions and drugs are required for control of symptoms, signs and/or nutritional deficiency;	Appropriate dietary restrictions and drugs do not completely control symptoms, signs, and/or nutritional state.	Symptoms are not controlled by treatment;
and	**and**	**or**	**or**
Weight can be maintained at the desirable level;	Loss of weight below the "desirable weight"* does not exceed 10%.	There is 10-20% loss of weight below the "desirable weight" which is ascribable to a disorder of the upper digestive tract.	There is greater than a 20% loss of weight below the "desirable weight" which is ascribable to a disorder of the upper digestive tract.
or			
There are no sequelae after surgical procedures.			

*See Table 2.

struction. Five years ago he had a resection of the esophagogastric junction for cancer. Although there is no evidence of recurrence of the tumor, he has developed severe stenosing esophagitis. Surgical correction was attempted but was unsuccessful. At present, gastrostomy tube is used for feeding. While the patient previously maintained a weight of 150 lb (68.1 kg), he now weighs 110 lb (49.9 kg). Dilation of the stricture is required about once a month to accommodate salivary secretions.

Diagnosis: Stenosing esophagitis.

Impairment: 55% impairment due to stenosing esophagitis and 10% impairment due to gastrostomy, which combine to 60% impairment of the whole person (see Combined Values Chart).

Comment: Symptoms and signs of disease have progressed despite exhaustive treatment, and further therapy can be only palliative. Weight loss has exceeded 20% of the desirable level. The prognosis is poor.

Stomach and Duodenum

Symptoms and signs of impairment include nausea, vomiting, pain, bleeding, obstruction, certain types of malassimilation, diarrhea, weight loss, and nutritional deficiencies that can include hematologic and neurologic manifestations.

Objective procedures useful in establishing impairment of the stomach and duodenum include, but are not limited to: (1) fluoroscopy and radiography employing contrast materials; (2) peroral endoscopy; (3) cytology and/or biopsy; (4) gastric secretory tests; (5) assimilation tests; and (6) stool examination.

Criteria for evaluating permanent impairment consequent to disease or injury of the stomach or duodenum are those listed in Table 1.

Example of Class 1 Impairment of the Whole Person: A 28-year-old man complains of having had intermittent epigastric pain and burning over a five-year period. There is no history of nausea, vomiting, hematemesis, or melena. The man's height with shoes on is 5 ft 11 in (1.80 meters), and weight is 160 lb (72.6 kg). An upper gastrointestinal study reveals a deformed duodenal bulb without an ulcer crater or evidence of gastric retention.

Diagnosis: Duodenal ulcer, in remission.

Impairment: 5% impairment of the whole person.

Comment: Symptoms have been remittent, and the disease has been uncomplicated. Dietary restriction usually has not been necessary. Desirable weight and activities have been maintained.

Example of Class 2 Impairment of the Whole Person: The patient, a 40-year-old man with a small frame body build, had intermittent ulcer symptoms over a period of ten years. Bleeding occurred on three occasions. Blood replacement was necessary twice. The man was hospitalized about once a year for a period of one to two weeks. He consistently refused surgery. He had one episode of transient pyloric obstruction. At present, continual treatment is required. The patient's height with shoes on is 5 ft 8 in (1.73 meters), and weight, 130 lb (59.0 kg), which is 7% below desirable weight. Radiographs of the upper gastrointestinal tract reveal a marked cloverleaf deformity of the duodenum with an ulcer crater 3 mm in diameter.

Diagnosis: Active duodenal ulcer with history of complications.

Impairment: 15% impairment of the whole person.

Comment: The disease has been complicated, and symptoms have recurred despite medical therapy. There has been interference with the performance of daily activities. In this case, the patient has adamantly declined a surgical remedy, although this might appreciably lessen his impairment.

Example of Class 3 Impairment of the Whole Person: A 50-year-old woman had a gastric resection for a duodenal ulcer two years ago. She now complains of episodes of light-headedness, sweating, and palpitation occurring 15 minutes after meals. The symptoms are partly relieved by diet and by lying down. Since the operation, her weight has decreased to approximately 15% below desirable weight.

Physical examination reveals a woman weighing 100 lb (45.4 kg) and standing 5 ft 3 in (1.60 meters) tall. A well-healed upper abdominal scar is present. The remainder of the physical examination is not remarkable. Upper gastrointestinal radiographs reveal evidence of a 70% gastric resection and a normally functioning gastrojejunostomy without evidence of ulceration.

Diagnosis: Postgastrectomy dumping syndrome.

Impairment: 30% impairment of the whole person.

Comment: The patient has symptoms impairing the

Table 2
DESIRABLE WEIGHTS IN ENGLISH AND METRIC
BY SEX, HEIGHT AND BODY BUILD
(INDOOR CLOTHING WEIGHING 5 LB (2.3 KG) FOR MEN AND 3 LB (1.4 KG) FOR WOMEN;
AND SHOES WITH 1 IN (2.5 CM) HEELS)*

Men

Height in cm	Weight lb (kg)		
	Small Frame	Medium Frame	Large Frame
62 (157)	128-134 (58.0-60.7)	131-141 (59.2-63.9)	138-150 (62.5-67.8)
63 (160)	130-136 (59.0-61.7)	133-143 (60.3-64.9)	140-153 (63.5-69.4)
64 (163)	132-138 (60.0-62.7)	135-145 (61.3-66.0)	142-156 (64.5-71.1)
65 (165)	134-140 (60.8-63.5)	137-148 (62.1-67.0)	144-160 (65.3-72.5)
66 (168)	136-142 (61.8-64.6)	139-151 (63.2-68.7)	146-164 (66.4-74.7)
67 (170)	138-145 (62.5-65.7)	142-154 (64.3-69.8)	149-168 (67.5-76.1)
68 (173)	140-148 (63.6-67.3)	145-157 (65.9-71.4)	152-172 (69.1-78.2)
69 (175)	142-151 (64.3-68.3)	148-160 (66.9-72.4)	155-176 (70.1-79.6)
70 (178)	144-154 (65.4-70.0)	151-163 (68.6-74.0)	158-180 (71.8-81.8)
71 (180)	146-157 (66.1-71.0)	154-166 (69.7-75.1)	161-184 (72.8-83.3)
72 (183)	149-160 (67.7-72.7)	157-170 (71.3-77.2)	164-188 (74.5-85.4)
73 (185)	152-164 (68.7-74.1)	160-174 (72.4-78.6)	168-192 (75.9-86.8)
74 (188)	155-168 (70.3-76.2)	164-178 (74.4-80.7)	172-197 (78.0-89.4)
75 (190)	158-172 (71.4-77.6)	167-182 (75.4-82.2)	176-202 (79.4-91.2)
76 (193)	162-176 (73.5-79.8)	171-187 (77.6-84.8)	181-207 (82.1-93.9)

Women

Height in cm	Weight lb (kg)		
	Small Frame	Medium Frame	Large Frame
58 (147)	102-111 (46.2-50.2)	109-121 (49.3-54.7)	118-131 (53.3-59.3)
59 (150)	103-113 (46.7-51.3)	111-123 (50.3-55.9)	120-134 (54.4-60.9)
60 (152)	104-115 (47.1-52.1)	113-126 (51.1-57.0)	122-137 (55.2-61.9)
61 (155)	106-118 (48.1-53.6)	115-129 (52.2-58.6)	125-140 (56.8-63.6)
62 (157)	108-121 (48.8-54.6)	118-132 (53.2-59.6)	128-143 (57.8-64.6)
63 (160)	111-124 (50.3-56.2)	121-135 (54.9-61.2)	131-147 (59.4-66.7)
64 (163)	114-127 (51.9-57.8)	124-138 (56.4-62.8)	134-151 (61.0-68.8)
65 (165)	117-130 (53.0-58.9)	127-141 (57.5-63.9)	137-155 (62.0-70.2)
66 (168)	120-133 (54.6-60.5)	130-144 (59.2-65.5)	140-159 (63.7-72.4)
67 (170)	123-136 (55.7-61.6)	133-147 (60.2-66.6)	143-163 (64.8-73.8)
68 (173)	126-139 (57.3-63.2)	136-150 (61.8-68.2)	146-167 (66.4-75.9)
69 (175)	129-142 (58.3-64.2)	139-153 (62.8-69.2)	149-170 (67.4-76.9)
70 (178)	132-145 (60.0-65.9)	142-156 (64.5-70.9)	152-173 (69.0-78.6)
71 (180)	135-148 (61.0-66.9)	145-159 (65.6-71.9)	155-176 (70.1-79.6)
72 (183)	138-151 (62.6-68.4)	148-162 (67.0-73.4)	158-179 (71.6-81.2)

*Source: 1979 Body Build Study, Society of Actuaries and Association of Life Insurance Medical Directors of America, 1980.
Copyright © 1983, The Metropolitan Life Insurance Company

performance of normal activities despite dietary restriction. She is unable to maintain weight within a 10% range of the desirable level.

Example of Class 4 Impairment of the Whole Person: A 62-year-old man had a total gastric resection three years ago for carcinoma of the stomach. After the surgical procedure he complained of anorexia and developed progressive weight loss and signs of nutritional deficiency.

Physical examination reveals a malnourished, elderly male. He is 5 ft 9 in (1.75 meters) tall and weighs 116 lb (52.7 kg). An upper abdominal scar is present, but no masses are palpable. The tongue is smooth and glistening. Slight pedal edema is present. Laboratory studies disclose anemia and hypoproteinemia. A satisfactory esophagojejunal anastomosis is demonstrated by radiography.

Diagnosis: Postoperative absence of the stomach with esophagojejunal anastomosis.

Impairment: 60% impairment due to gastric resection with esophagojejunal anastomosis, which is to be combined with an appropriate value for the anemia (see Chapter 5) to determine impairment of the whole person.

Comment: The patient's weight loss exceeds 20% of the desirable level, and there are signs of marked nutritional deficiency. The patient clearly is unable to perform activities of normal daily living.

Small Intestine

Symptoms and signs of impairment include pain, diarrhea, steatorrhea, bleeding, obstruction and weight loss, which often are associated with general debility and other extra-intestinal manifestations.

Objective procedures useful in establishing impairment of the small intestine include, but are not limited to: (1) fluoroscopy and radiography employing contrast materials; (2) peroral mucosal biopsy; and (3) measures of intestinal assimilation, for example, test for fecal fat excretion and urinary d-xylose excretion, C^{14} breath test, serum bile acid determination and Schilling test.

Criteria for evaluating permanent impairment of small intestine function are those listed in Table 1.

Example of Class 1 Impairment of the Whole Person: Ten years ago, a 45-year-old man who weighed 160 lb (72.6 kg) required an operation because of recurrent and protracted abdominal pain, fever, and distention. Approximately 30 cm of the terminal ileum were resected; the histologic findings were consistent with regional enteritis. There has been no recurrence of the preoperative symptoms. The patient maintains a weight of 155 lb (70.3 kg) on an unrestricted diet and has two to three soft stools daily. Radiographs of the remaining small intestine are normal.

Diagnosis: Partial ileal resection for regional enteritis.

Impairment: 0% impairment of the whole person.

Comment: There has been no recurrence of symptoms that indicated disease of the small intestine 10 years ago. The patient maintains normal activity and requires no therapy.

Example of Class 2 Impairment of the Whole Person: A 64-year-old woman, who is 5 ft 1 in (155 cm) tall, five years ago suffered diarrhea, weight loss and vague abdominal pain, had a macrocytic anemia, and had small intestinal diverticula demonstrated by radiograph. Prior to her illness she weighed 120 lb (54.4 kg). All symptoms cleared on parenteral treatment with cyanocobalamin (vitamin B_{12}) and oral tetracycline. Two years ago, mild diarrhea recurred for three weeks and again subsided after oral therapy with tetracycline. Radiographs now reveal numerous jejunal diverticula. Nutrition is normal, and her weight is maintained at 110 lb (49.9 kg). There are no symptoms on an unrestricted diet while the patient continues to take parenteral cyanocobalamin.

Diagnosis: Diverticulosis of the jejunum.

Impairment: 15% impairment due to diverticulosis of the jejunum, which is to be combined with an appropriate value for the anemia to determine impairment of the whole person.

Comment: This patient can perform the activities of daily living, but she is dependent on continuing therapy.

Example of Class 3 Impairment of the Whole Person: This 38-year-old man, 5 ft 3 in (1.60 meters) tall, has diarrhea and loss of stamina, and had a 15% decrease in weight from 130 to 110 lb (59.0 to 49.9 kg) after a partial resection of the ileum involved with regional enteritis. Three to four bouts of partial intestinal obstruction each year have not required surgical intervention. Radiographs of the small intestine disclose changes consistent with regional enteritis. Impaired intestinal absorption is confirmed by appropriate tests. Dietary restriction, vitamin supplements, anti-diarrheal agents, and on occasion corticosteroid therapy, have been required to help the patient maintain a reasonably satisfactory state of health.

Diagnosis: Recurrent regional enteritis with intestinal malabsorption and recurring partial intestinal obstruction after partial ileal resection.

Impairment: 40% impairment of the whole person.

Comment: The nutritional status of this patient has been impaired, and his weight deficit exceeds 10% of the desirable level, despite dietary and drug therapy.

Example of Class 4 Impairment of the Whole Person: A 35-year-old woman developed volvulus, which required removal of a large portion of the jejunum and ileum one year ago. She now requires continuous dietary control with supplemental nutrition and use of drugs to diminish abdominal pains and diarrhea.

Tetany and dehydration require frequent hospitalizations for fluid and electrolyte repletion. Stamina is diminished. Her weight remains 87 lb (39.5 kg), and it should be at least 127 lb (57.6 kg) for her height of 5 ft 5 in (1.65 meters) and medium build. Absorption of d-xylose and fat is impaired.

Diagnosis: Intestinal malabsorption secondary to extensive small-bowel resection for volvulus.

Impairment: 75% impairment of the whole person.

Comment: This patient's nutritional status has been markedly impaired by an irreversible defect of the small intestine. Her weight loss exceeds 20% of the desirable level, and her performance of daily activities is seriously impaired.

Colon, Rectum, and Anus

Symptoms and signs of impairment include pain, constipation, diarrhea, tenesmus, incontinence, bleeding, suppuration, appearance of fissures and fistulas, and varying degrees of fecal incontinence; systemic manifestations may include fever, weight loss, debility, and anemia.

Objective procedures useful in establishing impairment of the colon and rectum include, but are not limited to: (1) digital and endoscopic examination including anoscopy, proctoscopy, sigmoidoscopy, and colonoscopy; (2) fecal microscopy and culture; (3) biopsy; and (4) fluoroscopy and radiography with contrast materials.

Criteria for evaluating permanent impairment in function of the colon and rectum are those listed in Table 3.

Example of Class 1 Impairment of the Whole Person: A 50-year-old woman has a protracted tendency to have mildly erratic bowel action with alternating constipation and diarrhea. Stools, while varying in consistency, contain no pathologic products. Proctosigmoidoscopy shows clear mucosa; barium enema examination outlines a normal colon with several diverticula in the sigmoid segment associated with circular muscle spasm.

Diagnosis: (1) Functional gastrointestinal disorder, that is, irritable bowel syndrome; and (2) diverticulosis coli.

Impairment: 0% impairment of the whole person.

Comment: The symptoms, while occasionally annoying, have not interfered with the patient's necessary activities; her treatment requires only minor dietary adjustment.

Example of Class 2 Impairment of the Whole Person: A 28-year-old woman gives a ten-year history of recurring ulcerative colitis. During exacerbations, she has moderate diarrhea with abdominal discomfort and passes small amounts of blood. Sigmoidoscopy shows a granular, slightly friable bowel. Barium enema examination of the colon shows some loss of haustral markings in the descending and sigmoid colon. Fever and anemia are not present. Hospitalization has not been required. Her symptoms respond to a restricted diet, sedation, antispasmodics, constipating agents, and moderate limitation of activities.

Diagnosis: Mild ulcerative colitis, limited to descending colon, sigmoid and rectum.

Impairment: 15% impairment of the whole person.

Comment: The disease has been remittent, and the symptoms only occasionally have interfered with necessary activities; symptomatic and supportive therapy has adequately controlled the disease.

Example of Class 3 Impairment of the Whole Person: A 35-year-old man has had Crohn's disease since the age of 19. He has been hospitalized on several occasions, requiring intensive therapy with transfusion of packed red blood cells because of anemia. His symptoms include intermittent abdominal cramps and diarrhea with occasional perianal suppuration. Examination discloses Crohn's disease affecting the terminal ileum, segments of the colon, and the perianal area. He declines elective proctocolectomy. He continues his sedentary occupation, but his weight is consistently 20% below the desirable level.

Diagnosis: Crohn's enterocolitis.

Impairment: 35% impairment due to Crohn's disease, which is to be combined with an appropriate value for the anemia to determine the impairment of the whole person.

Comment: The disease, while remittent to varying degrees, interferes with the patient's pursuit of normal activities. He will require continuing treatment. His nutritional status is impaired.

Example of Class 4 Impairment of the Whole Person: A 42-year-old woman has a 12-year history of chronic, recurring, ulcerative colitis that requires

Table 3
CLASSES OF COLONIC AND RECTAL IMPAIRMENT

Class 1 0-5% Impairment	Class 2 10-20% Impairment	Class 3 25-35% Impairment	Class 4 40-60% Impairment
Signs and symptoms of colonic or rectal disease are infrequent and of brief duration;	There is objective evidence of colonic or rectal disease or anatomic loss or alteration;	There is objective evidence of colonic or rectal disease or anatomic loss or alteration;	There is objective evidence of colonic and rectal disease or anatomic loss or alteration;
	and There are mild gastrointestinal symptoms with occasional disturbances of bowel function, accompanied by moderate pain;	**and** There are moderate to severe exacerbations with disturbance of bowel habit, accompanied by periodic or continual pain;	**and** There are persistent disturbances of bowel function present at rest with severe persistent pain;
and Limitation of activities, special diet or medication is not required;	**and** Minimal restriction of diet or mild symptomatic therapy may be necessary;	**and** Restriction of activity, special diet and drugs are required during attacks;	**and** Complete limitation of activity, continued restriction of diet, and medication do not entirely control the symptoms;
and No systemic manifestations are present and weight and nutritional state can be maintained at a desirable level;	**and** No impairment of nutrition results.	**and** There are constitutional manifestations (fever, anemia, or weight loss).	**and** There are constitutional manifestations (fever, weight loss, and/or anemia) present;
or There are no sequelae after surgical procedures.			**and** There is no prolonged remission.

intensive therapy, limitation of activities, and numerous blood transfusions. As a result of malnutrition, infection, and transfusions, and as a further complication of her inflammatory bowel disease, the patient has developed jaundice and hepatomegaly. Extensive and severe involvement of the colon is demonstrated by sigmoidoscopic and radiographic studies. Fever and anemia persist. In the opinion of her physicians, surgery cannot be performed now because of her general debility and disease that involves several systems.

Diagnosis: Ulcerative colitis with associated liver disease.

Impairment: 60% impairment due to ulcerative colitis, which is to be combined with appropriate values for the liver disorder and anemia to determine impairment of the whole person.

Comment: The severe inflammatory bowel disease has been complicated by hepatobiliary disease. The patient's normal activities have been seriously impaired. It is possible that with intensive nutritional rehabilitation, a surgical remedy can be attempted, following which the impairment may be lessened.

Enterocutaneous Fistulas

Permanent enterocutaneous fistulas of the gastrointestinal tract, biliary tract, or pancreas, secondary to diseases of these structures, are evaluated as a part of the organ system primarily involved. Permanent, surgically-created stomas usually are provided to compensate for anatomic losses and to allow either for ingress to or egress from the digestive tract.

If a patient has a permanent surgically-created stoma, one of the values in the following table should be combined, using the Combined Values Chart, with a value based on criteria related to the involved organ.

Surgical Stoma	% Impairment of the Whole Person
Esophagostomy	10-15
Gastrostomy	10-15
Jejunostomy	15-20
Ileostomy	15-20
Colostomy	5-10

Criteria for evaluating permanent impairment of the anus are listed in Table 4.

Example of Class 1 Impairment of the Whole Person:
Five years ago a 45-year-old man had an acute pararectal abscess drained surgically. A fistula in ano resulted, with chronic drainage and recurrent bouts of acute infection. One year later a fistulectomy was performed. Since that time the man noted no recurrence of drainage or infection. Examination discloses a well-healed anal scar with distortion, but no weakness, of the anal sphincter.

Diagnosis: Healed fistula in ano.

Impairment: 0% impairment of the whole person.

Comment: The patient had documented anal disease that was appropriately treated and had a satisfactory resolution. His normal activities are not impaired.

Example of Class 2 Impairment of the Whole Person:
A 32-year-old woman has had Crohn's disease of the colon for 14 years, generally well controlled by medical therapy. However, during one exacerbation, a pararectal abscess developed that ruptured spontaneously and led to the development of a chronic fistula in ano. In addition, the patient experienced acute pain and bleeding at stool, and three years ago was found to have a chronic fissure in the posterior midline of the anal canal. Now, symptoms related to anal dysfunction occasionally recur, but generally they are well controlled by treatment. Surgery for the anal disorders is contraindicated in view of the patient's colonic disease.

Diagnosis: Chronic fistula in ano, chronic anal fissure, moderate intermittent impairment of anal function, associated with Crohn's disease of the colon.

Impairment: 10% impairment due to anal disorders, which is to be combined with an appropriate value for the colonic disorder to determine impairment of the whole person.

Comment: Anal function has been impaired but symptoms have been amenable to treatment when required. Her ability to perform normal activities has been only slightly impaired.

Example of Class 3 Impairment of the Whole Person:
Ten years ago a 56-year-old man developed a severe pararectal abscess that ruptured spontaneously. During the ensuing three years multiple recurrent infections occurred, with the opening of fistulous tracts in four other areas surrounding the anus. Surgical repair was undertaken in two stages, but this made necessary incision and excision of substantial portions of the sphincter. Recovery was complicated by severe wound infection. Since that time, the patient has had no recurrence of infection. However, he has had complete absence of fecal control. Although he practices daily rectal irrigations, he still soils himself almost daily. Examination discloses complete anatomic loss of sphincteric functions.

Diagnosis: Total anal incontinence secondary to anatomic loss of sphincter; complete loss of anal function.

Impairment: 25% impairment of the whole person.

Comment: The patient has uncontrollable fecal incontinence not amenable to further anorectal therapy.

Table 4
CLASSES OF ANAL IMPAIRMENT

Class 1 0-5% Impairment	Class 2 10-15% Impairment	Class 3 20-25% Impairment
Signs of organic anal disease are present or there is anatomic loss or alteration;	Signs of organic anal disease are present or there is anatomic loss or alteration;	Signs of organic anal disease are present and there is anatomic loss or alteration;
or There is mild incontinence involving gas and/or liquid stool;	**and** Moderate but partial fecal incontinence is present requiring continual treatment;	**and** Complete fecal incontinence is present;
or Anal symptoms are mild, intermittent, and controlled by treatment.	**or** Continual anal symptoms are present and incompletely controlled by treatment.	**or** Signs of organic anal disease are present and severe anal symptoms unresponsive or not amenable to therapy are present.

Liver and Biliary Tract

Symptoms and signs of hepatobiliary impairment include pain, nausea, vomiting, anorexia, loss of strength and stamina, reduced resistance to infection, jaundice, and pruritus. Complications of advanced liver disease include ascites, anasarca, portal vein hypertension leading to esophageal varices and hemorrhage, and severe metabolic disturbances leading to hepatic encephalopathy and renal failure.

Objective procedures useful in establishing hepatobiliary impairment include, but are not limited to: (1) radiography employing contrast materials, including percutaneous and endoscopic cholangiography, and nuclide scintigraphy; (2) ultrasonography; (3) computerized tomography (CT scan); (4) angiography; (5) liver biopsy; and (6) selected laboratory tests to assess various functions of the liver and biliary ducts.

Criteria for evaluating permanent impairment of the liver and biliary tract are listed in Table 5.

Example of Class 1 Impairment of the Whole Person: A 30-year-old man with a history of excessive alcohol consumption was hospitalized five years ago because of delirium tremens, fever, and jaundice. A liver biopsy revealed extensive fatty metamorphosis with steatonecrosis and minimal periportal fibrosis. Since being released from the hospital, he has drunk no alcoholic beverages, has felt well, and his strength and appetite have been excellent. Physical examination now shows a well-developed, muscular man without evidence of jaundice or ascites. The liver edge is firm and rounded and can be palpated 3 cm below the right costal margin. Liver function studies reveal: serum bilirubin 0.4 mg/100 ml; serum albumin 4.5 mg/100 ml; serum globulin 2.5 mg/100 ml; SGOT 35 units.

Diagnosis: Slight hepatomegaly, probably due to fatty metamorphosis and portal fibrosis.

Impairment: 0% impairment of the whole person.

Comment: The pre-existing disease was documented, but recovery was satisfactory with only minimal evidence of residual liver impairment. The patient requires no treatment other than abstinence from alcohol, and he is able to engage in the activities of normal living.

Example of Class 2 Impairment of the Whole Person: A 35-year-old man had acute viral hepatitis 10 years ago followed by a protracted convalescence.

For the past 6 to 7 years the disease has been quiescent, and the patient has had no jaundice, ascites, or gastrointestinal bleeding. His strength and nutritional state have been satisfactory except for limited stamina. Physical examination shows that he is well nourished and has good muscular development; several small spider angiomata are on the left shoulder; the liver is enlarged 4 cm below the right costal margin and has a firm, rounded edge; the spleen is palpable 1 cm below the left costal margin. Liver function studies reveal: serum bilirubin 2.1 mg/100 ml; serum albumin 4 gm/100 ml; serum globulin 4 gm/100 ml; SGOT 70 units. The serum hepatitis-B surface antigen and core antibody are positive. Liver biopsy shows chronic active hepatitis without cirrhosis.

Diagnosis: Chronic active hepatitis B.

Impairment: 15% impairment of the whole person.

Comment: There is evidence of chronic active hepatitis and limited stamina, but the patient has been able to perform daily activities. Liver impairment is documented but of slight to moderate degree.

Example of Class 3 Impairment of the Whole Person: A 48-year-old man had viral hepatitis at age 15, followed by recurrences of jaundice at ages 22 and 30. For the past six months he has had an intermittently poor appetite and an increase in fatigue. He has noted a slight yellowing of the skin. Physical examination shows that he appears to be chronically ill and minimally jaundiced. Several spider angiomata are seen on his neck and thorax. The liver and spleen are slightly enlarged. No ascites or edema are present. Laboratory studies reveal a normal blood count and urinalysis, serum bilirubin 2.8 mg/100 ml, serum albumin 3 gm/100 ml, serum globulin 4 gm/100 ml, and SGOT 180 units. Hepatitis B surface antigen and core antigen are absent from the serum. Examination of tissue obtained by needle biopsy shows chronic active hepatitis with extensive distortion of lobular architecture.

Diagnosis: Non-A, non-B chronic active hepatitis, and cirrhosis.

Impairment: 40% impairment of the whole person.

Comment: There is evidence of chronic, active, and probably progressive liver disease. The patient's ability to perform normal activities has been impaired.

Table 5—CLASSES OF LIVER AND BILIARY TRACT IMPAIRMENT

Class 1 0-10% Impairment	Class 2 15-25% Impairment	Class 3 30-50% Impairment	Class 4 Greater Than 50% Impairment
Liver Impairment			
There is objective evidence of persistent liver disease even though no symptoms of liver disease are present; and no history of ascites, jaundice, or bleeding esophageal varices within 3 years;	There is objective evidence of chronic liver disease even though no symptoms of liver disease are present; and no history of ascites, jaundice, or bleeding esophageal varices within 3 years;	There is objective evidence of progressive chronic liver disease, or history of jaundice, ascites, or bleeding esophageal or gastric varices within the past year;	There is objective evidence of progressive chronic liver disease, or persistent ascites or persistent jaundice or bleeding esophageal or gastric varices, with central nervous system manifestations of hepatic insufficiency;
and Nutrition and strength are good;	**and** Nutrition and strength are good;	**and** Nutrition and strength may be affected;	**and** Nutritional state is poor.
and Biochemical studies indicate minimal disturbance in liver function;	**and** Biochemical studies indicate more severe liver damage than Class 1.	**or** There is intermittent hepatic encephalopathy.	
or Primary disorders of bilirubin metabolism are present.			
Biliary Tract Impairment			
There is an occasional episode of biliary tract dysfunction.	There is recurrent biliary tract impairment irrespective of treatment.	There is irreparable obstruction of the bile tract with recurrent cholangitis.	There is persistent jaundice and progressive liver disease due to obstruction of the common bile duct.

Example of Class 4 Impairment of the Whole Person:
A 55-year-old woman has had repeated attacks of acute cholecystitis. She has experienced recurrent bouts of right upper quadrant pain, fever, jaundice, dark urine, nausea, vomiting and severe pruritus. Laboratory studies are consistent with the presence of chronic biliary obstruction and permanent liver damage. Esophageal varices are demonstrated by radiography. Abdominal exploration discloses irreparable obstruction of the common bile duct. A liver biopsy reveals advanced biliary cirrhosis.

Diagnosis: Biliary cirrhosis, secondary to obstruction of common bile duct.

Impairment: 85% impairment of the whole person.

Comment: The patient has sustained severe and irreparable impairment of the liver and biliary tract function. Her ability to perform normal activities has been seriously impaired.

Pancreas
Symptoms and signs of impairment of pancreatic function include pain, anorexia, nausea, vomiting, diarrhea, steatorrhea, jaundice, weight loss, muscle wasting, debility, and diabetes. Impairment from the endocrine function of the pancreas is discussed in Chapter 10.

Objective procedures useful in establishing impairment of pancreatic function include, but are not limited to: (1) radiography including plain or scout films of the abdomen, ultrasonography, CT scan, and endoscopic pancreatography; (2) determination of plasma glucose and glucose tolerance; (3) assay of pancreatic enzyme activity in blood, urine, and feces; (4) sweat electrolyte test; and (5) selected secretory tests such as the secretion test, and cytology.

Criteria for evaluating permanent impairment of pancreatic function are those listed in Table 1.

Example of Class 1 Impairment of the Whole Person:
A 45-year-old woman has had epigastric pain associated with an elevated serum amylase once or twice annually for the past three years. Despite a cholecystectomy for gallstones two years ago, the attacks continue to occur, usually after eating a large meal or drinking alcoholic beverages. A diet restricted in fat has corrected the patient's exogenous obesity but has not reduced her weight below a normal level. No clinical or laboratory evidence of pancreatic insufficiency is present.

Diagnosis: Recurrent pancreatitis.

Impairment: 5% impairment of the whole person.

Comment: The pre-existing disease was documented and treated appropriately. There is no present evidence of residual pancreatic impairment, and the patient is able to perform normal activities.

Example of Class 2 Impairment of the Whole Person:
A 35-year-old, 6 ft 3 in (1.90 meters) man of medium build required partial pancreatectomy because of cyst formation and recurrent inflammation of the pancreas, after he was thrown against the steering wheel in an automobile crash. Despite treatment with pancreatic exocrine supplementation, he notes intermittent diarrhea and decreased stamina. He now weighs 164 lb (74.5 kg), while he previously had a weight of 180 lb (81.7 kg). Epigastric and back pain are sufficiently severe to require hospitalization once or twice a year. Steatorrhea is present.

Diagnosis: Chronic pancreatitis and exocrine insufficiency subsequent to trauma, with partial pancreatectomy.

Impairment: 20% impairment of the whole person.

Comment: Pancreatic exocrine function has been impaired, but the patient has been able to maintain a weight within 10% of his desirable weight. However, the patient's ability to perform normal activities has been somewhat impaired.

Example of Class 3 Impairment of the Whole Person:
Subsequent to a cholecystectomy and partial pancreatectomy, and despite dietary restriction and abstinence from alcohol, a woman who is 45 years old and 5 ft 8 in (1.73 meters) tall has had frequently recurring, severe, abdominal pain requiring medication for relief. Insulin is used daily for the control of diabetes mellitus. There has been a 15% reduction in weight below her desirable weight of 135 lb (61.3 kg) despite pancreatic exocrine supplementation.

Diagnosis: Chronic pancreatitis.

Impairment: 40% impairment due to chronic pancreatitis, which is to be combined with an appropriate value for the diabetes mellitus to determine the impairment of the whole person.

Comment: Both exocrine and endocrine functions of the pancreas have been impaired, and continuing treatment is required. The patient has been unable, despite treatment, to regain weight within 10% of the desirable level.

Example of Class 4 Impairment of the Whole Person:
A 47-year-old man first noted apathy, irritability, confusion, and "drunken behavior" six months ago. Total pancreatectomy and duodenectomy (Whipple procedure) subsequently were performed for an insulin-producing islet-cell tumor of the head of the pancreas. The patient now has a malabsorption syndrome with steatorrhea, partially controlled by pancreatic exocrine supplements. His diabetes is brittle and controlled only with difficulty by insulin.

Diagnosis: Pancreatic insufficiency subsequent to total pancreatectomy.

Impairment: 70% impairment due to pancreatic insufficiency, which is to be combined with an appropriate value for the diabetes mellitus to determine impairment of the whole person.

Comment: This patient's ability to perform normal activities has been seriously impaired by total loss of the pancreas, and his symptoms are controlled only partially by intensive therapy.

References

1. Bockus HL (ed): *Gastroenterology*, ed 3. Philadelphia, WB Saunders Co, 1976.

2. Sleisenger MH, Fordtran JS (eds): *Gastrointestinal Disease*, ed 3. Philadelphia, WB Saunders Co, 1983.

3. Schiff L, Schiff ER (eds): *Diseases of the Liver*, ed 5. Philadelphia, JB Lippincott, 1982.

4. Cecil R: *Cecil's Textbook of Medicine*, ed 16, Wyngaarden JB, Smith LH, Jr (eds). Philadelphia, WB Saunders Co, 1982.

Chapter 9

The Reproductive and Urinary Systems

Introduction

This chapter provides criteria for evaluating the effects that permanent impairment of the urinary and/or reproductive systems has on the ability of an individual to perform the activities of daily living. The chapter discusses, in turn, (1) the upper urinary tract, and urinary diversions; (2) the bladder; (3) the urethra; (4) male reproductive organs; and (5) female reproductive organs.

Before using the information in this chapter, the reader is urged to consult the Preface to the Guides, which provides a general discussion of the purpose of the Guides, and of the situations in which they are useful; and discusses techniques for the evaluation of the patient and for report preparation.

Upper Urinary Tract

The parenchyma of the kidneys produces urine, which is conducted by the renal calyces, pelves, and ureters to the urinary bladder. The kidney is an important homeostatic regulatory organ. The manner in which renal and conduit abnormalities may affect the whole person can range from a clinically undetectable homeostatic change, to marked specific and generalized manifestations of deterioration of nephron reserve and urine transport.

Symptoms and signs of impairment of function of the upper urinary tract: These may include changes in micturition; edema; impairment of physical stamina; loss of weight and appetite; anemia; uremia; loin, abdominal, or costovertebral angle pain; chills and fever; hypertension and its complications; abnormalities in the appearance of the urine or its sediments; and biochemical changes in the blood. Renal disease may be revealed only on the basis of laboratory investigation.

Objective techniques useful in evaluating function of the upper urinary tract: Two clinically useful determinations of renal function, the renal clearance of endogenous creatinine and the 15-minute intravenous phenolsulfonphthalein (PSP) test, can ordinarily serve as guidelines for evaluating function of the upper urinary tract.

The glomerular filtration rate, which measures renal clearance of endogenous creatinine, gives a quantitative estimate of the total functioning nephron population. The reliability of clearance tests of renal function is improved by longer periods of urine collection; therefore, measurement of the 24-hour endogenous creatinine clearance should be used. The normal ranges of creatinine clearance are 130 to 200 liters/24 hr (90 to 139 ml/min) in men, and 115 to 180 liters/24 hr (80 to 125 ml/min) in women.

The 15-minute intravenous PSP test, although affected by stasis in conduit transport of urine, is a clinically useful determination of the general adequacy of renal tubular transport mechanisms. For the test to be valid, the patient must be adequately hydrated and precisely 1 cc of solution containing 6.0 mg of PSP must be injected intravenously, preferably by tuberculin syringe. The normal dye excretion is 25% or more in the urine within 15 minutes.

If there are any discrepancies in these two tests, that is, if the glomerular filtration rate is out of proportion to the PSP test, indicating tubular-glomerular imbalance, then it may be desirable to perform additional investigations, such as metabolic studies, serum and urine biochemical determinations, osmolalities, concentration and dilution tests, urinalyses, cultures, radiographic investigations, isotope renograms, and scans.

Assessment of parenchymal disfigurement and/or conduit abnormality, which by virtue of clinical manifestations impair the function of the whole person, may require such diagnostic procedures as endoscopy with study of both or of individual kidneys, biopsy, arteriography, and uroradiography.

Criteria for Evaluating Impairment of the Upper Urinary Tract

In most instances of stable loss of upper urinary tract function, diminution in creatinine clearance is commensurate with depression of PSP excretion. If a discrepancy exists between these two tests, then additional diagnostic studies should be performed to determine which test is most representative of the loss of upper urinary tract function, and the results of that test should be used in determining the degree of impairment.

From a physiologic point of view, an individual with a solitary kidney may have no actual impairment of renal function; nevertheless, with that condition there exists an absence or loss of the normal safety factor that may be of potential significance in evaluating impairment, depending on the cause of the condition. The individual with a solitary kidney, regardless of cause, should be rated as having 10% impairment of the whole person because of a structural loss of an essential organ. This value is to be combined with any other permanent impairment, including any impairment in the remaining kidney, to determine the individual's impairment.

Deterioration of renal function requiring either peritoneal dialysis or hemodialysis would indicate severe impairment in the range of Class 4 Impairment, or 65% to 90% (see below). Successful renal transplantation may result in marked improvement of renal function, to the level of Class 2 Impairment, or 15% to 30%. However, transplant recipients require continuous observation and medication, which may add to their impairment. For this reason, and at the discretion of the evaluating physician, 0% to 5% may be added to the figure for impairment of renal function. Furthermore, impairment from complications of the disease or therapy, such as Cushingoid changes and osteoporosis, must be evaluated as they arise and combined with the renal impairment rating. Combining of ratings should be done as prescribed in the Combined Values Chart.

Class 1—Impairment of the Whole Person, 0-10%:
A patient belongs in Class 1 when (a) diminution of upper urinary tract function is present, as evidenced by creatinine clearance of 75 to 90 liters/24 hr (52 to 62.5 ml/min) or PSP excretion of 15% to 20% in 15 minutes; OR (b) intermittent symptoms and signs of upper urinary tract dysfunction are present that do not require continuous treatment or surveillance.

Example 1: When a 22-year-old man was 12 years of age, he developed backache, fever, hematuria, headache, and hypertension during an epidemic of ß-hemolytic streptococcal tonsilitis. He was edematous and oliguric, and renal functions were depressed. The urine contained numerous red blood cells and red blood cell casts, and he passed 2.4 gm protein per 24 hours. The creatinine clearance was 72 liters/24 hr (50 ml/min).

After a severe illness with a long convalescence, the man improved and was well except for microscopic hematuria, which persisted for months but finally cleared. Six months after the illness, the creatinine clearance was 130 liters/24 hr (90 ml/min).

Current studies reveal a healthy man with no evidence of renal disease by biopsy and a creatinine clearance of 158 liters/24 hr (110 ml/min).

Diagnosis: Healthy man with kidneys that are completely recovered from poststreptococcal acute glomerulonephritis.

Impairment: 0% impairment of the whole person.

Example 2: A 40-year-old man had an acute episode of renal colic and later passed a small stone. He had two prior episodes of colic with spontaneous passage of stones. Urograms were interpreted as normal; no evidence of metabolic disease was present. Urine, creatinine clearance, and PSP determinations were within normal limits.

Diagnosis: Recurrent ureteral calculi.

Impairment: 5% impairment of the whole person.

Class 2—Impairment of the Whole Person, 15-30%:
A patient belongs in Class 2 when (a) dimunition of upper urinary tract function is present, as evidenced by creatinine clearance of 60 to 75 liters/24 hr (42 to 52 ml/min) or PSP excretion of 10% to 15% in 15 minutes; OR (b) although creatinine clearance is greater than 75 liters/24 hr (52 ml/min), and PSP excretion is more than 15%

in 15 minutes, symptoms and signs of upper urinary tract disease or dysfunction necessitate continuous surveillance and frequent treatment.

Example 1: A 45-year-old man with a history of nephritis as a child underwent an emergency appendectomy and drainage of an appendiceal abscess. Despite an adequate urinary output during the postoperative period, the serum creatinine rose to 2.8 mg/100 ml. Convalescence was prolonged; his anemia subsided gradually and physical stamina returned slowly.

Now, six months postoperatively, the patient feels well and is able to engage in most of his usual daily activities. The urine shows a trace of protein (0.75 gm/24 hr). Excretory urograms show no architectural abnormality, but the creatinine clearances range from 60 to 70 liters/24 hr (42 to 49 ml/min), and the PSP excretion ranges between 15% and 20% in 15 minutes.

Diagnosis: Asymptomatic persistent proteinuria as a result of childhood nephritis aggravated by surgery.

Impairment: 15% impairment of the whole person.

Example 2: A 50-year-old woman had a successful operation for parathyroid adenoma. However, she continues to have periodic attacks of pyelonephritis occasioned by residual calculi in both kidneys and she passes stones sporadically. The infrequent clinical attacks of pyelonephritis respond to antibiotics. The symptoms of her urinary tract infection are controlled by continuous medication. The creatinine clearance is stable at approximately 65 liters/24 hr (45 ml/min) and the PSP excretion at 10% in 15 minutes. The bilateral pyelocalyceal deformities and the size of the kidneys, as delineated by excretory urography, have not changed appreciably in a three-year period.

Diagnosis: Renal calculi and bilateral chronic pyelonephritis.

Impairment: 30% impairment due to upper urinary tract impairment, which is to be combined with an appropriate value for parathyroid impairment to determine the impairment of the whole person.

Example 3: A 52-year-old man had surgical reconstruction of his left lower ureter because of severe damage to its function from retroperitoneal fibrosis. Despite apparently normal architecture

and function of the kidney on the side of the ureteral repair, vesicoureteral reflux can be demonstrated, and repeated attacks of pyelonephritis occur whenever antibacterial medication is discontinued. The creatinine clearance is 100 liters/24 hr (69 ml/min), and the PSP excretion is 25% in 15 minutes. Since the involved kidney is normal in appearance and shows no deterioration of function, no further surgical intervention is contemplated.

Diagnosis: Active, unilateral, chronic pyelonephritis, secondary to vesicoureteral reflux.

Impairment: 15% impairment of the whole person.

Example 4: A 28-year-old man with progressive chronic glomerulonephritis developed marked azotemia and oliguria requiring hemodialysis. Successful renal transplantation from his mother resulted in good renal function with creatinine clearance of 108 liters/24 hr. The patient is maintained on immuran and prednisone, requiring close observation for possible development of osteroporosis of the hip. The immunosuppression also increases the possibility of severe secondary infections.

Diagnosis: Functioning renal transplant.

Impairment: 25% impairment of the whole person due to renal disease and the need for continuous medication.

Comment: Should complications develop because of the therapy, the patient should be re-evaluated and the permanent impairment from the complications should be combined with the above impairment rating.

Class 3—Impairment of the Whole Person, 35-60%: A patient belongs in Class 3 when (a) diminution of upper urinary tract function is present, as evidenced by creatinine clearance of 40 to 60 liters/24 hr (28 to 42 ml/min) or PSP excretion of 5% to 10% in 15 minutes; OR (b) although creatinine clearance is 60 to 75 liters/24 hr (42 to 52 ml/min), and PSP excretion is 10% to 15% in 15 minutes, symptoms and signs of upper urinary tract disease or dysfunction are incompletely controlled by surgical or continuous medical treatment.

Example 1: A 52-year-old woman complained of chronic fatigue. On examination, she was found to have elevation of the serum creatinine and a moderate anemia. There was no clear-cut history of nephritis. A renal biopsy demonstrated diffuse proliferative glomerulonephritis. A high-dose excretory urogram delineated contracted kidneys with normal pyelocalyceal architecture. Results of urine culture were negative; creatinine clearance was 50 liters/24 hr (35 ml/min), and PSP excretion was 10% in 15 minutes.

Diagnosis: Chronic glomerulonephritis with contracted kidneys.

Impairment: 60% impairment due to upper urinary tract impairment, which is to be combined, using the Combined Values Chart, with an appropriate value for the anemia to determine the impairment of the whole person.

Example 2: A 48-year-old man has calculi in the minor calyces of both kidneys. He has a history of multiple endoscopic and open surgical procedures for stone removal. He has marked diminution in the size of one kidney and bilateral pyelographic architectural changes as a result of previous surgical procedures and recurrent pyelonephritis. Despite continuous antibacterial medication, the urine remains infected, and periodic episodes of chills, fever and back pain occur. Creatinine clearance is 65 liters/24 hr (45 ml/min) and PSP excretion is 10% in 15 minutes.

Diagnosis: Renal calculi with bilateral recurrent pyelonephritis.

Impairment: 50% impairment of the whole person.

Example 3: A 48-year-old man was injured in an automobile crash and developed hematuria. Blood pressure was 150/90 mm Hg. Radiologic studies revealed that the left kidney was damaged. No other abnormalities were noted. The man was kept at bed rest in a hospital for a week and then discharged.

Six months later, the man began to complain of severe headaches. The blood pressure was found to be 240/160 mm Hg, and malignant hypertensive retinopathy was noted. Investigation revealed a creatinine clearance of 40 liters/24 hr (28 ml/min) and definite evidence of left renovascular hypertension. The left kidney was removed. Biopsies from the right kidney revealed malignant hypertensive changes. The histology of the left kidney revealed ischemia and juxtaglomerular hypertrophy.

Immediately after surgery, the patient's blood

pressure fell to 170/110 mm Hg and, during the next six months, it leveled off at 155/95 mm Hg. The eyegrounds regressed to Grade II (Keith-Wagner classification), and creatinine clearance rose slowly to level off at 58 liters/24 hr (40 ml/min).

Diagnosis: Left nephrectomy for malignant hypertension due to post-traumatic renovascular ischemia of the left kidney; arteriolonephrosclerosis of the right kidney; and hypertensive vascular disease.

Impairment: 55% impairment due to arteriolonephrosclerosis and 10% impairment due to nephrectomy, which combine to 60% impairment of the urinary system; this should be combined with an appropriate value for the cardiovascular impairment to determine impairment of the whole person.

Class 4 — Impairment of the Whole Person, 65-90%: A patient belongs in Class 4 when (a) diminution of upper urinary tract function is present, as evidenced by creatinine clearance below 40 liters/24 hr (28 ml/min) or PSP excretion below 5% in 15 minutes; OR (b) although creatinine clearance is 40 to 60 liters/24 hr (28 to 42 ml/min), and PSP excretion is 5% to 10% in 15 minutes, symptoms and signs of upper urinary tract disease or dysfunction persist, despite surgical or continuous medical treatment.

Example 1: A 44-year-old man with a family history of polycystic renal disease experienced sudden loin pain and noted gross hematuria. During two years preceding the acute episode, the man's serum creatinine rose from 8 mg/100 ml to 10 mg/100 ml, and he was maintained on a protein-restricted diet. Until the episode he was working regularly and was relatively asymptomatic.

Examination now discloses that the creatinine clearance is 35 liters/24 hr (24 ml/min), and the PSP excretion is less than 5% in 15 minutes. Endoscopy and retrograde urograms show bilateral deformities characteristic of polycystic kidneys.

Diagnosis: Bilateral polycystic renal disease; advanced renal insufficiency.

Impairment: 70% impairment of the whole person.

Example 2: A young woman became anuric following severe abruptio placentae. A percutaneous renal biopsy was performed. Diagnosis was renal cortical necrosis, and periodic courses of peritoneal dialyses were instituted. After 49 days

TABLE 1—CLASSES OF UPPER URINARY TRACT IMPAIRMENT*

Class 1 Impairment 0-10%	Class 2 Impairment 15-30%	Class 3 Impairment 35-60%	Class 4 Impairment 65-90%
Diminution of upper urinary tract function is present as evidenced by creatinine clearance of 75 to 90 liters/24 hr (52 to 62.5 ml/min), or PSP excretion of 15% to 20% in 15 minutes.	Diminution of upper urinary tract function is present as evidenced by creatinine clearance of 60 to 75 liters/24 hr (42 to 52 ml/min), or PSP excretion of 10% to 15% in 15 minutes.	Diminution of upper urinary tract function is present as evidenced by creatinine clearance of 40 to 60 liters/24 hr (28 to 42 ml/min), or PSP excretion of 5% to 10% in 15 minutes.	Diminution of upper urinary tract function is present as evidenced by creatinine clearance below 40 liters/24 hr (28 ml/min), or PSP excretion below 5% in 15 minutes.
or	**or**	**or**	**or**
Intermittent symptoms and signs of upper urinary tract dysfunction are present that do not require continuous treatment or surveillance.	Although creatinine clearance is greater than 75 liters/24 hr (52 ml/min), or PSP excretion is more than 15% in 15 minutes, symptoms and signs of upper urinary tract disease or dysfunction necessitate continuous surveillance and frequent treatment.	Although creatinine clearance is 60 to 75 liters/24 hr (42 to 52 ml/min), or PSP excretion is 10% to 15% in 15 minutes, symptoms and signs of upper urinary tract disease or dysfunction are incompletely controlled by surgical or continuous medical treatment.	Although creatinine clearance is 40 to 60 liters/24 hr (28 to 42 ml/min), or PSP excretion is 5% to 10% in 15 minutes, symptoms and signs of upper urinary tract disease or dysfunction persists despite surgical or continuous medical treatment.

*NOTE: The individual with a solitary kidney, regardless of cause, should be rated as having 10% impairment of the whole person. This value is to be combined with any other permanent impairment (including any impairment in the remaining kidney) pertinent to the case under consideration. The normal ranges of creatinine clearance are: Males: 130 to 200 liters/24 hr (90 to 139 ml/min). Females: 115 to 180 liters/24 hr (80 to 125 ml/min). The normal PSP excretion is 25% or more in urine in 15 minutes.

of anuria and then oliguria, the urine output increased; on the 60th day the serum creatinine, which was 22 mg/100 ml, began to fall without peritoneal dialysis. Four months after the episode of anuria, the patient performs most of the activities of daily living despite severely compromised renal function. The creatinine clearance has leveled off at 11.5 liters/24 hr (8 ml/min).

Diagnosis: Renal cortical necrosis; severe chronic renal failure.

Impairment: 90% impairment of the whole person.

Example 3: A 56-year-old woman with chronic progressive glomerulonephritis is severely anemic, azotemic and oliguric and requires hemodialysis twice weekly. For one or two days after treatment she feels well and is able to perform household duties. On the days just prior to dialysis she is nauseated, lethargic, and edematous.

Diagnosis: Severe chronic renal failure.

Impairment: 90% impairment of the whole person.

This classification of upper urinary tract impairment is recapitulated in Table 1.

Urinary Diversion

Permanent, surgically-created forms of urinary diversion usually are provided to compensate for anatomic loss and to allow for egress of urine.

They are evaluated as a part of, and in conjunction with, the assessment of the involved portion of the urinary tract.

Irrespective of how well these diversions function in the preservation of renal integrity and the disposition of urine, the following values for the diversions should be combined with those determined under the criteria previously given for the portion of the urinary tract involved:

Type of Diversion	% Impairment of the Whole Person
Uretero-Intestinal	10
Cutaneous Ureterostomy Without Intubation	10
Nephrostomy or Intubated Ureterostomy	15

Example 1: A 56-year-old man with bilateral nephrostomies because of obliterative fibrotic ureteral disease had removal of renal calculi. An attempt to reconstitute normal conduit function through surgery was unsuccessful. Urinary infection cannot be eradicated, and the patient complains mildly of hematuria when the nephrostomy tubes are changed and of occasional episodes of fever and flank pain. He continues to engage in most activities of daily living. The creatinine clearance is approximately 50 liters/24 hr (35 ml/min) and the PSP excretion is between 5% and 10% in 15 minutes.

Diagnosis: Pyeloureteral disease requiring bilateral nephrostomy diversion.

Impairment: 65% impairment due to pyeloureteral disease and 15% impairment due to bilateral nephrostomies, which combine to give 70% impairment of the whole person.

Example 2: A 52-year-old woman, seven years after anterior pelvic exenteration and uretero-ileostomy for carcinoma of the cervix, has no evidence of recurrent cancer. She has had calculi removed from both kidneys and she experiences periodic episodes of pyelonephritis even on continual medication. Radiographic changes suggesting pyelonephritis are present. The creatinine clearance is approximately 60 liters/24 hr (24 ml/min) and PSP excretion is about 10% in 15 minutes.

Diagnosis: Uretero-ileostomy urinary diversion and chronic bilateral pyelonephritis.

Impairment: 65% impairment due to bilateral pyelonephritis, 10% impairment due to uretero-ileostomy, and 55% impairment due to pelvic exenteration, that is, excision of bladder, lower ureters, uterus, cervix, vagina, fallopian tubes, and ovaries, which combine to 85% impairment of the whole person.

Bladder

The bladder is a voluntary controllable reservoir for urine that normally permits the patient to retain urine for several hours.

Symptoms and signs of impairment of function of the bladder: These may include urinary frequency, painful voiding (dysuria), urgency, incontinence, involuntary retention of urine, hematuria, pyuria, crystalluria, passage of urinary calculi, and a suprapubic mass.

Objective techniques useful in evaluating function of the bladder: These include, but are not limited to, cystoscopy, cystography, voiding cystourethrography, cystometry, uroflometry, urinalysis, and urine cultures.

Criteria for Evaluating Permanent Impairment of the Bladder

When evaluating permanent impairment of the bladder, the status of the upper urinary tract must also be considered. The appropriate impairment values for both should be combined using the Combined Values Chart in order to determine the extent of impairment of the whole person.

Class 1—Impairment of the Whole Person, 0-10%: A patient belongs in Class 1 when the patient has symptoms and signs of bladder disorder requiring intermittent treatment with normal function between episodes of malfunction.

Example: A 41-year-old woman was treated with radium 20 years ago for uterine fibroids. Recent episodes of urinary bleeding due to postradiation telangiectasia of the bladder required emergency hospitalization and vessel fulguration under anesthesia. The episodes occurred at intervals of from one to two weeks to six months. Between attacks, findings from blood and urine studies were normal. After each episode the patient was able to resume usual activities within seven days.

Diagnosis: Postradiation telangiectasia of the bladder.

Impairment: 10% impairment of the whole person.

Class 2—Impairment of the Whole Person, 15-20%: A patient belongs in Class 2 when (a) there are symptoms and/or signs of bladder disorder requiring continuous treatment; OR (b) there is good bladder reflex activity, but no voluntary control.

Example 1: A 47-year-old man developed such progressive urinary frequency that he was voiding at intervals of every 10 to 15 minutes day and night. A diagnosis of interstitial cystitis was established, but the usual treatment, bladder dilation with various agents, was ineffective. The upper urinary tract was normal and uninfected. After a ureterosigmoidostomy the man was able to resume his usual activities.

Diagnosis: Contracted, fixed bladder requiring urinary diversion.

Impairment: 15% impairment due to contracted fixed bladder and 10% impairment due to ureterosigmoidostomy, which combine to 24% impairment of the whole person.

NOTE: The removal of the bladder for any reason and a resultant urinary diversion should be assigned a similar rating of impairment, that is, one of about 24%.

Example 2: A 42-year-old man with chronic renal infection resistant to antibiotic therapy developed a severe cystitis requiring him to empty his bladder at intervals of less than 30 minutes and making necessary his use of a urine collection device. His general physical condition was excellent; his urine contained numerous white blood cells and a few red blood cells.

The man refused urinary diversion through a surgical procedure. As a result, he cannot retain his urine long enough to permit him to perform many activities of daily living.

Diagnosis: Chronic cystitis.

Impairment: 20% impairment due to cystitis, which is to be combined with an appropriate value for the upper urinary tract disorder to determine the impairment of the whole person.

Class 3—Impairment of the Whole Person, 25-35%: A patient belongs in Class 3 when the bladder has poor reflex activity, that is, there is intermittent dribbling, and no voluntary control.

Class 4—Impairment of the Whole Person, 40-60%: A patient belongs in Class 4 when there is no reflex or voluntary control of the bladder, that is, there is continuous dribbling.

Urethra

In the female, the urethra is a urinary conduit containing a voluntary urethral sphincter. In the male, the urethra is a conduit for urine and seminal ejaculations that possesses a voluntary urethral sphincter and propulsive musculature.

Symptoms and signs of impairment of function of the urethra: These include dysuria, diminished urinary stream, urinary retention, incontinence, extraneous or ectopic openings, periurethral mass or masses, and diminished urethral caliber.

Objective techniques useful in evaluating function of the urethra: These include, but are not limited to, urethroscopy, urethrography, cystourethrography, endoscopy, urethrometry, and cystometrography.

Criteria for Evaluating Permanent Impairment of the Urethra

When evaluating permanent impairment of the urethra, one must also consider the status of the upper urinary tract and bladder. The values for all parts of the urinary system should be combined using the Combined Values Chart to determine the extent of impairment of the whole person.

Class 1—Impairment of the Whole Person, 0-5%: A patient belongs in Class 1 when symptoms and signs of urethral disorder are present that require intermittent therapy for control.

Example: As a result of an injury, a 27-year-old man has a urethral stricture that requires dilation every few weeks. Between dilation he is free of symptoms, and he has difficulty only when the urethra gradually constricts, when he notices increasing difficulty in voiding. There is no upper urinary tract infection.

Diagnosis: Traumatic urethral stricture.

Impairment: 5% impairment of the whole person.

Class 2—Impairment of the Whole Person, 10-20%: A patient belongs in Class 2 when there are symptoms and signs of a urethral disorder that cannot be effectively controlled by treatment.

Example 1: A 23-year-old man experienced considerable laceration of the ventral surface of the penis that created a surgically uncorrectable fistula. He was able to perform most of the activities of daily living, but could not void normally. He could ejaculate with sexual sensation, but the fistula was so situated that impregnation of his wife was impossible.

Diagnosis: Urethral fistula.

Impairment: 15% impairment due to urethral fistula and 10% impairment due to impaired sexual function, which combine to 24% impairment of the whole person.

Example 2: After an automobile crash, a 31-year-old man experienced a urethral stricture that necessitated weekly or biweekly urethral dilations. Because of the magnitude of the injury to the urethra, corrective surgery was ineffective. Repeated urinary tract infections secondary to urethral dilations continued to occur, and pyelonephritis developed. The man's creatinine clearance is 65 liters/24 hr (45 ml/min), and PSP excretion is 10% in 15 minutes.

Diagnosis: Traumatic urethral stricture with chronic pyelonephritis.

Impairment: 20% impairment due to urethral stricture and 25% impairment due to upper urinary tract damage, which combine to 40% impairment of the whole person.

Example 3: A 21-year-old factory worker was crushed between a lift and a wall. His bony pelvis was fractured, his urethra was totally severed at the apex of the prostate, and his perineum was severely lacerated. Immediate reconstructive urethral surgery was unsuccessful, and one year after the injury a ureterosigmoidostomy was necessary, which resulted in hydronephrosis of the right kidney and repeated urinary tract infections. Later, this diversion was converted to a conduit, and renal infection occurred only sporadically thereafter.

At present, the worker is totally impotent. The pelvic fracture is healed and there is no evidence of musculoskeletal impairment, but because of occasional urinary tract infections the man periodically is unable to perform some activities of daily living. Creatinine clearance is 70 liters/24 hr (49 ml/min).

Diagnosis: Severed urethra, hydronephrosis with recurring urinary tract infections, and impotency.

Impairment: 20% impairment due to severed urethra, 30% impairment due to upper urinary tract impairment, 10% impairment due to uretero-ileostomy, and 30% impairment due to loss of sexual function, which combine to 65% impairment of the whole person.

Male Reproductive Organs

The male reproductive organs include the penis, scrotum, testes, epididymides, spermatic cords, prostate, and seminal vesicles. The values of impairment of the male reproductive organs are given in the following sections for men 40 to 65 years of age. These values may be increased by 50% of a given value for those below the age of 40 years, and decreased by 50% for those over the age of 65 years. For instance, a 50% increase of a 20% impairment equals a 30% impairment.

Penis

The penis has sexual functions of erection and ejaculation, and urinary functions. The latter are discussed in the section on urethra.

Symptoms and signs of impairment of function of the penis: These include abnormalities of erection and sensation, and partial or complete penile loss.

Criteria for Evaluating Permanent Impairment of the Penis

When evaluating impairment of the penis, it is necessary to consider impairment of both the sexual and the urinary functions. The degree of impairment of sexual function should be determined in accordance with the criteria that follow, and it should be combined with the appropriate value for an impairment of urinary function that is present to determine the impairment of the whole person.

Class 1—Impairment of the Whole Person, 5-10%: A patient belongs in Class 1 when sexual function is possible, but there are varying degrees of difficulty of erection, ejaculation, and/or sensation.

Example: A 32-year-old man suffered a compressive injury to the penile shaft. Healing occurred with partial cicatrization of the left mid corpus cavernosum. Bowstring curvature to the left occurs during erections. Sensation and ejaculation are normal, but pain results if intercourse is not very carefully consummated.

Diagnosis: Fibrosis of left mid corpus cavernosum, post-traumatic.

Impairment: 10% impairment of the whole person, which takes into consideration the patient's age.

Class 2—Impairment of the Whole Person, 10-15%: A patient belongs in Class 2 when sexual function is possible and there is sufficient erection, BUT ejaculation and sensation are absent.

Example: A 28-year-old man suffered a fractured pelvis with wide separation of the symphysis pubis, perivesical and periprostatic hematomas, and a tear of the prostatomembranous urethra. These injuries responded well to reparative surgery, and there was no subsequent urinary difficulty. Erection and intercourse are possible, but sexual sensation and ejaculation are absent.

Diagnosis: Post-traumatic urethral and genital insufficiency.

Impairment: 15% impairment of the whole person, which includes consideration for the patient's age.

Class 3—Impairment of the Whole Person, 20%: A patient belongs in Class 3 when no sexual function is possible.

Example: An 18-year-old boy suffered traumatic dislocation of the penis. Corporal repair and urethroplasty have preserved genital appearance and urethral function, but erection is not possible.

Diagnosis: Post-traumatic vascular and neurological penile insufficiency.

Impairment: 30% impairment of the whole person, which considers the patient's age.

Scrotum

The scrotum covers, protects, and provides a suitable environment for the testes.

Symptoms and signs of impairment of function of the scrotum: These include pain, enlargement, lack of testicular mobility, and inappropriate location of the testes.

Objective techniques useful in evaluating function of the scrotum: These include, but are not limited to, observation, palpation, and testicular examination.

Criteria for Evaluating Permanent Impairment of the Scrotum

Class 1—Impairment of the Whole Person, 0-5%:
A patient belongs in Class 1 when there are symptoms and signs of scrotal loss or disease and there is no evidence of testicular malfunction, although there may be testicular malposition.

Example: A 38-year-old man had an injury resulting in loss of all scrotal skin. Split-thickness skin graft reconstructions gave a good cosmetic result. At present, there is no evidence of testicular malfunction, but testicular mobility is affected, and the patient experiences discomfort during exercise and in certain positions.

Diagnosis: Ablation of scrotal skin; split-thickness skin graft reconstruction of the scrotum.

Impairment: 5% impairment of the whole person, which includes due consideration of the patient's age.

Class 2—Impairment of the Whole Person, 10-15%:
A patient belongs in Class 2 when (a) there are symptoms and signs of architectural alteration or disease such that the testes must be implanted in other than a scrotal position to preserve testicular function, and pain or discomfort is present with activity; OR (b) there is total loss of the scrotum.

Example: A 50-year-old man suffered extensive burns of the lower extremities, genitals, and abdomen. Skin grafting to the abdomen and lower extremities was satisfactory; however, it was necessary to transplant the testicles to the thighs to permit adequate skin coverage of the scrotal area.

Diagnosis: Burn ablation of the scrotum.

Impairment: 15% impairment of the whole person.

Testes, Epididymides, and Spermatic Cords

The testes produce spermatozoa, synthesize male steroid hormones, and provide the appearance and psychological badge of maleness. The epididymides and spermatic cords transport the spermatozoa.

Symptoms and signs of impairment of function of the testes, epididymides, and spermatic cords: These include local or referred pain; tenderness and change in size, contour, position, and texture; and abnormalities of testicular hormones and seminal fluid.

Objective techniques useful in evaluating function of the testes, epididymides, and spermatic cords: These include, but are not limited to, vasography; lymphangiography, spermatic arteriography and venography; biopsy; semen analysis; and studies of follicle-stimulating, ketosteroid, and hydroxysteroid hormones.

Criteria for Evaluating Permanent Impairment of Testes, Epididymides, and Spermatic Cords

Class 1—Impairment of the Whole Person, 0-5%:
A patient belongs in Class 1 when (a) symptoms and signs of testicular, epididymal, and/or spermatic cord disease are present and there is anatomic alteration; AND (b) continuous treatment is not required; AND (c) there are no abnormalities of seminal or hormonal function; OR (d) a solitary testis is present.

Example: A 36-year-old man has had repeated episodes of epididymo-orchitis due to recurrent prostatitis. He has symptoms of discomfort between attacks and clinical evidence of chronic epididymitis. He does not desire vas deferens ligation, because his seminal fluid is normal and he may desire additional children.

Diagnosis: Chronic epididymitis secondary to chronic prostatitis.

Impairment: 5% impairment due to epididymitis and 5% impairment due to prostatitis, taking into consideration the patient's age, which combine to give 10% impairment of the whole person.

Class 2—Impairment of the Whole Person, 10-15%:
A patient belongs in Class 2 when (a) symptoms and signs of testicular, epididymal and/or spermatic

cord disease are present and there is anatomic alteration; AND (b) frequent or continuous treatment is required; AND (c) there are detectable seminal or hormonal abnormalities.

Example: A 33-year-old man had evidence of interference with testicular blood supply after trauma, experiencing acute onset of swelling of the testes, hydrocele formation, and intense pain. One testis atrophied, and the other diminished in size. Procreative efforts, previously successful in producing offspring, were unavailing. At present, there are no systemic hormonal changes, but semen analysis reveals oligospermia.

Diagnosis: Testicular atrophy and oligospermia.

Impairment: 15% impairment of the whole person, which includes due consideration for the patient's age.

Class 3—Impairment of the Whole Person, 15-20%: A patient belongs in Class 3 when trauma or disease produces bilateral anatomical loss, or there is no detectable seminal or hormonal function of the testes, epididymides, or spermatic cords.

Example: A 17-year-old boy was injured by a farm machine, sustaining amputation of the scrotum and its contents.

Diagnosis: Traumatic gonadal ablation.

Impairment: 30% impairment due to gonadal ablation and 23% impairment due to scrotal loss, which include due consideration for the patient's young age, and 5% impairment due to lack of an endocrine gland; all values combine to give 49% impairment of the whole person.

Prostate and Seminal Vesicles

The prostate and seminal vesicles are involved with transport, nutritional modification, and maintenance of adequate environment for spermatozoa and semen. Impairment associated with urinary function is discussed in the section on urethra.

Symptoms and signs of impairment of function of the prostate and seminal vesicles: These may include local or referred pain; tenderness; changes in size and texture; disturbances in function of spermatic cords, epididymides and testes; oligospermia; hemospermia; and urinary abnormalities.

Objective techniques useful in evaluating function of the prostate and seminal vesicles: These include,

but are not limited to, urography, endoscopy, ejaculatory duct catheterization, vasography, biopsy, and examination of prostatic excretions and of hormone excretion patterns.

Criteria for Evaluating Permanent Impairment of the Prostate and Seminal Vesicles

Class 1—Impairment of the Whole Person, 0-5%: A patient belongs in Class 1 when (a) there are symptoms and signs of prostatic and/or seminal vesicular dysfunction or disease; AND (b) anatomic alteration is present; AND (c) continuous treatment is not required.

Example: A 42-year-old man has had many episodes of acute prostatitis. He has episodes of mild perineal discomfort that occasionally require medication for pain.

Diagnosis: Chronic prostatitis with acute febrile episodes.

Impairment: 5% impairment of the whole person.

Class 2—Impairment of the Whole Person, 10-15%: A patient belongs in Class 2 when (a) frequent severe symptoms and signs of prostatic and/or seminal vesicular dysfunction or disease are present; AND (b) anatomic alteration is present; AND (c) continuous treatment is required.

Example: After drainage of a prostatic abscess, a 34-year-old man has continual symptoms and signs of prostatitis that he can tolerate only with the constant use of antibacterial medication.

Diagnosis: Recurrent acute and chronic prostatitis.

Impairment: 15% impairment of the whole person, which includes due consideration for the patient's age.

Class 3—Impairment of the Whole Person, 15-20%: A patient belongs in Class 3 when there has been ablation of the prostate and/or seminal vesicles.

Female Reproductive Organs

The female reproductive organs include the vulva, vagina, cervix, uterus, fallopian tubes, and ovaries. The degree of impairment of the female reproductive system is influenced by age, and especially by whether the woman is in the childbearing age group. The physiologic differences of premenopausal and postmenopausal women are considered in establishing the criteria in this chapter for evaluating the impairment of female reproductive organs.

Vulva-Vagina

The vulva has cutaneous, sexual, and urinary functions. The latter has been discussed in the section on the urethra. The vagina has a sexual function and serves as a birth passageway.

Symptoms and signs of impairment of function of the vulva-vagina: These include loss or altered sexual sensation; complete or partial absence; presence of vulvovaginitis, vulvitis, vaginitis, cicatrization, ulceration, stenosis, atrophy, hypertrophy, neoplasia, dysplasia, and/or spasm; difficulty with sexual intercourse, urination, and/or vaginal delivery; and secondary effects on underlying perineal structures.

Criteria for Evaluating Permanent Impairment of the Vulva-Vagina

Class 1—Impairment of the Whole Person, 0-10%: A patient belongs in Class 1 when (a) symptoms and signs of disease or deformity of the vulva and/or vagina are present that do not require continuous treatment; AND (b) sexual intercourse is possible; AND (c) the vagina is adequate for childbirth during the premenopausal years.

Example: An obese 38-year-old married woman who has given vaginal birth to three living children experiences recurrent chronic dermatitis of the genitocrural area. At intervals, she requires treatment for intense pruritus and active dermatitis. Her discomfort is more marked during warm and humid weather. Laboratory cultures for fungal diseases are negative. The patient does not have diabetes. There is a remission of symptoms when her weight is controlled, when she avoids tight clothing, and when she observes careful hygienic measures. Sexual intercourse is possible if precautions are observed to avoid excessive vulvar irritation.

Diagnosis: Dermatitis of vulva, intertrigo.

Impairment: 0% impairment of the whole person.

Class 2—Impairment of the Whole Person, 15-25%: A patient belongs in Class 2 when (a) symptoms and signs of disease or deformity of the vulva and/or vagina are present that require continuous treatment; AND (b) sexual intercourse is possible with varying degrees of difficulty; AND (c) during the premenopausal years, adequacy for vaginal delivery is limited.

Example: A 34-year-old married woman developed a rectovaginal fistula incidental to vaginal delivery of her second child. This was corrected surgically, but the woman developed severe vaginal stenosis. She required intermittent dilatation of the vagina under anesthesia and the continuous use of vaginal creams. These measures made sexual intercourse possible, but it was extremely painful and the patient lacked sexual sensation. A third pregnancy ended with cesarean section because vaginal delivery was deemed hazardous.

Diagnosis: Stenosis, vaginal, postoperative, severe.

Impairment: 20% impairment of the whole person, which includes due consideration for the patient's age.

Class 3—Impairment of the Whole Person, 30-35%: A patient belongs in Class 3 when (a) symptoms and signs of disease or deformity of the vulva and/or vagina are present that are not controlled by treatment; AND (b) sexual intercourse is not possible; AND (c) during the premenopausal years, vaginal delivery is not possible.

Example: A para 2 30-year-old woman was injured in an automobile crash and suffered a severe traumatic laceration of the vagina, bladder, and rectum, leading to development of a vesicorecto-vaginal fistula. The vaginal depth was restricted to 2 cm, and a sinus tract 5 mm in diameter led to the cervix and provided escape for menstrual blood, feces, and urine. Sexual intercourse was impossible and pregnancy was deemed impossible. The recommended surgery was refused by the patient.

Diagnosis: Vesicorectovaginal fistula with partial absence of vagina.

Impairment: 35% impairment due to vaginal impairment, which includes consideration for the patient's age, and which is to be combined with appropriate values for the bladder and rectal impairments to determine the impairment of the whole person.

Cervix-Uterus

The cervix serves as a passageway for spermatozoa and menstrual blood, maintains closure of the uterus during pregnancy, and serves as a portion of the birth canal during vaginal delivery. The uterus is influenced during reproductive years by hormones that are elaborated by the ovaries. It serves as the organ of menstruation, a means of transportation of the spermatozoa, and the container of the products of fertilization. The uterus supplies the power for the first and third stages of labor and, in part, for the second stage.

Symptoms and signs of impairment of function of the cervix-uterus: These include abnormalities of menstruation, fertility, pregnancy, or labor; excessive size, stenosis, or atresia of the cervical canal; cervical incompetency during pregnancy; noncyclic hemorrhage; uterine displacement; dysplasia; and neoplasia.

Objective techniques useful in evaluating function of the cervix-uterus: These include, but are not limited to, cervical mucus studies; vaginal, cervical, and intrauterine cytologic smears; biopsy; gas insufflation; probing and measuring with calibrated sounds; radiologic studies using radiopaque contrast media; blood and urine hormone studies; basal body temperature recordings; studies on sperm concentration, mobility, and viability; dilatation and curettage of the uterus; microscopic study of the endometrium; gynecography; culdoscopy; placental localization techniques; and intra-amniotic pressure studies.

Criteria for Evaluating Permanent Impairment of the Cervix-Uterus

Class 1—Impairment of the Whole Person, 0-10%: A patient belongs in Class 1 when (a) symptoms and signs of disease or deformity of the cervix and/or uterus are present that do not require continuous treatment; OR (b) cervical stenosis, if present, requires no treatment; OR (c) there is anatomic loss of the cervix and/or uterus in the postmenopausal years.

Example 1: An obese 22-year-old married woman experienced menarche at age 14. Her menstrual cycles varied between 21 and 87 days until the age of 19, when they occurred between intervals of 26 to 40 days. Her menstrual periods averaged between two and three days, with no noncyclic bleeding. After medical treatment and good weight control, she reported her menstrual cycles became regular at 28 to 32-day intervals.

After 1½ years of marriage, during which no contraceptives were used, the woman became pregnant. During the second and third months of gestation, there was uterine bleeding that subsided with bed rest and medication. The pregnancy terminated spontaneously at 38 weeks with the delivery of a living infant weighing 2.6 kg (5 lb 12 oz). Menstrual periods after delivery averaged 32 days between cycles. Cytologic vaginal smears showed diminished hormone production. The uterus was small in size but normal in position and contour.

Diagnosis: Immature uterine development secondary to hormone deficiency.

Impairment: 0% impairment of the whole person.

Example 2: A 60-year-old married woman developed slight vaginal spotting of blood incidental to the lifting of heavy objects. Clinical examination disclosed no obvious pathologic lesion. The findings on cytologic, cervical, and vaginal smear studies were positive for malignant cells. On biopsy, carcinoma-in-situ was found. The cervix and uterine fundus were surgically removed.

Diagnosis: Carcinoma-in-situ of the cervix; absence of cervix and uterine fundus in a postmenopausal patient.

Impairment: 10% impairment of the whole person.

Class 2—Impairment of the Whole Person, 15-25%: A patient belongs in Class 2 when (a) symptoms and signs of disease or deformity of the cervix and/or uterus are present that require continuous treatment; OR (b) cervical stenosis, if present, requires periodic treatment.

Example: As the result of extensive cauterization of the cervix, a para 2 30-year-old woman developed partial stenosis of the cervix and incomplete retention of menstrual blood. Because of prolongation of menstruation and dysmenorrhea, cervical dilatation was necessary at two- to four-month intervals. After two years, pregnancy occurred and resulted in the vaginal delivery of a healthy, full-term infant.

Diagnosis: Incomplete cervical stenosis.

Impairment: 15% impairment of the whole person.

Class 3—Impairment of the Whole Person, 30-35%: A patient belongs in Class 3 when (a) symptoms and signs of disease or deformity of the cervix and/or uterus are present that are not controlled by treatment; OR (b) cervical stenosis is complete; OR (c) anatomic or complete functional loss of the cervix and/or uterus occurs in premenopausal years.

Example: As a result of a vaginal delivery, a 34-year-old woman suffered from severe prolapse of the uterus, which required surgical repair of the anterior and posterior vaginal walls, extensive amputation of the cervix, and posterior fixation of the uterus by plication of the broad ligaments. With careful management, three subsequent pregnancies were achieved, each of which ended in spontaneous abortion between 12 and 16 weeks' gestation, the result of premature dilation of the cervix. Objective evidence that there was almost no cervix indicated that a repair of the cervical incompetence was impossible.

Diagnosis: Partial absence of cervix; cervical incompetence.

Impairment: 30% impairment of the whole person.

Fallopian Tubes-Ovaries

The fallopian tubes transport ova and spermatozoa. The ovaries develop and release ova and elaborate female hormones.

Symptoms and signs of impairment of function of the fallopian tubes-ovaries: These include vaginal bleeding or discharge; stenosis of the tubes; abnormal morphology; pelvic mass; neoplasm; absent, infrequent, or abnormal ovulation; abnormal elaboration of hormones and menstrual dysfunction.

Objective techniques useful in evaluating function of the fallopian tubes-ovaries: These include, but are not limited to, air insufflation tests, cervical and vaginal cytologic smears, culdoscopy, pelvic roentgenography, hysterosalpingography, gynecography, ovarian biopsy, blood and urine hormonal assays, and basal temperature studies.

Criteria for Evaluating Permanent Impairment of the Fallopian Tubes-Ovaries

Any associated endocrine impairment should be evaluated in accordance with criteria set forth in Chapter 10, The Endocrine System.

Class 1—Impairment of the Whole Person, 0-10%: A patient belongs in Class 1 when (a) symptoms and signs of disease or deformity of the fallopian tubes and/or ovaries are present that do not require continuous treatment; OR (b) only one fallopian tube and/or ovary is functioning in the premenopausal years; OR (c) there is bilateral loss of function of the fallopian tubes and/or ovaries in the postmenopausal years.

Example: A 28-year-old married woman failed to become pregnant after six years of marriage, even though contraceptives were not used. Physical examination disclosed evidence of slight nodularity in the region of the fallopian tubes. Gas insufflation studies indicated partial stenosis of the tubes. Hysterosalpingography indicated tubal patency. After two years of treatment, the patient became pregnant and delivered a normal living infant.

Diagnosis: Partial stenosis of fallopian tubes.

Impairment: 5% impairment of the whole person.

Class 2—Impairment of the Whole Person, 15-25%: A patient belongs in Class 2 when symptoms and signs of disease or deformity of the fallopian tubes and/or ovaries are present that require continuous treatment, but tubal patency persists and ovulation is possible.

Example: A 27-year-old para 2 woman developed generalized peritonitis following a rupture of the bowel incurred in an automobile crash. Because of the infection, she underwent a unilateral salpingo-oophorectomy. Subsequently, there was evidence of irregular and infrequent ovulation. Pelvic examination showed the presence of fibrous adhesions in the adnexal area. With treatment, ovulation and cyclic hormone elaboration occurred. A normal pregnancy ensued, resulting in the birth of a living infant. Continuous treatment was required to maintain a regular ovulatory cycle.

Diagnosis: Anovulatory menstruation; unilateral salpingo-oophorectomy.

Impairment: 15% impairment due to anovulatory menstruation and 10% impairment due to unilateral salpingo-oophorectomy, which combine to give 24% impairment of the whole person.

Class 3—Impairment of the Whole Person, 30-35%: A patient belongs in Class 3 when (a) symptoms and signs of disease or deformity of the fallopian tubes and/or ovaries are present and there is total loss of tubal patency or total failure to produce ova in the premenopausal years; OR (b) bilateral loss of the fallopian tubes and/or ovaries occurs in the premenopausal years.

Example: A 32-year-old mother of two children had severe pelvic infection. Diagnostic studies indicated total occlusion of the fallopian tubes at the level of the uterine cornu. A bilateral salpingectomy was performed.

Diagnosis: Bilateral salpingectomy.

Impairment: 30% impairment of the whole person.

References

1. Campbell MF: *Campbell's Urology*, ed 4,
   Harrison JH, Gittes RF, Perlmutler AD, Stamey
   TA, Walsh PC (eds). Philadelphia, WB Saunders
   Company, 1979.

2. Glenn JF, Boyce WH (eds): *Urologic Surgery*, ed
   2. Hagerstown, MD, Harper and Row Publishers
   Inc, 1975.

3. Danforth, DN (ed): *Textbook of Obstetrics and
   Gynecology*, ed 3. New York, Harper and Row
   Publishers Inc, 1977.

Chapter 10

The Endocrine System

Introduction

The purpose of this chapter is to provide physicians with criteria they can use to evaluate permanent impairment of the endocrine system.

The endocrine system is composed of the hypothalamic-pituitary complex, thyroid, parathyroids, adrenals, islet tissue of the pancreas, and gonads. The secretions of these ductless glands are hormones that regulate the activity of organs or tissues of the body. Examples of such regulation include control of growth, bone structure, sexual development and function, metabolism, and electrolyte balance. The various endocrine glands are usually interdependent, and a disorder of one gland may be reflected by dysfunction in one or more of the other endocrine glands which, in turn, may affect other body systems. This possibility should be considered when evaluating permanent impairment of the whole person.

Impairments involving the endocrine system usually result from altered hormonal secretion by one or more endocrine glands, or from the elaboration of hormonal substances by non-endocrine tissue. Dysfunction may be associated with morphologic changes in the endocrine gland or glands involved, such as atrophy, hypertrophy, hyperplasia, or neoplasia; or there may be no demonstrable morphologic changes.

The causes of abnormal secretion are not considered in this chapter; rather, the limitations that continued endocrine dysfunction places on the patient's efficiency in activities of daily living are considered. Abnormal secretion of hormones usually can be corrected by treatment. When continuous treatment is necessary to maintain the patient, some degree of impairment may exist, even though the patient carries on most of the activities of daily living.

On the other hand, abnormal findings in other body systems may be associated with hypersecretion or hyposecretion of hormones, and some of these findings may persist indefinitely, even after therapy of the underlying hormonal dysfunction. Such impairment should be evaluated in accordance with criteria in the appropriate chapters, and, when appropriate, impairment ratings of other body systems should be combined with impairment ratings based on this chapter, using the Combined Values Chart to determine impairment of the whole person.

Neoplasms of the endocrine glands may produce nonhormonal permanent impairments manifested by pain or by effects involving other body systems. Such impairments should be evaluated with criteria set forth in the chapters concerning the respective body systems. It is recognized that, in addition to the abnormalities discussed in this chapter, others may occur that involve the endocrine system. If such abnormalities produce permanent impairment, the physician should attempt to assign a value based on the degree of the impairment and one that is consistent with established values.

The focus of this chapter is evaluation of physical impairment that may result from endocrine dysfunction. Since many of the endocrine abnormalities produce cosmetic and/or psychological abnormalities, the evaluator may wish to consider the criteria for impairment from mental and behavioral disorders that are discussed in Chapter 12. Similarly, many of the abnormalities require chronic replacement medications, perhaps for the lifetime of the individual. At the discretion of the evaluating physician, an added impairment of 0% to 5% may be allotted for this aspect of an endocrine disorder.

Before using the information in this chapter, the reader is urged to consult the Preface to the Guides, which provides a general discussion of the purpose of the Guides, and of the situations in which they are useful; and discusses techniques for the evaluation of the patient and for report preparation.

Hypothalamic-Pituitary Axis

The intimate relationship between the hypothalamus and the pituitary requires that they be regarded as a unit. The hypothalamus produces chemical factors, such as releasing and inhibitory hormones, that influence anterior pituitary function, and factors that serve as hormones in their own right, such as anti-diuretic hormone (ADH) and oxytocin. The anterior lobe of the pituitary gland produces trophic hormones that control the activity of the thyroid gland (thyroid stimilating hormone, TSH), the adrenal gland (adrenocorticotropic hormone, ACTH), and the gonads (luteinizing hormone, LH, and follicle stimulating hormone, FSH).

Growth hormone is responsible for growth prior to epiphyseal closure and contributes to glucose homeostasis in the adult. Prolactin is necessary for lactation. The posterior lobe of the pituitary is an extension of hypothalamic neurons. ADH regulates the fluid balance of the body through its ability to influence the excretion of water. At present, there is no clearly understood function for oxytocin.

Permanent impairment due to altered function of the thyroid gland, adrenal glands and gonads will be discussed in subsequent sections of this chapter.

Symptoms and Signs of Impairment of the Hypothalamic-Pituitary Axis

Hypothalamic and pituitary diseases can cause impairments through structural abnormalities or through alterations in hormone production. Structural changes resulting in visual field abnormalities, temporal lobe seizures, frontal lobe abnormalities, headaches, obstructive hydrocephalus, or non-endocrine hypothalamic dysfunction are considered in the section on the central nervous system in Chapter 2.

Hypersecretion of the anterior lobe may be evidenced by (a) prolactin hypersecretion due to a micro- or macro-adenoma (prolactinoma), the most common cause; and (b) growth hormone hypersecretion due to pituitary adenoma. Prolactin excess *per se* results in hypogonadism, manifest in the female by oligo-menorrhea, infertility, variable estrogen deficiency, and decreased libido, and in the male by decreased libido, impotence and/or infertility. Impairment from prolactin excess is equivalent to hypogonado-tropic deficiency of the appropriate end organ, that is, secondary ovarian failure in the female and testicular failure in the male. Gonadal failure is discussed further in the reproductive section of this chapter.

Growth hormone hypersecretion results in gigantism prior to epiphyseal closure and in acromegaly in the adult. The manifestations of acromegaly include enlargement of the hands and feet, coarseness of facial features, and prognathism. Fatigue and increased perspiration are common symptoms. Acromegaly of long duration leads to morbidity from degenerative arthritis and to shortened life expectancy due to increased mortality from cardiovascular causes. Growth hormone excess may lead to glucose intolerance, or may precipitate or exacerbate diabetes mellitus.

Hyposecretion of the anterior lobe may cause isolated or multiple hormone deficiencies known as hypopituitarism. The deficiencies may be parital or complete. In childhood, hypopituitarism may be genetic, congenital, due to infiltrative disease, related to craniopharyngioma, due to a pituitary adenoma, or of unknown cause. In the adult years, pituitary tumors, infarction, particularly post partum, and surgical or radiotherapeutic interventions are the most common causes.

Hypopituitarism that begins in childhood leads to short stature, failure to enter puberty, and symptoms of thyroid and cortisol deficiency. In the adult, hypogonadism, manifested by impotence and amenorrhea, and thyroid hormone and cortisol deficiency appear. Post partum pituitary infarction results in an inability to lactate. Hypopituitarism in the diabetic results in decreasing insulin requirements. Pallor, fatigue, lethargy, weight loss and weakness are also common symptoms.

Hyperfunction of the posterior lobe, which causes the syndrome of inappropriate antidiuretic hormone secretion (SIADH), may result from a variety of central nervous system disorders. However, it is rarely permanent. Inability of the kidneys to secrete a water load leads to hyponatremia if water intake is not restricted. Fatigue, lethargy progressing to confusion, coma and seizures may result, depending upon the degree of hyponatremia.

Hypofunction of the posterior lobe results in ADH deficiency, causing diabetes insipidus. Hypofunction usually stems from disease involving the hypothalamus and/or pituitary stalk, and less commonly from disease of the pituitary gland itself. It may be hereditary, or it may be related to trauma, surgery, metastatic tumors, craniopharyngioma, histiocytosis X, or other conditions, or of unknown origin. If thirst is unimpaired, diabetes insipidus is predominantly an inconvenience, because of polyuria, polydipsia and nocturia. If thirst is impaired due to concomitant hypothalamic disease, then severe hypernatremia may result, leading to mental depression or even coma.

Objective Techniques Useful in Evaluating Function of the Hypothalamic-Pituitary Axis

Structural abnormalities are evaluated by computerized tomography (CT scan), roentgenograms of the sella turcica, or polytomography. If a tumor is suspected, pneumoencephalography or metrizamide cisternography may be necessary to evaluate its extent. Angiography is required on occasion. Visual field examinations by perimetry complete the structural evaluation.

Hormonal function must be assessed, often by stimulation or suppression testing. In children, roentgenography for bone age to compare with physiologic and height age is useful.

Growth hormone deficiency is assessed by measuring the hormone in blood after stimulation testing with insulin, L-DOPA, arginine or other agents. ACTH, and hence cortisol insufficiency, are assessed by stimulating testing with insulin or metyrapone. Baseline studies of cortisol function are of little utility.

The diagnosis of secondary hypothyroidism (pituitary and hypothalamic hypothyroidism) is made by demonstrating low concentrations of peripheral thyroid hormones without elevation of TSH. In this circumstance, roentgenograms of the skull and tests of pituitary function are needed to distinguish a hypothalamic from a pituitary origin. Secondary gonadal insufficiency, that is, hypogonadotropic hypogonadism or pituitary hypogonadism, requires the demonstration of end organ failure, with low testosterone in the male and low estrogen in the female, and low or normal levels of the gonadotropins LH and FSH.

ADH insufficiency requires the documentation of urine hypo-osmolality in the face of a stimulus to urine concentration, usually through water restriction. Subsequently, one must demonstrate an increase in urine osmolality in response to ADH administration. Prolactin deficiency is documented by low basal levels of the hormone and failure to rise after injection of thyrotropin-releasing hormone (TRH), chlorpromazine or other stimulating agents.

Growth hormone excess is documented by failure to suppress growth hormone concentration after a glucose load. Prolactin excess is documented by measurement of elevated basal levels, and often by failure to rise after TRH injection. The SIADH is documented by hyponatremia with inappropriately elevated urine osmolality in the presence of normal cardiac, renal, adrenal, and thyroid function.

Criteria for Evaluating Permanent Impairment of Hypothalamic-Pituitary Axis

The assessment of permanent impairment of the whole person from disorders of the hypothalamic-pituitary axis requires evaluation of (1) primary abnormalities related to growth hormone, prolactin, or ADH; (2) secondary abnormalities in other endocrine glands, such as thyroid, adrenal, and gonads, and; (3) structural and functional disorders of the central nervous system caused by anatomic abnormalities of the pituitary. Thus, the physician must evaluate each disorder separately, using guides in this chapter or in other chapters, such as those on the nervous system, visual system, and mental and behavioral disorders, combining the impairment ratings according to the Combined Values Chart.

Class 1—Impairment of the Whole Person, 0-10%:
A patient with hypothalamic-pituitary disease belongs in Class 1 when the disease can be controlled effectively with continuous treatment.

Example: A 19-year-old man developed severe thirst and increased frequency of urination after head trauma, from which he had otherwise fully recovered. His fluid intake and output ranged from 4 to 7 liters per day. Nocturia occurred 4 to 7 times, and thirst during the night was marked. His general health was excellent, except for fatigue related to interrupted sleep. On initial assessment, serum osmolality was 292 mOsm/kg and serum sodium concentration was 142 meq/L; urine osmolality was 120 mOsm/kg, and specific gravity was 1.003. There was no glycosuria. An attempt at water deprivation led to severe thirst with a serum osmolality of 302 mOsm/kg and urine osmolality of 150 mOsm/kg. After an initial ADH injection, urine osmolality rose to 450 mOsm/kg and urine volume diminished.

At first, management consisted of self-administered injections of pitressin tannate in oil every other day, which lowered the patient's urine output to 1200 ml/24 hours and prevented nocturia. More recently he has been maintained with good results on 0.1 ml twice daily of desamino-8-D arginine vasopressin (DDAVP), a long acting nasal spray. On this regimen he feels well and his urine output is well controlled. Symptoms recur if a dose of DDAVP is missed. No other endocrine disease has been found, and he is able to carry out the usual activities of daily living.

Diagnosis: Traumatic diabetes insipidus, controlled by treatment.

Impairment: 5% impairment of the whole person.

Class 2—Impairment of the Whole Person, 15-20%:
A patient with hypothalamic-pituitary disease belongs in Class 2 when the symptoms and signs are inadequately controlled by treatment.

Example: A 57-year-old man developed fatigue, hyperhidrosis, headaches, carpal tunnel syndrome and enlargement of his hands, feet and nose. He also complained of pain in his knees and back and of decreased libido. He was found to have an enlarged sella turcia with suprasellar extension of a pituitary tumor, although there were no visual field abnormalities. His growth hormone level of 575 ng/ml was markedly elevated.

Despite an attempt at surgical excision and subsequent therapy with ionizing radiation, the man's growth hormone remained elevated at 100 ng/ml. He was unable to tolerate bromocriptine therapy. His testosterone level was low, but thyroid and adrenal function remained normal. His headaches were relieved, but symptoms of fatigue, excess perspiration, and joint discomfort continued. Libido improved with bi-monthly injections of testosterone. The carpal tunnel syndrome required surgical therapy, which was successful.

Diagnosis: Acromegaly, moderately severe, inadequately controlled by therapy.

Impairment: 15% impairment due to acromegaly, and 5% impairment due to testosterone deficiency, which combine to 19% impairment of the whole person.

Class 3—Impairment of the Whole Person, 25-50%:
A patient with hypothalamic-pituitary disease belongs in Class 3 when severe symptoms and signs persist despite treatment.

Example: A 55-year-old man was seen initially at age 45 for an enlarged sella turcica. Evaluation revealed testosterone deficiency and no suprasellar extension of his tumor. The patient was not treated and was lost to follow-up. Later he was hospitalized with complaints of excruciating headache, visual loss, and impotence. On physical examination, his beard was markedly diminished, and a female escutcheon was noted. Testing of visual fields showed nearly complete loss of vision in the left eye and a temporal field defect in the right with some macular involvement. A skull roentgenogram revealed a massively enlarged sella turcica. A CT scan showed extensive suprasellar growth of the tumor with a suggestion of hemorrhage into the tumor.

The patient underwent emergency transsphenoidal

pituitary decompression under coverage with glucocorticoids. Despite the decompressive procedure, vision in the left eye returned only to finger counting, and temporal field loss in the right eye continued. Preoperative prolactin concentration was 1000 ng/ml. Postoperative prolactin remained elevated at 660 ng/ml. In the postoperative period, a course of 4800 R to the sella turcica was given with ionizing radiation. Subsequent evaluation revealed elevated prolactin concentration of 280 ng/ml, low testosterone concentration, deficient cortisol response to hypoglycemia, and decreased thyroid function. Visual abnormalities were unchanged. The patient was unable to tolerate bromocriptine. Headaches were mild but persistent. Despite testosterone administration, the patient remained impotent.

Diagnosis: Prolactinoma (prolactin-secreting pituitary adenoma) with pituitary apoplexy, secondary panhypopituitarism, and partial blindness.

Impairment: 10% impairment due to pituitary dysfunction, 10% impairment due to secondary adrenal dysfunction, and 5% impairment due to secondary testosterone impairment, which combine to 23% impairment due to endocrine dysfunction; 33% impairment due to visual problems; and 10% impairment due to persistent headache. All of these combine to give 53% impairment of the whole person.

Thyroid

The thyroid gland, by its secretion of thyroid hormones, influences the metabolic rate of many organ systems throughout the body. Pathologic conditions causing impairments are hypersecretion and hyposecretion.

Symptoms and Signs of Impairment of Function of the Thyroid

Hypersecretion by the thyroid gland results in hyperthyroidism and may be manifested by nervousness, weight loss, heat intolerance, goiter, tachycardia, palpitation, diarrhea, tremor, and muscle weakness. Eye changes, such as exophthalmos, may be present.

Hyposecretion by the thyroid gland results in hypothyroidism and may be manifested by slowing of mental processes, lethargy, weakness, cold intolerance, dry skin, constipation, and myxedema. Late complications include myocardial insufficiency, effusions into body cavities, and coma. Hypothyroidism in infancy, including cretinism, may be associated with failure of skeletal and brain development and permanent mental retardation.

Objective Techniques Useful in Evaluating Function of the Thyroid

Useful techniques include, but are not limited to, determination of (1) circulating thyroid hormones, total thyroxine (TT_4), free thyroxine (FT_4), triiodothyronine (T_3) and free triiodothyronine (FT_3); (2) circulating pituitary thyrotropin (TSH) level before and after stimulation with the hypothalamic thyrotropin-releasing hormone (TRH); (3) radioiodine uptake of the thyroid gland; and (4) the radio-triiodothyronine (T_3) resin or red blood cell uptake.

Criteria for Evaluating Permanent Impairment of the Thyroid

Hyperthyroidism is not considered to be a cause of permanent impairment, because the hypermetabolic state in practically all patients can be corrected permanently by treatment. After remission of hyperthyroidism, there may be permanent impairment of the visual or cardiovascular systems, which should be evaluated using the chapters of this book for those systems.

Hypothyroidism in most instances can be satisfactorily controlled by the administration of thyroid medication. Occasionally, because of associated disease in other organ systems, full hormone replacement may not be possible.

Class 1—Impairment of the Whole Person, 0-10%:
A patient belongs in Class 1 when (a) continuous thyroid therapy is required for correction of the thyroid insufficiency or for maintenance of normal thyroid anatomy; AND (b) there is no objective physical or laboratory evidence of inadequate replacement therapy.

Example: A 45-year-old woman with symptoms of mild hypothyroidism had the diagnosis made by needle biopsy of lympho-epithelial goiter (Hashimoto's thyroiditis). She requires daily therapy with 0.20 mg of L-thyroxine to maintain a normal-sized thyroid, although her symptoms of hormone deficiency are relieved by a lower dose.

Diagnosis: Hashimoto's thyroiditis controlled by treatment.

Impairment: 5% impairment of the whole person.

Class 2—Impairment of the Whole Person, 15-20%:
A patient belongs in Class 2 when (a) symptoms and signs of thyroid disease are present, or there is anatomic loss or alteration; AND (b) continuous thyroid hormone replacement therapy is required for correction of the confirmed thyroid insufficiency; BUT (c) the presence of a disease process in another body system or systems permits only partial replacement of the thyroid hormone.

Example: A 65-year-old man has severe hypothyroidism with pronounced mental slowing, loss of memory, and apathy. He also has severe coronary artery disease with angina pectoris that can be precipitated by walking as little as 50 ft. TT_4 is 0.5 μg/100ml, and TSH is 100 μU/ml. Repeated trials and careful adjustment of doses of L-thyroxine disclose that a dose larger than 0.05 mg per day causes definite aggravation of his angina. Significant general debility from the hypothyroidism persists.

Diagnosis: Partially treated hypothyroidism.

Impairment: 20% impairment due to hypothyroidism, which is to be combined with an appropriate value for the cardiovascular impairment to determine the impairment of the whole person.

Parathyroids

The secretion of parathyroid hormone from the four parathyroid glands regulates the levels of serum calcium and phosphorus, which are essential to the proper functioning of the skeletal, digestive, renal, and nervous systems. The major abnormalities of the glands include hyperfunction, hypofunction, and carcinoma.

Symptoms and Signs of Impairment of Function of the Parathyroids

Hypersecretion of parathyroid hormone, or hyperparathyroidism, may be due to the hyperfunctioning of one gland, as with an adenoma, or of all four glands, as with hyperplasia, or due to a parathyroid carcinoma. Manifestations include lethargy, constipation, nausea, vomiting and polyuria, and in extreme cases, bone pain, renal calculi, renal failure, and coma.

Hyposecretion of parathyroid hormone, or hypoparathyroidism, may be due to inadvertent removal of the parathyroid glands during thyroidectomy, or idiopathic, that is, due to unknown causes. Manifestations include chronic tetany, paresthesias, and seizures, and, particularly in idiopathic cases, cataracts, chronic moniliasis of the skin, alopecia, and hypofunction of other endocrine organs; the latter state may be associated with hypothyroidism, diabetes mellitus or adrenal insufficiency.

Objective Techniques Useful in Evaluating Parathyroid Function

Techniques of evaluating parathyroid gland function include determinations of serum calcium, phosphorus, albumin, creatinine and parathyroid hormone levels, of calcium concentration in urine, and of urinary cyclic AMP response to intravenously administered parathyroid hormone. Intravenous pyelography and skeletal roentgenography may be useful.

Criteria for Evaluating Permanent Impairment of the Parathyroids

In most cases of hyperparathyroidism, surgical treatment results in correction of the primary abnormality, although secondary symptoms and signs may persist, such as renal calculi or renal failure, which should be evaluated according to criteria set forth in Chapter 9. If surgery fails, or if the patient cannot undergo surgery, the patient may require long-term therapy, in which case the permanent impairment may be classified according to the following:

Severity of Hyperparathyroidism	% Impairment of the Whole Person
Symptoms and signs are easily controlled with medical therapy	0-10
There is persistent mild hypercalcemia, with mild nausea and polyuria	15-20
There is severe hypercalcemia, with nausea and lethargy	55-100

Hypoparathyroidism is a chronic condition of variable severity that requires long-term medical therapy in most cases. The degree of severity determines the degree of permanent impairment, according to the following:

Severity of Hypoparathyroidism	% Impairment of the Whole Person
Symptoms and signs easily controlled by medical therapy	0-5
Intermittent hypercalcemia and/or hypocalcemia, and more frequent symptoms in spite of careful medical attention	10-20

Adrenals

Each adrenal gland consists of a cortex and a medulla. The adrenal cortex synthesizes and secretes adrenal cortical hormones. These hormones partici-

pate in the regulation of electrolyte and water metabolism and in the intermediate metabolism of carbohydrate, fat and protein. They also affect inflammatory response, cell membrane permeability, and antigen-antibody reactions, and play a role in the development and maintaining of secondary sexual characteristics. The adrenal medulla synthesizes and secretes primarily epinephrine, which functions in the regulation of blood pressure and cardiac output and, to some extent, affects the intermediate metabolism of the body.

Adrenal Cortex

Impairment of the whole person may result from hypersecretion or hyposecretion of the cortical hormones. Such an abnormality may be associated with dysfunction of another endocrine gland, for instance, the pituitary. If this occurs, impairment from the adrenal abnormality is evaluated together with the other dysfunction, using criteria set forth in the appropriate section of this chapter and the Combined Values Chart.

Symptoms and Signs of Impairment of Function of the Adrenal Cortex

Hypersecretion of adrenal cortical hormones results from hyperplasia or from benign or malignant tumors of the adrenal cortex. The symptoms and signs of adrenal cortical disease may arise from hypersecretion of one or more of the following hormones: (1) glucocorticoid; (2) mineralocorticoids; (3) androgens; and (4) estrogens. In some instances, there may be hypersecretion of hormones in one category and hyposecretion of those in another.

Iatrogenic Cushing's syndrome secondary to nonphysiologic doses of glucocorticoids administered for systemic diseases such as bronchial asthma, systemic lupus erythematosis, or rheumatoid arthritis, is the most common syndrome of adrenal hormonal excess.

Among the diseases caused by hypersecretion of the adrenal cortical hormones are Cushing's syndrome, the adrenogenital syndrome, and primary aldosteronism. Hypersecretion of the adrenal cortex due to hyperplasia may be associated either with a tumor of the anterior pituitary gland or with a malignant tumor arising outside the endocrine system that causes ectopic ACTH secretion.

Hyposecretion of adrenal cortical hormones may be primary, resulting from surgical removal or destruction of the adrenals, as with Addison's disease, or secondary, resulting from decreased production of corticotropin. Therapy is guided by the number of hormonal deficiencies, which may be single, as in hypoaldosteronism, or multiple, as in adrenocortical destruction. One normal adrenal gland can compensate for loss of the other.

Objective Techniques Useful in Evaluating Function of the Adrenal Cortex

These include: (1) measurement of adrenal cortical hormones in the urine, such as, 17-ketosteroids, 17-hydroxycorticoids, free cortisol, and aldosterone and of hormones in the plasma such as cortisol, and aldosterone; (2) measurement of ACTH, serum electrolytes, plasma glucose and creatinine; (3) measurement of the effects of suppression and stimulation of adrenal cortical function; and (4) radiography of the adrenal glands, CT scan, arteriography, and venography of the skull, including polytomography of the sella turcica and of the spine.

Criteria for Evaluating Permanent Impairment of the Adrenal Cortex

Hypoadrenalism is a lifelong condition that requires long-term replacement therapy with glucocorticoids and/or mineralocorticoids for proven hormonal deficiencies. Impairments should be classified according to the following scheme:

Severity of Hypoadrenalism	% Impairment of the Whole Person
Symptoms and signs controlled with medical therapy	0-10
Symptoms and signs controlled inadequately, usually during the course of acute illnesses	15-50
Severe symptoms of adrenal crisis during major illness, usually due to severe glucocortocoid deficiency and/or sodium depletion	55-100

Hyperadrenocorticism due to the chronic side effects of nonphysiologic doses of glucocorticoids (iatrogenic Cushing's syndrome) is related to dosage and duration of treatment and includes osteoporosis, hypertension, diabetes mellitus and the effects involving catabolism that result in protein myopathy, striae, and easy bruising. Permanent impairment may range from 0% to 100%, depending on the severity and chronicity of the disease process for which the steroids are given. On the other hand, with diseases of the pituitary-adrenal axis, impairment may be classified as:

Severity of Hyperadrenocorticism	% Impairment of the Whole Person
Minimal, as with hyperadrenocorticism that is surgically correctable by removal of a pituitary or adrenal adenoma	0-10
Moderate, as with bilateral hyperplasia that is treated with medical therapy or adrenalectomy	15-50
Severe, as with aggressively metastasizing adrenal carcinoma	55-100

Adrenal Medulla

The adrenal medulla is probably not essential to the maintenance of life or well-being. Hence, its absence does not constitute impairment of the whole person. Hyperfunction of the adrenal medulla may stem from pheochromocytomas, or rarely, from hyperplasia of the chromaffin cells. Pheochromocytomas may arise at any site in the body that has sympathetic nervous tissue. The presence of a pheochromocytoma is usually associated with paroxysmal or sustained hypertension. Approximately 10% of pheochromocytomas are malignant. Pheochromocytomas may be multiple in an individual and may occur in families in association with medullary carcinoma of the thyroid and hyperplasia of the parathyroid, constituting the syndrome of multiple endocrine neoplasms, Type II.

Objective Techniques Useful in Evaluating the Function of the Adrenal Medulla

These include: (1) measurement of unmetabolized urinary catecholamines, including total catecholamines, epinephrine and norepinephrine, and of their degradation products in urine, vanillylmandelic acid (VMA) and metanephrines; (2) measurement of the plasma catecholamines, epinephrine, norepinephrine and dopamine; and (3) radiography of the adrenals, including arteriography, venography and CT scan.

Criteria for Evaluating Permanent Impairment of the Adrenal Medulla

Permanent impairment from pheochromocytoma may be classified using the following table:

Severity of Pheochromocytoma	% Impairment of the Whole Person
Minimal, as when the duration of hypertension has not led to cardiovascular disease and a benign tumor can be removed surgically	0-10

Moderate, as with inoperable malignant pheochromocytomas, if signs and symptoms of catecholamine excess can be controlled with blocking agents 15-50

Severe, as with widely metastatic malignant pheochromocytomas, in which symptoms of catecholamine excess cannot be controlled 55-100

Pancreas (Islets of Langerhans)

Insulin and glucagon are among the hormones secreted by the islets of Langerhans. Both hormones are required for the maintenance of normal metabolism of carbohydrate, lipid and protein. Impairment of the whole person may result from a deficiency or an excess of either hormone. Removal of normal pancreatic tissue during the resection of an islet cell neoplasm does not constitute endocrine impairment if, after the operation, carbohydrate tolerance is normal.

Symptoms and Signs of Impairment of Function of the Pancreatic Islets

Abnormalities of islet cell function may be manifested by high plasma glucose levels, as in diabetes mellitus, or by low plasma glucose, as in hypoglycemia. Diabetes mellitus is classified into two main groups: insulin dependent (Type I) diabetes and non-insulin dependent (Type II) diabetes. People with insulin dependent diabetes mellitus, if untreated, will progress to stupor, coma, and death. This type of diabetes mellitus usually begins in the young, but it may occur at any age. People with non-insulin dependent diabetes generally are over 40 years old and overweight.

The main complications of diabetes mellitus and their associated impairments are: (1) retinopathy, causing visual impairment; (2) nephropathy, causing renal impairment; (3) arteriosclerosis, causing arteriosclerotic heart disease, and cerebrovascular and peripheral vascular disease; and (4) neuropathy.

Hypoglycemia occasionally causes impairment. Hypoglycemia may result from excessive insulin that is either produced endogenously or administered by injection. Hypoglycemia may be manifested by weakness, sweating, tachycardia, headache, muscular incoordination, blurred vision, loss of consciousness, and convulsions. Prolonged hypoglycemia or repeated severe attacks of hypoglycemia may lead to mental deterioration.

Objective Techniques in Evaluating Impairment Related to Diabetes Mellitus

These include, but are not limited to: (1) determination of fasting and postprandial plasma glucose levels; (2) determination of hemoglobin A_1c; (3) measurements of cholesterol and other lipids; (4) electrocardiogram; (5) ophthalmological examination; (6) tests of renal and bladder function; (7) Doppler testing of the peripheral circulation; (8) radiographs of chest, gastrointestinal tract, pelvis, or extremities, including arteriograms; and (9) neurological testing.

Criteria for Evaluating Permanent Impairment Related to Diabetes Mellitus

Class 1—Impairment of the Whole Person, 0-5%: A patient with diabetes mellitus belongs in Class 1 if he or she has non-insulin dependent (Type II) diabetes mellitus that can be controlled by diet; the person may or may not have evidence of diabetic microangiopathy, as indicated by the presence of retinopathy and/or albuminuria greater than 30 mg/100 ml.

Example 1: Medical examinations disclosed 1+ glycosuria in a moderately obese 40-year-old man. Fasting plasma glucose was 160 mg/100 ml on two occasions. Retinal examination revealed no diabetic retinopathy and there was no albumin in the urine. After three months on a special diet, the man's weight was normal, and his fasting plasma glucose was 110 mg/100 ml.

Diagnosis: Non-insulin dependent (Type II) diabetes mellitus controlled by diet, without evidence of diabetic microangiopathy.

Impairment: 0% impairment of the whole person.

Example 2: An obese 45-year-old woman had elevated fasting plasma glucose, and physical examination disclosed retinal microaneurysms and dot and blot hemorrhages. There was no impairment of vision.

Diagnosis: Non-insulin dependent (Type II) diabetes mellitus with early diabetic retinopathy.

Impairment: 5% impairment of the whole person.

Class 2—Impairment of the Whole Person, 5-10%: A patient belongs in this classification when there is diagnosis of non-insulin dependent (Type II) diabetes mellitus; and when satisfactory control of the plasma glucose requires both a restricted diet and hypoglycemic medication, either an oral agent or insulin. Evidence of microangiopathy, as indicated by retinopathy or by albuminuria of greater than 30 mg/100 ml, may or may not be present.

Example 1: A 55-year-old man had the diagnosis of non-insulin dependent (Type II) diabetes mellitus without retinopathy or proteinuria. Although he lost weight on a prescribed diet, his plasma glucose could not be maintained within normal limits on diet alone. When he was on a restricted diet and an oral agent, his fasting serum glucose was 120 mg/100 ml.

Diagnosis: Non-insulin dependent (Type II) diabetes mellitus controlled by diet and oral agent.

Impairment: 5% impairment of the whole person.

Example 2: A 50-year-old man has had non-insulin dependent (Type II) diabetes mellitus for 5 years. At the onset of the disease, he had a fasting plasma glucose of 190 mg/100 ml when on a restricted diet and an oral hypoglycemic agent. Four years ago his right leg was amputated above the knee because of severe peripheral vascular disease that led to gangrene of the foot.

At present, the man adheres to a prescribed diet and takes 16 units of NPH insulin daily. On this regimen, his fasting plasma glucose is 125 to 140 mg/100 ml. He has no symptoms, nor does he spill sugar or acetone.

Diagnosis: Non-insulin dependent (Type II) diabetes mellitus with complications, requiring insulin to control hyperglycemia. Plasma glucose is satisfactorily controlled by diet and one daily injection of insulin.

Impairment: 10% impairment due to non-insulin dependent (Type II) diabetes mellitus, and 36% impairment due to amputation above the knee joint, which combine to give 42% impairment of the whole person.

Class 3—Impairment of the Whole Person, 15-20%: A patient belongs in this class when insulin dependent (Type I) diabetes mellitus is present with or without evidence of microangiopathy.

Example 1: A 33-year-old teacher has had insulin dependent (Type I) diabetes mellitus for 5 years.

She originally presented with polyuria, polydipsia, and weight loss, and with a plasma glucose of 400 mg/100 ml and marked ketonuria. The condition is satisfactorily controlled with a prescribed diet and an injection of insulin before both breakfast and dinner. There is no evidence of microangiopathy.

Diagnosis: Insulin dependent (Type I) diabetes mellitus satisfactorily controlled by insulin and diet.

Impairment: 15% impairment of the whole person.

Example 2: A 40-year-old woman had onset of insulin dependent (Type I) diabetes mellitus 20 years ago, when she had polydipsia, polyuria, weight loss and plasma glucose of 350 mg/100 ml. At present, the condition is satisfactorily controlled with diet and a daily injection of insulin. Physical examination discloses that background retinopathy is present.

Diagnosis: Insulin dependent (Type I) diabetes mellitus with diabetic microangiopathy and no visual impairment.

Impairment: 20% impairment of the whole person.

Example 3: A 45-year-old man has had insulin dependent (Type I) diabetes mellitus for 25 years. He has proliferative retinopathy, and he has an elevated creatinine level and a diminished creatinine clearance. His plasma glucose is controlled by a mixture of NPH and regular insulin given twice daily, 12 units before breakfast and 6 units before dinner. Ophthalmological examination reveals 70% impairment of vision of the right eye and 63% impairment of the left, which combine to give 65% impairment of the visual system.

Diagnosis: Insulin dependent (Type I) diabetes mellitus with complications; plasma glucose is satisfactorily controlled by diet and insulin.

Impairment: 20% impairment due to diabetes mellitus, and 65% impairment due to visual impairment, which should be combined with an appropriate value for the renal impairment to determine impairment of the whole person.

Class 4—Impairment of the Whole Person, 25-40%: A patient belongs in Class 4 when the patient has the diagnosis of insulin dependent (Type I) diabetes mellitus, and when hyperglycemic and/or hypoglycemic episodes occur frequently in spite of conscientious efforts of both the patient and his or her physician.

Example 1: A 24-year-old male farmer has had labile insulin dependent (Type I) diabetes mellitus for ten years. His physical activities vary greatly from day to day. Despite adherence to a prescribed diet that includes between-meal and bedtime snacks, and despite a carefully planned insulin program with both morning and evening injections, home plasma glucose tests vary greatly, and at times there are severe insulin reactions without warning. He is 10% underweight, but he shows no clinical or laboratory evidence of complications.

Diagnosis: Insulin dependent (Type I) diabetes mellitus, not adequately controlled by diet and insulin.

Impairment: 35% impairment of the whole person.

Example 2: A 35-year-old woman has had poorly controlled insulin dependent (Type I) diabetes mellitus for 15 years. Although fasting plasma glucose is often greater than 200 mg/100 ml, and the urine usually contains sugar, severe hypoglycemic reactions occur unpredictably several times a week. The patient is malnourished on a 3,000-calorie diet, which is combined with injections of 30 units of Lente insulin before breakfast and 10 units of Lente insulin before supper. She becomes fatigued easily, and she complains bitterly of burning pain in the feet and of difficulty in walking. Vibratory sensation and deep tendon reflexes are absent below the knees. Examination of the fundi reveals numerous microaneurysms, but there is no visual impairment.

Diagnosis: Insulin dependent (Type I) diabetes mellitus, with complications, not adequately controlled by diet and insulin.

Impairment: 40% impairment due to diabetes mellitus and 15% impairment due to peripheral neuritis, which combine to 49% impairment of the whole person.

Objective Techniques Useful in Evaluating Impairment Related to Hypoglycemia

These include, but are not limited to: (1) measurement of plasma glucose after overnight or longer periods of fasting; (2) measurement of plasma insulin after overnight fasting on several occasions; (3) roentgenograms of skull, chest, and abdomen; (4) tests of liver function; and (5) tests of adrenocortical and pituitary gland function.

Criteria for Evaluating Permanent Impairment Related to Hypoglycemia

Class 1—Impairment of the Whole Person, 0%: A patient has Class I impairment when surgical removal of an islet-cell adenoma results in complete remission of the symptoms and signs of hypoglycemia, and there are no post-operative sequelae.

Example: The wife of a 45-year-old man noted that with increasing frequency he had a bad temper upon arising that improved after breakfast. He did not use alcohol or tobacco. At 11:30 a.m. one morning, while at work, he suddenly became disturbed and lost consciousness. Upon emergency admission to a hospital, his plasma glucose level was 20 mg/100 ml. In spite of a high carbohydrate intake that included a large feeding at bedtime, he remained weak and irritable before breakfast, and his fasting plasma glucose never exceeded 35 mg/100 ml.

An abdominal examination and a chest radiograph disclosed no abnormalities, and pituitary, adrenal and liver functions were normal. During an operation, a benign insulinoma 1.5 cm in diameter was excised from the head of the pancreas; the patient developed a pancreatic fistula that took three months to close. He was asymptomatic thereafter.

Diagnosis: Benign functioning islet-cell adenoma (insulinoma), with complete remission after an operation.

Impairment: 0% impairment of the whole person.

Class 2—Impairment of the Whole Person, 5-50%: A patient with symptoms and signs of hypoglycemia has Class 2 impairment of the whole person ranging from 5% to 50%, depending on the degree of control obtained with diet and medications; and on how the condition affects activities of daily living.

Example: A 55-year-old man manifested alarming personality changes within a few weeks' time and had a seizure. A diagnosis of insulinoma was made. Laparotomy revealed an islet-cell adenocarcinoma, 5 cm in diameter, in the tail of the pancreas, with metastases in the liver. The spleen and main tumor mass were resected. The man experienced no impairment of hepatic function, and recovery from surgery was uneventful except for persistence of mild fasting hypoglycemia. This responded well to frequent feedings of a high-protein, high-carbohydrate diet and 40 mg of prednisone taken daily. Three months after returning to work, he still had occasional transient mental lapses, during one of which the plasma glucose level was 28 mg/100 ml. When the daily dosage of prednisone was raised to 60 mg, the symptomatic hypoglycemia improved, but manifestations of Cushing's syndrome became more prominent.

Diagnosis: Metastatic islet-cell adenocarcinoma, with incomplete control of symptoms.

Impairment: 50% impairment due to hypoglycemia and 10% impairment due to steroid-induced Cushing's syndrome, which combine to give 55% impairment of the whole person.

The Gonads

The gonads produce spermotozoa or ova and also produce the sex hormones, which affect physical and sexual development and behavior. The interstitial cells of the testes produce male hormones. The most significant hormones of the ovaries are estrogen from the follicles and progesterone from the corpora lutea. Changes in function of the gonads can be produced by tumors, trauma, infection, scarring, and surgical removal. Gonadal function may vary with changes in the pituitary-hypothalamus axis.

Symptoms and Signs of Impairment of Function of the Gonads

Precocious puberty in the male results in early, rapid growth and accelerated skeletal maturation. Occasionally a tendency toward this condition is familial. Precocious puberty in the female may be caused by an ovarian tumor, but usually a cause is not found; it can result in accelerated skeletal maturation. Some ovarian tumors may also cause masculinization. Certain ovarian conditions produce heavy and irregular menstrual periods.

Testicular hypofunction results in eunuchoidism or eunuchism. Symptoms are diminished sexual function, failure to develop or maintain secondary sexual characteristics, and, if there is onset before adolescence, growth of the body beyond the usual age because of delayed epiphyseal closure. There is usually lack of endurance and strength.

Ovarian hypofunction, with onset in preadolescence, may be characterized by primary amenorrhea, poor development of secondary sexual characteristics, and growth beyond the usual age due to delayed maturation of the skeleton. The menopause is a natural occurrence in older women, but it also can follow surgical removal of the ovaries. It may be accompanied by hot flashes, and by symptoms such as irritability, fatigue, and headaches. Osteoporosis and other changes may occur during later years.

Objective Techniques Useful in Evaluating Function of the Gonads

Useful techniques of evaluation include, but are not limited to: (1) measurements of plasma gonadotropins, testosterone, estrogen, and progesterone, and occasionally urinary 24-hour 17-ketosteroids; (2) radiographic determinations of bone age in children and adolescents; (3) evaluation of sella turcica size by radiography; (4) studies of sex chromatin and chromosomes; (5) testicular biopsy; (6) semen examination; (7) study of vaginal cytology; (8) culdoscopy or laparoscopy; (9) endometrial biopsy; and (10) ovarian biopsy.

Criteria for Evaluating Permanent Impairment of the Gonads

A patient with anatomic loss or alteration of the gonads that results in an absence, or abnormally high level, of gonadal hormones would have 0% to 5% impairment of the whole person. Impairment due to inability to reproduce, and other impairments associated with gonadal dysfunction, should be evaluated in accordance with the criteria set forth in Chapter 9.

Example 1: A 12-year-old girl complained of severe menorrhagia during the preceding 6 months. She had experienced vaginal bleeding since the age of 9 years, at which time breast development began and pubic hair appeared. Also at that time, there was a spurt of growth, which slowed and then stopped during the 12th year. On physical examination her height was 4 ft 11 in (150 cm).

The girl's bone age was 17 years, and it seemed unlikely that she would grow taller. Urinary gonadotropin values were in the low normal range, while levels of urinary estrogens were elevated. The right ovary was enlarged to about five times its normal size. The ovary was removed surgically and found to contain a benign granulosa cell tumor. The left ovary was the size of an infant's and without visible follicles. A year after the operation, the patient had regular, normal menses.

Diagnosis: Precocious puberty caused by granulosa cell tumor of ovary.

Impairment: 0% impairment due to precocious puberty. The impairment of the whole person would be determined by the loss of one ovary. Note: Short stature in not considered a cause of impairment.

Example 2: A 31-year-old man complained of lack of sexual development and function, of a high-pitched voice, and of having no beard. He was tall, and had relatively long arms and legs. The penis was tiny and the scrotum and testes were small. The bone age was 18 years, the plasma testosterone was 70 ng/ml, and the plasma gonadotropins were low.

The man responded well to continuous treatment with testosterone. The penis became larger and there was adequate sexual functioning. The man had an increase in body and facial hair, and the voice became deeper. He continued to work as a railroad freight handler after the treatment.

Diagnosis: Hypogonadotropic hypogonadism.

Impairment: 5% impairment of the whole person.

Mammary Glands

The mammary glands make, store, and secrete milk. Absence of the mammary glands does not cause impairment of the whole person in males, but in females it will prevent nursing. In some endocrine disorders there may be galactorrhea in the female and gynecomastia in the male. Gynecomastia in the male may be accompanied by galactorrhea.

A female patient in the childbearing age with absence of the breasts, a patient with galactorrhea sufficient to require the use of absorbent pads, and a male patient with painful gynecomastia that interferes in the performance of daily activities, each would have 0% to 5% impairment of the whole person.

Metabolic Bone Disease

Metabolic bone disease, such as osteoporosis, vitamin D-resistant osteomalacia, and Paget's disease, may require continuous therapy. These conditions, unless accompanied by pain, skeletal deformity, or peripheral nerve involvement, should be rated at 0% impairment of the whole person. When continuous hormone and mineral therapy gives complete relief of symptoms, impairment of the whole person may be considered to be 3%. When continuous therapy is required to relieve pain, and the activities of daily living are restricted because of pain, the rating should be 5% to 15% impairment of the whole person. Any associated loss of motion should be evaluated in accordance with the criteria set forth in Chapter 1, which concerns the extremities and spine, and with those in Chapter 2, which concerns the nervous system.

Example: A 68-year-old woman has severe osteoporosis of the axial skeleton and, to a lesser extent, of the extremities. She has considerable local pain with motion of the spine, along with some generalized back ache and spasm related to partial collapse of T4 and T12. Pain persists in spite of prolonged therapy with anabolic agents, estrogens, vitamin D, and calcium.

Diagnosis: Postmenopausal osteoporosis with incomplete symptomatic control.

Impairment: 15% impairment of the whole person.

References

1. Williams RH (ed): *Textbook of Endocrinology*, ed 6. Philadelphia, WB Saunders Company, 1981.

2. Fely P, Baxter J, Broadus A, Frohman L: *Endocrinology and Metabolism*. New York, McGraw Hill, 1981.

3. Rifkin H, Raskin P (eds): *Diabetes Mellitus*. New York, American Diabetes Association, 1981.

4. Federman DD: Endocrinology, in Rubenstein E, Federman DD (eds): *Scientific American Medicine*. New York, Scientific American Inc, 1982.

Chapter 11

The Skin

Introduction

This chapter provides criteria for evaluating the effect that permanent impairment of the skin and its appendages has on an individual's ability to perform or participate in the activities of daily living, including occupation.

The functions of the skin include: (1) providing a protective body covering; (2) participating in sensory perception, temperature regulation, fluid regulation, electrolyte balance, immunobiologic defenses, and resistance to trauma; and (3) regenerating the epidermis and its appendages.

The protective functions include, for example, barrier defenses against damage by chemical irritants and allergic sensitizers, invasion by micro-organisms, and injuries by ultraviolet light. Temperature regulation involves the proper function of the small blood vessels and sweat glands. The barrier defense against fluid loss is related to the intactness of the stratum corneum.

Immunobiologic defenses of the skin prevent and control infections by bacteria, viruses, or fungi. Alterations of skin sensory perception include pruritus, the decrease or loss of sensation, and hyperesthesia. Cutaneous and systemic disorders can alter one or more of these functions. An established deviation from normal in any of the functions may result in an anatomic or functional abnormality or loss and constitute a permanent impairment.

Permanent impairment of the skin is any anatomic or functional abnormality or loss, including an acquired immunologic capacity to react to antigens that persists after medical treatment and rehabilitation, and after a length of time sufficient to permit regeneration and other physiologic adjustments. The degree of permanent impairment of the skin may not be static. Therefore, findings should be subject to review, and the patient's impairment should be re-evaluated at appropriate intervals.

Evaluation of impairment is usually possible through the exercise of sound clinical judgment based on a detailed medical history, a thorough physical examination, and the judicious use of diagnostic procedures. Laboratory aids include procedures such as patch, open, scratch, intracutaneous and serologic tests for allergy; Wood's light examinations and cultures and scrapings for bacteria, fungi and viruses; and biopsies.

Before using the information in this chapter, the reader is urged to consult the Preface to the Guides, which provides a general discussion of the purpose of the Guides, and of the situations in which they are useful; and discusses techniques for the evaluation of the patient and for report preparation.

Methods of Evaluation of Impairment

In the evaluation of permanent impairment resulting from a skin disorder, the actual functional loss is the prime consideration, although the extent of cosmetic or cutaneous involvement may also be important.

Impairments of other body systems, such as behavioral problems, restriction of motion or ankylosis of joints, and respiratory, cardiovascular, endocrine, and gastrointestinal disorders, may be associated with a skin impairment. When there is permanent impairment in more than one body system, the degree of impairment for each system should be evaluated separately and combined, using the Combined Values Chart, to determine the impairment of the whole person.

Manifestations of skin disorders may be influenced by physical and/or chemical agents that a patient may encounter. While the avoidance of these irritant agents, possibly through a change in occupation, might alleviate the manifestations of the skin disorder, the presence of a skin disorder should be recognized and evaluated in accordance with the criteria below.

Pruritus

Pruritus is frequently associated with cutaneous disorders. It is a subjective, unpleasant sensation that provokes the desire to scratch or rub. The sensation is closely related to pain, in that it is mediated by pain receptors and pain fibers when they are weakly stimulated. However, the itching sensation may be intolerable. Like pain, it may be defined as a unique complex made up of afferent stimuli interacting with the emotional or affective state of the individual and modified by that individual's past experience and present state of mind.

The sensation of pruritus has two elements, peripheral neural stimulation and central nervous system reaction, which are extremely variable in make-up and in time. The first element may vary from total absence of sensation to an awareness of stimuli as either usual or unusual sensations. The second element is also variable and is modified by the person's state of attentiveness, past experience, motivation at the moment, and stimuli such as exercise, sweating and changes in temperature.

In evaluating pruritus associated with skin disorders, the physician should consider (1) how the pruritus interferes with the individual's performance of the activities of daily living, including occupation; and (2) to what extent the description of the pruritus is supported by objective skin findings, such as lichenification, excoriation, or hyperpigmentation. Subjective complaints of itching that cannot be substantiated objectively may require specialized referral.

Disfigurement

Disfigurement is an altered or abnormal appearance. This may be an alteration of color, shape, or structure, or a combination of these. Disfigurement may be a residual of injury or disease, or it may accompany a recurrent or ongoing disorder. Examples include giant pigmented nevi, nevus flammeus, cavernous hemangioma and alterations in pigmentation.

With disfigurement there is usually no loss of body function and little or no effect on the activities of daily living. Disfigurement may produce either social rejection or impairment of self-image, with self-imposed isolation, life-style alteration or other behavioral changes. If, however, impairment due to disfigurement does exist, it is usually manifested by a change in behavior such as the individual's withdrawal from society. Then, it should be evaluated in accordance with the criteria set forth in Chapter 12.

In some patients with altered pigmentation there may be loss of body function and interference in the activities of daily living, which should be evaluated in accordance with the criteria below.

The description of disfigurement is enhanced by good color photographs showing multiple views of the defect. The probable duration and permanency of the altered appearance should be stated.

The possibility of improvement in the altered appearance through medical or surgical therapy, and the extent to which the alteration can be concealed cosmetically, such as with hair pieces, wigs, or cosmetics, should be described in writing and should be depicted with photographs if possible.

Scars

Scars are cutaneous abnormalities that result from the healing of burned, traumatized, or diseased tissue, and they represent a special type of disfigurement. Scars should be described by giving their dimensions in centimeters and by describing their shape, color, anatomical location, and evidence of ulceration; their depression or elevation, which relates to whether they are atrophic or hypertrophic; their texture, which relates to whether they are soft and pliable or hard and indurated, thin or thick and smooth or rough; and their attachment, if any, to underlying bone, joints, muscles or other tissues. Good color photography with multiple views of the defect enhances the description of scars.

The tendency of a scar to disfigure should be considered in evaluating whether impairment is permanent, or whether the scar can be changed, made less visible, or concealed. Function may be restored without improving appearance, and appearance may be improved without altering anatomical or physiological function. Assignment of a percentage of impairment because of behavioral changes related to a scar should be done according to the criteria set forth in Chapter 12.

If a scar involves the loss of sweat gland function, hair growth, nail growth, or pigment formation, the effect of such loss on performance of the activities of daily living should be evaluated. Furthermore, any loss of function due to sensory deficit, pain, or discomfort in the scar area should be evaluated according to the criteria in Chapter 2. Loss of function due to limited motion in the scar area should be evaluated according to criteria in Chapter 1, or, if chest wall excursion is limited, in Chapter 3.

Patch Testing—Performance, Interpretation and Relevance

Patch testing is not a substitute for an adequately detailed history. Nevertheless, when properly performed and interpreted, patch tests can make a significant contribution to the diagnosis and management of contact dermatoses.

The physician must be aware that patch testing can yield false positive and false negative results. Selecting the proper concentration of the suspected chemical, the proper vehicle, the proper site of application, and the proper type of patch are critical in assuring validity of the procedure. Making such selections and determining the relevance of the test results require considerable skill and experience.

A positive or negative patch test result should not be accepted at face value until the details of the testing procedures have been evaluated. While appropriate test concentrations and vehicles have been established for many common sensitizers, for most chemicals in existence there are *no* established vehicle and concentration standards. Further details about patch testing and its pitfalls are discussed in standard texts.

Criteria for Evaluating Permanent Impairment of the Skin

Class 1—Impairment of the Whole Person, 0-5%: A patient belongs in Class 1 when (a) signs or symptoms of skin disorder are present; AND (b) with treatment, there is no limitation, or minimal limitation, in the performance of the activities of daily living, although exposure to certain physical or chemical agents might increase limitation temporarily.

Example 1: A 48-year-old white man has operated a unit manufacturing silver nitrate for 20 years. Five years ago he noted bluish discoloration of the inner canthi of his eyes, which progressed so that presently the sclerae, face, and arms are now decidedly bluish, and the unexposed skin shows a slightly bluish tint. There is also bluish pigmentation in the posterior nasal passages and around the turbinates and the fauces. Although he is aware of the condition, it does not bother him. His general health is good, and the remainder of the physical examination shows no abnormalities. The results of laboratory studies are within normal limits. Skin biopsy of the arm confirms the diagnosis of argyria.

Diagnosis: Argyria.

Impairment: 0% impairment of the whole person.

Comment: If impairment from cosmetic disfigurement also existed, it would be manifested by behavioral changes, which should be evaluated in accordance with the criteria set forth in Chapter 12.

Example 2: Three years ago a 62-year-old man developed a lichenoid purpuric dermatosis of the legs that was biopsied. He experienced no pruritus, and he received specific medication. Six months later an incomplete, annular, infiltrative lesion that caused no symptoms developed in the right antecubital fossa. A biopsy established the diagnosis of mycosis fungoides. Complete blood count and bone marrow and liver biopsies were normal. The lesion responded well to 300 rads of x-ray therapy.

Diagnosis: Mycosis fungoides.

Impairment: 0% impairment of the whole person due to mycosis fungoides.

Example 3: A 27-year-old male worker in a small paint manufacturing company developed acute contact dermatitis of the hands and arms. He related onset and exacerbations to preparation of batches of latex paint. Patch testing revealed a strong, allergic reaction to a 0.1% petrolatum mixture of a non-mercurial preservative, 2-n-4-isothiazolin-3-one, used by the company in its latex paints. The patient was unable to avoid latex paint completely, and his dermatitis continued. When he left the company to seek other employment, his dermatitis resolved completely.

Diagnosis: Allergic contact dermatitis due to a latex paint preservative.

Impairment: 0% impairment of the whole person.

Comment: The preservative to which the worker was allergic was manufactured for use only in latex paints. It is used widely in the paint manufacturing industry but not in other industries. The patient was restricted from employment in industries where he would come in contact with the offending chemical but there was no limitation in the performance of activities of daily living. Although this worker has 0% impairment of the whole person, he may be disabled under some state workers' compensation statutes.

Example 4: A 52-year-old janitor had episodes of transient dermatitis of the hand from the detergents he used in wet work duties over the past thirteen years. About ten years ago, depigmentation developed on the sides of most fingers and over the dorsa of the hands and distal forearms. Recently, other areas of depigmentation became apparent on the upper torso and thighs.

The janitor used a germicidal disinfectant that contained para-tertiary butyl phenol (TBP). Patch tests revealed a 2+ reaction to TBP 1% in petrolatum but not to other common industrial allergens. A month later, the site of the positive patch test became depigmented. Ultraviolet light therapy in combination with oral 8-methoxypsoralen (PUVA therapy) failed to stimulate re-pigmentation over a one year period. Covering with cosmetics was unsatisfactory.

The janitor also was required to perform outdoor maintenance work. Sunburn frequently occurred in the areas lacking pigmentation. Early actinic changes with wrinkling, bruising and scaling of the skin were present.

Diagnosis: Occupational leukoderma due to a phenolic chemical, TBP.

Impairment: 5% impairment of the whole person.

Comment: This rating does not consider any impairment of the man's self-image or of social relationships that might develop, nor the effects that these might have on the worker's future occupational situation.

Class 2—Impairment of the Whole Person, 10-20%: A patient belongs in Class 2 when (a) signs and symptoms of skin disorder are present; AND (b) intermittent treatment is required; AND (c) there is limitation in the performance of some of the activities of daily living.

Example 1: An eczematous eruption developed beneath the wedding ring on the fourth finger of the left hand of a 28-year-old housewife shortly after the birth of her first child six years ago. The eruption gradually spread to involve areas on several fingers of both hands despite treatment and avoidance of all jewelry. The eruption persisted for several months, then subsided slowly. A severe flare-up of hand dermatitis occurred after the birth of her second child two years later. Presently, chronic low-grade dermatitis persists despite special precautions. Intermittent treatment is required to control the dermatitis. The patient has no previous history of eczema, hay fever, or asthma, and no family history of atopy. Her general health is good. Patch tests performed with various food, household, cosmetic, and diagnostic and therapeutic contactant tray materials were nonreactive.

Diagnosis: Chronic dermatitis of the hands, from undetermined multiple contact factors.

Impairment: 10% impairment of the whole person.

Comment: While the history of atopy is negative, the clinical events are highly suggestive of an atopic cutaneous reaction of recurrent nature. Allergic contact dermatitis was not demonstrated but the cutaneous reaction to low grade irritant agents seems clear.

Example 2: A 25-year-old man who has a family history of "eczema" and hay fever has had a recurrent pruritic eruption since the age of one month, when it was characterized by oozing lesions of the face, scalp, neck, and upper extremities. A diagnosis of infantile eczema was made shortly after the onset. He had periods of relatively complete remission, but even during these periods, lichenified patches in his antecubital, popliteal, and nuchal areas persisted. Exacerbations were severe at age 14, when he entered high school, and increased in frequency during college. In the past three years, he had two episodes requiring hospitalization. These were characterized by a pruritic, red papular eruption of the face, neck, upper trunk, and shoulders, followed by scaling and dryness.

When the eruptions flare, they respond to the frequent application of topical steroids, to oatmeal starch baths, oral antihistamines, and occasional courses of ataractics. When his acute eczematous eruption subsides, he benefits from the application of a nonmedicated emollient cream to the dry scaling areas. Extensive patch and scratch tests do not elicit significant positive reactions. His condition is made worse by cold weather, marked changes in environmental temperature, and stressful situations in his job or at home. No residual scarring occurs. Exacerbations may require confinement for as long as seven days, either at home or in the hospital, along with treatment by a physician.

Diagnosis: Atopic dermatitis.

Impairment: 15% impairment of the whole person.

Comment: Attacks of atopic dermatitis are precipitated by a variety of excitants often of a chemical nature. The need for frequent hospitalization and absence from work may require evaluation of the mental health status.

Example 3: A 45-year-old white man developed an eczematous eruption on his left arm and hand during spring, four years ago. The eruption was treated effectively by admitting him to the hospital and giving topical medications. After the man's discharge, the condition flared up, involving the right side of his face and neck and the left forearm to the bottom of his work shirt sleeve. The eruption responded incompletely to treatment but subsided in the fall. It returned the next spring and subsided in the winter, but during the next two years it persisted throughout the year. Further history was that the eruption on the exposed areas subsided to some degree when the man was off work but flared up within a day after his return, even on the night shift. He worked in the warehouse of a paperbox factory and handled only printed paper cartons. Illumination of the work area was exclusively by banks of fluorescent tubes contained in low-hanging fixtures.

Medical examination disclosed evidence of chronic dermatitis. There were no positive reactions from extensive patch tests with materials from the patient's work, home or personal activities, or from those in the standard screening tray. The minimal erythema dose (MED) was significantly decreased. Photo patch tests with halogenated salicylanilides and fragrances were negative. However, within 6 hours after he was exposed to 5 minutes of light from an 8-watt fluorescent bulb, a severe erythema and edema developed in the exposed area. Five days later, this area was eczematous. Tests for urinary porphyrins were within normal limits.

Whenever the man was exposed to fluorescent light or sunlight, the eruption recurred. It was necessary for him to change jobs and to avoid all ultraviolet light exposure, including fluorescent lighting. He could be kept comfortable by intermittent use of topical corticosteroids and of a benzophenone sunscreen. Exacerbations occurred periodically that required treatment.

Diagnosis: Persistent photodermatitis, elicited and aggravated by ultraviolet light, including exposure to fluorescent light.

Impairment: 20% impairment of the whole person.

Comment: The presence of a light receptor being applied to the skin periodically or being contacted at work remains obscure, but the reactivity to light is well demonstrated. Clinically this case could represent a persistent light reactor.

Example 4: One year ago a 32-year-old black woman developed a 2 cm area of erythema and induration of the right malar eminence. One month later, similar spots appeared on the left side of her forehead, on the left cheek, at the right external auditory meatus, and at the interior aspect of the pinna of the left ear. At first the spots were erythematous and indurated, but then they became scaly and hyperpigmented, progressing to hypopigmentation with atrophic changes and some hair loss. Hyperpigmentation persisted at the margins of the lésions.

The patient limited her exposure to sunlight, and except for occasional mild pruritus, the lesions were asymptomatic. Various ointments and antimalarial medications were prescribed, but there was no improvement of the lesions. The patient became depressed about her appearance and her friends reported that she avoided them and seemed withdrawn.

Diagnosis: Discoid lupus erythematosus.

Impairment: 15% impairment due to discoid lupus erythematosus, which is to be combined with an appropriate value for the behavioral disorder to determine the impairment of the whole person.

Example 5: A 30-year-old white man was employed in a rare metals refining plant. Inadvertently he was splashed with concentrated liquid zirconium chloride over the face, scalp, and neck. Immediately he was washed, and then he was taken to the hospital, where he remained for two days. Healing and epithelialization occurred without complications. He returned to work 22 days after the episode.

Examination one year after the incident discloses well demarcated areas of depigmentation on the right side of the face, extending from behind the right ear to the center of the face, and from the mid-temple area of the scalp to the chin. There are smaller areas of depigmentation on the left side of the neck and behind the right ear. Maximum dimensions of the depigmented areas on the right side of the face are 16 cm by 11 cm. There are narrow collars of hyperpigmentation around the depigmented areas.

Neurological examination indicates that all of the depigmented areas are hypersensitive to cold, heat, pinprick, and touch, and for some of these areas, low-temperature stimuli are mistakenly identified as "hot" and "burning." In contrast to the adjacent normal skin, the depigmented areas sunburn easily, causing considerable discomfort. When the patient is operating a kiln in the plant or approaching a furnace, the affected side develops a stinging sensation. In the affected areas there is occasional muscle twitching.

The patient experiences considerable embarrassment when attempting to explain his disfigurement, and he avoids many kinds of social activities in which he previously participated. Examinations show that there has been no change during the last 6 months in the pigment loss, hyperesthesia, and intolerance to sunlight and warmth. Plastic surgery is not indicated.

Diagnosis: Chemical leukoderma after zirconium chloride burn.

Impairment: 20% impairment due to leukoderma, which is to be combined with an appropriate value for the behavioral problem to determine impairment of the whole person.

Class 3 — Impairment of the Whole Person, 25-50%: A patient belongs in Class 3 when (a) signs and symptoms of skin disorder are present; AND (b) continuous treatment is required; AND (c) there is limitation in the performance of many activities of daily living.

Example 1: Twenty-two months ago, a 50-year-old woman developed a persistently sore mouth. An examination revealed many eroded lesions of the tongue and oral mucous membranes. Subsequently, the patient noted the appearance of vesicles, and then bullae, over the face, trunk, and extremities. In the hospital, the diagnosis of pemphigus vulgaris was made, this being substantiated by histologic, immunofluorescent, and cytologic procedures. Oral administration of steroids brought about a prompt remission of the disease.

A month after the hospital admission, the patient was discharged on steroid therapy. Bullae reappeared when withdrawal of the steroid was attempted, and therapy with azothiaprine was started. Oral erosions continued to appear, and therapy with cytoxan and then methotrexate also failed to control the disease. The patient experienced difficulty in eating and swallowing and was forced to puree her food. The debilitating effects of her disease also interfere with her speech and sleep.

Diagnosis: Pemphigus vulgaris.

Impairment: 25% impairment of the whole person.

Example 2: For the last 6 years, a 45-year-old man has had a persistent pruritic dermatitis involving both ankles, forearms, and hands, and occasionally the face and neck. These areas are excoriated and lichenified. He has had recurrent bouts of pyogenic infection, and on occasion regional nodes have become swollen and tender.

At the time of onset, the man's work as a nurseryman included general greenhouse activity, such as planting, weeding, watering, fertilizing, and spraying with numerous pesticides and antifungal agents. Some of the chemicals were found to be primary irritants. Initially, the man's dermatitis responded to topical therapy and to his avoiding irritants, but the condition would flare up after re-exposure. Eventually, avoiding incriminated agents and changing jobs was not followed by the subsiding of symptoms, which caused neurodermatitis, or the "itch-scratch" syndrome. Warm environments, sweating and stress provoked episodes of severe itching. The man had no history of a prior dermatologic problem.

Three years ago, the patient began to have episodes of headache and memory loss, and to note periods of tenseness and apprehension accompanied by nausea and vomiting. He was treated intermittently for the mental disturbances, with little improvement of the neurodermatitis.

The patient has not engaged in nursery work for the past three years. He finds it difficult to tolerate other kinds of work, claiming they make his dermatitis worse. He is gainfully employed no more than six months during the year. At home he has been unable to perform household maintenance chores and to participate in social and recreational activities, and he has experienced difficulty sleeping.

Diagnosis: Persistent neurodermatitis secondary to occupational contact dermatitis.

Impairment: 30% impairment due to the skin disorder, which is to be combined with an appropriate value for the behavioral disorder to determine the impairment of the whole person.

Example 3: A 28-year-old man has had acne vulgaris for the past 12 years. He has not responded to the conventional methods of treatment. During the last five years he has developed large cystic lesions and draining sinuses on his face, neck, and upper trunk. This has been accompanied by fever and aching joints. Scarring is severe. The large lesions on his back and chest have made it difficult for him to rest comfortably. In warm weather, clothing irritates his skin. He has had difficulty sleeping, participating in social and recreational activities, and in obtaining employment. Sweating also aggravates the skin disorder considerably.

Diagnosis: Acne vulgaris, acne conglobata; post-acne scar formation.

Impairment: 30% impairment of the whole person.

Comment: A new systemic therapy for severe recalcitrant acne vulgaris, 13-Cis Retinoic Acid (Accutane®), has just been released by the Food and Drug Administration. This therapy offers hope of significantly reducing the extent of impairment in this patient.

Example 4: A 22-year-old woman entered the hospital with fever, malaise, arthralgia, painful hands and feet and marked erythema, and edema of the face, the V of the neck, and the areas of the back not covered by her bathing suit. She also complained of abdominal pain and nausea. The acute episode was precipitated by a trip to the seashore, where she had sunbathed for several hours.

On physical examination, she had erythema, edema and scaling of exposed body areas, generalized annular, atrophic plaques involving the trunk, palms and soles. The liver was tender to palpation, and there was an apical systolic murmur. Funduscopic examination revealed perivascular hemorrhages and fluffy exudates. Laboratory tests showed hemolytic anemia, leukopenia, hypocomplementemia, hyperglobulinemia, albuminuria, hematuria, a positive lupus erythematosus cell test, and a high antinuclear antibody titer.

Steroid therapy was begun, and the patient responded well. However, the hematuria and albuminuria persisted, and she had to be maintained on steroids. She remained very tired most of the time, especially after slight exertion. Plaquenil therapy was begun for the severe cutaneous involvement with only a partial improvement of her palms and soles. She has considerable difficulty grasping, standing and walking because of the severe skin disease.

Diagnosis: Systemic lupus erythematosus.

Impairment: 50% impairment due to lupus erythematosus, which is to be combined with appropriate values for impairments of the other involved systems, namely, the hematopoietic, urinary, and visual systems, to determine the impairment of the whole person.

Class 4—Impairment of the Whole Person, 55-80%: A patient belongs in Class 4 when (a) signs and symptoms of skin disorder are present; AND (b) continuous treatment is required, which may include periodic confinement at home or other domicile; AND (c) there is limitation in the performance of many of the activities of daily living.

Example 1: A 55-year-old man, who had been employed for 30 years as a parts clerk at a construction company warehouse, while at work injured his right leg severely in an automobile crash. The injury was followed by a deep vein thrombophlebitis of the right leg that required six months of total and partial bed rest, both in a hospital and at home.

After recovery, the man began to work at a chemical company. He wore an elastic stocking, but his right leg began to swell more and more each day. Four days after starting work, he spilled a can of caustic drain cleaner, causing second and third degree burns over 20% of the right lower leg. He was hospitalized for 12 weeks until the burn healed, leaving a scar but no thickening or contracture.

After four months, the man returned to work at the chemical company, but in spite of using elastic support stockings and diuretics, the edema in his leg became intolerable. He was unable to stay on his feet more than four hours at a time without significant swelling and discomfort. He began to develop stasis dermatitis with ulceration. Periodic treatment with Unna paste boots and occasional admissions to the hospital healed the ulcers only temporarily. After 5 years at the chemical company, he quit work and applied for workers' compensation benefits, alleging total disability.

At the time of evaluation the following were noted. Below the right knee there were marked pitting edema, post-inflammatory hyperpigmentation, scar formation and ulceration. A large hypopigmented, atrophic, scaly scar, measuring 10 cm by 20 cm, on which there was no sensation of light touch, was found laterally, beginning 8 cm above the ankle and extending upward 20 cm. A stasis ulcer measuring 7 cm by 5 cm was noted over the right medial malleolus.

Diagnosis: Post-thrombophlebitis syndrome with stasis dermatitis and ulceration; scar formation secondary to chemical burn.

Impairment: 55% impairment of the whole person.

Comment: Future episodes of phlebitis, cellulitis and ulceration are to be expected. Diligent medical care will be required indefinitely.

In similar cases, a physician may be asked to apportion a percentage of the overall impairment between the two injuries. The reader is referred to the discussion of apportionment in the Preface.

Example 2: Raynaud's phenomenon was first observed in a 38-year-old man about 5 years ago. Four years ago, he noted difficulty in swallowing, and then he developed swelling and tightening of the skin of the fingers, which gradually and progressively worsened. Dressing and feeding became progressively more difficult.

Examination discloses that the patient has increased pigmentation with telangiectasia, primarily on the face, forearms, and dorsal surface of his hands. He has a "pinched facies," and the skin over most of the body is hidebound. Chest excursion is limited. The fingers are held in flexion, and the patient has ulcerations on the distal phalanges of both index fingers. He is unable to extend his fingers because of stiffness, tightness, and pain.

The patient's weight is 20% below the desirable weight for height and age. Complete blood cell count is within normal limits, except for a sedimentation rate of 40 mm/hr. Urinalysis is normal, and the lupus erythematosus cell test and serologic test for syphilis are negative. An electrocardiogram and a chest roentgenogram are interpreted as normal. Roentgenographic examinations reveal a mild stenosis of the esophagus and disturbed peristaltic activity.

Diagnosis: Acrosclerotic scleroderma, mild stenosis of esophagus, and flexion deformity of fingers, with chronic ulcerations.

Impairment: 55% impairment due to scleroderma, which is to be combined with appropriate values for the stenosis of the esophagus and the flexion deformities to determine the impairment of the whole person.

Example 3: A 32-year-old white man was first admitted to the hospital because of a widespread pustular eruption associated with an acute conjuctivitis and severe arthritis of all joints of the hands, wrists, knees, ankles, and toes. He stated that he had been in good health until two months before this admission, when he developed an erythematous scaly eruption of the pretibial areas, which then spread to involve his upper extremities and hand. Shortly thereafter he developed pain, swelling, and erythema of the knees, and a urethral discharge. No organisms were grown in culture. The joints of the hands and feet were warm, red, and tender, with minimal swelling. A skin biopsy was compatible with exudative psoriasis. He was treated with topical therapy with no response, but he improved on systemic steroids and cytotoxic agents.

At the time of discharge, he was thought to have either Reiter's syndrome, keratoderma blennorhagica, or pustular psoriasis with psoriatic arthritis.

He was rehospitalized three months later with an acute and severe exacerbation of his skin eruption with severe pain, swelling and deformity of all joints of his extremities. A skin biopsy again was diagnostic of exudative psoriasis. Radiographic examination of the hands and wrists demonstrated marked bony demineralization of the carpal bones and the proximal and distal heads of the metacarpals and all the phalanges. Joint space narrowing and periosteal reaction were present in the metacarpal bones of both hands. Flexion deformities were present in both hands. Five months later, after some improvement, he was discharged from the hospital. Presently, oral doses of steroids and cytotoxic agents are required for controlling the disease. He continues to have periodic flare-ups of his arthritis and psoriasis, which require hospitalization.

Diagnosis: Pustular psoriasis with psoriatic arthritis.

Impairment: 60% impairment due to psoriasis, which is to be combined with appropriate values for the limitations of joint motion to determine the impairment of the whole person.

Comment: The clinical features of Reiter's syndrome and pustular psoriasis may overlap. The presence of conjunctivitis and urethritis favors the former; small joint arthritis of the hands and feet favors psoriasis. The finding of HLA-B27 antigen in about 65% of cases of Reiter's syndrome, as well as in most patients with pustular psoriasis, indicates a further link between these conditions. Both may relapse and adversely affect the activities of daily living.

Example 4: A 56-year-old white man was admitted to the hospital because of a generalized pruritic eruption. His condition began 20 years ago with pruritic patches on his back and extremities. Despite topical therapy the eruption gradually became generalized, and many patches became infiltrated plaques. Recently nodular lesions have developed. Past treatment has included topical nitrogen mustard, PUVA and electron beam therapy.

Physicial examination revealed a generalized eruption consisting of erythematous scaly plaques, some of which were quite infiltrated. There were also many excoriations found on the trunk and extremities and nodular tumors on his face and soles of his feet. Palpable axillary and inguinal lymph nodes were noted.

Laboratory tests showed normal values for fasting blood sugar, blood urea nitrogen, creatinine, uric acid, alkaline phosphatase, bilirubin, cholesterol, prothrombin time, sedimentation rate and platelet counts. A skin biopsy confirmed a diagnosis of mycosis fungoides. There were no abnormalities found in bone marrow aspiration, and the results of serology, rheumatoid factor, antinuclear factor and ECG were negative. A biopsy specimen from an axillary lymph node showed mycosis fungoides infiltrating the node.

The chest radiograph showed some tortuosity of the thoracic aorta. The heart was normal in size and shape.

The patient was given a cytotoxic agent intravenously daily for five days with excellent results, followed by oral doses of the same cytotoxic agent. Moderate control of his eruption has been obtained with the cytotoxic agent and radiation therapy.

Diagnosis: Mycosis fungoides.

Impairment: 75% impairment of the whole person.

Comment: Late stage, wide spread mycosis fungoides requires close medical surveillance. Morbidity is considerable, and the prognosis is poor. In most patients there is interference with some activities of daily living and they succumb within two to five years.

Example 5: A 35-year-old male technician inadvertently had exposures of about 12,000 rads to the hands and forearms while working on an x-ray machine. Within hours, an intense bluish-purple erythema appeared on the hands and wrists that was followed rapidly by the development of large, tense blisters filled with serous exudate. Treatment was symptomatic, and over the next few weeks the exposed areas became pigmented and atrophic, showing telangiectasia. Later, after only minor trauma, the exposed areas would develop large, tender ulcerations that would only partly heal.

During the next two years, the technician developed contractures that made it impossible for him to resume employment. He had to protect the affected skin from even minor injury, and he developed many limitations in his ability to care for himself. He became depressed and often thought of suicide. Excision of the ulcers and skin grafting were unsuccessful, the grafts quickly breaking down.

Diagnosis: Chronic radiation dermatitis with ulceration and scarring of both hands.

Impairment: 80% impairment due to radiation dermatitis, which is to be combined with appropriate values for the mental disorder to determine the impairment of the whole person.

Comment: The effects of such radiation exposure are life long and progressive. Repeated skin ulceration will occur and adversely affect the activities of daily living and survival.

Class 5—Impairment of the Whole Person, 85-95%: A patient belongs in Class 5 when (a) signs and symptoms of skin disorder are present; AND (b) continuous treatment is required, which necessitates confinement at home or other domicile; AND (c) there is severe limitation in the performance of the activities of daily living.

Example 1: A 12-year-old girl has had photophobia for 8 years. At the age of 5 years, she developed marked pigmentation of sun-exposed areas of the face, chest, arms, and legs. Since then, she has developed generalized freckling of the skin, several areas of telangiectasia, and multiple basal and squamous cell epitheliomas. The condition is progressing in severity, and the patient requires continuous observation and treatment. She has been confined to the home for the past year. Laboratory tests for blood and urine show normal values. Fecal and urinary porphyrin studies were negative.

Diagnosis: Xeroderma pigmentosum.

Impairment: 85% impairment of the whole person.

Comment: Xeroderma pigmentosum is a progressive disease with ultimate impairment approaching 100%. Development of metastatic carcinoma from squamous cell carcinomas or malignant melanoma can be expected, leading to early death.

Example 2: A 19-year-old boy developed bullous lesions shortly after birth; these have been present continuously since then, except for very minor and short remissions. Bullae appear after the slightest trauma and, at times, without apparent trauma, and heal with severe scarring. The boy's fingers now are tapered stumps. Bullae are present almost constantly in the mouth and pharnyx, probably to the level of the esophagus. The boy requires continuous hospitalization. His weight is 40% below the desirable weight for his height. Roentgenography shows stricture of the esophagus.

Diagnosis: Epidermolysis bullosa dystrophica.

Impairment: 90% impairment due to epidermolysis bullosa dystrophica, which is to be combined with appropriate values for the stricture of the esophagus and the finger stumps to determine the impairment of the whole person.

Comment: This autosomal recessive disorder is one of the most impairing of all hereditary diseases, with impairment approaching 100%. Appropriate values for psychiatric complications should be combined with the physical features of this disorder.

Example 3: A 25-year-old black man suffered burns on his body from a gasoline explosion three years prior to being seen by a dermatologist for impairment evaluation. He stated that he needed to soak 30 minutes a day with a teaspoon of alcohol and a teaspoon of Ivory soap in the water, after which he coated his body with Vaseline, but he still experienced considerable amount of itching. He felt that he could not work with heavy equipment and be outdoors, because when he is out in the sun or in the heat he is not able to perspire and he becomes dizzy. However, he sweats extensively on his face. He has difficulty with writing, walking and with nonspecialized hand activities because of scar formation. His ability to participate in group activities is greatly limited.

On physicial examination approximately 85% of his body was involved in some dermatologic disease, including residual of burn scars; graft sites and donor sites; depigmentation in the axillae, palms, dorsum of the hands and ankles; partial destruction of the left ear; and thickened fingernails. The cheeks were mildly involved and there was essentially no involvement of the neck and of a three inch band around his waist. There was some hypertrophic scar formation involving approximately 20% of the individual skin.

Diagnosis: Residual skin damage with extensive scarring secondary to a gasoline explosion.

Impairment: 90% impairment of the whole person.

Comment: Approximately two years later, the patient was again seen by the dermatologist. He stated that his workers' compensation had been discontinued over a year ago. He also stated that the Social Security Administration had sent him to another physician for an evaluation of his problem and that physician told him he could return to work. As a result, the Social Security Administration discontinued his payments and he consulted an attorney.

Physical examination revealed no essential change in the skin except for minimal repigmentation in some areas. His subjective complaints were the same and he still used Vaseline all over his body twice a day with soaking in the tub thirty minutes a day. The evaluation of the impairment of the whole person remained the same at 90%.

The criteria for evaluating permanent impairment due to skin disorders are recapitulated in Table 1.

Table 1 IMPAIRMENT CLASSIFICATION FOR SKIN DISEASE

Class 1 0-5% Impairment	Class 2 10-20% Impairment	Class 3 25-50% Impairment	Class 4 55-80% Impairment	Class 5 85-95% Impairment
A patient belongs in Class 1 when signs or symptoms of skin disorder are present	A patient belongs in Class 2 when signs and symptoms of skin disorder are present	A patient belongs in Class 3 when signs and symptoms of skin disorder are present	A patient belongs in Class 4 when signs and symptoms of skin disorder are present	A patient belongs in Class 5 when signs and symptoms of skin disorder are present
and	**and**	**and**	**and**	**and**
with treatment, there is no limitation, or minimal limitation, in the performance of the activities of daily living, although exposure to certain physical or chemical agents might increase limitation temporarily.	intermittent treatment is required **and** there is limitation in the performance of some of the activities of daily living.	continuous treatment is required **and** there is limitation in the performance of many activities of daily living.	continuous treatment is required, which may include periodic confinement at home or other domicile **and** there is limitation in the performance of many of the activities of daily living.	continuous treatment is required, which necessitates confinement at home or other domicile **and** there is severe limitation in the performance of activities of daily living.

References

1. Adams RM: *Occupational Skin Disease*. New York, Grune and Stratton, 1982.

2. The *Cosmetic Benefit Study*. Washington, DC, The Cosmetic, Toiletry and Fragrance Association, 1978.

3. Key MM: Confusing compensation cases. *Cutis* 1967;3:965-969.

4. Maibach HJ, Gellin GA (eds): *Occupational and Industrial Dermatology*. Chicago, Yearbook Medical Publishers, 1982.

Chapter 12

Mental and Behavioral Disorders

Introduction

This chapter provides a set of five principles for assessing mental and behavioral impairment, and provides a table with specific factors that must be evaluated to arrive at an estimated degree of impairment due to mental or behavioral disorders. The discussion in the chapter is general enough to apply to persons who may have mental or behavioral disorders resulting from physical impairment of other organ systems, as well as to those whose mental or behavioral disorders do not involve organic dysfunction. The five principles are:

1. In assessing the impairment that results from any mental or physical disorder, readily observed, empirical criteria must be applied accurately. Only a structured, replicable examination will result in an informed judgment.

2. Diagnosis is among the factors to be considered in assessing the severity and possible duration of the impairment, but it is by no means the sole criterion.

3. In a way that is dissimilar to the evaluation of other organ systems, factors related to the individual's family, education, financial and social situations, and occupation must be taken into consideration, as well as the individual's existing level of functioning.

4. The underlying character and value system of the individual is of considerable importance in the outcome of the disorder, be it mental or physical. Motivation for improvement is a key factor in the outcome.

5. A careful review must be made of the treatment and rehabilitation methods that have been applied or are being used. No final judgment can be made until the whole history of the illness, the treatment, the rehabilitation phase, and the individual's current mental and physical status and behavior have been considered.

Principle 1:

In assessing the impairment that results from any mental or physical disorder, readily observed, empirical criteria must be applied accurately. Only a structured, replicable examination will result in an informed judgment.

Assessments are concerned with three major factors: the degree of impairment, the degree of disability, and the degree of handicap.

Impairment is a medical determination. It involves any anatomical or functional abnormality or any clinically significant behavior changes assessed on the basis of symptoms, signs, laboratory findings, and/or psychological tests. Such impairment is considered to be permanent if the evaluator considers it to be stable or non-progressing at the time of evaluation.

In a mental disorder, the impairment may be a demonstrable loss of an important function that is caused by an organic brain disorder, a functional thinking disorder, or an affective disorder. Impairment may be stable or variable, and it may be exacerbated by various psychosocial stressors. The severity of an impairment should be assessed at a time when the individual is on medication, if it is needed.

Disability refers to the functioning social or vocational level of an individual that has been altered by an impairment. An impaired individual may have a reduced ability to function within the environment. For instance, a person may be unable to perform normal tasks because of a persistent thought disorder, or be unable to relate productively to fellow workers because of anxiety or misperception of their actions or intentions.

The degree of a person's disability is reflected in the individual's daily activities, both vocational and social, the range of interests, the ability to take care of personal needs, and the ability to relate to others. Determining an equitable degree of disability may present the dilemma of distinguishing between individuals who are unable to work and those who are unwilling to work because of secondary gains they have received from their impairments. Secondary gain is considered further under Principle 4.

A person is **handicapped** when his or her ability to function socially and/or vocationally is absent or reduced because of persistent impairment, and no marked or fundamental change can be expected. A handicapped individual is unable to function satisfactorily because of a specific deficit, such as a thought disorder with misperception of reality, an affective disorder, or overwhelming anxiety in a situation that normally does not entail severe risk or threat. The degree of social or vocational handicap is in part determined by the individual's reaction to the impairment.

Rehabilitation is of particular importance to the individual whose degrees of impairment and disability have been determined and who now needs special guidance to achieve potential return to paid employment or work, or to other normal performance. Gruenberg's definition of work is that of an activity which, if not performed by one person, must be performed by someone else. This definition includes childcare, housework and other domestic chores, as well as work done outside the home for pay. It distinguishes between productive activities that are required by society and those that involve hobbies or recreation.

Principle 2:

Diagnosis is among the factors to be considered in assessing the severity and possible duration of the impairment, but it is by no means the sole criterion.

For diagnostic and descriptive criteria, the evaluator should use the Diagnostic and Statistical Manual of Mental Disorders (ed 3), commonly known as DSM III.

DSM III calls for a multiaxial evaluation. Each of the five axes refers to a different class of informa-tion. The first three axes constitute the official diagnostic evaluation. The last two offer predictive values depending upon circumstances.

Axis I: This includes clinical syndromes and conditions that, while not attributable to a mental disorder, are a focus of treatment because they may affect the outcome of the mental disorder.

Axis II: This includes personality disorders and specific developmental disorders. The principal diagnosis may be either on Axis I or Axis II; when Axis II represents the principal diagnosis, it should be indicated with the phrase, "Principal Diagnosis." If both axes are used and no further information is given, the principal diagnosis is assumed to be related to Axis I.

Axis III: This includes physical disorders or conditions that may be relevant to the understanding and management of the individual.

Axis IV: This relates to severity of psychosocial stressors and offers a means of prognosis; for instance, the prognosis may be better if the disorder developed as the consequence of a severe stress than if it had developed after only minimal apparent stress.

Axis V: This relates to the highest level of adaptive functioning shown by the individual during the past year and the individual's use of leisure time. Axis V information often has predictive value, especially if the individual has returned to his or her previous level of functioning after an episode of illness.

In the description of mental disorders, the term "functional" means that the cause of the disorder is as yet unknown or uncertain; that is, the disorder is recognized mainly because of the manner in which the individual functions and is not recognized as being due to the dysfunction of a specific organ or system. It must be recognized that even if a disorder is termed "functional," it nevertheless may cause severe impairment. The word "functional" is not used if an organic cause of the disorder can be identified.

Functional disorders, however uncertain their etiology, can be treated successfully, although their improvement may be gradual and take a long time, especially if the disorder is a deep-seated one with onset over a long period.

In judging the degree of mental impairment, it is important to recognize that there are various types of mental disorders, each of which, like a physical disorder, has its own natural history and unique characteristics. Stress-related depression, for instance, is often a short-term, self-limiting illness that may clear up when the stressful situation is relieved. Other affective disorders have their own patterns of recurrence and chronicity and often respond well to therapeutic interventions. Somatic and psychological treatment and adequate supervision are important in all affective disorders, because one outcome of partial treatment may be suicide or attempted suicide.

The schizophrenias are typically chronic disorders. Their onset can be insidious and recognized only in retrospect.

Certain organic mental disorders, such as brain damage and lifelong mental retardation, are chronic. Treatment consists of minimizing the response to the pathology; for some patients, achieving only a degree of capability or habilitation may be a valid goal.

It is apparent that some major mental disorders are chronic. The term "remission" rather than "cure" is used to indicate improvement, and remission may be intermittent, long-term, or short-term, and may occur in stages rather than all at once. The degree of impairment may vary considerably in different patients, and the severity of the impairment is not necessarily related to the diagnosis. Indeed, diagnosis alone is of limited relevance to the objective assessment of psychiatric impairment, because it does not permit sufficient insight into the nature of the impairment.

The types of mental dysfunctioning in various disorders are curiously similar, regardless of the specific diagnosis. Just as "fever" and "pain" are seen in different kinds of physical disorders, so "anxiety" and "hostility" may be observed in different kinds of mental disorders.

Principle 3:
In a way that is dissimilar to the evaluation of other organ systems, factors related to the individual's family, education, financial and social situations, and occupation must be taken into consideration, as well as the individual's existing level of functioning.

The evaluator must consider the age, level of education, and social matrix of the individual, as well as the length of the onset of the illness, the length of its acute phase, and whether the person is currently having symptoms or is in remission. Vital to all these determinations is a comprehensive medical and psychiatric history.

The evaluator must consider the impaired individual's past and present functioning, and potential for future functioning; specifically, the evaluator must consider how well the individual has functioned during the past year or since the onset of illness, and how long he or she has been able to maintain the highest level of functioning. In this evaluation, the activities of daily living are important. These include self-care, responsibility toward other members of the household, and responsibility toward the community at large. For instance, has the individual maintained more or less "normal" behavior, including a reasonable degree of socialization? Maintaining good social relationships, particularly with family or friends, has important prognostic significance.

The patient's present vocational functioning must be investigated. What skills are intact, and what limitations exist? Is the individual marginally employable, or not employable at all at the former level? Is the patient employable at a lower level of skill than before the illness started?

In making judgments about degrees of impairment, it is important to consider the patient's social situation and how it contributes to, or detracts from, possible improvement. For example, consider the plight of the long-term patient with a major psychosis who is in an institution. The patient is given medication and earnestly exhorted to take it regularly. This is one of the few demands made upon the patient, in addition to prohibition of violent or angry behavior that may injure himself or others. Under the tranquilizing effects of medication, the patient may become a "good patient," one who gives no trouble but who is increasingly indistinguishable from other patients.

Once the role of "good patient" becomes firmly established, the social service department may attempt to place the person in the community, perhaps with relatives or in a halfway house. Here the individual will resume the career of "good patient," coming periodically to the institution to renew a supply of medication, and still not giving anyone trouble. Encounters with an overworked institutional staff may be superficial, the increasingly anonymous individual will receive the medications, and little attention will be paid to the possibility of psychiatric and vocational rehabilitation.

An evaluator discerning such a social pattern will recognize that depersonalization, the primary foe of improvement, has led to the institutionalization of the patient if he or she is in a hospital; benign neglect if at home or in a community facility; and possible overmedication or inappropriate medication if the patient has seldom or never been re-evaluated. But if the evaluator recognizes that there is still a possibility of further rehabilitation, with partial restoration to a higher degree of self-help or vocational ability, the evaluator may decide not to rate the patient's impairment until more appropriate rehabilitative measures have been taken.

Purely descriptive evaluations are not adequate in making determinations of impairment. Regardless of the diagnosis, the evaluator is charged with making judgments about the severity and possible future course of the existing impairment. To help the evaluator make such judgments, this chapter provides a table listing the personal characteristics and abilities on which the evaluation of impairments should be based. Table 1 will help the evaluator make specific judgments based on elements of the mental status examination and on the activities of daily living; classify the amount of treatment or vocational potential and the expected duration of impairment; and estimate the overall potential for the individual's rehabilitation.

The mental status examination, which is central to the total evaluation, will help to determine to what degree observed deficits might affect vocational handicap—severely, moderately, or not at all. Judgment, for instance, is important, not only as to whether it is intact or impaired, but also as to whether the individual should even be called upon to make autonomous decisions at work. Behavior, closely related to the degree of anxiety that the individual suffers, may be mildly to severely disordered, and may or may not prove to be disabling in a vocational sense. Finally, the evaluator must judge the degree and possible duration of the impairment: is it partial or total; is it likely to be a short-term or a long-term problem; and is it likely to get worse over time?

Principle 4:
The underlying character and value system of the individual is of considerable importance in the outcome of the disorder, be it mental or physical. Motivation for improvement is a key factor in the outcome.

The issue of motivation cannot be ignored as a connecting link between impairment and handicap. For some people, poor motivation is a major cause for continuing malfunction. The underlying character of the individual may be the dominant factor in whether or not he or she is likely to benefit from rehabilitation.

Personality characteristics usually remain unchanged throughout adult life. An individual who tends to be dependent may become more dependent as the course of the illness proceeds, and one who is inclined to act out conflicts may develop a constant pattern of antisocial behavior. Indeed, the pathological development of an underlying character trait may become even more pronounced and more significant than the actual illness.

Internal events, that is, psychological reactions, can influence physical and mental illness. Thus, the degree of handicap in the social and vocational context is not necessarily the same as the degree of impairment. The handicap may be greater or less than the impairment might warrant, and the individual's performance may fall short of, or exceed, that usually associated with the impairment. Handicaps arising because of impairments put the individual at a disadvantage by limiting individuals and preventing them from fulfilling normal roles.

Here the complex issue of "secondary gain" arises, involving not only the amount of compensation or financial benefit that may be awarded, but also the individual's lifestyle. The individual's motivation to recover and to be self-sufficient will either diminish or enhance the quality of life, in terms of social and vocational activities. Impairment plus poor motivation may add up to an almost total handicap, while impairment plus good motivation may result in a minimal handicap.

Often it is difficult for an evaluator to separate impairment and motivation. The evaluator may be able to see some clues in the clinical or family history, but these are likely to be only suggestive. The individual's daily activities can offer clues. Does he or she lead a rather steady, harmonious life, or an erratic kind of life? Recently has there been a steady worsening of his or her coping abilities? Very tenacious leanings toward dependency, hidden or overt, may influence any patient's chosen life-style, regardless of background.

Principle 5:

A careful review must be made of the treatment and rehabilitation methods that have been applied or are being used. No final judgment can be made until the whole history of the illness, the treatment, the rehabilitation phase, and the individual's current mental and physical status and behavior have been considered.

Of paramount importance to the evaluator is the degree of vocational limitation suffered by the individual, which may range from minimal to total. The severity of an impairment may vary with the course of the illness, and when an individual is ready for discharge, vocational skills may be intact, or the individual may have slight, moderate, or severe limitations that may or may not be reversible. The evaluator must judge the possible duration of any remaining impairment; whether remission will be fast or slow; whether it will be partial or total; and whether it will remain stable or get worse. Upon such considerations will depend the final decision about degree of impairment.

Rehabilitation is a *sine qua non* in treating most patients who have recovered or are recovering from the acute phase of mental disorder, especially a major mental disorder. Even if it is not possible to effect total "remission" or "cure," the outcome may be considered worthwhile if the individual has been able to move from one degree of impairment to one of a lesser degree.

For some persons, poor motivation seems to be a major cause for continuing impairment. Yet, with proper rehabilitative measures it seldom is necessary to speak of permanent total impairment, except in some patients with organic illnesses. Determination of permanent impairment is often imprecise, and rarely is there certainty that it exists. The use of such a determination is pessimistic, providing an adverse prediction that may well be self-fulfilling.

An important aspect of rehabilitation is the recognition that an individual on certain types of medication may be able to sustain a satisfactory degree of functioning, whereas without medication, he or she might fail to do so. For instance, there may be only a slight problem in the thinking process while the patient is taking suitable medication, but a severe one if the patient is not taking medication. Another vital part of the rehabilitation effort is to educate family and potential employers about the importance of maintenance doses of the medication, as well as about the possibility that the patient may re-experience symptoms while taking or not taking medication.

Another consideration is that an employer needs reassurance that a worker on proper medication and in the proper job is a safe worker. An example is the control of epileptic seizures with medication. Education of the patient's family, employer and fellow workers in such matters is vital and is properly a part of the rehabilitation process.

There are various degrees of impairment, and "total rehabilitation" may not be possible. To use an example from physical medicine, it is impossible for an amputated leg to be replaced, and the affected individual cannot hope to regain perfect, pre-injury ambulation. But a well-fitted prosthesis, accompanied by training in its use, can greatly improve ability to walk. If, in addition, the individual obtains suitable private or public transportation, he or she may well be totally restored to gainful employment, unless total ambulation is a requirement of the job. Even if it is, an employer could provide alternative tasks, or modify existing tasks so that they can be performed successfully by an amputee who makes skillful use of a suitable prosthesis.

Obviously, the analogy between the loss of a limb and the loss of capability resulting from a mental disorder has limitations. Nonetheless, it is important to recognize that residual impairment from a mental disorder may be just as real and severe as impairment resulting from a physical disorder or injury. The link between motivation and recovery may need strengthening in individuals impaired either by physical or mental illnesses, and this is a task for rehabilitation psychiatry. The provision by the employer of alternative tasks, or the modification of existing work conditions, may be an important part of restoration to vocational ability for a patient with mental illness, just as it is for one with a physical illness, or for one with an illness that combines elements of both.

When considering the total background of the individual and his or her underlying character and value system, it must be remembered that educational levels and financial resources of family members cannot be ignored. The evaluator should assess the usefulness of family influences, and if rehabilitation efforts are to be continued, the evaluator may wish to recommend the inclusion of the family in the endeavor.

A Method of Evaluating Psychiatric Impairment

Solutions to the many dilemmas encountered in determining the degree of impairment resulting from a psychiatric illness can only be sought through the application of consistent and observable criteria that must be considered in relation to one another.

The table that follows, when used according to the best clinical judgment of the evaluator, will aid in the evaluation of an individual, and it should be used after all diagnostic, clinical, treatment, and rehabilitation factors have been explored.

An example follows the table that gives the overall rating of a patient based upon the mental status and upon the current condition as observed by the evaluator. The rating is based upon observed attributes and phenomena that are somewhat interrelated, and it necessarily must be considered to be somewhat subjective.

Table 1
EVALUATION OF PSYCHIATRIC IMPAIRMENT

Class of Impairment	1	2	3	4	5
Percentage of Impairment	0% to 5%	10% to 20%	25% to 50%	55% to 75%	over 75%
MENTAL STATUS					
Intelligence	Normal or better	Mildly Retarded	Moderately Mildly Retarded	Moderately Severely Retarded	Severely Retarded
Thinking	No Deficit	Slight Deficit	Moderate Deficit	Moderately Severe Deficit	Severe Deficit
Perception	No Deficit	Slight Deficit	Moderate Deficit	Moderately Severe Deficit	Severe Deficit
Judgment	No Deficit	Slight Deficit	Moderate Deficit	Moderately Severe Deficit	Severe Deficit
Affect	Normal	Slight Problem	Moderate Problem	Moderately Severe Problem	Severe Problem
Behavior	Normal	Slight Problem	Moderate Problem	Moderately Severe Problem	Severe Problem
ACTIVITIES OF DAILY LIVING					
Ability	Self-sufficient	Needs Minor Help	Needs Regular Help	Needs Major Help	Quite Helpless
REHABILITATION OR TREATMENT POTENTIAL					
Potential	Excellent	Good	Good for Partial Restoration	Condition Static	Condition Will Worsen

EXAMPLE OF PSYCHIATRIC IMPAIRMENT PROFILE

Category	Impairment Description	Impairment Class
Mental Status		
Intelligence	Normal	1
Thinking	Moderately severe deficit; cannot draw rational conclusions from single statements.	4
Perception	Slight deficit; however, shows no signs of delusions.	2
Judgment	Moderately severe deficit; engages in self-defeating behavior.	4
Affect	Between moderate and severe deficit; mood swings from hostile to friendly.	4
Behavior	Moderate to severe deficit; see Affect.	4
Activities of Daily Living	Self-sufficient	1
Rehabilitation or Treatment Potential	Good for partial restoration	3
Collective Impairment*	Moderate to severe 55% to 75%	4

*Whole-person Impairment Rating: Patient is vocationally unemployable and will remain so. Socially, the patient is moderately impaired, but the degree of impairment varies from time to time, depending upon the amount of stress to which the patient is subjected and upon whether the patient takes prescribed medication regularly.

REFERENCES

1. Gruenberg EM: The social breakdown syndrome—some origins. *AM J Psychiat* 123:1481-1489, 1967.

2. Lamb HR, Rogawski AS: Supplemental security income and the sick role. *AM J Psychiat* 135:1221-1224, 1978.

3. Mikkelson EJ: The psychology of disability. *Psychiatric Annals* 7:74-75, 1977.

4. Nagi S: Disability and Rehabilitation. Columbus, Ohio, Ohio State University Press, 1969.

5. Nussbaum, K, Puig JG, Schneidmuhl AM Shaffer JW: Psychiatric impairment under social security. *AM J Forensic Psychiat* 2:39-45, 1981-82.

6. World Health Organization: *International Classification of Impairments, Disabilities and Handicaps*, Geneva, World Health Organization, 1980.

7. Committee on Nomenclature and Statistics: *Diagnostic Statistical Manual of Mental Disorders*, (ed 3). Washington DC, American Psychiatric Association, 1980.

Appendix A

Reports

Reports

A clear, accurate and complete report is essential to support a rating of permanent impairment. The following list identifies the kinds of information that should be contained in the report:

Medical evaluation includes:

1. Narrative history of the medical condition(s) with specific reference to onset and course of the condition, findings on previous examinations, treatments, and responses to treatment.

2. Results of the most recent clinical evaluation, including any of the following that were obtained:
- physical examination findings
- laboratory test results
- electrocardiogram
- radiographic studies
- rehabilitation evaluation
- mental status examination and psychological tests
- other special tests or diagnostic procedures

3. Assessment of current clinical status, and statement of plans for future treatment, rehabilitation and re-evaluation.

4. Diagnoses and clinical impressions.

5. Estimate of the expected date of full or partial recovery.

Analysis of the findings includes:

1. Explanation of the impact of the medical condition(s) on life activities.

2. Narrative explanation of the medical basis for any conclusion that the medical condition has, or has not, become static or well-stabilized.

3. Explanation of the medical basis for a conclusion that the individual is, or is not, likely to suffer sudden or subtle incapacitation as a result of the medical condition.

4. Explanation of the medical basis for any conclusion that the individual is, or is not, likely to suffer injury or harm or further medical impairment by engaging in activities of daily living or any other activity necessary to meet personal, social, and occupational demands.

5. Explanation of any conclusion that restrictions or accommodations are, or are not, warranted with respect to daily activities or any other activities that are required to meet personal, social, and occupational demands. If restrictions or accommodations are necessary, there should be an explanation of their therapeutic or risk-avoiding value.

Comparison of the results of analysis with the impairment criteria includes:

1. Description of specific clinical findings related to each impairment, with reference to how the findings relate to the criteria described in the chapter. Reference to the absence of, or to the examiner's inability to obtain, pertinent data is essential.

2. Comparison of specific clinical findings to the specific criteria that pertain to the particular body system, as they are listed in the Guides.

3. Explanation of each percent of impairment rating, with reference to the applicable criteria.

4. Summary list of all impairment ratings.

5. Combined or "whole person" rating, when more than one impairment is present.

Appendix B

Glossary

Correct standardized usage of terminology related to the evaluation of medical impairment and disability is essential. Semantic distinctions between terms assume legal importance. This Glossary provides definitions of terms that are used in the Guides, and definitions of other terms related to impairment and disability evaluations that may be of interest to the reader although they are not mentioned in the Guides. To assist the reader in distinguishing the evaluation of impairment from that of disability, the Glossary is in two sections: the first section contains terms related to impairment; the second section contains terms related to disability evaluation, workers' compensation, and employability.

Impairment

1. Activities of Daily Living

Activity	Example
Self care and personal hygiene	Urinating, defecating, brushing teeth, combing hair, bathing, dressing oneself, eating
Communication	Writing, typing, seeing, hearing, speaking
Normal living postures	Sitting, lying down, standing
Ambulation	Walking, climbing stairs
Travel	Driving, riding, flying
Nonspecialized hand activities	Grasping, lifting, tactile discrimination
Sexual function	Having normal sexual function and participating in usual sexual activity
Sleep	Restful nocturnal sleep pattern
Social and recreational activities	Ability to participate in group activities

2. Apportionment: Apportionment is the determination of the degree to which each of various occupational or nonoccupational factors has contributed to a particular impairment. For each alleged factor, two criteria must be met:

(a) The alleged factor could have caused the impairment, which is a *medical* decision, and

(b) in the particular case, the factor did cause the impairment, which is a *nonmedical* determination.

3. Clinical Evaluation: The clinical evaluation is the collection of data by a physician for the purpose of determining the health status of an individual. The data includes information obtained by history; clinical findings obtained from a physical examination; laboratory tests including radiographs, electrocardiograms, blood tests and other special tests and diagnostic procedures; and measurements of anthropometric attributes and physiologic and psycho-physiologic functions.

4. Disfigurement: Disfigurement is an altered or abnormal appearance. It may be an alteration of color, shape, or structure, or a combination of these. Disfigurement may be a residual of an injury or disease, or it may accompany a recurrent or chronic disorder of function or disease. It may produce either social rejection or impairment of self-image, with self-imposed isolation, alteration of life style, or other changes in behavior.

5. Impairment: Impairment is the loss of, loss of use of, or derangement of any body part, system or function.

Permanent impairment is impairment that has become static or well stabilized with or without medical treatment, or that is not likely to remit despite medical treatment of the impairing condition.

Evaluation or rating of impairment is an assessment of data collected during a clinical evaluation and the comparison of those data to the criteria contained in the Guides.

6. Intensity and Frequency: The intensity and the frequency of occurrence of symptoms or signs occasionally are useful in rating impairment. These can be graded as follows:

Intensity is:
(a) *minimal* when the symptoms or signs constitute an annoyance but cause no impairment in the performance of particular activity:

(b) *slight* when the symptoms or signs can be tolerated but would cause some impairment in the performance of an activity that precipitates the symptoms or signs:

(c) *moderate* when the symptoms and signs would cause marked impairment in the performance of an activity that precipitates the symptoms or signs;

(d) *marked* when the symptoms or signs preclude any activity that precipitates the symptoms or signs.

Frequency is:
(a) *intermittent* when the symptoms or signs occur less than 25% of the time when awake;

(b) *occasional* when the symptoms or signs occur between 25% and 50% of the time when awake;

(c) *frequent* when the symptoms and signs occur between 50% and 75% of the time when awake;

(d) *constant* when symptoms and signs occur between 75% and 100% of the time when awake.

Disability, Workers' Compensation and Employability

1. Aggravation and Causation: Aggravation and causation are related to the nonmedical determination that a factor that *can* cause a particular impairment in fact *did* cause the impairment (see Apportionment). In many benefit systems, causation and aggravation must be determined before entitlements are provided. In contrast to their involvement in traumatic injuries, the roles of occupational or environmental factors in causing or aggravating disorders of the various body systems often are not obvious to the lay person; thus evaluating their roles usually requires expert medical opinion. The expert's comments should include the identification of the specific environmental forces or agents and the dates and duration of their actions. An accurate chronicle of the clinical course of the disorder,

with dates, times and locations of environmental events, is helpful in the evaluation of causation and aggravation.

An aggravation, in order to have the legal impact of a causation, must be substantial and permanent, not merely speculative. Five types of aggravations are:

(a) an occupational disorder aggravated by a supervening nonoccupational disorder;

(b) an occupational disorder aggravated by a supervening other occupational condition arising out of and in the course of employment by the same employer;

(c) an occupational disorder aggravated by a supervening other industrial condition arising out of and in the course of employment by a different employer;

(d) an occupational disorder aggravated by a pre-existing nonoccupational condition;

(e) an occupational disorder aggravating a pre-existing nonoccupational condition.

2. Disability: Disability is the limiting loss or absence of the capacity of an individual to meet personal, social, or occupational demands, or to meet statutory or regulatory requirements.

Permanent disability occurs when the degree of capacity becomes static or well stabilized and is not likely to increase in spite of continuing medical or rehabilitative measures. Disability may be caused by medical impairment or by nonmedical factors.

Evaluation or rating of disability is a nonmedical assessment of the degree to which an individual does or does not have the capacity to meet personal, social, or occupational demands, or to meet statutory or regulatory requirements.

3. Employability: Employability is the capacity of an individual to meet the demands of a job and the conditions of employment.

4. Employability Determination: Employability determination is a management assessment of the individual's capacity to meet the demands of a job and the conditions of employment. The management carries out an assessment of performance capability to estimate the likelihood of performance failure and an assessment of the likelihood of future liability in case of human failure. If either likelihood is too great, then the individual will not be considered employable in a particular job.

5. Medical Determination Related to Employability:

The medical determination of employability is a statement by a physician about the relationship of an individual's health to the demands of a specific job, such as the demands for performance, reliability, integrity, durability, and overall useful service life as defined by the employer. The physician must ensure that the medical evaluation is complete and detailed enough to obtain the clinical information needed to draw valid conclusions. The physician's tasks are: to identify impairments that could affect performance and to determine whether or not the impairments are permanent; and to identify impairments that could lead to sudden or gradual incapacitation, further impairment, transmission of a communicable disease, or other adverse conditions.

In estimating the risk factors, the physician should indicate whether or not the individual represents a greater risk to the employer than someone without the same medical condition, and indicate the limits of the physician's ability to predict the likelihood of an untoward occurrence.

6. Possibility and Probability:
Possibility and probability are nonspecific terms without true statistical or legal meanings. They refer to the likelihood that an injury or illness was caused by a stipulated employment or other event. *Possibility* sometimes is used to imply a likelihood of less than 50%. *Probability* sometimes is used to imply a likelihood of greater than 50%.

Appendix C

Sleep and Arousal Disorders

Method of Evaluation

While it has been known that disorders of sleep and arousal can cause impairment, until recently physicians have been hampered by the lack of a nosological scheme describing standard diagnostic criteria for such disorders. The development of a comprehensive diagnostic classification now enables physicians to base their diagnostic determinations on common terminology, accepted methods of evaluation and standard signs and symptoms. The classification appears in Table 1.

TABLE 1

OUTLINE OF DIAGNOSTIC CLASSIFICATION OF SLEEP AND AROUSAL DISORDERS

A. Disorders of initiating and maintaining sleep (DIMS), or insomnias

1. Psychophysiological
   a. Transient and situational
   b. Persistent

2. Associated with psychiatric disorders
   a. Symptom and personality disorders
   b. Affective disorders
   c. Other functional psychoses

3. Associated with use of drugs and alcohol
   a. Tolerance to or withdrawal from CNS depressants
   b. Sustained use of CNS stimulants
   c. Sustained use of withdrawal from other drugs
   d. Chronic alcoholism

4. Associated with sleep-induced respiratory impairment
   a. Sleep apnea DIMS syndrome
   b. Alveolar hypoventilation DIMS syndrome

5. Associated with sleep-related (nocturnal) myoclonus and "restless legs"
   a. Sleep-related (nocturnal) myoclonus DIMS syndrome
   b. "Restless legs" DIMS syndrome

6. Associated with other medical, toxic and environmental conditions

7. Childhood-onset DIMS

8. Disorders associated with other DIMS conditions
   a. Repeated REM sleep interruptions
   b. Atypical polysomnographic features
   c. Not otherwise specified

9. No DIMS abnormality
   a. Short sleeper
   b. Subjective complaints without objective findings
   c. Not otherwise specified

B. Disorders of Excessive Somnolence (DOES)

1. Psychophysiological
   a. Transient and situational
   b. Persistent

2. Associated with psychiatric disorders
   a. Affective disorders
   b. Other functional disorders

3. Associated with use of drugs and alcohol
   a. Tolerance to or withdrawal from CNS stimulants
   b. Sustained use of CNS depressants

4. Associated with sleep-induced respiratory impairment
   a. Sleep apnea DOES syndrome
   b. Alveolar hypoventilation DOES syndrome

5. Associated with sleep-related (nocturnal) myoclonus and "restless legs"
   a. Sleep-related (nocturnal) myoclonus DOES syndrome
   b. "Restless legs" DOES syndrome

6. Narcolepsy

7. Idiopathic CNS hypersomnolence

8. Associated with other medical, toxic, and environmental conditions

9. Other DOES conditions
   a. Intermittent (periodic) syndromes
      i. Kleine-Levin syndrome
      ii. Menstrual-associated syndrome
   b. Insufficient sleep
   c. Sleep drunkenness
   d. Not otherwise specified

10. No DOES abnormality
    a. Longer sleep
    b. Subjective complaint without objective findings
    c. Not otherwise specified

C. Disorders of the Sleep-Wake Schedule

1. Transient
   a. Rapid time zone change ("jet lag") syndrome
   b. "Work-shift" change in usual sleep-wake schedule

2. Persistent
   a. Frequently changing sleep-wake schedule
   b. Delayed sleep phase syndrome
   c. Advanced sleep phase syndrome
   d. Non-24 hour sleep-wake syndrome
   e. Irregular sleep-wake pattern
   f. Not otherwise specified

D. Dysfunctions Associated with Sleep, Sleep Stages, or Partial Arousals (Parasomnias)

1. Sleepwalking (somnambulism)

2. Sleep terror

3. Sleep-related enuresis

4. Other dysfunctions
   a. Dream anxiety attacks (nightmares)
   b. Sleep-related epileptic seizures
   c. Sleep-related bruxism
   d. Sleep-related headbanging
   e. Familial sleep paralysis
   f. Impaired sleep-related penile tumescence
   g. Sleep-related painful erections
   h. Sleep-related cluster headaches and chronic paroxysmal hemicrania
   i. Sleep-related abnormal swallowing syndrome
   j. Sleep-related asthma
   k. Sleep-related cardiovascular symptoms
   l. Sleep-related gastroesophageal reflux
   m. Sleep-related hemolysis (paroxysmal nocturnal hemoglobinuria)
   n. Asymptomatic polysomnographic finding
   o. Not otherwise specified

Adapted from: Association of Sleep Disorders Centers Sleep Disorders Classification Committee: *Diagnostic Classification of Sleep and Arousal Disorders*, ed 1, in *Sleep* 1979;2:1-137. Copyright © 1979 Raven Press Books, Ltd.

Diagnostic evaluation includes taking a detailed medical history and performing a physical examination and appropriate laboratory tests. The history should include a daily sleep log or diary cataloging the time of retiring, estimated time to fall asleep, occurrence of nocturnal awakening and daytime naps and the use of hypnotic or analeptic medications. Often the patient is not aware of the severity of the problem, and for that reason reports from the bed partner and other informants may be useful.

For the purpose of rating the patient's impairment, it is essential not only to assess performance decrements but also the psychosocial impact of the sleep disorder and treatment for it. For example, a permanent tracheostomy for sleep apnea, and the impotence caused by drugs prescribed for cataplexy, may constrict social interaction, hamper participation in sports, and limit affective expression.

The physical examination should be thorough and geared to the evaluation of the upper airways, the nervous system, and, if there are abnormal hemodynamics, the cardiovascular system.

Special laboratory tests for these disorders include the multiple sleep latency test (MSLT) and polysomnography (PSG), which simultaneously assess multiple physiologic variables while the patient sleeps. This testing can be done only in sleep laboratories, and it often requires more than one night's or day's evaluation to get an accurate assessment of the patient's sleep patterns. PSG is especially useful in making a definitive diagnosis of most sleep and arousal disorders; it is discussed in more detail under the later section on sleep apnea.

The standardized MSLT assessment technique provides a quantitative measure of sleepiness, the factor most often responsible for functional impairment in sleep apnea, narcolepsy and other sleep and arousal disorders. The MSLT consists of a daytime series of five 20 minute nap opportunities at 2 hour intervals during which the patient is asked to "try to sleep." Sleep latency, defined as the time from lights out to the first minute of sleep, is averaged across the 5 naps and is a measure of sleepiness or sleep tendency.

The rationale for the MSLT is based on the simple, straightforward assumption that the sleepier an individual is the faster he or she will fall asleep. Clearly, the tendency to fall asleep can change from moment to moment depending on a diverse set of factors including external stimulation, activity level, motivation and so on. Therefore, the standard conditions of the MSLT are designed to minimize transient alerting and promote the measurement of an underlying physiological tendency to fall asleep. Extensive testing of groups of normal controls and patients with sleep apnea and narcolepsy have established that the MSLT is sensitive in detecting and quantifying sleepiness. In brief, an average sleep latency of 4 minutes is in the pathological range while a sleep latency value of 10 minutes is the normal range.

Permanent impairments due to sleep and arousal disorders are related to (1) the central nervous system, especially to diminished attention and cognitive function; (2) the cardiovascular system, especially to pulmonary and systemic hypertension, arrhythmias, cardiomegaly and congestive heart failure, and polycythemia associated with chronic nocturnal hypoxia of the sleep apnea syndromes; and (3) mental and behavioral disorders that may be associated with or result from chronic sleep deprivation. Impairment ratings related to the above three systems are described in Chapters 2, 4 and 12.

In this section, the examples will illustrate the rating of sleep disorders related primarily to the central nervous system. The examining physician, however, should evaluate each organ system and combine the respective impairment ratings using the Combined Values Chart, to derive the impairment of the whole person.

Disorders of Initiating and Maintaining Sleep (DIMS, Insomnias)

The insomnias, or disorders of initiating and maintaining sleep, are a heterogeneous group of conditions. The patient's report of difficulty falling asleep, trouble staying asleep, or both, and the history of disturbed sleep, diminished sleep, and non-restorative sleep, are complaints of insomnia, not diagnoses. Due to the large overlap in amount of sleep that is obtained by normal individuals and by persons with insomnia, the physician cannot refer to a table showing normal duration of sleep time, in order to determine if a patient has insomnia.

The insomnias are common disorders. Estimated prevalence in the general population is high, and studies have shown that approximately 20% of patients seen by a wide variety of medical

specialists complain of insomnia. The origins of the complaints come from organic or psychogenic disorders, or from a combination of both. The strength and interaction of triggering factors, the features that maintain the condition, and the possibility of constitutional predisposition are complex matters.

Diagnosis and rational treatment are facilitated by systematically assessing the patient's sleep-wake pattern and determining the response of the patient's sleep schedule to psychological and social challenges, the effect of changes in sleep-wake habits, and the response to trials of sedative and psychoactive medications. To track these various effects, a daily sleep log is invaluable. In order to assure that maximum medical treatment has preceded the assessment of permanent impairment, a substantial period of time is required to allow for the evaluation of clinical response to treatment(s). In addition, periodic reassessment of the insomnia is necessary, because the severity of the condition may vary.

Example: A 60-year-old married, childless woman stated that for the past 20 years she had difficulty falling asleep and staying asleep. Chronic use of hypnotics, tranquilizers, and alcohol was of little help. She reported that her average time to fall asleep (sleep latency) was 90 minutes, and that her average nightly sleep time of four hours was fragmented by one or two long periods of wakefulness. Daytime consequences of the sleeplessness included reduced concentration, functioning at a reduced speed, inefficiency, and tiredness.

Self-deprecation and interpersonal difficulties had been long-standing problems for this patient. The product of a "crazy family," she was "hated" by her mother, and she witnessed intense feuding between her two older siblings, who didn't speak to each other for 10 years during their teens and early twenties. The patient's two years of psychoanalysis were of no help. Further psychotherapy helped her switch from barbiturates to a non-barbiturate sedative, and she learned that a major motive for her habituation to hypnotics was to reduce the intensity of the severe self-punitive ruminations and agitation that preoccupied her during nocturnal awakenings. Attempts at drug withdrawal were only partially successful.

In the sleep laboratory, PSG recordings on two nights were obtained and showed a very low sleep efficiency (sleep time/recording time X 100) of 40%

and 55%. The awake time resulted from a combination of moderately long sleep latencies and one or two long nocturnal awakenings. These laboratory findings were consistent with the reported complaint.

The treatment consisted of improving sleep with regular, rational sleep hours, reducing alcohol consumption, and curtailing use of hypnotics. The patient showed some improvement during many months of follow-up. Total sleep time was increased by an hour, and daytime complaints diminished. However, sleep remained fragmented, nocturnal awakenings were filled with distressing ideas, daytime functioning was still compromised, sense of well-being was impaired, daytime stress still exacerbated the insomnia, and anticipation of sleepless nights preoccupied her during the day.

Diagnosis: (1) Disorders of initiating and maintaining sleep with symptoms, and personality disorder; (2) depressive disorder; and (3) obsessive-compulsive personality.

Impairment: 15% impairment due to daytime cognitive decrements, to be combined with an appropriate rating for the personality disorder to arrive at an impairment rating of the whole person.

Disorders of Excessive Somnolence (DOES) (Sleep Apnea and Narcolepsy)

The chief symptoms of the DOES group are: (1) excessive sleepiness during the waking period; (2) reduced attention, concentration and psychomotor performance; (3) tendency to nap; (4) increase in total sleep time per 24 hours; and (5) impaired arousal or awakening.

Sleep Apnea DOES Syndrome

Sleep apnea is defined as a disorder associated with at least 30 apneic episodes during 7 hours of nocturnal sleep. Apnea, or an apneic episode, is the cessation of airflow lasting at least 10 seconds, and the apnea index is the number of apneic episodes occurring per hour of sleep. The major syndromes caused by breathing abnormalities during sleep are obstructive sleep apnea, central sleep apnea, and Cheyne-Stokes respiration.

In central apnea there is cessation of both airflow and respiratory movements. This may be present in normal individuals at the time of sleep onset or during rapid eye movement (REM) sleep. In obstructive apnea there is cessation of airflow due to upper airway obstruction, despite persistent

respiratory movements. Mixed apnea can be manifested by a central apnea early in an episode, followed by an obstructive apnea later in the same episode. In Cheyne-Stokes respiration there are regular cycles of crescendo-decrescendo tidal volume breathing separated by central apnea or hypopnea (reduction in tidal volume).

These syndromes may prevent progression through the normal stages of sleep, producing frequent arousals and leading to insomnia or to daytime hypersomnolence. Hypoxia during obstructive sleep apnea is generally more severe than hypoxia from central sleep apnea or Cheyne-Stokes respiration. Chronic nocturnal hypoxemia may contribute to the daytime pulmonary and systemic hypertension and the mental confusion often found in such patients.

In the obstructive sleep apnea syndrome, the patient's bed partner when questioned usually will describe episodes of intermittent loud, sonorous snoring that are followed by silence lasting from 30 to 100 seconds or longer, during which the bed partner may notice struggling motions of the thorax and abdomen. The silent period is terminated by a loud snore, and airflow resumes with a few additional snores. The periods are repeated throughout the night as often as 500 times. Mild thrashing of the limbs is common, as are talking and walking during sleep. These features, combined with the noisy, loud snoring, frequently lead the bed partner to take refuge in another room.

Disturbance of normal nighttime sleep is caused by frequent arousals at the termination of apneic periods, and it is rare for patients with obstructive sleep apnea to achieve deep, sustained sleep. In mild cases, daytime somnolence may be limited to certain times, such as the postprandial period or when viewing television. In severe cases, the irresistible urge to sleep may lead to virtual incapacitation and endanger the life of the patient and perhaps the lives of others. For example, inappropriate onset of sleep while driving may be associated with automobile crashes. In critical stages of this disorder, it may be difficult to differentiate severe somnolence from the semi-comatose state.

Morning headaches are common with this type of apnea, and they may gradually disappear over several hours. Headaches in association with nausea and confusion may prompt physicians to suspect an intracranial lesion. Personality changes such as agitated depression, and hostility often occur. Problems at work arise because of intellectual deterioration and difficulty in mental concentration because of the chronic sleep disturbance and deprivation. Reduced libido and impotence are frequently present. Obstructive sleep apnea occurs with a much greater frequency in men, particularly in middle aged men, than in women.

The patient who suffers from obstructive sleep apnea is often obese and may have a short neck and large jowls. A narrowed posterior pharyngeal aperture, a hypertrophied or long uvula, and prominent tonsils may be present. Nasal obstruction, manifested by narrowing or collapse of the nares with forced inspiration through the nose, is often present.

Polysomnography

The definitive diagnosis of sleep apnea rests upon the analysis of nocturnal sleep stages using electroencephalography (EEG), electro-oculography (EOG), and digastric (chin) electromyography (EMG); breathing pattern and pleural pressure swings; and oxygen saturation. Electrocardiographic and leg electromyographic monitoring are complementary procedures. The standard monitoring procedure is called polysomnography.

Most of the noninvasive devices used to detect thoracoabdominal movement, such as pneumobelts, mercury in silastic strain gauges, or electrical impedance pneumograms, are not fully reliable during sleep, because they provide only qualitative information. To enhance reliability, these devices often are used in conjunction with nasal and oral

Figure 1. Polysomnographic Tracing of Mixed Apnea

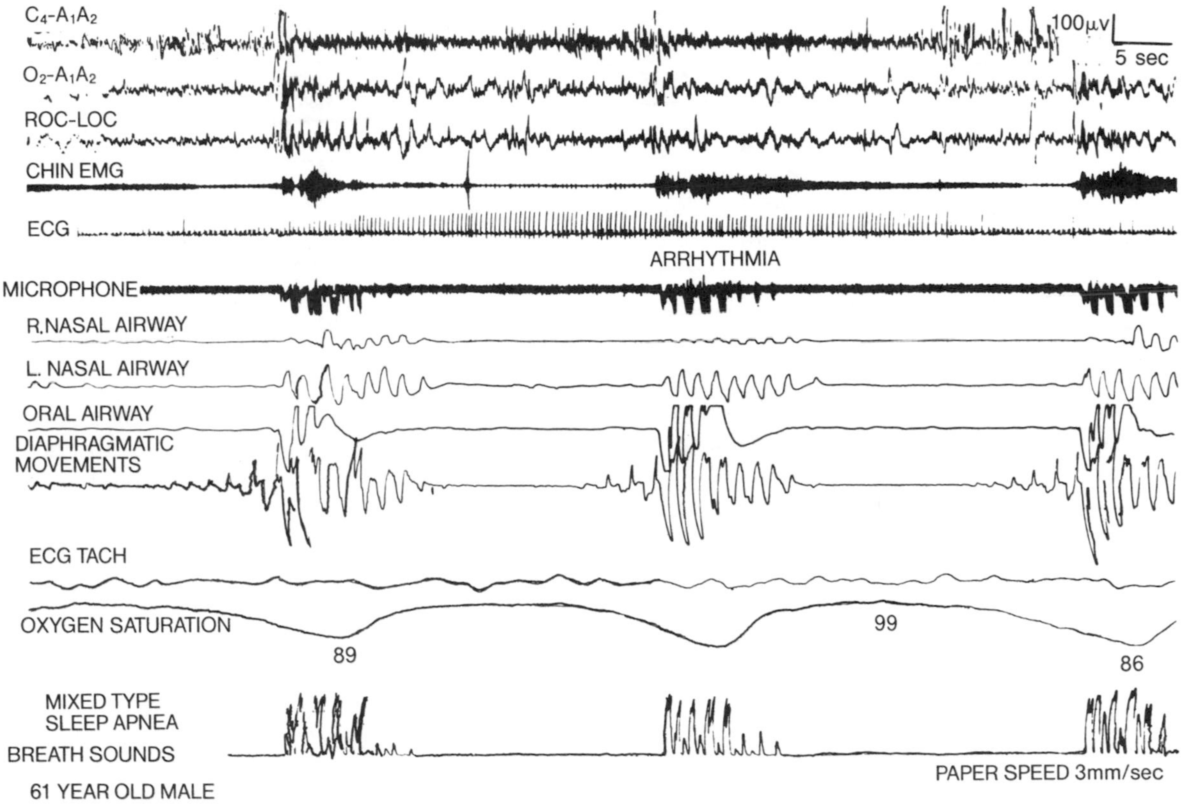

Legend
C_4-A_1A_2 and O_2-A_1A_2: Electroencephalogram (EEG) leads
ROC and LOC: Right and left outer canthus (electroculogram-EOG) leads
CHIN EMG: Chin electromyogram
ECG: Electrocardiogram
R & L NASAL & ORAL AIR WAY: Right & Left nasal & oral thermistors
ECG TACH: Electrocardiographic tachometer

thermistors, which detect airflow by measuring changes in temperature between room and expired air. These devices are slightly obtrusive and also are only qualitative indicators that may overestimate or underestimate airflow. However, if continuous monitoring of oxygen saturation with ear oximetry is also used, diagnosis of the frequency, duration and type of apnea generally can be made with such systems.

An example of a polysomnographic recording of a series of combined central and obstructive apneas, called mixed apnea, is illustrated in Figure 1. Wide pen excursions on the right and left nasal airway and oral airway, concurrent with diaphragmatic movements, indicate air exchange with respiratory effort for approximately 12 seconds. At the same time the microphone detects loud snoring. Following this period a central apnea ensues, characterized by no diaphragmatic movements and no airflow, for 15 seconds. Respiratory efforts then begin in the absence of airflow for 7 seconds. This phase is the obstructive apnea component of mixed apnea. Oxygen saturation falls into the 80% range shortly after the apnea. The entire sequence repeats itself in the next segment of the recording.

Monitoring for apneas also can be accomplished with the respiratory inductive plethysmograph. This device records changes of rib cage and abdominal cross-sectional areas, which can be calibrated semiquantitatively to tidal volume by summing the rib cage and abdominal excursions. Therefore it is useful in discriminating hypopneic episodes.

Historically, recordings of physiologic parameters during sleep included intrapleural pressure measured with an intraesophageal balloon catheter (P_{ESOPH}). This differentiated obstructive from central apneas, because wide variations in intrapleural pressure occurred in the former but were absent in the latter. But the discomfort associated with swallowing an esophageal balloon catheter limited its application, and at present it is infrequently employed.

A noninvasive technique that substitutes for intraesophageal pressure is based upon surface inductive plethysmography (P_{SIP}). The transducer of this device consists of a loop of insulated wire fixed to the skin of the suprasternal fossa with collodion or tape. Qualitative changes of intrapleural pressure are reflected by the degree of excursion of the suprasternal fossa during inspiration and expiration.

Figures 2a, 2b and 2c are examples of pressure tracings obtained in patients with obstructive sleep apnea, mixed obstructive and central apnea, and Cheyne-Stokes respiration, respectively. Figure 2a illustrates a recording of obstructive apnea that is terminated by a hyperpneic period and followed by another obstructive apnea. In the apneic phase the excursions of the rib cage (RC) and abdomen (ABD) are equal and opposite, causing absence of fluctuations in their summation tracing ($SUM(V_T)$). Respiratory effort is indicated by swings of intrapleural pressure during the obstructive apneic period as reflected by the fluctuations of P_{ESOPH} and P_{SIP}. The termination of the apnea is marked by the cluster of deep breaths in the mid-portion of the recording.

If the calibration of respiratory inductive plethysmography and tidal volume is not tight, and if the sum of the RC and ABD tracings indicates reduced tidal volumes interspersed with brief periods of hyperpnea, then P_{ESOPH} or P_{SIP} may be helpful in evaluating respiratory effort and the presence of partial or complete obstruction. An example is seen in Figure 2b.

At the beginning of the mixed apnea in Figure 2b (middle one-third of the tracing), no fluctuations are present on the P_{ESOPH} and P_{SIP} or on the respiratory inductive plethysmographic tracings, $SUM(V_T)$, RC and ABD. The high frequency oscillations on P_{ESOPH} are cardiac in origin. In the last third of the tracing, obstructive apnea is indicated by the fluctuation of P_{ESOPH} and P_{SIP} in the absence of changes in $SUM(V_T)$.

In contrast to Figure 2a, the absence of change in the $SUM(V_T)$ tracing is a result of the absence of changes in, rather than opposing movements of, the RC and ABD tracings. Figure 2b illustrates the importance of monitoring intrapleural pressure to differentiate central from obstructive apnea, especially when paradoxical thoracoabdominal fluctuations are minimal, which occurs in about 15% of patients with an obstructive apnea.

Figure 2c shows Cheyne-Stokes respiration, which consists of regularly recurring cycles with a gradual increase in tidal volume, then a gradual decrease in tidal volume, and finally a period of apnea or of hypopnea. The periodic nature of the crescendo-decrescendo respiratory fluctuations and of the central apnea or hypopnea, in conjunction with absent or diminished intrapleural pressure swings, clearly characterizes this pattern.

Figure 2 Pressure Tracings of Three Syndromes of Breathing Abnormalities During Sleep

a. Obstructive Sleep Apnea

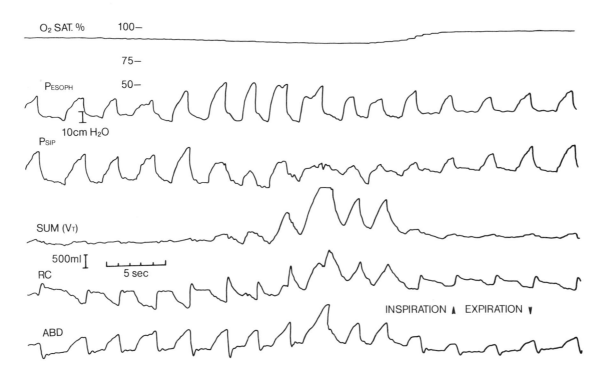

b. Mixed Apnea

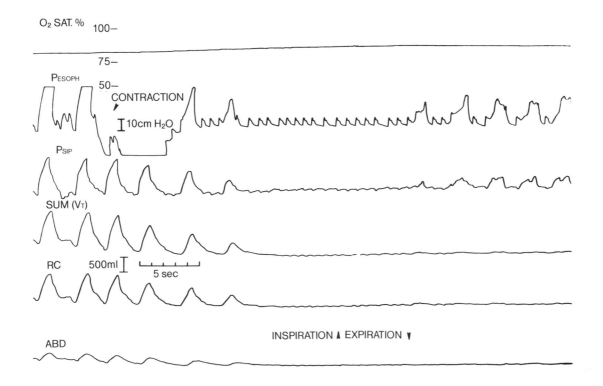

c. Cheyne-Stokes Respiration

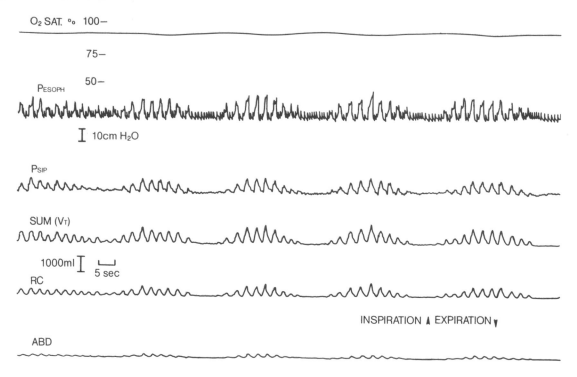

Legend

O₂SAT   :Oxygen saturation
PESOPH   :Intrapleural pressure as measured by intraesophageal balloon*
PSIP   :Intrapleural pressure as measured by surface inductive plethysmography
SUM(VT) :Summation of respiratory inductive plethysmography tracings (RC + ABD)
RC   :Rib cage excursion
ABD   :Abdominal excursion

*Because of the discomfort associated with the use of intraesophageal balloons, PESOPH is shown here
 for illustrative purposes, and is not recommended to be used in all evaluations of breathing abnormalities
 during sleep.

Oxygen saturation is measured noninvasively and continuously with ear oximetry. Values less than 50% may be observed during prolonged obstructive or mixed apneas as a result of the prolonged holding of breath, the shrinking lung volume, and the increasing ventilation/perfusion disparity. With central apnea or partial obstruction, oxygen saturation rarely falls below 80%, because with uptake of fresh air, lung volume does not change dramatically. There is no consensus about criteria for defining significant hypoxemia or oxygen desaturation; various cut-off values, such as 4% or 10% decreases from baseline saturation levels, have been used by different investigators to indicate significance.

At least 240 minutes of total sleep time is desirable for the diagnosis of a sleep disorder during a recording session that is carried out at the usual time of sleep. A single daytime nap study is usually unsatisfactory, because REM sleep, the stage during which the most severe breathing abnormalities are seen, is less likely to occur. In addition, the short recording session is not adequate to document the extent of the disorder. Two nights of recording may be necessary, because the strange environment and the monitoring devices of the first night's studies may disturb the patient's sleep patterns.

Normal adult males below the age of 50 years have an average of seven episodes (range 1-25) of central apnea per night, and females have an average of 2.1 episodes (range 0-5); these rarely last longer than 30 seconds. There is evidence that asymptomatic men and women who are older than 50 years, have increasing numbers of central and obstructive apneic episodes.

Example: A 63-year-old male editor had a history of 15 years of excessive daytime sleepiness. This resulted in reduced work performance, falling asleep at social functions, and, more recently, inability to drive a car safely. For many years the patient consumed an average of 8 ounces of alcohol every evening. His wife often slept in a separate room because of his loud snoring.

Physical examination disclosed that the patient was obese and had a deviated nasal septum. Blood pressure was 130/85 mm Hg; there was a normal sinus rhythm by ECG, and there was no evidence of cardiomegaly. In the sleep laboratory during a 7-hour period, the patient had 384 mixed or obstructive apneic episodes that were from 10 to 50 seconds in length, and he had only mild oxygen desaturation.

Tracheostomy was discussed with the patient, but he declined, believing that his imminent retirement would reduce the impact of the sleepiness and that other restrictions of his activities were tolerable. The patient was encouraged to reduce his weight and to avoid drinking alcoholic beverages.

Diagnosis: Sleep apnea DOES syndrome and alcoholism.

Impairment: 20% impairment due to excessive daytime sleepiness.

Comment: The patient will require close follow-up to assess deterioration in cardiovascular function and to assess progress in losing weight and in avoiding alcohol.

Narcolepsy

The symptoms of narcolepsy include: (1) recurrent attacks of excessive daytime sleepiness and sleep episodes; (2) sudden muscle weakness, or cataplexy; (3) sleep paralysis; and (4) hypnogogic hallucinations. Although narcolepsy generally does not progress in severity, it is a chronic, life-long illness without complete remission.

The major and usually most incapacitating feature of narcolepsy is the episodic sleepiness during

daytime, which varies in severity among patients and may fluctuate over a period of time in the same patient. Many of the clinical features of the sleep apnea DOES syndrome are applicable to this condition. The treatments presently available to aid alertness are limited, and some residual sleepiness often remains following treatment. In contrast, the treatments for cataplexy, sleep paralysis, and hypnogogic hallucinations are more satisfactory.

Although the clinical picture of narcolepsy may be classic and unequivocal, a substantial proportion of patients will need to have a PSG to confirm the clinical impression. The occurrence of rapid eye movement (REM) sleep within 15 minutes of falling asleep, which is called a sleep-onset REM period, during an afternoon nap or a nocturnal recording is strongly suggestive of narcolepsy. Retiring time and waking up time for the major sleep period must be stabilized for at least a week prior to recording. A MSLT is diagnostically useful. Ideally the patient should be drug free from 10 to 14 days before the test.

Example: A 42-year-old divorced mother of two children stated that she has had a "constant feeling of drowsiness all my life." She described a pattern of four 15 minute sleep periods each day, during which she has vivid dreams. She described, and others have observed, occurrence of cataplexy about 3 times per day, especially in response to laughter or other types of acute emotional arousal. In addition, she experienced sleep paralysis and hypnogogic hallucinations. The patient had a history of recurring episodes of endogenous depression, and although she was intelligent, educated and motivated, she had a checkered employment history due to daytime sleepiness, cataplexy and depression.

In the sleep laboratory, the patient had two sleep-onset REM periods during each of three nocturnal PSG recordings. During a MSLT she had two sleep-onset REM periods with an average sleep latency of 2.9 minutes, which is very short and clearly pathological.

To treat the sleepiness, the patient takes dextroamphetamine, methylphenidate and pemoline separately or in various combinations. At best, however, she still requires two or three obligatory naps per day, and the sleepiness continues to interfere with her ability to do paper work, to read and engage in other sedentary activities, and to hold a job. The cataplexy has been abolished by the use of imipramine, but the patient must constrict her emotional arousal to avoid small cataplectic episodes. Avoidance of arousing situations compromises her social life.

Diagnosis: Narcolepsy and recurrent endogenous depression.

Impairment: 15% impairment due to narcolepsy and 20% impairment due to depression, which combine to 32% impairment of the whole person.

Disorders of the Sleep-Wake Schedule

In disorders of the sleep-wake schedule there is a misalignment between sleep and wake behaviors and the individual's preference for and the social necessity of timing of these behaviors. The patient describes the problem as an inability to sleep when he or she desires, needs, or expects to. Similarly, wakefulness occurs at odd hours or is uncomfortable because of sleepiness.

The temporal positioning of sleep and wakefulness contributes to the pattern of rhythmic variations in other physiological functions, such as maintaining body temperature and neuroendocrine functions. The reverse is also true. If one elects to reposition sleep-wake behavior, as with a "shift-work" or a time zone change leading to "jet lag," other physiological processes initially remain in their former temporal positions. Reestablishment of in-phase relationships may take days to several weeks. Therefore, in assessing the degree of impairment, the physician must take into account the transition period following a sleep-wake schedule change.

Example: A 34-year-old female psychotherapist has had for most of her life difficulty falling asleep at night and difficulty waking in the morning. Recently, her sleep-onset time varied from 3:00 AM to 5:30 AM, and she did not awaken until 1:00 PM. Hypnotics did not help her fall asleep at an earlier hour.

While she was being evaluated, the patient was able to maintain a regular sleep-wake schedule for two weeks that consisted of lights out at 6:00 AM and lights on and out of bed at 3:30 PM. Chronotherapy was then carried out at home. For 6 days, the patient went to bed three hours later each day. At the end of the treatment, the patient chose to set her sleep time as lights out at 2:00 AM and lights on at 10:00 AM.

The patient has maintained the 2:00 AM to 10:00

AM schedule for a 17-week period. However, she continued to exhibit a tendency to develop the delayed sleep phase disorder, and therefore she had to pay rigorous attention to sleep scheduling in order to maintain the desired sleep phase position within the 24-hour day. She also had to avoid events that would result in her getting to bed later than the 2:00 AM bedtime.

Diagnosis: Delayed sleep phase syndrome.

Impairment: 5% impairment of the whole person.

Comment: Although patients such as this one can avoid daytime sleepiness by rigorously adhering to a sleep schedule, there remains a strong life-long tendency to revert to the delayed sleep phase syndrome. Therefore the impairment is permanent.

Dysfunctions Associated with Sleep, Sleep Stages or Partial Arousals (Parasomnias)

This is a heterogeneous group of disorders in which some motor behavior or mental experience, such as nightmares and sleep terrors, occurs during sleep. The experience itself may be pathological, such as a sleep-related seizure, or it may be disassociated from the conscious, alert state that is its usual context, as with sleepwalking.

A number of these conditions, such as sleep-related enuresis, have a developmental course in which they decrease in frequency or stop completely with increasing age. Therefore, these conditions must be monitored into adulthood and periodically reevaluated to determine their permanence, before impairment can be rated.

An all night PSG is used to document the occurrence of the parasomnias. For example, if sleep-related epileptic seizures were suspected, simultaneous EEG and video monitoring might help establish the connection, if any, between epileptiform activity and behavioral signs.

Example: A 32-year-old female laboratory technician complains of "nightmares a few times each week" that began when she was age 19 years old. Typically the episodes occur within the first hour of sleep; she sits up and screams, feels her heart racing, and feels she cannot breathe. The screaming continues for a minute and the patient recalls no dream content. She is reluctant to sleep in other persons' houses, lest an episode occur and embarrass her. During adolescence, depersonalization and derealization experiences occurred frequently. At present, she is overly impulsive and has severe marital problems.

Physical and neurological examinations were within normal limits. No event occurred on the night of a PSG recording, which was unremarkable. Diazepam 5 mg at the hour of sleep was initially dramatically effective, virtually eliminating the night terror episodes. Six months later, several episodes occurred, which required an increase in dose to 7.5 mg. Night terror episodes continued at the rate of one or two every 6 months.

Diagnosis: (1) Night terror; (2) personality disorder type undetermined (Atypical, DSM III).

Impairment: 5% impairment of the whole person.

Comment: The impairment rating is not based upon daytime hypersomnolence but upon the patient's mental and behavioral disorders that are associated with sleep. Impairment is rated according to the criteria of Chapter 12.

References

1. Weitzman ED: Disorders of sleep and the sleep-wake cycle, in Isselbacher KJ, Adams RD, Braunwald E, et al (eds): *Update I: Harrison's Principles of Internal Medicine* (ed 9). New York, McGraw Hill, 1981, pp 245-263.

2. Association of Sleep Disorders Centers Sleep Disorders Classification Committee: *Diagnostic Classification of Sleep and Arousal Disorders*, ed 1, in *Sleep* 1979;2:1-137.

3. Guilleminault C, Dement WC (eds): *Sleep Apnea Syndrome*, New York, Alan R. Liss, 1978.

4. Guilleminault C, Dement WC, Passouant P (eds): *Narcolepsy*, New York, Spectrum Publications, 1975.

5. Tobin MJ, Cohen MA, Sackner MA: Breathing abnormalities during sleep. *Arch Intern Med* 1983;143:1221-1228.

6. Mitler MM: The multiple sleep latency test as an evaluation for excessive somnolence, in Guilleminault C (ed): *Sleep and Waking Disorders: Indications and Techniques*. Reading MA, Addison-Wesley Publishing Inc, 1982, pp 145-153.

COMBINED VALUES CHART

The values are derived from the formula: A + B (1 − A) = combined value of A and B, where A and B are the decimal equivalents of the impairment ratings. In the chart all values are expressed as percents. To combine any two impairment values, locate the larger of the values on the side of the chart and read along that row until you come to the column indicated by the smaller value at the bottom of the chart. At the intersection of the row and the column is the combined value.

For example, to combine 35% and 20% read down the side of the chart until you come to the larger value, 35%. Then read across the 35% row until you come to the column indicated by 20% at the bottom of the chart. At the intersection of the row and column is the number 48. Therefore, 35% combined with 20% is 48%. Due to the construction of this chart, the larger impairment value must be identified at the side of the chart.

If three or more impairment values are to be combined, select any two and find their combined value as above. Then use that value and the third value to locate the combined value of all. This process can be repeated indefinitely, the final value in each instance being the combination of all the previous values. In each step of this process the larger impairment value must be identified at the side of the chart.

1	2
2	3	4
3	4	5	6
4	5	6	7	8
5	6	7	8	9	10
6	7	8	9	10	11	12
7	8	9	10	11	12	13	14
8	9	10	11	12	13	14	14	15
9	10	11	12	13	14	14	15	16	17
10	11	12	13	14	15	15	16	17	18	19
11	12	13	14	15	15	16	17	18	19	20	21
12	13	14	15	16	16	17	18	19	20	21	22	23
13	14	15	16	16	17	18	19	20	21	22	23	23	24
14	15	16	17	17	18	19	20	21	22	23	23	24	25	26
15	16	17	18	18	19	20	21	22	23	24	24	25	26	27	28
16	17	18	19	19	20	21	22	23	24	24	25	26	27	28	29	29
17	18	19	19	20	21	22	23	24	24	25	26	27	28	29	29	30	31
18	19	20	20	21	22	23	24	25	25	26	27	28	29	29	30	31	32	33
19	20	21	21	22	23	24	25	25	26	27	28	29	30	30	31	32	33	34	34
20	21	22	22	23	24	25	26	26	27	28	29	30	30	31	32	33	34	34	35	36
21	22	23	23	24	25	26	27	27	28	29	30	30	31	32	33	34	34	35	36	37	38
22	23	24	24	25	26	27	27	28	29	30	31	31	32	33	34	34	35	36	37	38	38	39
23	24	25	25	26	27	28	28	29	30	31	31	32	33	34	35	35	36	37	38	38	39	40	41
24	25	26	26	27	28	29	29	30	31	32	32	33	34	35	35	36	37	38	38	39	40	41	41	42
25	26	27	27	28	29	30	30	31	32	33	33	34	35	36	36	37	38	39	39	40	41	42	42	43	44
26	27	27	28	29	30	30	31	32	33	33	34	35	36	36	37	38	39	39	40	41	42	42	43	44	45	45
27	28	28	29	30	31	31	32	33	34	34	35	36	36	37	38	39	39	40	41	42	42	43	44	45	45	46	47
28	29	29	30	31	32	32	33	34	34	35	36	37	37	38	39	40	40	41	42	42	43	44	45	45	46	47	47	48
29	30	30	31	32	33	33	34	35	35	36	37	38	38	39	40	40	41	42	42	43	44	45	45	46	47	47	48	49	50
30	31	31	32	33	34	34	35	36	36	37	38	38	39	40	41	41	42	43	43	44	45	45	46	47	48	48	49	50	50	51
31	32	32	33	34	34	35	36	37	37	38	39	39	40	41	41	42	43	43	44	45	45	46	47	48	48	49	50	50	51	52	52
32	33	33	34	35	35	36	37	37	38	39	39	40	41	42	42	43	44	44	45	46	46	47	48	48	49	50	50	51	52	52	53	54
33	34	34	35	36	36	37	38	38	39	40	40	41	42	42	43	44	44	45	46	46	47	48	48	49	50	50	51	52	52	53	54	54	55
34	35	35	36	37	37	38	39	39	40	41	41	42	43	43	44	45	45	46	47	47	48	49	49	50	51	51	52	52	53	54	54	55	56	56
35	36	36	37	38	38	39	40	40	41	42	42	43	43	44	45	45	46	47	47	48	49	49	50	51	51	52	53	53	54	55	55	56	56	57	58
36	37	37	38	39	39	40	40	41	42	42	43	44	44	45	46	46	47	48	48	49	49	50	51	51	52	53	53	54	55	55	56	56	57	58	58	59
37	38	38	39	40	40	41	41	42	43	43	44	45	45	46	46	47	48	48	49	50	50	51	51	52	53	53	54	55	55	56	57	57	58	58	59	60	60
38	39	39	40	40	41	42	42	43	44	44	45	45	46	47	47	48	49	49	50	50	51	52	52	53	54	54	55	55	56	57	57	58	58	59	60	60	61	62
39	40	40	41	41	42	43	43	44	44	45	46	46	47	48	48	49	49	50	51	51	52	52	53	54	54	55	55	56	57	57	58	59	59	60	60	61	62	62	63
40	41	41	42	42	43	44	44	45	45	46	47	47	48	48	49	50	50	51	51	52	53	53	54	54	55	56	56	57	57	58	59	59	60	60	61	62	62	63	63	64
41	42	42	43	43	44	45	45	46	46	47	47	48	49	49	50	50	51	52	52	53	53	54	55	55	56	56	57	58	58	59	59	60	60	61	62	62	63	63	64	65	65
42	43	43	44	44	45	45	46	47	47	48	48	49	50	50	51	51	52	52	53	54	54	55	55	56	57	57	58	58	59	59	60	61	61	62	62	63	63	64	65	65	66	66
43	44	44	45	45	46	46	47	48	48	49	49	50	50	51	52	52	53	53	54	54	55	56	56	57	57	58	58	59	60	60	61	61	62	62	63	64	64	65	65	66	66	67	68
44	45	45	46	46	47	47	48	48	49	50	50	51	51	52	52	53	54	54	55	55	56	56	57	57	58	59	59	60	60	61	61	62	62	63	64	64	65	65	66	66	67	68	68	69
45	46	46	47	47	48	48	49	49	50	51	51	52	52	53	53	54	54	55	55	56	57	57	58	58	59	59	60	60	61	62	62	63	63	64	64	65	65	66	66	67	68	68	69	69	70
46	47	47	48	48	49	49	50	50	51	51	52	52	53	54	54	55	55	56	56	57	57	58	58	59	60	60	61	61	62	62	63	63	64	64	65	65	66	67	67	68	68	69	69	70	70	71
47	48	48	49	49	50	50	51	51	52	52	53	53	54	54	55	55	56	57	57	58	58	59	59	60	60	61	61	62	62	63	63	64	64	65	66	66	67	67	68	68	69	69	70	70	71	71	72
48	49	49	50	50	51	51	52	52	53	53	54	54	55	55	56	56	57	57	58	58	59	59	60	60	61	62	62	63	63	64	64	65	65	66	66	67	67	68	68	69	69	70	70	71	71	72	72	73
49	50	50	51	51	52	52	53	53	54	54	55	55	56	56	57	57	58	58	59	59	60	60	61	61	62	62	63	63	64	64	65	65	66	66	67	67	68	68	69	69	70	70	71	71	72	72	73	73	74
50	51	51	52	52	53	53	54	54	55	55	56	56	57	57	58	58	59	59	60	60	61	61	62	62	63	63	64	64	65	65	66	66	67	67	68	68	69	69	70	70	71	71	72	72	73	73	74	74	75	75
	1	2	3	4	**5**	6	7	8	9	**10**	11	12	13	14	**15**	16	17	18	19	**20**	21	22	23	24	**25**	26	27	28	29	**30**	31	32	33	34	**35**	36	37	38	39	**40**	41	42	43	44	**45**	46	47	48	49	**50**

Percentage conversion table.

50	49	48	47	46	45	44	43	42	41	40	39	38	37	36	35	34	33	32	31	30	29	28	27	26	25	24	23	22	21	20	19	18	17	16	15	14	13	12	11	10	9	8	7	6	5	4	3	2	1	
76	76	76	77	77	78	78	79	79	80	80	81	81	82	82	83	83	84	84	85	85	86	86	87	87	88	88	89	89	90	90	91	91	92	92	93	93	94	94	95	95	96	96	97	97	98	98	99	99	100	**50**
75	76	76	76	77	77	78	78	79	79	80	80	81	81	82	82	83	83	84	84	85	85	86	86	87	87	88	88	89	89	90	90	91	91	92	92	93	93	94	94	95	95	96	96	97	97	98	98	99	99	49
75	75	75	76	76	77	77	78	78	79	79	80	80	81	81	82	82	83	83	84	84	85	85	86	86	87	87	88	88	89	89	90	90	91	91	92	92	93	93	94	94	95	95	96	96	97	97	98	99	99	48
74	74	75	75	76	76	77	77	78	78	79	79	80	80	81	81	82	82	83	83	84	84	85	85	86	86	87	87	88	88	89	89	90	90	91	92	92	93	93	94	94	95	95	96	96	97	97	98	98	99	47
74	74	74	75	75	76	76	77	77	78	78	79	79	80	81	81	82	82	83	83	84	84	85	85	86	86	87	87	88	88	89	89	90	90	91	91	92	92	93	94	94	95	95	96	96	97	97	98	98	99	46
73	73	74	74	75	75	76	76	77	77	78	79	79	80	80	81	81	82	82	83	83	84	84	85	85	86	86	87	87	88	88	89	89	90	90	91	91	92	93	93	94	94	95	95	96	96	97	97	98	99	**45**
73	73	73	74	74	75	75	76	76	77	78	78	79	79	80	80	81	82	82	83	83	84	84	85	85	86	86	87	87	88	88	89	89	90	90	91	91	92	92	93	93	94	94	95	96	96	97	97	98	99	44
72	72	73	73	74	74	75	75	76	77	77	78	78	79	79	80	81	81	82	82	83	83	84	84	85	85	86	86	87	87	88	88	89	90	90	91	91	92	92	93	93	94	95	95	96	96	97	97	98	98	43
72	72	72	73	73	74	74	75	76	76	77	77	78	78	79	80	80	81	81	82	82	83	83	84	84	85	86	86	87	87	88	88	89	89	90	90	91	91	92	93	93	94	94	95	95	96	97	97	98	98	42
71	72	72	72	73	73	74	75	75	76	76	77	77	78	79	79	80	80	81	81	82	82	83	84	84	85	85	86	86	87	87	88	88	89	90	90	91	91	92	92	93	93	94	95	95	96	96	97	99	99	41
71	71	71	72	72	73	74	74	75	75	76	77	77	78	78	79	79	80	80	81	82	82	83	83	84	84	85	85	86	86	87	88	88	89	89	90	90	91	91	92	93	93	94	94	95	95	96	97	98	98	**40**
70	70	71	71	72	72	73	73	74	74	75	76	76	77	77	78	79	79	80	80	81	81	82	82	83	84	84	85	85	86	86	87	87	88	89	89	90	90	91	91	92	92	93	93	94	95	95	96	99	99	39
70	70	70	71	71	72	72	73	73	74	75	75	76	76	77	77	78	78	79	80	80	81	81	82	82	83	83	84	85	85	86	86	87	87	88	88	89	89	90	91	91	92	93	93	94	95	95	96	99	99	38
69	69	70	70	71	71	72	72	73	74	74	75	75	76	77	77	78	78	79	79	80	80	81	81	82	82	83	84	84	85	85	86	86	87	87	88	88	89	90	91	91	92	92	93	94	94	95	97	98	99	37
69	69	69	70	70	71	71	72	73	73	74	74	75	75	76	77	77	78	78	79	79	80	80	81	82	82	83	83	84	84	85	86	86	87	87	88	88	89	89	90	91	91	92	92	93	94	94	95	99	99	36
68	68	69	69	70	71	71	72	72	73	73	74	75	75	76	77	77	78	78	79	79	80	81	81	82	82	83	83	84	84	85	86	86	87	88	88	89	89	90	90	91	92	92	93	94	94	95	96	99	99	**35**
68	68	68	69	70	70	71	71	72	72	73	73	74	75	75	76	76	77	78	78	79	79	80	81	81	82	82	83	83	84	85	85	86	86	87	88	88	89	89	90	90	91	92	93	93	94	95	96	99	99	34
67	67	68	69	69	70	70	71	71	72	73	73	74	74	75	75	76	77	77	78	79	79	80	80	81	82	82	83	84	84	85	85	86	86	87	87	88	89	89	90	91	91	92	93	93	94	95	96	97	99	33
67	67	68	68	69	69	70	70	71	72	72	73	73	74	75	75	76	76	77	78	78	79	79	80	81	81	82	82	83	84	84	85	85	86	86	87	88	88	89	90	90	91	92	92	93	94	95	95	98	99	32
66	67	67	68	68	69	69	70	71	71	72	72	73	74	74	75	76	76	77	77	78	78	79	80	80	81	82	82	83	84	84	85	86	86	87	87	88	89	89	90	91	91	92	93	94	94	95	96	99	99	31
66	66	66	67	68	68	69	69	70	71	71	72	73	73	74	75	76	76	77	77	78	78	79	80	80	81	82	83	83	84	84	85	86	86	87	87	88	89	90	90	91	92	92	93	94	95	95	96	99	99	**30**
65	65	66	66	67	68	68	69	69	70	71	71	72	73	73	74	75	75	76	77	77	78	78	79	80	80	81	82	82	83	84	84	85	86	86	87	87	88	89	90	91	91	92	93	93	94	95	96	99	99	29
65	65	66	66	67	67	68	68	69	70	70	71	72	72	73	74	74	75	76	76	77	77	78	79	80	80	81	82	82	83	84	84	85	86	86	87	88	88	89	90	90	91	92	93	94	94	95	96	99	99	28
64	65	65	66	66	67	68	68	69	69	70	71	72	72	73	74	75	75	76	77	77	78	79	79	80	80	81	82	82	83	84	85	85	86	87	87	88	89	89	90	91	92	92	93	94	95	96	96	97	99	27
64	64	65	65	66	67	67	68	68	69	70	70	71	72	73	73	74	74	75	76	77	77	78	79	79	80	81	81	82	83	84	84	85	86	87	87	88	89	89	90	91	92	93	93	94	95	96	96	98	99	26
63	64	64	65	66	66	67	67	68	69	70	70	71	72	72	73	74	75	75	76	76	77	78	78	79	80	81	81	82	83	84	84	85	86	86	87	88	89	89	90	91	92	93	93	94	95	96	96	99	99	**25**
63	64	64	65	66	66	67	67	68	69	70	70	71	72	72	73	74	75	75	76	76	77	78	79	79	80	81	81	82	83	84	85	85	86	87	88	88	89	89	90	91	92	93	94	95	95	96	97	98	99	24
62	63	63	64	65	65	66	67	68	68	69	70	71	71	72	73	74	75	75	76	77	78	78	79	80	81	81	82	83	83	84	85	85	86	87	88	88	89	90	91	91	92	93	94	95	95	96	97	98	99	23
62	63	63	64	65	65	66	66	67	68	69	70	70	71	72	73	74	74	75	76	76	77	78	79	80	80	81	82	83	83	84	85	86	86	87	88	88	89	90	90	91	92	93	94	95	95	96	97	98	99	22
61	62	63	63	64	64	65	66	67	68	68	69	70	71	72	72	73	74	75	75	76	76	77	78	79	80	81	81	82	83	83	84	85	86	87	87	88	89	89	90	91	92	93	93	94	95	96	97	98	99	21
61	61	62	62	63	64	65	66	66	67	68	69	70	70	71	72	73	74	74	75	76	77	78	78	79	80	81	82	82	83	84	85	86	86	87	88	88	89	90	91	91	92	93	94	95	96	97	98	98	99	**20**
60	60	61	61	62	63	64	64	65	66	67	68	68	69	70	71	72	73	73	74	75	76	76	77	78	79	80	81	81	82	83	84	85	85	86	88	88	89	89	90	91	92	93	94	95	96	97	98	98	99	19
60	61	61	62	63	64	64	65	66	66	67	68	69	70	70	71	72	73	74	74	75	75	76	77	78	79	80	81	82	82	83	84	85	86	86	87	88	89	90	91	91	92	93	94	95	96	97	98	98	99	18
59	60	60	61	62	63	63	64	65	66	67	67	68	68	69	70	71	72	73	73	74	75	76	77	78	79	80	80	81	82	83	83	84	85	86	87	88	89	90	90	91	92	93	94	95	96	97	98	98	99	17
59	60	60	61	61	62	63	64	64	65	66	67	68	68	69	70	71	71	72	73	74	75	75	76	77	78	79	80	81	82	83	83	84	85	86	87	88	88	89	90	91	92	93	94	95	96	97	98	98	99	16
58	59	59	60	61	62	63	63	64	65	66	67	68	69	69	70	71	72	73	74	75	75	76	77	78	78	79	80	81	82	83	84	84	85	86	86	87	88	89	90	91	92	93	94	95	96	97	97	98	99	**15**
58	58	59	60	60	61	62	63	64	65	66	66	67	68	69	70	71	72	72	73	74	75	76	77	77	78	79	80	81	82	83	84	85	85	86	87	88	89	90	90	91	92	93	93	94	95	96	97	99	99	14
57	58	59	59	60	61	62	63	63	64	65	66	67	68	69	70	70	71	72	73	74	75	76	76	77	78	79	80	81	82	83	84	85	86	86	87	88	88	89	90	91	91	93	93	95	95	97	97	98	99	13
57	58	58	59	59	60	61	62	63	64	64	65	66	67	68	69	70	71	72	73	73	74	74	75	76	77	78	79	79	80	82	82	83	84	85	86	86	87	89	89	90	91	92	93	94	95	96	97	98	99	12
56	57	57	58	59	60	61	62	63	63	64	65	66	67	67	68	69	70	71	72	73	74	74	75	76	77	78	78	79	80	81	82	83	84	85	86	86	87	88	89	90	91	92	93	94	95	96	96	98	99	11
56	57	57	58	59	60	60	61	62	63	64	65	66	66	67	68	69	69	70	71	72	73	74	75	76	77	78	78	79	80	81	82	83	84	85	86	87	87	88	89	90	92	92	94	94	96	96	98	98	99	**10**
55	55	56	57	58	59	60	61	62	63	64	65	65	66	67	68	69	70	71	72	73	74	75	75	76	77	78	78	79	80	81	82	83	84	85	86	87	88	89	90	91	92	93	93	94	95	96	96	98	99	9
55	55	56	56	57	58	59	60	60	61	62	63	63	64	65	66	67	68	69	70	71	72	72	73	74	75	76	77	78	79	80	81	82	83	83	84	85	86	88	88	89	90	91	93	93	95	96	97	98	99	8
54	54	55	55	56	57	58	59	60	61	61	62	63	64	65	66	67	67	68	69	70	71	72	73	74	75	76	77	78	79	80	80	81	82	83	85	85	86	87	88	90	90	92	93	94	95	96	97	98	99	7
54	54	55	56	57	58	59	59	60	61	61	62	63	64	65	66	67	68	69	70	71	72	72	73	74	75	76	77	77	78	79	80	81	82	83	84	85	86	87	88	90	90	92	93	94	95	96	97	98	99	6
53	53	54	54	55	56	57	58	59	60	61	62	62	63	64	65	66	67	68	69	70	71	72	73	74	75	76	76	77	78	79	80	81	82	83	84	85	86	88	89	90	91	92	93	94	95	96	98	99	99	**5**
53	53	54	55	56	57	58	59	60	61	62	63	63	64	65	66	67	68	68	69	70	71	72	73	74	75	76	77	78	79	80	81	82	83	84	85	86	87	88	89	90	91	92	93	94	96	96	98	98	99	4
52	52	53	54	55	56	57	58	58	59	60	61	62	63	64	65	66	67	68	69	70	71	72	73	74	76	77	78	78	79	80	81	82	83	84	85	86	87	88	89	90	91	92	93	94	95	96	97	98	99	3
52	53	53	54	55	56	57	58	59	60	61	62	63	64	65	66	67	68	69	70	71	72	73	74	75	76	77	78	79	80	81	82	83	84	85	86	87	88	89	90	91	92	93	94	95	96	97	98	99	2
51	52	52	53	54	55	56	57	58	59	60	61	62	63	64	65	66	67	68	69	70	71	72	73	74	75	76	77	78	79	80	81	82	83	84	85	86	87	88	89	90	91	92	93	94	95	96	97	98	99	1
51	52	53	54	55	56	57	58	59	60	61	62	63	64	65	66	67	68	69	70	71	72	73	74	75	76	77	78	79	80	81	82	83	84	85	86	87	88	89	90	91	92	93	94	95	96	97	98	99	
55					**60**					**65**					**70**					**75**					**80**					**85**					**90**					**95**										

241

COMBINED VALUES CHART (continued)

	51	52	53	54	55	56	57	58	59	60	61	62	63	64	65	66	67	68	69	70	71	72	73	74	75	76	77	78	79	80	81	82	83	84	85	86	87	88	89	90	91	92	93	94	95	96	97	98	99
51	76																																																
52	76	77																																															
53	77	77	78																																														
54	77	78	78	79																																													
55	78	78	79	79	80																																												
56	78	79	79	80	80	81																																											
57	79	79	80	80	81	81	82																																										
58	79	80	80	81	81	82	82	82																																									
59	80	80	81	81	82	82	82	83	83																																								
60	80	81	81	82	82	82	83	83	84	84																																							
61	81	81	82	82	82	83	83	84	84	84	85																																						
62	81	82	82	83	83	83	84	84	84	85	85	86																																					
63	82	82	83	83	83	84	84	84	85	85	86	86	86																																				
64	82	83	83	83	84	84	85	85	85	86	86	86	87	87																																			
65	83	83	84	84	84	85	85	85	86	86	86	87	87	87	88																																		
66	83	84	84	84	85	85	85	86	86	86	87	87	87	88	88	88																																	
67	84	84	84	85	85	85	86	86	86	87	87	87	88	88	88	89	89																																
68	84	85	85	85	86	86	86	87	87	87	88	88	88	88	89	89	89	90																															
69	85	85	85	86	86	86	87	87	87	88	88	88	89	89	89	89	90	90	90																														
70	85	86	86	86	87	87	87	87	88	88	88	89	89	89	90	90	90	90	91	91																													
71	86	86	86	87	87	87	88	88	88	88	89	89	89	90	90	90	90	91	91	91	92																												
72	86	87	87	87	87	88	88	88	89	89	89	89	90	90	90	90	91	91	91	92	92	92																											
73	87	87	87	88	88	88	88	89	89	89	89	90	90	90	91	91	91	91	92	92	92	92	93																										
74	87	88	88	88	88	89	89	89	89	90	90	90	90	91	91	91	91	92	92	92	92	93	93	93																									
75	88	88	88	89	89	89	89	90	90	90	90	91	91	91	91	92	92	92	92	93	93	93	93	94	94																								
76	88	88	89	89	89	89	90	90	90	90	91	91	91	91	92	92	92	92	93	93	93	93	94	94	94	94																							
77	89	89	89	89	90	90	90	90	91	91	91	91	91	92	92	92	92	93	93	93	93	94	94	94	94	94	95																						
78	89	89	90	90	90	90	91	91	91	91	91	92	92	92	92	93	93	93	93	93	94	94	94	94	95	95	95	95																				
79	90	90	90	90	91	91	91	91	91	92	92	92	92	92	93	93	93	93	93	94	94	94	94	95	95	95	95	95	96																			
80	90	90	91	91	91	91	91	92	92	92	92	92	93	93	93	93	93	94	94	94	94	94	95	95	95	95	95	96	96	96																	
81	91	91	91	91	91	92	92	92	92	92	93	93	93	93	93	94	94	94	94	94	94	95	95	95	95	95	96	96	96	96	96																
82	91	91	92	92	92	92	92	92	93	93	93	93	93	94	94	94	94	94	94	95	95	95	95	95	96	96	96	96	96	96	97	97															
83	92	92	92	92	92	93	93	93	93	93	93	94	94	94	94	94	94	95	95	95	95	95	95	96	96	96	96	96	96	97	97	97	97														
84	92	92	92	93	93	93	93	93	93	94	94	94	94	94	94	95	95	95	95	95	95	96	96	96	96	96	96	96	97	97	97	97	97	97													
85	93	93	93	93	93	93	94	94	94	94	94	94	94	95	95	95	95	95	95	96	96	96	96	96	96	96	97	97	97	97	97	97	97	98	98												
86	93	93	93	94	94	94	94	94	94	94	95	95	95	95	95	95	95	96	96	96	96	96	96	96	97	97	97	97	97	97	97	97	98	98	98	98											
87	94	94	94	94	94	94	94	95	95	95	95	95	95	95	95	96	96	96	96	96	96	96	96	97	97	97	97	97	97	97	98	98	98	98	98	98	98										
88	94	94	94	94	95	95	95	95	95	95	95	95	96	96	96	96	96	96	96	96	97	97	97	97	97	97	97	97	97	98	98	98	98	98	98	98	98	99									
89	95	95	95	95	95	95	95	95	95	96	96	96	96	96	96	96	96	96	97	97	97	97	97	97	97	97	97	98	98	98	98	98	98	98	98	98	99	99	99								
90	95	95	95	95	96	96	96	96	96	96	96	96	96	96	97	97	97	97	97	97	97	97	97	97	98	98	98	98	98	98	98	98	98	98	99	99	99	99	99	99							
91	96	96	96	96	96	96	96	96	96	96	96	97	97	97	97	97	97	97	97	97	97	97	98	98	98	98	98	98	98	98	98	98	98	99	99	99	99	99	99	99	99						
92	96	96	96	96	96	96	97	97	97	97	97	97	97	97	97	97	97	97	98	98	98	98	98	98	98	98	98	98	98	98	98	99	99	99	99	99	99	99	99	99	99	99					
93	97	97	97	97	97	97	97	97	97	97	97	97	97	97	98	98	98	98	98	98	98	98	98	98	98	98	98	98	99	99	99	99	99	99	99	99	99	99	99	99	99	99	100				
94	97	97	97	97	97	97	97	97	98	98	98	98	98	98	98	98	98	98	98	98	98	98	98	98	99	99	99	99	99	99	99	99	99	99	99	99	99	99	99	99	99	100	100	100			
95	98	98	98	98	98	98	98	98	98	98	98	98	98	98	98	98	98	98	98	99	99	99	99	99	99	99	99	99	99	99	99	99	99	99	99	99	99	99	99	100	100	100	100	100	100		
96	98	98	98	98	98	98	98	98	98	98	98	98	99	99	99	99	99	99	99	99	99	99	99	99	99	99	99	99	99	99	99	99	99	99	99	99	99	100	100	100	100	100	100	100	100	100	
97	99	99	99	99	99	99	99	99	99	99	99	99	99	99	99	99	99	99	99	99	99	99	99	99	99	99	99	99	99	99	99	99	99	100	100	100	100	100	100	100	100	100	100	100	100	100	100
98	99	99	99	99	99	99	99	99	99	99	99	99	99	99	99	99	99	99	99	99	99	99	99	99	100	100	100	100	100	100	100	100	100	100	100	100	100	100	100	100	100	100	100	100	100	100	100
99	100	100	100	100	100	100	100	100	100	100	100	100	100	100	100	100	100	100	100	100	100	100	100	100	100	100	100	100	100	100	100	100	100	100	100	100	100	100	100	100	100	100	100	100	100	100	100

Index